THE RELUCTANT ADMIRAL

THE RELUCTANT ADMIRAL

Yamamoto and the Imperial Navy

HIROYUKI AGAWA

Translated by JOHN BESTER

KODANSHA INTERNATIONAL LTD.
Tokyo, New York, San Francisco

This is a translation, with some abridgment approved by the author, of the work published in Japanese by Shinchosha in 1969 under the title *Yamamoto Isoroku*.

Published by Kodansha International Ltd., 2–12–21 Otowa, Bunkyo-ku, Tokyo 112 and Kodansha International/USA, Ltd., 10 East 53rd Street, New York, New York 10022 and 44 Montgomery Street, San Francisco, California 94104.

Quality Printing and Binding by:
Berryville Graphics
P.O. Box 272
Berryville, VA 22611 U.S.A.

CHRONOLOGY

1884   Born in Nagaoka, Niigata Prefecture, sixth son of Takano Sadayoshi, a former samurai.

1901   Enters Naval Academy at Etajima.

1904   Graduates from Naval Academy.

1905   Participates in Battle of Japan Sea on board warship *Nisshin*. Seriously wounded. Ensign.

1914   Enters Navy Staff College. Lieutenant.

1915   Lieutenant commander.

1916   Graduates from Navy Staff College. Registered as adopted son of late Yamamoto Tatewaki, whose surname he adopts.

1918   Marries (the marriage is to produce two sons and two daughters).

1919–21 Stationed in U.S.A. Commander.

1923   Visits Europe and U.S.A. Captain.

1924   Second-in-command of Kasumigaura Aviation Corps. So far has been gunnery specialist, but now becomes increasingly interested in aviation.

1926–28 Naval attaché at Japanese embassy in Washington.

1928   Captain of cruiser *Isuzu*, then captain of aircraft carrier *Akagi*.

1930   Participates in London Naval Disarmament Conference. Rear admiral.

1930   Head of Technical Division of Aeronautics Department.

1933   Commander of First Carrier Division (on board *Akagi*).

1934   Japanese delegate to preliminary talks for London Naval Conference. Vice admiral.

1935   Head of Aeronautics Department.

1936   Navy vice-minister.

1939   Commander in chief of the Combined Fleet.

1940   Admiral.

1943   Killed in action in South Pacific.

EDITOR'S NOTE:
All Japanese names in this book (except the author's) are given in the Japanese order—surname first, followed by the given name. It should also be noted that references to persons as "still surviving" etc. are translations from the Japanese text of 1969 and may no longer hold true.

THE RELUCTANT ADMIRAL

ONE

1

I have by me as I write a faded group photograph. It shows Yamamoto Isoroku in the days when he was still a captain, together with more than twenty others who had graduated from the Naval Academy in the same year as he. It was taken in the middle or late 1920s, and the place seems to have been the entrance to some naval officers' club.

In addition to Yamamoto, one can identify various other men, then in the prime of life, who were later to become admirals holding key posts in the Japanese Imperial Navy and to influence the whole nation's fortunes. One of them wears a daredevil smile; the face of another, a tall man, glowers like a gargoyle above the rest; most of the group are typical specimens of the species sea-dog, half of them sporting moustaches in the fashion of the time. Yamamoto's upper lip, though, is clean-shaven. He is shorter than the rest, and his expression as captured by the camera is gentle, almost forlorn. The photographs of "Admiral Yamamoto Isoroku, commander in chief of the Combined Fleet," that became so familiar in the wartime press gave a rather different impression—due partly, no doubt, to the efforts of those who took them and published them. But here at least he is seen as frankly short, slightly stooping, and faintly dejected-looking.

If one were to bring together a group of people who did not know what Yamamoto looked like, and to ask them which of these twenty-odd men was the one who in later years was to plan the attack on Pearl Harbor and oversee the fleet that carried it out, I doubt whether any of them would be able to pick out the right one.

Yamamoto Isoroku was, in fact, a physically small man. On April 18, 1943, when he left the east airstrip on Rabaul on what was to be his last journey, Petty Officer Hayashi Hiroshi, chief pilot of the second land-based attack plane that accompanied his, saw him for the first time. Hayashi, a large man himself, confesses to having thought, "Why, the C. in C.'s only half my size!"

Yamamoto was five feet three inches tall and weighed around 125–130 pounds. His bone structure, it seems, had an almost feminine delicacy; according to the proprietress of a restaurant who knew him well, he had fingers like a pianist's. Unlike a pianist, though, he had only eight fingers. The generally accepted story is that during the Battle of the Japan Sea a Russian shell scored a direct hit on the warship *Nisshin*, on which Yamamoto was serving as a cadet, and severed the middle and index fingers of his left hand at the base. Yamamoto himself wrote: "With a great roar, a shell scored a direct hit on the forward 8-inch gun that still remained. Billows of acrid smoke covered the forward half of the vessel, and I felt myself almost swept away by a fierce blast. I staggered a few steps—and found that the record charts that had been hanging round my neck had disappeared, and that two fingers of my left hand had been snapped off and were hanging by the skin alone."

This suggests that he too believed the same thing for many years. But the truth seems to be that one of the *Nisshin*'s own guns burst—a thing that happens when the steel of the barrel, weakened after heating by repeated firing and sudden cooling as cold waves break over it, becomes unable to contain the gases produced by an explosion. Whether the cause, though, was an enemy shell or an accident on board his own ship, Yamamoto was known in the geisha district of Shimbashi as "Eighty Sen," since the regular charge for a geisha's manicure—all ten fingers—was one yen. And besides the missing fingers, his body bore other shocking scars of the same accident.

With Yamamoto, smallness of physique did not matter. The photo already mentioned shows his face to have been clean-cut and intelligent, with nothing weak about it. The absence of any suggestion of the fiery military leader in no way implies that he was not a suitable commander in chief for the Combined Fleet.

In other ways, a study of the photo will inspire various emotions in anyone who knows the period in question. Admiral Inoue Shige-yoshi, the blunt-spoken head of the Naval Affairs Bureau at the time when Yamamoto was navy vice-minister, divided admirals into first-grade and second-grade ones, and of the four (a rare number) pro-

2

duced by this particular class—Shiozawa, Yoshida, Yamamoto, and Shimada—only Yamamoto made first grade.

Yoshida Zengo, Yamamoto's predecessor as C. in C. of the Combined Fleet, returned to the Navy Ministry as minister when Yamamoto left it. Yamamoto seems to have felt that Yoshida could be trusted to carry on the work that he and Minister Yonai had been doing; but Yoshida left the post before long.

Shimada Shigetaro became navy minister on the formation of the Tojo government and remained in the post from the beginning of the war, through the time of Yamamoto's death in action, until the moment when Tojo reluctantly gave up power in July 1944, following the fall of Saipan. He followed Tojo's orders so slavishly that he was privately referred to as "Tojo's lackey."

One cannot help feeling that it would have been better if Yamamoto, at some appropriate time, had himself returned to government. If only he had left the fleet and become navy minister, Japan's fate might well have been different (though in that case some Japanese assassin might, quite early on, have saved an American fighter pilot the trouble of killing him later). In fact, to examine Yamamoto's career and its relation to the last war is to wonder time and again what would have happened "if . . ." And it is with one small instance of the "ifs" presented by Yamamoto's life that I would like to begin this story.

2

It happened—or, more accurately, did not happen—on the very day that Yamamoto was appointed by the emperor as commander in chief of the Combined Fleet.

In Japan, the name Sorimachi Eiichi is familiar to quite a number of people by now. He went to the same middle school in Nagaoka as Yamamoto and, though five years younger, was one of his oldest friends in his home district. Sorimachi's two-volume work *Yamamoto Isoroku: The Man* goes into great detail concerning Yamamoto's family background, birth, and upbringing, and though it displays a partisan tendency to see every pockmark as a dimple and to omit most things unfavorable to its subject, it contains much material unavailable elsewhere.

On the morning of August 30, 1939, Sorimachi boarded the Tokyo-bound express at Shibata Station on the main Uetsu line. Seated in the second-class car he found an old acquaintance, Ishiwara Kanji, in major general's uniform. Greeting Ishiwara, he asked where he was going. Ishiwara replied that he had been appointed commander of the Sixteenth Division and was on his way to Tokyo. He was to have an audience with the emperor, and intended to advise him that the present war (the China Incident) should not be allowed to continue; he also intended to tell princes Chichibu and Takamatsu the same thing.

"I know this car's loaded with military policemen in plain clothes and political police," he said, "but it won't stop me saying that this business will ruin Japan if we go on with it."

"Actually," he went on, "I'm hoping to see Vice-Minister Yamamoto too. He's the only man in the navy who could stop the war. . . . I'd like to go and see him on September 3—perhaps you could call him later and let him know I'm coming."

Ishiwara, who had been on nodding terms with Yamamoto for some time, was looked on as something of a heretic within the army. An ardent follower of the teachings of Nichiren, he believed that some 2,500 years after the Buddha's death—around the year 2000—what would now be called a "world government" would be realized, but that war on an unprecedented scale would take place as part of the process leading to it. It was he who had planned the Manchurian Incident, with the idea of creating a kind of ideal state in Manchuria in which "the five races would live in harmony." In these respects, there may have been something of a gap between his outlook and Yamamoto's, but at the outbreak of the China Incident he had immediately called for a policy of localization. His feeling was that troops should not be committed until mankind's "final war," and that the incident should be settled quickly so as to avoid any immediate confrontation with America and Britain. Here, at least, he would probably have found a fairly sympathetic listener in Yamamoto.

"How long will you be in Tokyo?" asked Sorimachi in a low voice, warned that the military and political police were probably listening. ". . . I see. I'll let Yamamoto know at once." Their conversation for the remaining hour and a half until the train reached Nagaoka was desultory, and at Nagaoka Station they parted.

Sorimachi's own business was to give a lecture at a primary school in a village that lay in the hills some way back from Miyauchi, the next station after Nagaoka. The lecture started at three and lasted until around dusk, when Sorimachi and the others concerned were given a meal at the home of a local bigwig on a hill overlooking the village. As they were eating, a man from the village office arrived, all out of breath, with an urgent message for Sorimachi. The office people had heard a report on the radio that Vice-Minister Yamamoto had been appointed commander in chief of the Combined Fleet, and that he had been to the palace for the investment ceremony. The village headman and all the others present rose excitedly to their feet at the news and gave three cheers. Sorimachi himself immediately went back down to the village, in high spirits, and returned by taxi to his home in Nagaoka, where he put in a call to Tokyo. When it came through, he offered Yamamoto his congratulations, and the two men talked for a while before Sorimachi remembered the message from Ishiwara, which the excitement of the moment had made him temporarily forget. He told Yamamoto of the meeting in the train, and of Ishiwara's message.

"Unfortunately," said Yamamoto, "I have to leave tomorrow to join the fleet, so I can't see him. But give him my regards next time you meet, will you?"

If Yamamoto's appointment as commander in chief had been only four or five days later, the meeting that Ishiwara had hoped for would probably have taken place. If only it had, the course of the China Incident—indeed, Japan's whole future—might have been rather different. One can never know; but one small possibility was thereby extinguished. Yamamoto went to sea, and from then until his death was never to meet Ishiwara again.

3

At 5:30 that afternoon, Yamamoto, having been to the Imperial Palace to be invested as commander in chief of the Combined Fleet and the First Fleet, returned to the red brick building that housed the Navy Ministry.

The newspapers of the day gave great prominence to his first remarks on assuming his new post, with headlines declaring, "Setting Sail Again on the Seven Seas after Six Years Ashore: Yamamoto, the Stern, Silent Admiral." One typical article had this description

5

to offer: "Sturdy frame clothed in spotless white uniform; manly features, solemn with emotion and resolve; confident stride. . . . Thus the vice admiral entered the ministry to give his press conference. Today, unusually for him, he drained his beer at one draft, with every appearance of pleasure, then delivered his first pronouncement as commander in chief: 'There have been all kinds of problems, but I have done what I could. I have no comments to make. I feel overwhelmed at the great task with which I have been so undeservedly entrusted, but I mean to do my humble best in the service of His Imperial Majesty. For a navy man, the post of C. in C. of the Combined Fleet is the greatest honor possible, and my mind is made up accordingly.' "

The article, which is accompanied by a photograph of Yamamoto flashing dazzlingly white teeth, goes on in the same vein but succeeds in saying little more than this, which was just about as much as any newspaper at the time could have said.

Yamamoto, who had served as vice-minister in four successive governments—under Hirota, Hayashi, Konoe, and Hiranuma—was extremely popular with the reporters attached to the Navy Ministry. "Whatever questions you ask me," he told them, "I'll always reply at least 'Yes' or 'No.' But I expect you to keep faith with me." He was willing to talk to them about comparatively sensitive matters; in time, even reporters detailed to the prime minister's official residence came to feel they had not got to the heart of a matter unless they dropped in to see Vice-Minister Yamamoto at the Navy Ministry. He was invariably straightforward, and disliked diplomatic lies. Sometimes, apparently, he would express himself in what might seem an oddly pugnacious way. "I hate his guts," he would say of someone or other, or "Only an asshole would say a thing like that. Get him in here."

He would often put in an appearance in the office of the Kokuchokai (Black Current Society) in the Navy Ministry; this Kokuchokai was the oldest reporters' club in Japan, and was frequented by some of the most able among the newsmen attached to the various ministries. Yamamoto would play *shogi* (Japanese chess) and chat with them, and was always willing to receive them at the vice-minister's residence; however late the hour, he would provide them with whisky and cigars, and when they left would come to the entrance hall to see them off. One reason why these meetings were so often held late at night was that Yamamoto himself came home at all hours, having disappeared for destinations unknown once work was over for the day.

The reporters responsible for gathering news from the navy knew very well what the "all kinds of problems" to which he referred were, and how he had "done what he could." They knew, too, that he could almost certainly make all kinds of comments if he chose. But it was not possible to say this clearly in their articles. Either way, he was attractive as a person, and an important news source into the bargain, and the reporters regretted seeing the man whom they had referred to informally as "Isoroku" go off to sea. The day before, the Combined Fleet had sent Fujita Motoshige, senior aide to command, to Tokyo in order to see off Vice Admiral Yoshida Zengo and bring back the new commander in chief Once they had left the flagship *Nagato*, Yoshida and Fujita both changed to civilian clothes for the train journey to Tokyo, but the press got wind of them nonetheless and swarmed onto the night train in the hope of getting Yoshida to air his hopes and impressions on becoming navy minister, and Fujita was kept hard at work all night fending them off.

At 7:10 A.M. on the twenty-ninth, they arrived at Tokyo Station, where Lieutenant Commander Sanematsu Yuzuru, an aide from the Navy Ministry, had come to meet them. They proceeded to the navy minister's official residence, where Yonai Mitsumasa was waiting to receive Yoshida.

Yonai had had a bath readied, and while Yoshida was bathing Vice-Minister Yamamoto also put in an appearance. The three men talked as they ate breakfast together. This was not the first time that Fujita had met Yamamoto, since he had been on board the *Akagi* as divisional gunnery officer when Yamamoto had been the ship's captain. For the next three and a half months, however, he was to be in close contact with Yamamoto as an aide in charge of protocol and personnel.

The next day, when Fujita went to the vice-minister's residence to escort Yamamoto to the investment ceremony, he found that Yamamoto's wife Reiko was away in Karuizawa, and it was a maid who saw Yamamoto off as he came out of the house. A plainclothes military policeman accompanied them in the car as far as the Sakashita Gate of the Imperial Palace. He was waiting for them at the same place when they came away after the ceremony, and made to board Yamamoto's car again. But Yamamoto told Fujita that since he was no longer vice-minister he did not need a police guard, and Fujita sent the man packing. It was common knowledge in the Navy Ministry at the time that military policemen from the army acted not only as escorts but as spies as well.

The next day, on which Yamamoto left to join the fleet, happened to be his twenty-first wedding anniversary, but his wife was still away. He left home alone that morning, went to the Navy Ministry, then, accompanied by Fujita, made several courtesy calls in a ministry automobile before proceeding to Tokyo Station.

A little before 1:00 P.M. Yamamoto, wearing the Order of the Sacred Treasure, First Class, on the left breast of his white uniform, and preceded by the stationmaster of Tokyo Station, emerged onto the platform from the staircase reserved for VIPs, and passed through a throng of well-wishers who had come to see him off: prominent government officials and military men, personal acquaintances, press representatives—and the women from the Shimbashi geisha quarter who had accounted for his disappearance until late the night before.

As Yamamoto followed the stationmaster to the observation car at the rear of the train, he responded to those there to see him off with the smart salute that was later to become so famous. There was a red carpet at the entrance to the observation car, but Yamamoto himself seems to have had little taste for ceremony of this kind. Most people who knew him or served under him, if asked for an estimate of his character, replied without hesitation, "He was a man who hated pomposity." Yonai Mitsumasa replied quite simply, "Mischievous devil."

To Yamamoto, gambling and games of chance had always been more important than food or drink. "Every man has his faults," writes Takagi Sokichi, "and Admiral Yamamoto was no saint. Few men could have been as fond of gambling and games of chance as he. . . . *Shogi*, *go*, mahjongg, billiards, cards, roulette—anything would do. At parties and the like, although he could not drink, he would make up for it by organizing 'horse races' on paper and getting the younger officers accompanying him or the young women serving at a teahouse to bet fifty sen on the outcome."

Although Yamamoto could not take alcohol, he and his friend Hori

Teikichi would often visit two or three particular geisha houses in the Shimbashi and Tsukiji districts. It is generally agreed that the chief aim was to play cards or mahjongg with the women there; only a few of Yamamoto's closest friends knew that several years earlier his visits had already stepped beyond the bounds of mere "amusement." Whether his wife Reiko was one of those who knew or not is uncertain.

According to someone who went to the station to see Yamamoto off, a peculiarly sheepish expression passed across his face when his eyes met those of the Shimbashi women; they, at least, could detect the shyly embarrassed smile that played around the eyes in those "manly features, solemn with emotion and resolve." In another sense, it was as though he was saying—a favorite remark of his—"I may be 'Eighty Sen,' but I can play the great man when I have to."

As he came out on the deck of the observation car with his aide, the departure bell began to ring. At precisely one o'clock, the "Kamome" slowly drew out of the station, while the eyes of all those in the crowd on the platform focused on the single figure at the rear. In navy fashion, he took off his cap and waved it slowly in circles. Conspicuous among those on the platform—heaven knows how they had got there—was a group of three Nichiren-sect devotees who stood banging away on their paper drums until the train was out of sight.

During the two years and three months between then and the raid on Pearl Harbor, he was to come up to Tokyo again any number of times on business, but the capital was never to be his hometown or place of work again. He was fifty-five, the same age as his father Sadayoshi had been when he himself was born in 1884.

He sat on the sofa in the observation car, gazing with apparent emotion at the buildings of Yurakucho and Shimbashi as they slipped by, bright beneath the late August sun.

4

The "Kamome" stopped at Yokohama, Numazu, and Shizuoka, and it was dusk by the time the train finally reached Nagoya. During the early stages, a man in plain clothes, apparently a military policeman, had put in fitful appearances in the car, but he seemed to have left the train at Yokohama, and in his place Yamamoto had to deal with the crowds of people who were waiting at each stop to greet him. Presents—cigarettes at Yokohama, Odawara fish sausage at Numazu—were brought on board the observation car in large quantities. On each occasion Yamamoto got up and thanked those responsible, talking frankly and freely with all and sundry. But once the train started again and he was alone with his aide, he made no effort to dispel or conceal the depression apparent on his face. Something—whether the future of the nation, his family, or a woman was not clear—seemed to be weighing on his mind; possibly it was a little of each.

A certain woman had in fact boarded the ordinary first-class car of the "Kamome" that day without attracting notice. But Fujita writes simply, "When we left Tokyo Station, the C. in C. seemed terribly abstracted; I imagine he was feeling lonely," without making any direct reference to her.

At Nagoya, reporters from the Osaka papers boarded the train in the hope of eliciting some comments from Yamamoto, who had exchanged his uniform for a white linen suit. They asked him about the recently signed treaty of non-aggression between Germany and the Soviet Union—the matter that had occasioned the resignation of the Hiranuma government and the appointment of a new navy minister and vice-minister—and whether it did not strike him as rather repugnant to the Japanese ethical sense. "I can't comment on political matters," Yamamoto replied. "In theory," he added significantly, "morality in foreign affairs should mean doing what one knows to be right whether one is deceived or not. In human terms, that's a very fine attitude, but in a politician it's sometimes a mistake, don't you think?" Asked about the "new life" campaign then in progress, whose champions urged men to shave their heads and women to forgo permanent waves because of the "gravity of the situation," he replied: "What does it all matter? I myself have worn my hair short for years. I find it's less trouble, but I don't see what it has to do with any 'new life' whether one shaves one's head or wears one's hair long. Most officers in the Naval Air Corps wear their hair long and parted. If you bang your head, you hurt yourself less if you have hair. On the other hand, a slob's a slob, however close-cropped he may be. So either's OK, surely? It's the same with permanent waves. One reason women have them, I'm sure, is that it's more economical. So I don't see anything wrong with permanent waves—or with traditional Japanese hairstyles either. It's not worth making a fuss about."

At this point, a steward came to say that dinner was ready, and with a curt "Well, excuse me then," he went with Fujita to the dining car.

The "Kamome" arrived in Osaka at 9:20 P.M., and Yamamoto, the woman accompanying him, and his aide spent the night at the New Osaka Hotel. The Combined Fleet was anchored in Wakanoura Bay, having suspended exercises on account of the change in commander in chief. The Combined Fleet at the time was the third most powerful in the world; the harbors at Osaka and Kobe were both too small to accommodate the whole of it, and it was necessary for the First and Second Fleets to split up if they wished to enter those ports, but Wakanoura was big enough to take the whole fleet at once.

The next morning, Yamamoto said good-bye to his companion at the barrier of Nanba Station and took a train of the Nankai Private Railway to Wakanoura. Here, the C. in C.'s launch, a small steam vessel, was waiting at the pier. It was a fine, hot day. Yamamoto disappeared into the tiny cabin, and at a command from the officer in charge, a young ensign whose cheeks were flushed with eagerness, the launch left the pier.

Offshore, the Combined Fleet, seventy or eighty vessels in all, lay at anchor, peacefully riding the sunny seas of Wakanoura Bay. Its flagship was the *Nagato*, which was to be Yamamoto's home, and headquarters of the Combined Fleet, until the *Yamato* came into service following the outbreak of the Pacific War.

As the launch carrying the new commander in chief approached the *Nagato*, the men who were to serve under him waited on board—on the inner side of the deck, looking from the gangway, the captains and staff officers of the fleets and divisions under his command; on the outer side of the same deck, the staff officers of the Combined Fleet command; and at right angles to these two lines, the captain, Fukudome Shigeru, and other officers of the *Nagato*.

After Yoshida Zengo had left the *Nagato* to become navy minister, there had been much discussion on board as to who would succeed him. The commander of the Second Fleet at the time was Toyoda

Soemu, and precedent would normally have dictated that he should be promoted to command the Combined Fleet. When Yamamoto Isoroku was appointed instead, many people, it seems, were surprised and impressed by the choice.

As the launch drew alongside the *Nagato*, Yamamoto leaped nimbly onto the ladder. The vice admiral's pennant that had been fluttering over the commander in chief's launch was lowered, and the commander in chief's pennant was raised on the mast of the *Nagato*. Simultaneously the flagship's band struck up the usual piece played in honor of the C. in C. Yamamoto came on board, then, returning the salutes of those waiting to greet him, disappeared down the C. in C.'s hatch and entered the C. in C.'s wardroom at the rear of the vessel, where the command staff officers and commanders of the fleets under him came to pay their respects.

The taking-over ceremony was relatively simple. As soon as it was over Yamamoto seemed relieved and, visibly brightening, began to chat freely. "I rather like being commander in chief," he told his aide. "One's popular. A navy vice-minister's just a high-grade office boy."

"High-grade office boy" or not, Yamamoto's period as navy vice-minister, and especially the last few months, had involved him in a succession of troublesome and depressing episodes. He was generally considered to be the prime cause of the navy's stubborn opposition to the Tripartite Pact; as such, he had been a target of rightist hostility and had stood in danger of his life. There is no doubt that, personally, he was relieved to find himself at sea again after six years ashore. To fill his lungs again with good sea air must have been a refreshing change.

In a letter written to Sasakawa Ryoichi on September 15, about two weeks later, he said:

> Ever since then the fleet has been in the Bungo Channel, engaged in training exercises around the clock, with all contact with land cut except for taking mail on board. By now this year's training is drawing to a close, and I have a feeling that the fleet is just about reaching the peak of its capabilities. I'm truly proud at having taken over such a fine fleet, yet at the same time I'm made more and more aware of the size of the job I have taken on and am afraid that it may prove beyond all my efforts.

Where events in the outside world are concerned, I know only what I can glean from the thrice-daily radio news and the newspapers that arrive every other day, and even these seem like distant mutterings from another world. By now I can turn my back on everything else and devote myself entirely to naval matters, and can sense the bracing effect this has both spiritually and physically.

Sasakawa Ryoichi, president of the Kokusui Domei, a nationalistic organization, was alone among rightist leaders of the day in respecting Yamamoto. He would often come to the Navy Ministry, wearing a formal crested kimono, to call on Yamamoto. He always referred to the latter as "*sensei*"—or Master—and even advised him on matters such as what to do if he were set on by a would-be assassin.

On the evening of the first day of September—the day on which Yamamoto took up his appointment with the fleet—he heard the news of the German invasion of Poland. At 7:15 P.M., Japan time, on September 3, England declared war on Germany. France followed suit six hours later. In a letter written to Shimada Shigetaro on September 4, he says: "The great upheaval now occurring in Europe makes me feel terrified when I think of our relationship with Germany and Italy."

On September 5, Yamamoto issued a message to the officers and men of the entire Combined Fleet. It began: "In assuming the grave responsibilities of commander in chief of the Combined Fleet in accordance with an unexpected command from His Imperial Majesty . . ." and ended: "The situation in Europe shows clear signs of developing into another worldwide conflict. The task facing the imperial navy in the days to come will be graver than ever. I look to all those under my command to take still greater care of their health, and to devote themselves night and day to training so as to maintain the power of the fleet at its height, enabling it to fulfill its duty in the national defense in conformity with the imperial will."

It is a purely formal message. It seems likely, in fact, that Yamamoto did little more than touch up a draft prepared by his staff; when anyone in a position like his wished to make some official pronouncement in Japan at the time, the question was not so much one of what he should say as of what he should not say. Reading the message carefully, it is possible to feel that he would really have liked to express some theory of a "non-belligerent navy" such as that expounded by another reluctant admiral, Kato Tomosaburo.

The Combined Fleet, however, gave not the slightest sign of inner dissension as a result of the fighting in Europe. On September 4 the recently formed Abe government issued a statement saying, "Japan intends not to intervene in the war that has recently broken out in Europe, but to devote itself exclusively to the solution of the China Incident. . . ." The daily routine of the fleet remained undisturbed, and Yamamoto—in striking contrast to his period as vice-minister —found himself with time on his hands.

Except when maneuvers were in progress, the commander in chief of the Combined Fleet in peacetime had comparatively little to do. Yamamoto found himself suggesting games of *shogi* with his staff officers, or ensconced in his private cabin busily writing letters and the specimens of calligraphy for which admirers so often asked him. The men of his part of the country have always had a reputation as hearty eaters, and the sea air now gave a sudden spur to his appetite. Breakfast for the Combined Fleet command was either Japanese-style or— for those who wanted it and told the orderly the night before— Western-style with coffee, porridge, and so on. The general consensus, however, was that "one cannot make war on porridge," and most people chose the regulation bean-paste soup and rice.

Luncheon was a full Western meal beginning with soup and ending with dessert, and employing both silver tableware and finger bowls. During the meal, for thirty minutes beginning at 12 : 05 P.M., the band on the afterdeck would provide music for the C. in C.'s enjoyment. This also served as the band's daily practice period, but the repertoire seldom included martial tunes such as the well-known "Battleship March"; the emphasis, rather, was on sentimental Japanese melodies and popular Western music. Yamamoto himself is said to have been particularly fond of "Shina no Yoru" ("China Night"). The rest of the ship's company would get lunch over quickly in order to go out on the afterdeck and listen to the music; it provided one of the chief relaxations on board the flagship, but only, of course, while the ship was at anchor.

The evening meal, Japanese-style again, included such delicacies as sea bream, either salted or broiled, savory egg custard, and sliced raw fish, and the galley made a point of employing cooks noted for their skill. The only drawback was that, since naval officers paid their own wardroom expenses, the younger officers who occupied the foot of the table found such luxuries a considerable strain on their purses.

At lunch and dinner the C. in C. and all his officers were, in principle, supposed to be present, the rectangular conference table in the C. in C.'s wardroom being transformed into a dining table by the addition of a white cloth. On a battleship like the *Nagato*, this wardroom made great use of teak, in the manner of the first-class saloon on a rather old-fashioned liner, the idea being that any guest, at any port anywhere in the world, could be welcomed aboard without disgrace.

The C. in C. sat at the center of one side of the table, with his chief of staff sitting opposite. The others at the table included the senior and other staff officers, the aides, the fleet codes officer, fleet meteorological officer, fleet engineer, fleet paymaster, fleet medical officer, fleet legal officer, and from time to time the captain of the *Nagato*. Yamamoto himself spoke little, but was in no way forbidding and smiled a lot. He also ate a lot. In the days of his predecessor, Admiral Yoshida, it was rare for dried sardines to appear on the table, but Yamamoto was inordinately fond of the *urume-iwashi* (a type of sardine) from Tosa. Whenever the fleet entered Sukumo Bay, he would have the supply officer buy large quantities and would munch them happily, head and all, constantly urging others to join him.

Yoshida had been a rather fussy, oversensitive man, unhappy unless everything was in order. He did not drink, and having no chance to let himself go, tended to find fault and take small things too much to heart. He made lavish use of the red pencil on the documents his staff prepared for him, and sometimes corrected personally the most minor details of signals. Even his staff officers were subject to frequent naggings. In short, it seems that he was already showing signs of the neuroses that were to affect him later.

In the cold season, when the fleet entered harbor at Beppu in Kyushu and everyone else was looking forward to eating blowfish accompanied by hot sake, Yoshida would anxiously question the chief medical officer as to whether it was really safe—and even then could rarely be persuaded to eat any. On leaving the *Nagato*, he commemorated the occasion by distributing photographs of himself to all his officers, but in some quarters at least they seemed to have been received with less than gratitude.

As his aide Fujita saw him, Yamamoto had an extremely tough side and an extremely easygoing side; his immediate impression was that the new C. in C. represented a considerable change from Yoshida, and that he was a man of formidable dimensions.

After a short time, the fleet left Wakanoura Bay and resumed its interrupted maneuvers. To get it out of harbor was no easy job, since Combined Fleet command, single-handed, had to shepherd a crowd of some eighty vessels of all sizes out of harbor in orderly fashion, and only navigation officers of the highest ability were qualified to serve on the staff. Each vessel's engines and anchor mechanism would have been readied well in advance. Eventually, the order would come: "Fifteen minutes before leaving port. Sea duty men to their stations," and the bows and bridge would suddenly spring to life.

A report would come in: "First vessel, Second Division, raising anchor."

Bugles would sound the "Prepare for sea."

A submarine group would lead the way out. The submarines played a lookout role, bringing up the rear when the fleet entered harbor and preceding it when it left. By this time the C. in C. would be up on the bridge, binoculars in hand, watching the procedure personally. Messengers from the navigation section would come to report the movements of individual vessels or divisions in loud voices:

"Fourth Division leaving port."

"*Takao, Atago, Chokai, Maya* leaving."

"*Ise* now leaving. *Hyuga, Fuso* leaving."

"*Akagi, Kaga, Soryu, Hiryu*, First and Second Carrier Divisions, leaving port."

Komoto Hironaka, who was an air staff officer and junior aide, has said, "The time I'd have liked to be commander in chief of the Combined Fleet was when we left harbor." There must, indeed, have been a very special emotion in watching such a great fleet start moving and in realizing that everything in sight was under one's own command. At such a time, any man might have been forgiven for puffing out his chest a little, but such tendencies were almost completely absent in Yamamoto. The younger officers on board the

Nagato would comment on this among themselves. "The new C. in C. doesn't put on airs," one would say. "He doesn't seem to like being made a fuss of," another would add. "I wonder how he'd react if there was a war and he found himself a conquering hero?" What seems to be a rare display of pride in him occurs in the following passage from a letter to Sorimachi in Nagaoka, which is quoted by Sorimachi himself: "I'm sure you'll always remember that the former Nagaoka clan, Nagaoka Middle School, and the Nagaoka-sha [a local scholarship society that had helped Yamamoto] have produced a commander in chief of the Combined Fleet for the Japanese Empire!" This seems to smack strongly of vulgarity.

In a different sense, Yamamoto was no doubt a vulgar character. But one searches in vain among the words and deeds of his mature years for any suggestion of interest in worldly advancement for its own sake, of the itch that makes some men want to be prime ministers or generals. The passage, in fact, jars completely with the normally held view of Yamamoto, and it is suggestive here that Sorimachi himself uses extravagantly emotional phraseology in his account of hearing the news of Yamamoto's appointment to the Combined Fleet: "Every drop of blood in my veins tingles with joy at this realization of the hopes cherished for seventy years past by the men of Nagaoka. . . . Society has changed; Nagaoka has changed; Japan has changed. . . . The moon is bright. Admiral Yamamoto is commander in chief! Nagaoka is suddenly a brighter place. The whole of Japan will be a brighter place!"

It seems quite possible, in the light of this, that Yamamoto said something with substantially the same sense but with a somewhat different nuance: "So the Nagaoka clan has finally produced a commander of the Combined Fleet! Don't you forget it!"

Yet it still seems rather odd for him to have said such a thing, even to an intimate friend from his own hometown. It may be—as is suggested by the constant references to Nagaoka in what Sorimachi has written—that one will never understand unless one views Nagaoka in a rather special light. There is no space here to go into the history of the place in detail, but the Nagaoka clan was one of those that went over to the "wrong" side—that of the former shogunate—in the Boshin War of 1868–69, and because of this the district had produced very few prefectural governors, generals, or admirals. The navy, for example, was for many years notoriously under the thumb of members of the former Satsuma clan, which had been on the side of the new government. Eventually, in the Showa era (1926–), this bias disappeared, and it is even said that those responsible deliberately avoided appointing anyone from Kagoshima Prefecture (former Satsuma) as head of the Personnel Bureau lest he should show regional favoritism. Yamamoto, however, was born the strong-willed son of a man who had once been an impoverished samurai of the Nagaoka clan; his father, eldest brother, and second eldest brother had all taken part in the Boshin War; all three had been wounded and had spent a long time drifting about northern Honshu. To the old-style "Nagaoka man," it seems, Nagaoka was something quite special and separate from either Choshu or Satsuma. The only men still surviving in Nagaoka who knew Yamamoto well are Sorimachi Eiichi, a Zen priest called Hashimoto Zengan, and a friend of the same age as Yamamoto called Toyama. At the time of a later, Satsuma-led uprising, Toyama's grandfather had declared as he left for battle, "Now we shall get our own back for the Boshin War. . . ."

There is no telling how aware Yamamoto himself was of the sufferings his father and brothers had undergone on account of the disgrace incurred by their having opposed the imperial forces, but it seems beyond doubt that, like Sorimachi, Yamamoto had a tendency to betray a slightly abnormal degree of emotion in any matter that concerned his home district.

TWO

1

The Combined Fleet, with its new commander in chief, sailed out of Wakanoura Bay, leaving dozens of white trails behind it on the waters of the bay. So began Yamamoto's life as master of a great body of ships and men. But it is necessary here to leave the Combined Fleet for a while and to go back five years further into the past. On September 7, 1934—just five years before the *Nagato* sailed from Wakanoura Bay—Yamamoto, who was then a rear admiral attached to the Naval General Staff and the Navy Ministry, was appointed chief delegate to represent the navy at the preliminary talks for the second London Naval Conference. This marked the beginning of Yamamoto's sudden emergence as a figure to be reckoned with within the navy. At roughly the same time, his name became known not only in Japan but in government and naval circles in America, England, and Germany.

According to what Sorimachi has written, the first public mention of his name was probably a piece of chitchat about him that appeared in an article published around 1927 or 1928 in the magazine *Bungei Shunju*, but the article in question cannot be traced. (In fact, novelist Tayama Katai had mentioned Yamamoto in writing a full twenty years earlier. In *True Stories of the Russo-Japanese War*, there is a reference to "Takano [Yamamoto's surname before adoption] Isoroku, a cadet in the navy who received an honorable wound in the great sea battle of May 27 and is at present convalescing in the Yokosuka Naval Hospital. . . ." But this is hardly relevant here.) The earliest reference apart from this that I have found is a "One Page Profile," with a sketched likeness, that appeared, also in *Bungei Shunju*, in October 1934. The author, whose name does not appear, writes as follows:

When it was decided to send Rear Admiral Yamamoto as chief

delegate representing the navy to the preliminary talks for the London Naval Conference, all those who knew him pinned great hopes on him as exactly the right man for the job. He is the perfect helmsman for Ambassador Matsudaira—in fact, being a man of firm purpose and practical ability, he is quite capable if the circumstances so demand of ignoring the ambassador and taking matters into his own hands. . . .

At the London Naval Disarmament Conference of 1930, four years ago, he had the experience of working under Vice Admiral Sakonji Seizo. He has also known the bitterness of failure in the form of the London Naval Treaty, which came as such a shock in naval circles and evoked such extraordinary protests at home. He is thoroughly acquainted, therefore, not only with what went on at the time but with the personality and methods of Ambassador Matsudaira. More particularly, he has recently left his post as commander of the First Carrier Division to become a member of the Committee for the Study of Disarmament Measures, and is a leading expert on disarmament questions, to which he has been devoting specialist study.

The imperial government is approaching the question of disarmament with a well-defined policy: that it will not yield an inch—even if, in the last resort, it has to give notice of abrogation of the Washington Naval Treaty—and that it will secure equal rights to arm in terms of total tonnage. Rear Admiral Yamamoto's chief role will probably be to convince the nations concerned that this basic spirit should be observed. Thanks to the experience gained during his spell as naval attaché at the embassy in America, he is careful about his pronouncements and always has his wits about him.

As would be expected in one who saw action [in the Russo-Japanese War] and had a narrow brush with death, he is not a man who scares easily. His brusque refusal to resort to flattery offends many people; but he is the kind of man who improves steadily with acquaintance.

This character sketch gives the impression that Yamamoto set off for London full of fire, determined not to "yield an inch," but in fact this was not so. The truth is that he tried many times to get out of going to London. Admittedly, once it was decided that he should go, he seems to have determined to devote all his energies to the conference, with the "enthusiasm and resolve" of one who, in his own small way, "was bearing responsibility for the future of the nation." Yet the "enthusiasm and resolve" may well have been rather different from that envisaged by the average reader of *Bungei Shunju*'s "One Page Profile." The phrases just quoted occur in a letter to the woman, already mentioned, who had surreptitiously boarded the limited express "Kamome" at the same time as Yamamoto.

We shall return to the letter later; the point here is that pride at having, in the short space of seventy years, raised the Japanese navy to the position of third most powerful in the world had gradually gone to the heads of some naval men, among whom there was a tendency—though not so marked as in the army—to belittle Anglo-American strength. Yamamoto could not go along with this. Since 1919, when he had been a lieutenant commander, he had been stationed twice in America and had visited Europe twice on official business. He was particularly well aware of America's real strength and of its national character; moreover, he liked the country. During his spell as naval attaché in Washington, on a picture postcard showing the cherry trees by the Potomac River and addressed to a former teacher, he says: "The Yoshino cherry here is in full bloom around now; it is almost more beautiful than at home, and seems to be saying sardonically that the 'Japanese spirit' is not a monopoly of our country. The pointed object in the center is the Washington Monument."

Around the same time, Lieutenant Commander Miwa Yoshitake, his junior assistant, told Yamamoto that he wanted to read the biography of some famous American to improve his English, and asked him whose biography he would recommend. "Lincoln, of course," Yamamoto replied. "I like Lincoln. I think he's great not just as an American, but as a human being. If you're going to read a biography, why don't you read his—there's a good one by Carl Sandburg."

This would be his third visit to Europe, and his second visit to London as a delegate to disarmament talks. He was aware, however, of the gap between his own ideas and the prevailing atmosphere within the navy, and he hesitated many times to accept the commission, feeling that he was not the right man to press Japan's claims to the bitter end in dealing with the Powers.

As it turned out, however, there was no other suitable candidate. The fact that he was friendly with Ambassador Matsudaira counted in his favor, as did the high reputation he had enjoyed in the other countries concerned ever since the London conference of 1930. Thus Yamamoto accepted his appointment as chief delegate.

2

At 3:00 P.M. on September 25, two weeks after the appointment, Yamamoto set sail from Yokohama on the *Hie-maru*, a packet ship on the North American route. The day before, a send-off party had been held for him at the navy minister's official residence. The navy minister of the day was Admiral Osumi Mineo, and Nomura Kichisaburo and other navy veterans were also present. The speech Yamamoto made to them included the following passage: "I accompanied Admiral Takarabe and Vice Admiral Sakonji to the first London Naval Disarmament Conference. At that time, so many requests for instructions were sent that, altogether, close to a million yen was spent on cables between Tokyo and London. This time I shall take my instructions with me, and I intend not to ask for further instructions while I am there. I hope you will understand. I shall give you a detailed report on my return, on the basis of which you can judge whether what I have done is satisfactory or not."

Yamamoto was a rear admiral at the time, a rank that might carry enormous weight within the fleet or the air corps but was still relatively junior in high navy circles in Tokyo. Thus his speech showed considerable courage. One thing must be added, though: the figure of "a million yen" is rather doubtful. The cost of telegrams between London and Tokyo at the time was one yen thirty-eight sen per word, or double that amount for urgent cables.

He was accompanied by three other men—Enomoto Shigeharu, a friend of Yamamoto's and secretary in the Navy Ministry Secretariat; Lieutenant Commander Mitsunobu Motohiro who acted as his aide; and Mizota Shuichi, attached to the Navy Ministry. Besides these, a petty officer, Yokokawa Akira, had left Yokohama on September 16 on the *Hakozaki-maru*, bound for London via Suez, taking with him their baggage, typewriters, coding machines, and so on. Of the four men, three are still alive and well, but Mitsunobu was killed during the war.

Mizota, generally known as "George Mizota," had gone to America with his parents at the age of nine and spent nearly twenty years there, graduating from the law department of Stanford University. He was an able and highly prized interpreter. In December 1941, with the outbreak of hostilities, he was virtually dismissed from the navy and obliged to live in retirement. It was probably felt that a man who had said that in any war with America Japan would inevitably be beaten could hardly be kept in the navy. (This approach was diametrically opposite to that of the Americans, who as soon as war began mobilized everyone who knew anything at all about Japan and launched courses in the Japanese language.)

Even so, it seems that somebody high up in the Navy Ministry foresaw that he would become necessary one day, for throughout the four wartime years his salary was sent to him regularly every month, without explanation. And sure enough, he was to play an important part in the navy's moves to wind up the war.

To Enomoto, Yamamoto said, "I need you of course to play *shogi* with, but I could make do perfectly well at the coming conference with Mizota alone."

Yokokawa, a graduate of the Torpedo School, who was not particularly good at either English or codes, was chosen to accompany Yamamoto because he happened to be working in an office attached to the First Section of the Naval Affairs Bureau, which was in charge of the disarmament question. It was a custom in the navy, whenever there was some international conference, to select an outstanding petty officer from each of the naval stations in turn and send him abroad with the title of "clerical assistant to the Foreign Ministry." Even so, the choice of Yokokawa to go to London seems to have struck many people as odd; the newspapers at the time gave the appointment great prominence, with photographs and captions on the lines of "Petty officer chosen to accompany disarmament delegate," or "Chief Petty Officer Yokokawa, keyed up for appearance in limelight, looks relaxed at home in unfamiliar civvy suit." The real reason for the "unfamiliar civvy suit" was that on board ship, in a petty officer's white uniform with hardly any markings, he would have been constantly mistaken for a steward.

On the day that Yamamoto's party—four of them, excluding Yokokawa—left, they had to put up with large numbers of unwelcome well-wishers who, whether in an attempt to exert pressure on Yamamoto or from some mistaken idea as to his intentions, turned up both at Tokyo Station and on the wharf at Yokohama. One of them even made his way into the cabin, hauled Yamamoto to his feet, unrolled a scroll, and began to read to him in a haranguing tone. Yamamoto reportedly listened with a very sour expression. In a letter addressed to Hori Teikichi and written on board the *Hie-maru* the day before it entered Seattle harbor, he gave vent to his feelings: "We land in America tomorrow. Many thanks for the cable you sent when we left. . . . I found it most unpleasant at Tokyo Station and Yokohama to have a lot of people from this or that league or association fussing around reading 'resolutions' and 'declarations.' It depresses and perturbs me to think that men like that pass as 'patriots'. . . ."

In Seattle, Yamamoto had Mitsunobu go and buy playing cards and poker chips. No sooner were they settled on board the Great Northern's transcontinental train than the game began in real earnest. Mizota knew how to play, but Mitsunobu and Enomoto did not. Yamamoto taught them, let them practice for just one game, then started playing for money. From then on until their arrival in Chicago, they spent so much time playing poker, bridge, and *shogi* that the car attendant began to look rather disgusted. At bridge, too, Yamamoto was a fast player and quick to sense his opponents' reactions. People who played with him say that if one vacillated even for a moment one had the feeling that he already knew what was in one's hand.

They stayed in Chicago for three nights. They arrived on a Saturday, so Yamamoto went to Evanston, on the northern outskirts of the city, to watch a football game between Iowa and Northwestern universities. Football was another thing he was fond of.

On board the New York Central train from Chicago to New York, the four men again spent their time playing cards, even passing up the chance to see the Niagara Falls as they went through Buffalo. In New York, they went to the Astor Hotel. The man who looked after them in New York, seeing to everything from their hotel reservations to their berths on the British liner *Berengaria*, was Captain Sakurai Tadatake, navy inspector in New York. A graduate of the Engineering College, he had attended the first London Naval Disarmament

Conference with Yamamoto as a member of the delegation. He was in New York at Yamamoto's recommendation, his job being to make a survey of aviation in America. Another man, Yamaguchi Tamon—later to be killed on the *Hiryu* during the Battle of Midway—who was serving as naval attaché in Washington, came to New York for talks and saw Yamamoto off from the banks of the Hudson River when he left on October 10.

The day before the *Berengaria* docked at Southampton, Yamamoto gave a "farewell banquet" on board. The menu, which is dated October 15, 1934, is headed "Dinner [sic] d'Adieu," and shows that "Rear Admiral Yamamoto and Guests" consumed "Clam Suimono, Prawn Tempura, Suki Yaki, Shitashimono, and Fresh Fruit." The party, which was held in a private first-class dining room, was given by Yamamoto for several fellow passengers including the former Czechoslovakian minister in Japan, who happened to be aboard. There can be few other examples of a Japanese-style dinner being served on board a liner on the Atlantic route. For dessert, they had green-tea ice cream made with powdered tea given them by a Japanese-American living in Chicago. When they summoned the French head chef to ask how he had managed such typical Japanese dishes as clam *suimono* (clear soup) and prawn tempura, he replied that he had studied for a week at the Japanese Club in New York, and, to demonstrate his prowess, produced out of the hat a variety of other things, from broiled eels to pickled eggplant, much to everybody's delight.

At 4:00 P.M. the next day, October 16—the twenty-seventh day after leaving Tokyo—the ship docked in Southampton, and the party of four, arriving in London that evening by the boat train, took up lodgings at Grosvenor House. Grosvenor House was one of the four hotels in London that were considered suitable for foreign envoys and ministers to stay at, and was regularly used by Japanese delegations. The rooms occupied by such delegations were always on the sixth floor.

The next morning, when Mizota rang the bell, he was surprised to see the same room waiter that he had had on the previous visit come in with a "Good morning, Mr. Mizota, very glad to see you, sir." To his greater surprise still he was asked, "Same breakfast, sir?" and when he doubtfully agreed was brought half a grapefruit,

brown bread, and weak American-style coffee with cold milk in it—
his favorite breakfast, just as he had had it before. In England, of
course, hotels like Grosvenor House prided themselves on providing
such service, yet quite apart from this the general attitude of both
government and public toward Yamamoto and his companions was
far from unfriendly. As was the custom, the Rising Sun flag hung over
the porch of Grosvenor House.

3

That day, Yamamoto had his first conference with Ambassador
Matsudaira, then went with him to pay courtesy calls on the British
foreign secretary and First Lord of the Admiralty. The following day,
October 18, he called on Lord Chatfield, chief of the Naval Staff. All
of these seem to have been purely formal visits.

Yamamoto's real work did not start until five days later, on the
twenty-third, when he had his first meeting with British representatives at 10 Downing Street, followed by a similar meeting with
American representatives at Claridges, where the Americans were
staying. In principle, the conference was due to be carried on in the
form of bilateral negotiations between Japan and Britain, Japan and
America, and America and Britain respectively.

It is not true however that, as some books state, these 1934 preliminary talks did not get going until after the arrival of Yamamoto
and his party in London. There had, in fact, been a preliminary round
of talks before this. It was in May of that year that British Foreign
Secretary Simon had first invited Japan, America, France, and Italy
to join in talks. Japan had promptly signaled its acceptance, and its
representatives engaged in negotiations from June on into July. The
chief representative was Ambassador Matsudaira Tsuneo, with the
embassy's naval attaché, Oka Arata, as technical adviser, together with
a captain who was dispatched in great haste from Japan.

In mid-July, however, after it had become clear that there was a
serious gap between the British and American views, talks were broken
off by agreement among the three nations. Thus when Yamamoto
arrived in London with Japan's new proposals, the conference was in
fact in recess, and the meetings that were begun on October 23 constituted the second round of preliminary talks.

As to the important question of what the Japanese position at the conference was, and in what direction Yamamoto bent his efforts, matters are too involved to allow of any easy explanation. Of course, with the demise of the Japanese navy as such eleven years later, questions of ratios and the like became totally irrelevant, and it may seem scarcely necessary to go into the troublesome details of the disarmament talks.

Nevertheless, if one is to understand Yamamoto's way of thinking, his subsequent actions, and the shifts in his psychology, one cannot overlook either the tortuous course of these negotiations or what lay behind them. In one sense or another, they are subtly related both to Pearl Harbor and to Midway.

4

The whole question of naval disarmament dates back, of course, to the Washington Conference of 1921–22. As is well known, this conference fixed the relative strengths of the British, U.S., and Japanese navies at five, five, and three respectively. It is also common knowledge by now that, as Herbert Yardley revealed in his book *Black Chamber*, all Japan's coded diplomatic cables at the time were being deciphered by the Americans. The Japanese navy was by no means united in its willingness to accept these relative strengths; the question became strongly divisive, and was to prove the ultimate cause of the emergence within the navy of what are known as the "treaty" and "fleet" factions.

An exhaustive account of the question is given by Tsunoda Jun in his *History of Three Generations of the Japanese Navy*. This work, together with other material written on the subject and firsthand accounts by survivors among those who had a hand in the proceedings, makes it clear, first of all, that—as America was aware at an early date thanks to its deciphering of Japanese cables—Kato Tomosaburo, the navy minister who attended the Washington Conference as Japanese plenipotentiary, was ready from the start to accept the proposed sixty percent ratio for Japan.

At the time, the Japanese plan to construct an 8–8 fleet (centered on eight battleships not more than eight years old, with eight battle cruisers) with America as the hypothetical enemy was being steadily transformed into reality, the central figure behind it being Kato himself. As a result of the plan, however, naval expenditure had by 1921 come to account for one-third of the total national budget. This meant that total military appropriations would swell to sixty percent of the total budget, and a limit had been reached in the economic burden that the nation could shoulder.

Kato thus found himself obliged to abandon construction of the fleet that he himself had championed. He arrived in Washington fully determined on this score, and promptly informed Ambassador Shidehara that the 8–8 fleet was impossible to realize and that he had been seeking a suitable excuse to give it up. He had, he said, discussed the point fully with Prime Minister Hara Kei.

The 8–8 fleet was to have given Japan a naval strength corresponding to seventy percent of America's, which would mean that although Japan might not be able to overwhelm America it would have—or so it was generally claimed—the minimum necessary to fight an attacking American fleet on equal terms in the West Pacific.

Thus for Japan to abandon the 8–8 fleet and accept a disarmament plan that would give it only sixty percent of the strength of the U.S. and Britain would also mean abandoning the basic assumption that America was the hypothetical enemy. By the time Kato left for the conference, he seems to have made up his mind quite clearly on this point. In a message to the Navy Ministry which he delivered verbally in Washington after agreement had been reached on most of the important matters pending, he put forward a concept that rejected the inevitability of war between Japan and the U.S. and postulated a "non-belligerent" navy:

> Defense is not a monopoly of the military, nor is war the prerogative of the military alone. Neither can easily attain its aims without a general mobilization of the whole nation. . . . One cannot, very broadly speaking, make war without money. . . . Even supposing Japan's armaments were to rival those of America in strength, the nation could not, as it did in the Russo-Japanese War, fight on a shoestring. Where then would the money come from? The answer is that there is no country other than America that could oblige Japan with the foreign credit required—and this would obviously not be forthcoming if America were the enemy. . . . The conclusion is that a contest between Japan and America is unthinkable. . . . At all costs

28

Japan should avoid war with America. . . . In view of this, I believe that the true aim of national defense at present should be to maintain a military strength commensurate with the nation's resources and to nurture that strength while using diplomatic means to avoid war.

Where the organization of the imperial navy following conclusion of a disarmament treaty is concerned, he puts forward a progressive viewpoint based on the idea of civilian control: "Sooner or later, the navy minister will have to be a civilian, and preparations should be made for that time. I envisage something on the lines of the English system." As Tsunoda points out, the underlying wisdom of this marks Kato's emergence as a statesman, rather than a mere politician.

It was Hori Teikichi—a commander in Kato's entourage in Washington at the time—who took down this message for transmission to the Navy Ministry. Among the navy men who belonged to the same tradition as Kato were Hori himself, Yamamoto, their seniors such as Taniguchi Naomi, Sakonji Seizo, Yamanashi Katsunoshin, and Yonai Mitsumasa, and their juniors such as Koga Mineichi and Inoue Shigeyoshi.

Hori Teikichi declares that the Washington Conference saved Japan, both internationally and economically. Koga Mineichi, similarly, believed that it was wrong to see Japan as being held down to six-tenths of Britain's and America's strengths; in terms of power and size, he stressed, it would be more correct to consider that Britain and America were voluntarily contenting themselves with ten-sixths of Japan's strength.

Nevertheless, views such as these were naturally seen in some quarters as representing an irritating weakness and subservience to the wishes of Britain and the United States. One man in particular— Admiral Kato Kanji, who had attended the conference as naval adviser and had insisted throughout that Japan should be permitted seven-tenths of America's strength—was vociferous in his complaints after returning home. These complaints were to find a ready hearing not only among younger officers in the navy but among large sections of the public as well.

As to why such protests, which for all their bravado remained unrealistic, should have found such favor in certain quarters, Tsunoda in his *History of Three Generations of the Japanese Navy* says: "Could the majority of people, who had been proclaiming—or having it dinned into their ears—night and day that the hypothetical enemy was America, and that an 8–8–8 fleet was necessary to cope with it, really be expected to switch overnight to a completely different view?"

There were other aspects of the matter, however, that seem to have played still more strongly on the general public's feelings. The battleship *Tosa*, which with a displacement of 39,900 tons was one of the most powerful battleships in the world at the time, was singled out for scrapping under the Washington Naval Treaty, and in February 1925, after a period of use in experiments, was scuttled in three hundred and fifty fathoms of water to the south of Sukumo Bay. It must have seemed intolerable to some people that the great vessel, built as it were with the blood and sweat of the Japanese people, should be sent to the bottom as a result of—as they saw it— pressure from England and America and the pusillanimity of their own leaders.

Shortly after this, Kato Kanji became vice-chief of the Naval General Staff, with Suetsugu Nobumasa under him. Kato Tomosaburo had died in the summer of 1923. With the removal of the latter's restraining hand on the ministry, the conflicts between the "fleet faction" led by Kato and Suetsugu, with its advocacy of hawkish policies toward America, and the "treaty faction" which followed Kato Tomosaburo's views became still more clearly defined, and the former was gradually to drive the latter out.

In short, some of the factors that were eventually to lead Japan to embark on the very war with America that Yamamoto predicted it must inevitably lose were already present at this period. And it is no wonder that when, at the 1930 London Naval Disarmament Conference held eight years after the Washington Conference, Japan found itself limited to six-tenths of the British and American strengths where auxiliary vessels as well as capital vessels were concerned, there should occur an outburst of public indignation, and that more and more people both within and outside the navy should see this restriction as an insult to Japan's status as a first-rate power and a grave threat to its defenses.

Even so, it would be wrong to assume that the hawkish element within the navy was in favor of immediate hostilities with America.

There were very few even among the most hawkish, at least until sometime around 1935, who were sufficiently bold and sufficiently ignorant to believe that Japan could really win a war against the United States. For example, Admiral Suetsugu Nobumasa, who became commander in chief of the Combined Fleet in November 1933, was forever currying favor with the young officers by mouthing anti-American and anti-British views, but it seems unlikely that even he, had he been questioned by the emperor, could have promised with any confidence to bring America to its knees in the event of war.

Hori Teikichi, who was chief of the Naval Affairs Bureau around the time of the 1930 London conference, disliked hearing people in the ministry, carried away by public sentiment, talking of Japan's "invincible fleet." "Remember how Spain's much-vaunted 'invincible Armada' was beaten by the English navy," he would often say. "Heaven knows what will happen to the navy if naval officers themselves start getting the same inflated notions as the general public." At that time, in fact, no professional navy man in any responsible post was willing to use words such as "invincible" lightly.

Each of them, in his own mind, recognized that the Japanese navy was essentially a defensive navy; at conferences of the time, whether they included the Naval General Staff, the Navy Ministry, or the fleet, arguments were concerned primarily with figures, and whether Japan's strength should be sixty percent or seventy percent of that of the two leading powers.

The same outlook seems to have prevailed within both the "treaty faction" and the "fleet faction." The more hawkish among navy men, however, also had their own—not necessarily emotional—viewpoints and theories which should, at least, be given a hearing.

As they saw things, sea power in wartime varied in direct proportion to the squares of the relative strengths of the nations concerned. Thus a proportion of 10:6 at a time of inactivity became 100:36 when the effect of movement was taken into account. It would not be possible for Japan to launch an attack on America and win, but should the American fleet move against Japan, Japan, to avoid defeat, would need ships in the proportion of at least 100:49—that is, vessels equivalent to seventy percent of the American fleet. Without them, the navy could not fulfill its responsibilities where national defense was concerned. Thus there was a strong feeling among such men that they had had enough of disarmament conferences, and an unwillingness to be bound any further by treaties and the like.

These men were extremely critical of Yamamoto both before and during the war, and have remained so ever since. Although Yamamoto is generally believed to have been loved and revered by everybody, this was not really the case. He had quite a number of enemies within the navy—and still has not a few even today. The picture of Yamamoto as a kind of idol worshiped by all former naval men without fail is no more than a pleasant fiction.

5

The question arises, then, of what Yamamoto himself really thought about the treaty question.

During the thirteen years between the Washington Conference of 1921–22 and the beginning of the unrestricted race to build ships, Japan participated in five international disarmament conferences in all. Washington was succeeded by a three-nation naval disarmament conference in Geneva in 1927, the London Naval Disarmament Conference of 1930, the disarmament conference sponsored in Geneva by the League of Nations in 1932–33, the preliminary talks of 1934 now under discussion, and the main London Naval Conference of 1935. Yamamoto was directly concerned with only two of these, the 1930 conference and the 1934 preliminary talks, but ever since going to London in 1930 he had been making a fairly exhaustive study of the disarmament question.

He had been stationed twice in America, moreover, and the chance to see for himself the Detroit automobile industry and the oil fields of Texas had convinced him, as he told people frequently, that for Japan to get involved in an unrestricted shipbuilding race with the U.S. would inevitably lead it to overstrain its resources.

As Yamamoto, Hori, and Inoue Shigeyoshi saw things, the intense discussions within the navy over a difference of a mere ten percent meant very little; they could not believe, in fact, that the seventy percent for which the hawks called could ever enable Japan to feel secure in its defenses where America was concerned.

Their attitude to the "N^2" equation was that if Japan and America went to war and the two fleets threw their whole weight against each other, the hundred percent fleet would be able to concentrate its attack on the seventy percent fleet, whereas the seventy percent fleet's attack would be scattered among its opponent's vessels. Moreover, when one took into account the other side's ability to construct vessels following the outbreak of war, and its industrial capacity as a whole, it was clear that the seventy percent would gradually be reduced to sixty, then fifty, then forty percent, until with time it finally vanished altogether. Thus even with a seventy percent navy Japan would still be obliged to stick to its policy of avoiding a conflict with the United States. It was not desirable of course that Japan should conclude a treaty unfavorable to itself; but still more undesirable was the possibility of finding itself without any treaty at all. International talks always involved compromising, and some compromise must be found, as favorable to Japan as possible, so that the limitation treaty as such could continue to exist. This, it seems, was Yamamoto's basic way of thinking.

6

The Washington Naval Treaty was due to expire in 1936. Should any one signatory give notice two years previous to this of its intention to abrogate the treaty, the treaty would automatically lapse in that same year, 1936.

The London Naval Treaty, similarly, was valid for only five years, and would expire in 1935. In this case, however, there was an agreement that the signatories should hold a conference one year before this date in order to discuss the future of the disarmament question. Thus England had proposed preliminary talks in London in 1934, so as to allow the five participants—Japan, England, America, France, and Italy—to prepare the ground for a new agreement on naval limitation. Of the five nations nominally concerned, France and Italy were, as naval powers, on a totally different level from the other three, and as such had little say in the outcome.

The prevailing mood in Japan at the time was that the Washington and London treaties could not be allowed to stand as they were, and the Japanese government had privately more or less decided to allow the Washington Naval Treaty to lapse. But it did not feel, it seems, that Japan should allow this to leave it without any treaty at all. It is interesting here to see what contemporary government documents such as the "Instructions to Be Given to the Imperial Delegate" and the "Imperial Government's Policy concerning the Preliminary Talks on Naval Disarmament" have to say. One finds, for example, the following passage: "Since the continued existence of the treaty concerning restrictions on naval armament signed in Washington in 1922 would be against the interest of the nation's defenses, and in view of the nation's basic policy concerning such restrictions, notification of Japan's intention to abrogate the treaty should be given by the last day of this year."

On the other hand, another passage reads: "On Japan's side, however, abrogation of the treaty does not mean that it is unwilling to see any agreement signed concerning the reduction of naval armaments."

And again: "Wishing to see the preliminary talks carried through in as friendly and effective a manner as possible, Japan is at the moment refraining from giving notice of its abrogation; it would be of considerable advantage in mollifying public opinion if the nations concerned were first to agree to give notice of their abrogation within the year, then to cooperate in making efforts to draw up a new treaty. The desirability of such a procedure should be explained, as the occasion arises, to the delegates of the countries concerned, and efforts should be made to steer things in this direction."

In other words, the government wished to do away with the Washington Naval Treaty and its 5–5–3 stipulation, yet was unwilling for Japan to incur the international opprobrium of having been the first to suggest it. If possible, it wanted all the signatories to give joint notice of the treaty's abrogation, then to join in concluding a new treaty that would leave no unpleasant emotional aftermath and would be a little more favorable to Japan.

Despite a rather overbearing tone, the contents of the documents are not, in themselves, particularly extreme. The instructions have one eye on opinion both at home and abroad, and at times seem almost timid. They talk, for example, of "avoiding unnecessarily irritating public opinion in the countries concerned," and of "paving the way for a new treaty sufficient to ensure the security of the nation's defenses while easing as far as possible the burden on the public." Precisely what kind of new disarmament agreement, then, did Japan hope to obtain once it had abrogated the Washington Naval Treaty? It wished to establish the principle of non-threat and non-aggression, and the form that this was to take was the laying down by Japan, England, and the U.S.—possibly with France and Italy as well—of a common limit which their naval power must not exceed, and which should be observed by all equally. In principle, the limit in question was to be kept as low as possible, weapons of attack were to be abandoned, and each country was to concentrate on improving its defensive armaments.

For this reason, the Japanese government had Yamamoto call for the scrapping of all aircraft carriers. It also agreed that, as a bargaining point in the negotiations, he could even go so far as to suggest the scrapping of all capital vessels. These were fairly drastic proposals, and Yamamoto probably did not believe for a moment that Britain and America would accept them as they stood. It was his own belief, moreover, that one day the air corps would come to dominate the fleet; thus Tokyo's idea that he should use the abolition of capital ships as a bargaining point while aiming, essentially, at the abolition of aircraft carriers would have seemed odd in his eyes. However, insofar as he had been appointed Japanese representative, he was a servant of the nation, and as such was in no position to make any deal that diverged too far from the lines laid down in his instructions from the government. (Yamamoto's position in London somewhat resembled that of Nomura Kichisaburo in Washington just before the outbreak of hostilities. The efforts that he made were directed toward finding some point of compromise with England and America within the lines laid down by his instructions, and to lay the foundations for the conclusion of a new agreement.)

7

Meetings took place on a number of occasions beginning at the end of October. The English side was represented by Prime Minister Ramsay MacDonald, together with Foreign Secretary Simon, First Lord of the Admiralty Eyres-Monsell, Chief of the Naval Staff Chatfield, Vice-Chief of the Naval Staff Little, and Foreign Office Counselor Craigie. The last-named was the Sir Robert Craigie who three years later was to go to Japan as ambassador.

The American representatives were Ambassador Norman Davis and Chief of Naval Operations Standley. Thus the teams Japan had to deal with both consisted of minister or ambassador and navy men with the rank of admiral. Japan had Ambassador Matsudaira, but the

35

chief naval representative, Yamamoto, was only a rear admiral. On November 15, during the course of the conference, he was promoted to vice admiral, but even so he was still outranked.

But though he may have been inferior in rank, Yamamoto's ability—still more, his sincerity—had given him a high reputation on the other side ever since, in 1930, he had visited London with the delegation headed by Takarabe and Sakonji. Kaya Okinori, who also participated in the 1930 conference as Finance Ministry representative, has said of Yamamoto: "However fierce the argument, he never showed stubborn pride, nor did he say things merely intended to please. Discussion with him never left an unpleasant aftertaste." It seems likely that the impression received by plenipotentiaries and delegates from the other countries was much the same as this. In dealing with foreigners, just as with the Japanese press, he told no lies and uttered no platitudes. He seems, in fact, to have succeeded in upsetting preconceived notions of the typical Japanese as a man not to be trusted, a man with an equivocal smile on his face and something quite different in his heart. It was this that enabled him, though only a vice admiral, to get along on equal terms with the more illustrious figures on the British and American sides.

Records still survive of the main points made in each of the discussions with the British and Americans, but there is no need to go into them in too much detail here. Yamamoto's manner of speaking was abrupt, but he would yield with grace whenever he saw fit and press a point without fear or hesitation if he thought it necessary. Enomoto Shigeharu, who was present with him, found his manner entirely refreshing. Yamamoto had a considerable command of English, and could hold his own at cocktail parties and other similar gatherings. On important questions, however, he invariably spoke in Japanese and had Mizota interpret for him. "It takes twice as long when you have an interpreter," he said, "and gives you time to watch the other man and consider your next move."

One day, the records show, Yamamoto was asked by the Americans why, when the Japanese had been satisfied with the 5–5–3 arrangement at the Washington Conference, they should start complaining about it now. In reply, he referred in detail to the strides made in aviation and technical advances in the refueling of vessels at sea; the times were different, he said, and distances on the oceans had shrunk. By now, it had become impossible to maintain a strategic balance with these ratios, even in the seas around Japan.

On another occasion, the Americans argued that equal naval strengths did not necessarily mean equal security, and suggested that the 5–3 ratio ought not to present any threat to Japan. "If America's five is no threat to Japan's three," Yamamoto countered, "then surely Japan's five should present no threat to America's five?"

All these exchanges, however, were full of bluffs and counterbluffs, the objective being to pave the way for a new agreement as favorable to Japan as possible; it does not follow that every exchange accurately represented Yamamoto's personal views on the subject.

Two letters that Yamamoto wrote to Miwa Yoshitake from Grosvenor House in London that year still survive. Miwa, who as already mentioned served as junior assistant while Yamamoto was naval attaché in America, was one of Yamamoto's favorite subordinates. He was also a born aviator. The first of the two letters is short and deals with unimportant matters such as the outcome of games of bridge that Yamamoto played with the American chief of Naval Operations, but the second is worth quoting at length, since it seems to give a good idea of Yamamoto's way of thinking:

Dear Lieutenant Commander Miwa:

Thank you for your letter of October 5. I am sorry not to have written before; it is not so much that I had no time as that the pressure of heavy responsibilities leaves me no inclination to take up my pen.

As I expected, it looks as though the conference is going to be fraught with difficulties; given my own poor abilities, and the state of Japan's national strength, it's going to be very difficult to carry our point of view.

One thing that has surprised me, though, is the willingness—however irksome they may privately find it—of the three British ministers, the American ambassador, and the chiefs of Naval Operations and the Naval Staff to listen politely, at least on the surface, to the foolish views being put forward by a youngster like myself; it shows what an immeasurable difference there is in Japan's strength now compared with the time of the Washington Conference, and I feel keenly that the time has come for this mighty empire rising in the east to devote itself, with all due circumspection, to advancing its own fortunes.

The example afforded before the Great War by Germany—which, if only it had exercised forbearance for another five or ten years, would by now be unrivaled in Europe—suggests that the task facing us now is to build up our strength calmly and with circumspection. Even though the present conference may not be successful, I sense that the day may not be so distant when we shall have Britain and the United States kowtowing to us.

For the navy, the most urgent task of all is to make rapid strides in the field of aviation. . . .

The letter is dated November 10, 1934. One wonders what Yamamoto meant in referring to "foolish views"; it seems likely that he meant something more than the self-depreciation common in Japanese when referring to one's own opinions. Yamamoto's surviving friends agree that it obviously refers to the "basic policy" of the imperial government which he was having to expound. One other thing clear from this letter, however, is that Yamamoto still held a very rosy view of Japan's future—even though, as the frequent use of the word "circumspection" shows, it was qualified by fear lest Japan should tread the path followed by Germany in the First World War.

8

Neither Britain nor America was at all disposed to accept the Japanese proposal for establishing a common limit to their strengths. There was a subtle difference, however, between the attitudes of each country to the Japanese plan. Britain's attitude to Japan had throughout been comparatively friendly and open to compromise, whereas America had been relatively distant and inflexible. Privately, even so, American representative Norman Davis was lamenting Yamamoto's acuteness. "I don't know whether it's because I'm inferior to Hughes or because Yamamoto is superior to Kato," he said, "but where in Washington America had the upper hand, this time it's Yamamoto who's beginning to get an edge over us." The Kato in question, of course, was Kato Tomosaburo, Japanese plenipotentiary to the Washington Conference. "Hughes" was Charles E. Hughes, who, as U.S. secretary of state, presided over the Washington Conference.

Unlike Japan, America and England preferred not to change their representatives at successive conferences dealing with the same question. Norman Davis, who had attended the U.S.-Japan communications conference in 1920, fourteen years earlier, seems to have been aware of Yamamoto's potential at that early date. There is a story that he went out of his way—he was undersecretary of state at the time—to ask Ambassador Shidehara the identity of the naval commander serving as the ambassador's aide, and commented, "You've got some good men in the Japanese navy!"

Robert Craigie, of the British Foreign Office, was another who set great store by Yamamoto. On his arrival in Tokyo as British ambassador in September 1937, Craigie created a stir by making a private call on Navy Vice-Minister Yamamoto even before his official call on the foreign minister. (This also, incidentally, provided material for those who slandered Yamamoto as a "running dog" of Britain and America.)

British representatives, Counselor Craigie included, had of course their own private reasons for seeming on the whole favorably disposed to Japan. There were two different views concerning the course Britain should take. One party believed that the Washington Naval Treaty could be left as it stood. The other—which seems to have had the upper hand—felt that in Washington Britain, traditionally the world's leading sea power, had been caught up with by newcomer America. If things went on as they were, Britain might eventually find itself left behind. At talks between Japan and Britain on October 30, Foreign Secretary Simon expressed great alarm at the idea that Japan might give notice of its intention to allow the Washington Naval Treaty to lapse, since the other nations would then be left without a treaty, which might well lead to an unrestricted race to build warships. "America at the moment," he added, in a warning to Japan that showed what was really on his mind, "has tremendous resources and is tremendously wealthy, and the president, I have heard, is determined, should the Washington treaty lapse, to spend huge sums on the construction of warships. This may well, in view of what one knows of the American national character, be the case. England itself would deplore such a development, having no desire whatsoever to embark on a shipbuilding race with the United States."

Where Japan made frequent use of the term "national prestige," Britain referred equally often to "vulnerability." The former, of course, referred to the damage that would be done to Japan's pride if it, as one of the three great naval powers, continued to be allowed only sixty percent of the strength of the other two. Britain itself attached great importance to "national prestige," and its representatives assured the Japanese of their full understanding of the position.

At the same time, however, the British pointed out that each nation's "vulnerability" varied in accordance with its situation. If the Japanese plan were adopted, a vulnerable nation such as Great Britain might find itself restricted to the same strength as other, relatively invulnerable nations, and the question that preoccupied the British was what reassurances the highly vulnerable countries would be given.

In translating the word "vulnerability" Mizota apparently used a Japanese term signifying "weakness" or "fragility." This does not fully convey the original sense of "having an Achilles' heel," but Yamamoto himself almost certainly grasped the sense of the word in the original—since the word "vulnerable" is commonly used in bridge.

With America, on the other hand, there were signs that it was hoping to drive Japan into a position where it would be forced to give notification, alone, of its abrogation of the Washington Naval Treaty. This would make it possible to put all the blame on Japan for failure to achieve disarmament. Should a treatyless period follow, with an unrestricted race to construct ships, it would be Japan and England that felt the pinch; America itself would be comparatively little affected. Yamamoto seems to have perceived this and to have been afraid of falling into the American trap. His only alternative in the long run apparently was to rely on the help of England, which was comparatively well disposed, in finding some line on which the two countries could compromise.

9

It should not be imagined, however, that Yamamoto's days in London were entirely burdened with care and bound by formalities. The conference, being in the nature of preliminary talks, had a fairly informal atmosphere, and despite the comparatively uncooperative American stand and occasional clashes of opinion that ruptured the talks temporarily, the general atmosphere was calm and amicable. Yamamoto managed to enjoy his stay in London; he willingly attended cocktail parties and dinners given by representatives of the other countries, went shopping in London—buying himself a high-quality snakewood walking stick—and played bridge with the American and British chiefs of the Naval Staff and Naval Operations, and relieved Admiral Chatfield of twenty pounds in the process.

One Saturday in November, he was invited to the prime minister's official country residence, Chequers, for a lunch party given by Ramsay MacDonald, and the question arose of what the Japanese guests should wear. Matsudaira was for going in morning dress, but naval attaché Oka objected that they would look silly in morning dress at a weekend gathering, so they eventually compromised on black jackets and striped trousers. When they arrived at Chequers, after a drive of thirty-eight miles through beautiful late autumn scenery, they found Ramsay MacDonald waiting for them in plus fours.

MacDonald was a widower, and his daughter Mary acted as hostess. Although the prime minister was far older than Yamamoto, his manner was extremely cordial; according to Enomoto the two men seemed, almost, to recognize each other as kindred spirits.

They were also invited to visit David Lloyd George at his home. The former premier—the first British prime minister of humble origin, known for a certain roughness in his speech and behavior— had very poor eyesight by now. He regretted being unable to see Yamamoto's face, and asked if he could touch it instead, so Yamamoto was obliged to stand still while Lloyd George stroked his features with a hairy hand rather like a bear's paw.

In London, once the day's talks—or official dinner—were over, Yamamoto and the rest would go back to their office at the Japanese embassy in Portland Square for a private conference, then return to their hotel in Grosvenor Square. They must have been tired by then, but Yamamoto would round up Enomoto, Mitsunobu, and Mizota for a game of poker or bridge, which would go on, if he had his way, until three in the morning. Mitsunobu, who always lost, would try to get out of it early by placing a pound note on the table and announcing, "When this is gone, I'm going to bed."

Each day brought a pile of letters from Japan. Yamamoto would reply to every one of them, even the letters from primary-school pupils inquiring if he was "doing his best for his country." His evenings were occupied with gambling, so he had only the dawn hours for writing letters and going through his papers. Some people have expressed wonder that Yamamoto should have written so many letters. One theory is that he was essentially a solitary man both before and during the war, and that letter-writing served to lessen his loneliness. Another holds that the letters were little more than a means of making himself popular. Either way, the fact is that he always replied, even to letters from children.

If Mizota and Enomoto found anything of interest as they read the newspapers over their morning coffee, they would take it along to Yamamoto's room. They themselves would still be in pajamas, but Yamamoto would already be dressed in a dark suit, sitting at his desk making preparations for the day's talks, or writing his eternal letters. They often wondered just when he found time to sleep. Yamamoto himself declared that, as a military man, he could go without food and rest if necessary; it seems, in fact, that he could get by for days on end with only four hours' sleep.

One morning in December, Yamamoto showed considerable alarm when Enomoto casually remarked that he had had a dream about Hori Teikichi; he obviously took it as a bad omen. It seems strange that such a rationally minded individual as Yamamoto should have been superstitious about dreams. Some people, admittedly—and particularly those who, like Yamamoto, are fond of games of chance—do seem to be able to sense, either in their waking or sleeping hours, something that is happening to someone close to them. One way or another, Hori had been on Yamamoto's mind ever since he left Tokyo, and if Enomoto's mention of his dream was enough to alarm him so much, one cannot help suspecting that he must have had some clear warning of what was going to happen to his friend. Hori, a contemporary of Yamamoto's at the Naval Academy, was one of his most trusted and admired associates. Among the countless letters from Yamamoto that survive, those in which he seems truly to have laid bare his soul are all addressed either to Hori, a few other close friends, or to one or two female acquaintances. According to Enomoto, "only Hori could have succeeded so well in taming and refining an impetuous 'country samurai' from Nagaoka."

Hori became a vice admiral in 1933, one year earlier than Yamamoto;

he shared the latter's views and was regarded with even greater loathing by the hawks of the day. Around that time, the members of the "fleet faction," with Admiral Kato Kanji presiding, were holding a series of meetings at a restaurant in Akasaka, at which they plotted to lay low once and for all the advocates of retention of the treaty. Some of those who attended, it seems, were prepared to go to fairly drastic lengths.

In January 1933, Osumi Mineo—in Tsunoda Jun's words, "the timeserving Osumi"—had become navy minister and, in deference to the faction led by Kato Kanji, Suetsugu Nobumasa, and Takahashi Sankichi, connived at the downfall of a number of officers of the orthodox faction established by Kato Tomosaburo. These included Yamanashi Katsunoshin as well as Taniguchi Naomi, Sakonji Seizo, and Terashima Takeshi. Finally, Hori Teikichi was suddenly relieved of his post on December 10, 1934, and, on the fifteenth, placed on the reserve list.

Before leaving Tokyo, Yamamoto had put in a good word for Hori with both the minister and Prince Fushimi, chief of the Naval General Staff. Prince Fushimi's reply, apparently, was that he never interfered in appointments; in the end, however, he did just that, being persuaded by the hawks within the Naval General Staff to believe slander against Hori and to have him fired. (Hori's detractors claimed that he had been guilty of cowardly behavior as commander of a Japanese flotilla at the time of the Shanghai Incident. No further details are available. It is a fact, however, that at the time of the fleet's shelling of shore batteries along the central China coast in support of the landing force, Hori delayed opening fire because a few civilians still seemed to be in the neighborhood of the batteries. Later, during the Korean War, when the Japanese Red Cross began a campaign to supply blood for the United Nations forces, it was Hori who asked why the Red Cross should give blood only to United Nations' troops and not to North Korean and Communist Chinese soldiers as well; such discrimination, he declared, ran counter to the spirit of the Red Cross. Episodes such as this may well give a clue to the nature of the earlier charges against him.)

When Yamamoto in London learned via a message from Yoshida Zengo, head of the Naval Affairs Bureau, that Enomoto's dream about Hori had in fact been an ill omen, he immediately wrote Hori a letter in which he deplored his dismissal and the "Sakano affair" as signs of an increasing tendency within the navy to passivity and appeasement of the army.

The "Sakano affair" refers to an episode that took place in June that year, when Rear Admiral Sakano Tsuneyoshi, head of the Naval Affairs Bureau Propaganda Department (later Information Division), incurred the wrath of Navy Minister Osumi and was dismissed his post. Sakano, born in the same year as Yamamoto, had graduated from the Naval Academy one year later than Yamamoto and Hori, whose views he shared. He is still alive and well, though advanced in years. "Until the time of the Manchurian Incident," he says, "the navy was clearly distinguishable from the army, but in the end it gradually became the same." On the question of a disarmament treaty, he says, "they were all worked up just because Japan wasn't allowed a few extra percent of tonnage—as though it was a defeat for Japan. They were preoccupied with the idea of war, without giving any thought to the national resources as a whole. Personally, I was sure they were wrong."

The episode occurred on June 1, the day on which the army's Ugaki Kazushige, who still held the post of governor-general of Korea, arrived in Tokyo in response to a campaign to set him up as prime minister. A prominent army figure, he was active behind the scenes in the political world, and had enemies both within the army and among the hawks in the navy; Admiral Kato Kanji had a particular dislike for him.

Asked for his views on the subject by Navy Ministry reporters of the Kokuchokai, Sakano made a statement saying that the navy was a "blank sheet" (not yet prejudiced either way) on the matter. The Kokuchokai was a kind of miniature of the navy in being divided between a "fleet faction" and a "treaty faction," and it happened that the reporter in charge that day held views close to those of the "fleet faction." Thus the article he wrote embellished Sakano's remarks so as to imply that the navy supported Ugaki.

Navy Minister Osumi Mineo was at the home of Fleet Admiral Togo, hero of the Russo-Japanese War, who was gravely ill at the time. On reading the article, Osumi flew into a rage and, summoning a section chief of the Personnel Bureau, ordered him to prepare papers putting Sakano on the reserve list. That evening, Sakano visited Osumi's private residence in order to explain things to him, but all he could get out of the minister was that it was not a good thing to say anything likely to offend Admiral Kato, who was a military councillor.

Sakano, being a member of the "treaty faction" and from the same part of the country as Ugaki, was held to have deliberately put in a word for the latter, and his original statement—which was merely intended to deny the possibility of any anti-Ugaki fervor within the navy—was taken in the end as infringing the principle of non-interference by naval officers in political affairs; thus he was dismissed from his post and given a warning.

A messenger came to Sakano, bringing word from his superiors that he should keep out of the public eye as far as possible for a while and promising to "make things right before long." When Sakano told Hori of this promise, Hori dismissed it as worthless. Sure enough, in the regular list of reappointments, Sakano, instead of being appointed commander of a minor naval station as had already been unofficially decided, was suddenly put on the reserve list, and Hori along with him.

Such are the general outlines of the "Sakano affair," which seems to have saddened and angered Yamamoto greatly, particularly since the same fate had befallen Hori, one of his closest friends. He called the dismissals "utterly stupid," and demanded to know "which was more important for the navy, a division of cruisers or a man like Hori Teikichi?" He also declared that he had lost all energy and enthusiasm for his work, and seemed in fact almost alarmingly despondent.

As soon as he learned what had happened, he realized what was behind it, and his dislike of and resentment toward members of the "fleet faction" for having fired Hori seem to have stayed with him until the end of his life. Nagumo Chuichi, later commander in chief of the force that attacked Hawaii, was one of those who allied himself with the men responsible for firing Hori; and in a statement opposing the London Naval Treaty, Nagumo's name appeared alongside that of Suetsugu Nobumasa. These are facts that should be remembered for the light they throw on later events.

One wonders, even so, whether this infighting within the navy was, in the long run, a product solely of differences in views on strategy and the limitation treaties. A certain former vice admiral, still alive today, has some interesting things to say on this score:

45

This is only my own idea, but it seems to me that questions of position, pride, and military pensions also played a part in producing the atmosphere prevailing at the time. An admiral normally led a comfortable life, able to employ two or three maids and with a Navy Ministry car at his disposal, but once he was put on the reserve list, all this came to an abrupt end. A fleet admiral retained his rank for life, but an ordinary admiral was retired, if I remember correctly, at sixty-five. Everyone, however able, was obliged to leave his job at that age. A man with a strong personality, still interested in worldly things but finding himself nearing retirement, inevitably began to kick against the inevitable. Unlike business leaders, few of them had many savings, so, being only human, they naturally wanted to retain their jobs as long as possible. That necessitated having a number of protégés who could be used in various ways to exert pressure for them; and naturally enough they hoped to bring about their rivals' early downfall. What gradually happened, in fact, was much the same as in the army—the sort of situation where middle-ranking officers came to exert influence over their seniors. For that reason I sometimes urged that the government should revise its ideas on military pensions, but I was invariably told that it was hopeless in a country as poor as Japan.

10

In London, the talks went on through November and December. The British were showing signs of wanting to prevent them from getting bogged down and of finding some way to a compromise. They even suggested that if quantitative restrictions proved impossible, an agreement should be signed providing at least for qualitative restrictions— limiting, for example, the tonnage of individual vessels and the caliber of their guns—as a means of relaxing the race to build ships. The American delegates, however, insisted that the London Naval Treaty should be amended and the Washington Naval Treaty retained in principle. When December came, they began to use Christmas as an excuse for talking of returning home temporarily. Yamamoto said that even if the talks were suspended it would be better to fix a date for reconvening, and suggested that the recess should last until March the following year; he himself would return to Japan in the interval. But the Americans said vaguely that there was no point in fixing a date for its own sake, and on December 20 Ambassador Davis, Chief of Naval Operations Standley, and the rest of the delegation left London for home.

During the period that followed, informal talks were to continue between Japan and Britain, and at one stage it was actually agreed that some solution might be possible by incorporating Japanese proposals into the British compromise plan and getting Britain to persuade America to agree to the result.

As Yamamoto had promised at his farewell party in Tokyo, he rarely sought fresh instructions from home, but twice in December—on the eleventh and the twenty-fifth—circumstances required him to cable Tokyo asking its views. However, there had been a subtle change in the atmosphere at home in the meantime. Although it seems that those in positions of real responsibility in the Naval General Staff were sound enough in their views, a special climate had been created by the hawkish younger officers and other officers on the reserve list, who insisted vociferously that if things were left to Yamamoto and he were inveigled into making some pledge or other Japan might find itself bound hand and foot at the main conference the following year. This was reflected in Tokyo's replies to Yamamoto's requests for instructions, which were distinctly cool and implied the hope that, at least while the talks were recessed, he would not take too much upon himself.

Nevertheless, Yamamoto persisted with his efforts into the New Year. The British side, too, seems to have been extremely reluctant to give up.

At the main conference in 1935, Yamamoto's place in London was to be taken by Nagano Osami, and according to those who accompanied him, Nagano was an entirely different kettle of fish. By now, moreover, both Britain and America had given up hope. Thus the conference was never more than a formality, and the crucial period for world naval disarmament—the period that decided whether or not the world should enter upon a treatyless term of unrestricted rivalry in building ships—was to prove to have been those three months, beginning in October 1934, during which Yamamoto had negotiated so doggedly.

In mid-January 1935, on the day after it had been decided to break off even the informal talks with Britain, Chief of the Naval Staff

Chatfield privately telephoned Mizota and asked for one more meeting with Yamamoto. He insisted, however, that it should be kept top secret, and that even Mizota should not attend. Early the next day, therefore, Mizota—who hitherto had never once left Yamamoto's side—set off in the chief delegate's car, wearing plus fours, in order to play golf. (Yamamoto's two missing fingers prevented him from getting a good grip on the club, and he never played.) A large number of reporters were keeping watch in the hotel lobby, but seeing Yamamoto's interpreter and car both go off, they dispersed, convinced that nothing more would happen that day.

Somewhat later, Yamamoto hailed a taxi and went off privately to meet Chatfield. There is no information as to what exchanges took place between the two men. What is certain, though, is that no definite agreement was reached. On January 28, Yamamoto and his party left Grosvenor House, the hotel in which they had spent three months, and, seen off by Ambassador Matsudaira, boarded a train at Victoria Station on the first leg of their trip across Siberia and back to Japan.

On this particular trip to Europe, Yamamoto did not stay over either in Paris or in his beloved Monaco. He did, however, spend one night in Berlin, having been requested to do so by the Japanese ambassador in Berlin, Mushanokoji Kintomo. This request, in fact, came not from Mushanokoji himself but indirectly from Nazi leaders. After the war, Mushanokoji published his reminiscences of Yamamoto; though sometimes inaccurate in their detail, they are extremely interesting, and the following account of this episode is based upon them.

It was the second year following Hitler's seizure of power, and Ribbentrop—a former wine merchant who was later to become German foreign minister, though at this stage an ordinary Nazi Party member—already seems to have wielded considerable influence within the party. He too, in a different way from Chatfield or Norman Davis, was very interested in what Yamamoto did in London. While the preliminary disarmament talks were in progress there, Ribbentrop, in conference with the German navy minister, planned to have Yamamoto stop over in Berlin on his way home for a meeting with Hitler. For this purpose, he dispatched a secretary to London to try to find out what was going on in the negotiations and at the same time to talk directly with Yamamoto and suggest that he visit Berlin for the proposed interview with Hitler.

Yamamoto seems to have had little enthusiasm for the proposal. Like Yonai Mitsumasa, he appears to have been deeply suspicious of Germany, at least as it was under the Nazis—which was, almost certainly, the reason why Ribbentrop was so keen to get him to Berlin. Apart from the direct contact, the Japanese embassy in Berlin was also asked to help arrange things. Mushanokoji discussed the matter several times with the Germans, as a result of which he telephoned the Japanese embassy in London the day before Yamamoto and his party were due to leave. He spoke first with Matsudaira, then got Yamamoto to the phone and told him, "I think you'd better meet Ribbentrop and the navy minister. As for Hitler, I know how you feel about him, and I myself don't think it would be a good idea for you both to meet, so I suggest you pay a purely courtesy call on the two other men."

Yamamoto accepted Mushanokoji's recommendation, and the following day, on a train via Holland, arrived at Berlin's Friedrichstrasse Station. "When he arrived at the station," Mushanokoji wrote later, "he smiled, but said scarcely a word. I introduced him to Ribbentrop, and then to the navy minister, but though his responses were crisp and created a good impression on the other side, he made absolutely no move to bring up subjects of conversation of his own accord. In this respect he was like Yonai. But I had the impression that he was considerably sharper than the latter had been." Doubtless Yamamoto was determined to keep his mouth shut and not say anything that the Nazis might take as a pledge. As we shall see later, despite the courtesy talks held between the Japanese and German navies on this occasion, when Yamamoto later became vice-minister he violently opposed the Tripartite Pact between Japan, Germany, and Italy.

That evening, a private dinner for Yamamoto and his party was given at the Japanese embassy. Again Yamamoto was extremely taciturn. However, when something turned the conversation to bridge, poker, and gambling, he suddenly became a different man and held forth at length.

After one night in Berlin, the party passed through Poland and into Russian territory, then boarded the Trans-Siberian Railway in Moscow.

Day and night throughout the whole interminable journey, Yamamoto played poker or bridge with Enomoto, Mitsunobu, and Mizota. It was the season of intense cold, and there were long stops at every station to permit inspection of rolling stock and removal of ice accumulated on the underside of the floors. In Novosibirsk, the Japanese consul was waiting with a large batch of *sushi* that his wife had made. When the train finally arrived, he and his wife hurried to Yamamoto's compartment, where they found him in the middle of a game with his colleagues, and cards and poker chips spread all around them. Yamamoto thanked the pair cordially for coming, delighted at having such a typical Japanese delicacy delivered in the middle of a Siberian winter.

11

Once the Manchurian border was crossed, there were well-wishers waiting to see them wherever the train passed. On February 7, Yamamoto and his party left Manchouli for Harbin, passed through Korea, and on the afternoon of February 12, 1935, amidst lightly falling snow, arrived back in Tokyo after an absence of five months. A large crowd of high officials, including Navy Minister Osumi and Foreign Minister Hirota Koki, was waiting to welcome them in Tokyo Station; Yamamoto and Osumi, however, must have greeted each other with very mixed feelings. Also on the platform were the usual women from the Shimbashi geisha quarter, and friends with whom Yamamoto had studied at Harvard. Walking past them, Yamamoto stuck his tongue out briefly when no one else was looking.

The stationmaster preceded him along the underground passage and out to the front approach to Tokyo Station, where a car was waiting to take him to the palace to sign his name in the visitors' book. However, when he saw the citizens of Tokyo lining the road in front of the station and on, past the Marunouchi Building, toward the Wadakura Gate of the palace, he got out of the car again and walked through the driving snow as far as the entrance to the palace. One could interpret this in two ways: he was a thoughtful man who was always ready to respond to the wishes of those about him; or he was consciously playing to the gallery. Probably it was a bit of both.

Two days later, on the morning of February 14, he went to the navy minister's residence to deliver his official report to Osumi in the presence of Prince Fushimi, chief of the Naval General Staff. In the afternoon, he made a similar report at a conference of military councillors. His official report to the emperor was dated February 19. For a long time, neither the original nor any copy of this document could be found, and it was presumed to have been destroyed either accidentally or deliberately at the palace or the Navy Ministry during the confusion of the immediate postwar period, but a copy of it eventually turned up among a heap of documents in the former army General Staff Headquarters. Since it is extremely long, I will omit entirely the parts dealing with the progress of the preliminary talks and quote here only the concluding section:

> At the preliminary talks, the representatives of all the nations concerned engaged in a frank and honest exchange of opinions in a consistently friendly atmosphere, working sincerely to discover some basis for a new treaty; there was no suggestion whatsoever of any two countries working together to put pressure on, or shut out, the third.
>
> The British in particular—though partly, presumably, because of their position as sponsors of the talks—showed a singular eagerness to bring about a disarmament agreement, and were unflagging in their efforts to ensure the smooth progress of negotiations.
>
> Thus both Britain and America listened with the greatest interest to what we had to say, and we were able to make a full exposition of the imperial government's basic policy. Nevertheless, the differences between the three countries' positions has so far made it impossible to reach any agreement.
>
> I deeply regret that it was not possible to persuade Britain and America to accept the imperial government's views, and am convinced of the necessity for still further efforts in this direction.
>
> In concluding this report, I am Your Imperial Majesty's most obedient servant,

Isoroku

It seems likely that the essence of what Yamamoto wished to say was in this last section. A former naval officer, at present engaged in research on the question, is of the opinion that the report to the emperor implied considerably more than it expressed on the surface. The firm denial of any collusion between Britain and the United States to bring pressure to bear on Japan, or to shut it out, constituted a strong protest—he believes—against the general trend of feeling at home at the time and against irresponsible speculation.

As a result of his five months' visit to London, Yamamoto found himself suddenly famous, but following his return the attitude of the leaders of the navy was distinctly unfriendly. Navy Minister Osumi, for example, made no serious attempt even to listen to what he had to say.

Where the instructions given to Yamamoto when he left for London were concerned, the emperor is said to have told Prime Minister Okada that in view of the demands of the army there might be no alternative but to settle for the type of solution they envisaged. However, he hoped that the abrogation of the Washington Naval Treaty would be handled in such a way as to avoid irritating the Powers unnecessarily. It seems probable that in his report to the emperor Yamamoto was trying to make Hirohito, at least, understand that a treatyless state of affairs must be avoided, that patient efforts in this direction were necessary, and that it would be a mistake to be carried away by the big talk of the men who had fired Hori and who were determined at all costs to do away with the limitation treaty.

THREE

1

Chief Petty Officer Yokokawa, who had been in London with Yamamoto and his party, arrived back in Yokohama on March 12, just one month later than the delegation. He had gone on his own from London to Paris, where he made various purchases at the request of Yamamoto and the others, then went to Marseilles and boarded the *Katori-maru* for Japan via Suez. The list of things he ordered through a Japanese agent in Paris included three dozen lipsticks for Lieutenant Commander Mitsunobu (a good-looking young man; Yokokawa confesses to wondering who were the lucky recipients of so many gifts), ten large bottles of perfume and thirty small bottles for Yamamoto and Mitsunobu together, and thirty-three boxes of Coty powder. Yet despite Yamamoto's lively generosity in stocking up on intimate gifts for women—and despite his preoccupation with gambling—Yokokawa's impression of him in London is of a man with a perpetually sad, solitary air. And the same impression remained even after Yamamoto had gone back to work in the Naval Affairs Bureau in Tokyo.

In his dimly lit room in the Navy Ministry, hemmed in by bookshelves, Yamamoto was, in fact, gloomy-looking and fretful. In name he was attached to both the Navy Ministry and the Naval General Staff, but in practice he had nothing to do. In all probability, this was the idlest period of his entire career. Significantly, Yamamoto went back to Nagaoka four times in the course of that year, sometimes staying as long as two weeks. If there had been work to do, he would never have taken things so easily. Some of the navy's hawks would probably have liked to go further and dismiss him once and for all, and Yamamoto himself seems often to have considered quitting the service around this time.

Hashimoto Zengan, a Zen priest at a temple in Nagaoka, says of

him that "when one was seated opposite him at a table, one had the feeling that he was laying all his inner workings in front of one and saying 'Here, take what you want.'"

"In one sense, though," he adds, "it was difficult really to know him. When he felt frivolous, nobody could be more so, yet he also had his muscularly austere, almost forbidding side." In conversations he had with Yamamoto around this time he could, he says, sense indirectly a strong dissatisfaction with the top men of the navy concerning the preliminary talks for the London Naval Conference.

The plenipotentiaries and other delegates whom Japan sent to international conferences such as the first London talks and the Geneva conference were invariably men of great ability, yet they were all, without exception, made to suffer on their return to Japan, being removed from their jobs on the grounds of some minor infringement or other of their instructions. Yamamoto had found himself in a similar position. Quite a few men within the navy sympathized with him and were indignant that this should have happened to someone who had been reluctant to go in the first place; but there was nothing to be done.

With Hori Teikichi dismissed and himself given the cold shoulder, Yamamoto had half a mind to throw in the towel and, as he sometimes told close friends, "go to Monaco and be a gambler."

According to Yamamoto's formula for gambling, he might well have been able to amass a considerable amount in the course of a year or two. Every two or three years, the Japanese training fleet's deep-water cruise took it to Europe. He would—he said, half in earnest—use the money he had earned as a gambler to give the young cadets who came to Europe a good time.

Hori tried frantically to dissuade Yamamoto from resigning. "What would happen to the navy if you were to quit?" he asked. It is not clear just when, during this year, Yamamoto gave up the idea, but it seems likely that the frequent visits he made to his beloved Nagaoka were partly responsible for calming his misgivings.

His first visit following his return to Japan was on April 13. His parents were already dead, but his elder brother Kihachi and elder sister Kazuko were still living there, and they made "Iso-sa," as they called him, thoroughly welcome. Even so, his brother, who was five years his senior, was careful not to let him forget his place in the

family and—at least when Isoroku was not in uniform—invariably positioned himself at the head of the table.

The day after he got home, Yamamoto gave a talk to the pupils of Sakanoue Primary School, his own old school, at the school's request. According to Sorimachi Eiichi, Yamamoto, on stepping up onto the dais, began by reciting in a loud voice the names of the principal and other teachers during his own days at school. "I'm deeply grateful," he declared with bowed head, "to these teachers, thanks to whose guidance I find myself, on returning here today, shouldering such a vital responsibility on behalf of the nation." Only then did he turn to the pupils and begin his talk.

If this is literally true, it is remarkably theatrical for a man like Yamamoto; so, incidentally, is the fact that Yamamoto put on full-dress uniform just to give a talk at a primary school. For a naval officer to dress like this in order to address a crowd of children might be likened to an author on a lecture tour insisting on giving his talks in a tuxedo.

Such things provide more fuel for complaint from former naval men who are critical of Yamamoto. They reveal, they claim, his show-manship—or if not showmanship, the peculiar effect that anything involving Nagaoka had on him. "Why should he always have put him-self out so much for his home district?" his critics ask. "To put it bluntly, didn't he exploit his position?"

The full-dress uniform could presumably be explained away by assuming that, having just returned to Japan and his home district, he had been to pay his respects to the Takano and Yamamoto family graves, and that he went straight on to his lecture without changing. But there are, in fact, a number of cases where he would seem to have used his authority in the navy for the benefit of fellow Nagaokans.

On one occasion there was a young man who was having trouble finding a job because of a poor degree. Hearing that his family was so impoverished that it would have difficulty in making both ends meet unless he found work, Yamamoto went specially to see the president of a certain company and asked him to take the young man on. The company, finding that his university record had in fact been far from impressive, made no move to employ him, but Yamamoto became importunate, and finally, around his sixth visit, he succeeded in badgering the president into agreeing.

This episode, however gratifying for the young man in question and for fellow Nagaokans, has an unpleasant ring to the unprejudiced outsider, whose distrust would be more than justified if the company proved to be one of those supplying weapons to the navy; but by now neither the company nor the not-so-gifted graduate are traceable.

In any case, Yamamoto himself thoroughly enjoyed this stay in Nagaoka. It was the season when the heavy snows melt at last and the plum, peach, and cherry trees seem to burst into flower all at once. Whenever he got back home, Yamamoto would lapse into the broad Nagaoka dialect and spend his time dropping in on old aquaintances or playing *shogi* with the head of the local young men's association. Usually he was accompanied by Sorimachi. On one occasion they went to nearby Niigata City, where the festival of the Hakusan Shrine was in progress. There they found an old woman selling broiled dumplings on skewers at one of the stalls that always line the approaches to shrines at such times. She was fanning the burning charcoal with a round paper fan, and a savory smell came wafting toward them. "Hey, look!" said Yamamoto. "They're just the kind they used to sell when we were kids. Let's have some." He refused the old woman's invitation to eat the dumplings seated in comfort at the back of the stall. "I've eaten broiled dumplings standing ever since I was a kid—they taste better that way," he said and, still standing, disposed of fifteen skewers.

At the entrance to Hakusan Park, they found a bean vendor toasting his wares. Attracted by the aroma again, Yamamoto got Sorimachi to buy some of these too. Then, warning his friend to keep an eye open for cars coming from the rear, he crossed the busy street throwing beans one at a time up into the air and catching them in his mouth. He was fifty-one at the time; as Morimura Isamu, who was with Yamamoto at Harvard, has said, he seems to have had a peculiarly childish streak in him.

2

Another dumpling of which Yamamoto was very fond was the three-colored kind sold at the teashops at Yukyuzan. During the Meiji period, the spot where Nagaoka Station now stands—formerly the site of the main donjon of Nagaoka Castle—was a public park. Here were sold the renowned three-colored dumplings made of red beans, soy-bean flour, and sesame, but Yamamoto's family was so poor that the young Takano Isoroku—as he was then—was lucky if he could enjoy them once a year at most. When he was a naval officer, he seems to have gone out of his way, almost as though getting even with society, to eat these delicacies that he had looked at so longingly as a child.

The cherry trees along the Kaji River were in full bloom. Borrowing a boat from an acquaintance, Yamamoto spent a day going down the river with his friends, enjoying the blossom and the sight of the distant, still snow-capped mountains. On the way, they encountered a string of blossom-viewers' boats coming upstream, towed by a motorboat. Seeing this, Yamamoto asked the two boatmen to row for all they were worth. The boat slid forward with extra speed, beginning to rock as it encountered the waves set up by the motorboat—and at just that moment Yamamoto moved briskly forward and, placing both hands on the prow, did a handstand.

It was a favorite trick of his. He had done it in the first-class saloon of the *Suwa-maru* on his first crossing to America, sixteen years earlier. Three or four days after sailing from Yokohama, the usual shipboard entertainment was held. At such times, Japanese passengers were usually very reluctant to perform for others, but the captain was just winding up the proceedings when the young lieutenant commander came forward and did a handstand on the balustrade of the saloon. The ship had a slow roll, and one slip would have meant a dangerous fall to the deck below, but not content with merely standing on his head, he borrowed two large plates from a steward, and putting them on the palms of his hands twirled them round and round, out sideways and above his head, finishing with a somersault, plates still on his hands. He was fond of showing off his handstands in dangerous places. The passengers on the blossom-viewing boats had no idea, of course, who he was, but heartily applauded his skill just the same.

After devoting about two weeks in Niigata Prefecture to such idle amusements, Yamamoto returned to Tokyo on April 28, but on May 26 went home to Nagaoka again, staying this time for about a week. He went again on July 31, and once more on November 21. On this last occasion, a certain cabinet minister happened to be in Nagaoka, and members of his entourage sent an invitation to Yamamoto to come to a restaurant and meet him. But Yamamoto declined, on the grounds that he was in discussion with the Nagaoka young men's association and could not get away.

It may be that he was beginning to feel rather sour at the way the world was treating him. The real reason behind his frequent visits home was that he felt "to be honest . . . utterly wretched working in Tokyo." The phrase comes from a letter written in the Navy Club at Kure on May 1 that year and addressed to Kawai Chiyoko—the "certain woman" mentioned earlier who surreptitiously boarded the limited express "Kamome" at the same time as he did. The letter is extremely long, but one part of it runs as follows:

> When I consider how the last three or four years have passed liked a dream, and picture to myself the ten, twenty, thirty still to come, life seems more and more like a fleeting illusion; I'm beset by a Buddhistic sense of impermanence, by the idea that fame and riches, love and hate, are all as evanescent as the morning dew.
>
> You say you're wretched because you're alone, but one could also say that in a world where so many people are helpless in the toils of society, not permitted even to die when they want to, the person who is alone among strangers is in a sense the most fortunate of beings. But thinking like this makes everything seem depressing: philosophical talk apart, if it's really true that you miss me and have faith in me, then in practice I consider myself really fortunate. The one thing that makes me miserable is that I'm so unsatisfactory for you, my sister and sweetheart.
>
> When I say I'm miserable, I'm not just imitating you or the *sensei* [see below]—it's a genuine sense of my own worthlessness when I consider myself dispassionately as an object of your affections. The more I see of you, so beautiful and beguiling, the more miserable I feel. Please don't think too badly of me.
>
> When I went to London, I was full of enthusiasm and resolve, feeling that in my own way I was bearing responsibility for the future of the nation, but though I put everything I had into the talks there, as time went by the people in the navy, not to mention the general public, began to be completely indifferent to what was happening. It gave me the feeling that I was being used as a tool—which was extremely unpleasant, and also brought

home to me still more my own aimlessness. To be honest, I feel utterly wretched working in Tokyo, and very resentful too.

In theory, it was *I* who wanted to be of help to you and to relieve your loneliness, and as a man I feel ashamed to find myself, on the contrary, weakly wanting to cry on your bosom. I also feel I'm letting you down, which makes me still more miserable.

This is the first time I've told anybody about these feelings of mine. Please don't tell anybody, will you!

Kawai Chiyoko was a geisha at the time, working at the Nojima-ya geisha house in Shimbashi under the professional name of Umeryu (Plum-Dragon). Her relationship with Yamamoto suddenly became close in 1934, just before he left for London. From then until his death, he was to love her with the freshness of spirit of a far younger man. During the war, however, and for nearly ten years afterward, the general public had no idea that he had such a mistress. The truth was first revealed in the *Weekly Asahi* of April 18, 1954. The magazine had heard through certain channels that a woman called Kawai Chiyoko, proprietress of a restaurant called Seseragi in Numazu, had a large number of love letters from Yamamoto and was willing to make them public. A *Weekly Asahi* reporter and photographer went to call on her in Numazu. She made them welcome and fetched out a bundle of letters to show them. She even read aloud some parts where the calligraphy was difficult for the young reporter to decipher. And she talked freely about herself. Her remarks, published in the April 18 issue, were introduced in the following fashion: "Most people, hearing talk of admirals and love affairs, will think of Nelson and Lady Hamilton. Few people can have suspected, though, that the life of Fleet Admiral Yamamoto concealed a very similar romance. We do not present what follows for its sensational appeal, but as a human record that shows that the semi-deified hero was, after all, a man like the rest of us."

Hori Teikichi, who was still alive and healthy at the time, got wind of the article just before publication and made an indirect request to the *Asahi* to suppress it. But the magazine was already in the presses. The article provoked an enormous reader response, and the *Asahi* was flooded with letters. Those who found the newly revealed facts disgraceful came predominantly from the younger age groups. "I was called up by the navy during the war," said one, "and found I couldn't even write a postcard to my relatives without running into all sorts of restrictions. How comforting to think that Admiral Yamamoto was writing all those long, long letters to his mistress from the front line!"

The letters that took the opposite view and seemed, if anything, pleased to find that Yamamoto had had such a human side came chiefly from older people. Kawai Chiyoko herself was also deluged with letters, expressions both of sympathy and criticism. The public response was probably rather too much for her, for she seldom agreed to interviews with the mass media after that.

3

One inevitably feels a certain constraint in writing about Chiyoko. She is now sixty-five. Following the failure of her restaurant Seseragi, she made a formal marriage, and is at present living quietly on the coast near Numazu, where she and her husband run an inn called Seseragi-so. To write about her, moreover, also necessitates touching on Yamamoto's family life, thus involving still greater difficulties, since his widow Reiko is still alive and well, as are his children. Nevertheless, any attempt to portray Yamamoto the man without involving his home and his relations with women is bound to fail.

Yamamoto's relationships with women other than Chiyoko had begun when he was still young—inevitably, perhaps, when one considers his life as a sailor. Watanabe Yasuji—one of the Combined Fleet staff officers in whom Yamamoto showed great personal interest and the man who went to bring home Yamamoto's remains following his death—defends Yamamoto vigorously. "For every woman Yamamoto had," he says, "I must have had fifty." Nor was Yamamoto the Don Juan type who flitted from one woman to another. According to Sasakawa Ryoichi, "he was extraordinarily innocent where women were concerned. If I was a reasonably successful student at college, Yamamoto was a first grader at primary school."

Although the geisha Umeryu was based in Shimbashi, she was not a native of the district, but was born in Nagoya in 1904. Her father was a stockbroker, and the years of her youth after leaving her girls' school were spent in comfortable circumstances, but while the family was living near Yoroibashi in Tokyo, the great earthquake of 1923 occurred. Her father's business went bankrupt, and she returned with her parents to Nagoya, where life was so difficult that at one stage the family contemplated committing suicide together. Eventually she became the mistress of a man called Ikoma, head of the Meiji Bank.

Two years later her mother died, followed by her father the next year. She went to Tokyo again, and rented a house where she became involved with a succession of men. This led to all kinds of complications, including threats to cut her hair off or throw acid at her, and in the end she tried, unsuccessfully, to kill herself with sleeping pills. Once she had recovered, she turned up in Shimbashi and asked to be trained as a geisha. This was in December 1932, when she was twenty-eight—approximately a year and a half before she became intimate with Yamamoto, assuming that this happened in the summer of 1934. At first, none of the geisha houses would have anything to do with her, feeling natural doubts about a woman who proposed to start a career in such a celebrated geisha district when she was already nearing thirty. But she was so persistent that she eventually won the day, and was taken on by the Nojima-ya with the professional name of Umeryu.

With such a late start, she was in no sense among the most accomplished of the district's geishas, but she made up for this by her sexual attractiveness. With a broad forehead and oval face, she had less the air of an ordinary geisha than of a high-class courtesan, and she began to win a reputation among habitués of the quarter. Before long, her name was being associated with those of various figures in the political and business worlds, and she had her own patrons. The celebrated artist Yokoyama Taikan was one of them, and it was he whom Yamamoto referred to as "*sensei*"—or Master—in the letter quoted above.

It was in the summer of 1933, the year after she became a Shimbashi geisha, that Umeryu first saw Yamamoto. The occasion was a party at a restaurant. Yamamoto, who was a rear admiral at the time, commanding the First Carrier Division, was wearing a white summer suit. He was having trouble getting the lid off a lacquered soup bowl, and Umeryu offered to help him. Glancing at his hands, she was startled, she says, to see that two fingers were missing on his left hand. Yamamoto, however, merely gave her a stare and said, "I can manage myself." She was to remember him, if none too favorably, because of this.

61

About a year later, in the summer of 1934, around the time when the question of whether Yamamoto should go to London or not was being discussed, she saw him again at a geisha house party. This time, he was in a rear admiral's uniform. She greeted him and reminded him of the incident with the soup bowl the previous summer. But again his reply was brusque in the extreme:

"Really? I don't recall. I can hardly remember every single woman I meet."

"*I* remember, because you were so unpleasant," she said.

"You mustn't mind him, Ume," Yoshida Zengo, who was sitting near them, said soothingly. "He's always like this."

A few days later, she again was summoned to a party at which Yamamoto and Yoshida were present. In the course of the conversation Yoshida, who was sitting next to Yamamoto, happened to ask her whether she was fond of cheese. "I love it," she said, whereupon Yamamoto suddenly declared: "I'll take you somewhere nice, then. Let's meet at the Imperial Hotel for lunch tomorrow."

"You'd better accept," urged Yoshida. "It's not often Yamamoto makes an offer like that!"

So the following day Umeryu and Yamamoto, now in uniform, had their first meal together. A few more unremarkable encounters, and one evening found them watching a romantic movie together at the Imperial Theater. It was there that Chiyoko, her hand clasped in Yamamoto's, announced that she didn't want to part from him yet, and suggested that she should take him on to a geisha house where she was expected. When they arrived she asked him to wait until she was through with her clients, and went off to another room.

The daughter of the proprietor of Nakamura-ya was called Furukawa Toshiko. Coming back from having her hair done, she looked into one of the rooms and saw a man with short, bristly hair sitting there in solitary state. It occurred to her at once, she says, that it was the Admiral Yamamoto whose photo she'd seen in the papers. It was that evening that Yamamoto first really got involved with Chiyoko and also became friendly with two other geishas, friends of Furukawa Toshiko and Chiyoko, called Kikutaro and Kikuya.

Yamamoto, however, was a military man with little money to spare and a reputation at stake, and it seems that even after this he insisted on treating Chiyoko as a "younger sister." Eventually, it was

Chiyoko herself who announced that she was tired of being his younger sister and asked him, in the old-fashioned phrase, "to take her hair down with his own hands." It was this that led to the use in his letter of the phrases "my sister and sweetheart" and "the excitement caused by the rapid development of our relationship."

This happened just before he left for London. From then on, their relationship could no longer be seen as a simple flirtation, and when Yamamoto boarded the *Hie-maru*—she came to Yokohama to see him off—the "blood was on fire in my veins."

4

He was no newcomer, even so, to the gentle art of amusing himself in the geisha quarter of Shimbashi. In fact, he enjoyed considerable popularity among the women who lived there. In the words of one who was in a geisha house at the time: "There were lots of naval men around, but we were all gone on Yamamoto-san." Until then, however, he had never been associated with any particular woman there.

According to Niwa Michi, who under the geisha name of Kosuga was one of the first to make his acquaintance, he gave the impression of being rather unapproachable and taciturn at first, but once he let himself relax he was something of a clown—the "mischievous devil" of Yonai's description, with a touch of the "big baby" in him as well.

He would hail a taxi in front of the Navy Ministry and tell the driver to go to the Ginza, holding up one gloved hand as he did so. The driver took this to mean an offer of fifty sen, which was quite a generous fare in those days. But when Yamamoto got out, he would hand over only thirty sen. If the driver complained, he would hold up his—now ungloved—left hand with its three surviving fingers and say, "Don't be silly—look!" Such things only happened, of course, when he was out of uniform.

On another occasion he was with Hori in the geisha quarter when Hori came in great consternation and told him that the geisha he had with him in his room had revealed that her father worked at the Naval Academy. Afraid for their reputations, they made discreet inquiries—and discovered that the father was in charge of cleaning out the Naval Academy toilets. Yamamoto was fond of telling such stories.

Yamamoto himself had little taste for formal geisha parties, whether large or small; he preferred to play cards in the small room leading off the entrance of a geisha house and have a bowl of plain salmon *chazuke* (salmon on boiled rice with hot tea poured over it). One day when he was still a captain, Kosuga had asked him to come and "try the *chazuke* at a geisha house." He came, and from then on he and Hori were forever turning up at Kosuga's to eat *chazuke* and take a midday nap.

Quite often, he had holes in his socks. And though he was particular about his appearance, his long underpants were not always particularly clean. The women would mend his socks and wash his underwear, and have it dry and ironed for him by the next time he came. Presumably it stimulated their motherly instincts.

5

The following passage is from a letter Yamamoto wrote to Chiyoko in September 1935: "I had a dream last night, though what prompted it I've no idea. I dreamed that we were driving along the coast at Nice, in the south of France. I thought how happy I'd be if only it were true."

Nice, of course, is not far from Monte Carlo. The dream and the letter both show very clearly how he was feeling at the time. Should he quit the navy or not? If he quit, should he go off to, say, Monaco? His mind was often weighed down with these questions, and at such times his only solaces were the familiar scenery back home in Nagaoka and the love of Kawai Chiyoko.

Yamamoto's days in Nagaoka were given over to such innocent amusements as cherry blossom viewing from the river, visiting the festival of the Hakusan Shrine, and so on. But on the way back to Tokyo he occasionally alighted at Minakami spa, where he joined up with Hori Teikichi, Kawai Chiyoko, and Furukawa Toshiko. It was in their company that he seemed most to let himself go, frolicking like a schoolboy and playing mahjongg or flower cards at the hotel until the early hours.

Yamamoto was fond of going for a bath at the very end of the day. At some time past midnight, he would excuse himself from the mahjongg game and with a cotton towel dangling from his hand go off to soak in the bath, which by now would have been taken over by the head clerk and hotel maids.

One reason for this was his dislike of letting those who knew him well see the lower half of his body, which was disfigured by scars left by more than a hundred and twenty fragments from the gun that burst during the Russo-Japanese War. "Whenever I go into a public bath, people think I'm a gangster," he would say. Once he was in the bath, though, he would linger there, chatting idly with the hotel employees —it was mixed bathing, of course—for as long as an hour at a time.

Once she was intimate with Yamamoto, Chiyoko became a devoted mistress in a way she never did, it seems, with other men. In addition to Yamamoto she had a patron, a man who had made a fortune in real estate; and both men were aware of and accepted each other's existence. She availed herself unabashedly of the patron's economic affluence, and he on his side gave freely. Yamamoto could not, and did not, use money so lavishly. One woman who was herself a geisha at the time and had the chance to observe their relationship has remarked that she often wondered "how Umeryu could put up with anyone like that." I myself have heard Furukawa Toshiko, recalling the old days, say to the now elderly Chiyoko, "Ume, you knew how to keep your heart and body separate, didn't you!" And Chiyoko smiled and nodded reminiscently.

Chiyoko was attractive, clever, and skilled at calligraphy, but, as we have seen, she was far from being one of the more accomplished geishas of the Shimbashi quarter. Nor was her background following the period in Nagoya at all clear. The mistresses of teahouses in the quarter looked askance at the way in which, when she finally got a good patron, the money he gave her went toward her relationship with Yamamoto. Those who still survive have little good to say of her in fact, and all kinds of unfavorable stories—some of them undoubtedly pure fiction— are told about her.

One naturally asks why Yamamoto, at an age when he should perhaps have known better, should have fallen so badly for such a woman. It is always difficult to pass judgment on affairs of the heart where others are concerned, but the only possible answers seem to be either to recall the saying that "mumps and love become more serious with age," or to look to Yamamoto's domestic life for some explanation.

Concerning Yamamoto's wife Reiko, Hori Teikichi once remarked —this was after the outbreak of war—that "Yamamoto's wife is the strongest person in Japan. She must be, because Yamamoto's supposed to be the strongest, and she's stronger than he is." After Yamamoto's death in action, Reiko was dubbed "Mrs. Fleet Admiral."

And though she was loving with their children, she seems to have been rather unfeeling in some ways.

Admiral Yamashita Gentaro was a cousin of Reiko's mother, and the Yamamotos and Yamashitas were on visiting terms. Fukazawa Motohiko, who as a college classmate of Yamashita's eldest son was in and out of the house almost like a member of the family, recalls hearing how Yamashita's wife Tokuko was at the Yamamotos' one day when Isoroku came home. He greeted her, then went off into another room to change into kimono. In those days, it was normal practice for a Japanese wife to wait on her husband at such times, but Reiko made no move to do so. "Reiko," said Tokuko reprovingly, "you ought to go and help him." But Reiko just said, "Ought I?" and remained completely unconcerned. Fukazawa also heard Tokuko relate, disapprovingly, that Yamamoto had to hand the maid her salary personally—another unthinkable thing in a traditional Japanese household at that time.

Yamamoto, on the other hand, was extremely attentive to the needs of others outside his home. His thoughtfulness toward the wives of subordinates was almost such as to invite misinterpretation. When he went abroad he brought them back perfumes and cosmetics as presents. Once, when a subordinate moved to a new house, he remembered that the man's wife had been eyeing a certain coffee set longingly, and bought it, taking it along personally as a present for them in their new house.

No doubt Yamamoto was intensely disappointed by his wife's lack of small attentions. But she, on her side, probably failed to realize what it was she did wrong. She once remarked sadly, "I never once so much as went for a walk with my husband."

6

When one examines the circumstances of their marriage more closely, it is evident that Yamamoto was selfish in his own way too. Around the time that a first meeting was arranged between him and Reiko at a hot-spring resort—at Hori Teikichi's instigation—Yamamoto wrote a letter to his elder brother in Nagaoka in which he says:

> Since leaving the Aizu Girls' School in 1913, she has been helping her mother in place of a maid in the family business, and has

never seen Tokyo. She is said to be strong, and able to put up with hardship.

The Makino family has already suggested one or two other matches, and former vice-minister Suzuki and other older men in the ministry and the navy have occasionally advised me to get married, but until I obtained your agreement the other day I have never been able to make up my mind to take a wife. Besides, the women have mostly been from so-called "prominent" families, and none of them would have been suitable for a man without property and with a very doubtful future. However, it seems that the girl I just spoke of might be a good match, so I'm thinking of taking a look at her, and if there's nothing wrong, settling for her. I hope you will approve.

He also says: "Her family seems to be very frugal in its habits. She herself stands about five foot one or two and is extremely sturdy; it looks as though she could put up with most hardships, which is why I'm in favor of the match."

All of this might give the impression that her ability "to put up with hardship" was her one attraction, and that it was this that had taken Yamamoto's fancy. The Makino family mentioned in the letter is the family of Count Makino, former head of the Nagaoka clan, and "former vice-minister Suzuki" is the Admiral Suzuki who later became prime minister. It seems that, although prospective partners from "prominent" families were suggested to him by various distinguished figures, Yamamoto had never once made any move to follow up these suggestions. One reason for this was that for many years he continued sending money to his family, as well as paying for the schooling of children of relatives and of his former teacher, so that it was a long time before he could afford to support a household of his own. Although the Yamamoto family into which he had been adopted had an illustrious history within the Nagaoka clan, it was desperately poor; far from making life easier for him the move had proved a burden.

It seems likely that Yamamoto's interest in the match was first aroused because the proposal had come this time from one of his closest friends. On the personal level, there are various theories as to what first took his fancy in Reiko—that the calligraphy of her letters impressed him; that after the first introduction, when Yamamoto was dozing in the summer heat on the train, she dutifully fanned him all the way. But the most important factor, probably, was that she came from Aizu Wakamatsu.

It was at Wakamatsu that Yamamoto's father, eldest brother, and second eldest brother had fought and been wounded in the Boshin War of the Meiji era, and it was there that his own adoptive father had been put to death. When he went there for his meeting with Rei-ko, he went to pay his respects at the "tomb of the unknown warriors"—who included his adoptive parent—and also visited the Amida Temple in the town, which is dedicated to the Nagaoka clan soldiers who died on the Aizu plain. The fact that Reiko came from a town so closely associated with Nagaoka might well have appealed to Yamamoto's sentimental feelings for his birthplace.

One can accept his wish to avoid the "so-called 'prominent' families"; but if he really thought that the prospective bride's being robust and able to withstand hardship, a Wakamatsu girl who had never seen Tokyo, justified a match that was "from above" and asking her to marry a man who had little confidence in his own future, then he seems to have been rather casual, even for an old-style military man, in his approach to married life.

It may well be, though, that one should not take Yamamoto's remarks at their face value, since he was extremely diffident about— which is in one sense to say extremely sensitive about—expressing his own feelings. In a piece entitled "In Memory of My Father Yamamoto Isoroku," published in the May 1966 issue of *Bungei Shunju*, Yamamoto's eldest son Yoshimasa quotes from a letter written by his father to his mother before their marriage. It contains the following unexpectedly gentle passage: "I am glad to hear that you and your family are all keeping well despite the heat of summer [the original Japanese is considerably more flowery in expressing this simple sentiment]. I am delighted that, thanks to everybody's efforts, everything has been arranged so successfully. Once we have obtained your mother's permission, we shall no longer have to consider each other as strangers, but can discuss anything at all with each other. I hope that on your side you will confide in me without hesitation. . . ."

Everything in fact was "arranged successfully," and the ceremony took place on August 31, 1918, at the Navy Club in Shiba, Tokyo.

Reiko was twenty-two, but Yamamoto, in his fourth year as a lieutenant commander, was already thirty-four, which was rather late for those days. The newly married couple took up residence in Akasaka Ward, Tokyo, in the same district as Hori Teikichi.

Four children were born to them during the next fourteen years—Yoshimasa in October 1922, Sumiko (a girl) in May 1925, Masako (a girl) in May 1929, and Tadao in November 1932. As was usual, the birth of successive children progressively strengthened Reiko's position as mistress of the house; strong-minded by nature, she got so that she would rarely withdraw anything she had once said, while Yamamoto, when a quarrel began, would retire to bed and draw up the quilts over his ears.

He seems to have been reluctant to introduce her into the company of others. If the wife of a subordinate inquired after her health, he would say brusquely, "Her? She's as strong as a horse." Sometimes, if he found that one of his officers had a photo of his wife in his cabin, he would say, "You're lucky to be in love with your wife. I threw in the sponge long ago."

Reiko was, in fact, relatively unhealthy. It seems likely again, however, that such deliberately curt expressions as "strong as a horse" should not be taken too literally. In the piece already quoted above, Yamamoto Yoshimasa writes: "Our home was always peaceful and warm, like a room that catches the sun in the winter. On the surface, Father seemed indifferent and undemonstrative, but beneath this was a proper concern for our welfare." This, one imagines, represents the truth as seen through a child's eyes. Indeed, the kind of married relationship that can continue for years on end without any rift, upheaval, or boredom must be a rare exception. It was in one such period of trial, no doubt, in the fifteenth year of his marriage, that Yamamoto unexpectedly encountered Kawai Chiyoko, the geisha Umeryu.

FOUR

1

If some rift had in fact developed between Yamamoto and his wife at that time, at least half the cause must be sought in his career. Too much of their time in the vital period following their marriage was spent apart, with no chance to get to really love and understand each other. On April 4, 1919, only eight months after their marriage, Yamamoto was posted to America, and on May 20 he sailed alone on the *Suwa-maru* to take up his post. It was during this voyage, at an evening's entertainment given on board, that he stood on his head on a balustrade in the first-class saloon.

For approximately two years until his return in July 1921, Yamamoto was absent from Japan and his newly founded household. In the succeeding years too, his duties frequently obliged him and his wife to live apart. In July 1923, he went on a tour of America and Europe lasting nine months, accompanying Admiral Ide Kenji, a military councillor. The two years from the beginning of 1926 until March 1928 were spent in America as naval attaché in the Japanese embassy. Once again, of course, he went without wife and children. All in all, roughly half the first ten years of his married life was spent abroad.

On one occasion during his period as naval attaché, he said to Miwa Yoshitake, his junior assistant, "A human being hasn't really grown up until he can live with loneliness and face it directly." On another occasion, when the wife of a high-ranking U.S. navy official asked him if he was not lonely without his family, he impressed her greatly by replying, "Oh yes, I'm lonely. But it's part of my job, so it can't be helped." Most Japanese would have replied, "Oh no, I'm not lonely—I'm enjoying life in America too much," and Yamamoto's frankness must have been a refreshing change.

70

Following Yamamoto's return from his second stay in America, when he was captain of the cruiser *Isuzu*, Lieutenant Commander Kondo Tamejiro, navigation officer, asked him what he did about sex while he was in America. Yamamoto claimed not to have wanted for outlets, but one wonders all the same. America in those days seemed infinitely farther away than it does today. Though he may have had the enterprise to ensure that he found "outlets," it is unlikely that they would have helped much in curing his loneliness. Nor is there any doubt that Reiko too, left alone at home, frequently felt intensely lonely. Even when her husband came back to Japan, it did not mean that he could settle down at home, since there was his work with the fleet. It could hardly be wondered at if, as a kind of defense against solitude, she gradually began to assert her own authority in the home.

The same kind of thing, of course, must have applied in the homes of many other naval officers; but Yamamoto's case seems to have been rather extreme. Largely by coincidence, it happened that every one of his promotions between the ranks of commander and vice admiral occurred while he was abroad. He became a commander in Cambridge, Massachusetts, a captain while he was on a tour of Europe and America, a rear admiral while on his way to London, and a vice admiral in London. There was no chance for Reiko to cook her husband the traditional "red rice," common on such auspicious occasions, even assuming she wanted to. At the very best, such an anomalous way of life could hardly have had a positive influence on the normal processes of assimilation, understanding, and maturing that occur in married life. This is not the place, however, to probe further into Yamamoto's marital relations. The important fact is that the entry into his life of Chiyoko aroused emotions in him, in his fifties, that might have suggested a much younger man.

For a long time after his return from the preliminary disarmament talks, Yamamoto was left to languish in sinecures, but finally, in a shake-up that took place on December 2, 1935, he was appointed chief of the Aeronautics Department of the Navy Ministry. The Aeronautics Department was the central agency in charge of general matters pertaining to naval aviation, and the new job meant that Yamamoto, who had been thinking of quitting the service, had at last made a comeback in an important post. As an individual, he might well have been happier if he had retired that year and taken Chiyoko abroad with him. And if he had, visitors to Nice or Cannes in later years might have pointed out the aged Japanese gambler, once a tolerably well known admiral in the imperial navy, who looked after Japanese travelers so well. But it was not to be.

Yamamoto, who seems to have been delighted with his new post, declared that he would be happy to hold it indefinitely—naturally enough, when one considers that he had long had a strong enthusiasm for aviation and believed that the Naval Air Corps was destined sooner or later to become the "Air Naval Corps."

Originally, it is true, he had had no training in this field. He completed the basic course at the Naval Gunnery School in 1908, and graduated from the advanced course of the same school in 1911. This would normally have made him a lifelong gunnery expert; but his two periods of duty in America—from 1919 to 1921 and from 1926 to 1928—directed his gaze toward the skies.

2

By the time he returned to Japan in 1921 following his first period in America, Yamamoto already seems to have been quite firmly convinced of the future importance of air armament. Shortly after this, he became an instructor at Navy Staff College—he was a commander by now—and expounded to his students a set of views that must have seemed positively eccentric at the time. No notes on his lectures have survived, but the general drift of his message was, first, that no navy could exist without oil and, second, that the future of airplanes was much greater than most people thought and that those responsible should awaken to the necessity of air armament.

As to the origins of these ideas, Takagi Sokichi writes in his book *Yamamoto Isoroku and Yonai Mitsumasa*:

> The sources of his ideas about the need to give priority to aviation are not clear, since he never let others know what he was reading or studying. However, from the time of World War I onward, the idea that control of the skies would eventually determine the outcome of naval battles had spread steadily in U.S. naval circles. The appearance of General Mitchell's *Winged Defense* in 1924 caused a stir among writers on military affairs,

72

and by the mid-1920s the idea of priority for air forces in sea battles was well established in American naval circles. So it seems likely that Yamamoto took a hint from the strategic concepts of the American army and navy during his stays in the States.

During this first stay in America, Yamamoto was naval representative and language officer. He studied as he chose, being officially registered in a Harvard class called "English E," which taught English to foreign students in America. He studied hard—and also, it seems, played hard.

Japan during the period following World War I was enjoying an unprecedented boom, and there were more than seventy Japanese students at Harvard alone. All kinds of stories are told about Yamamoto, but the only one that need concern us for the moment relates to his trip to Mexico to see the oil wells there.

It may seem self-evident that a naval officer stationed in another country should be interested in oil resources and the state of aviation, but in Japan around 1920 this was not necessarily so. Warfare at the time was only just emerging from the stage when aviators fought by throwing stones at each other in midair, and when the navy's dependence on coal was symbolized by the belching clouds of black smoke to be seen in the pictures of warships in the Russo-Japanese War. Yamamoto must therefore be credited with remarkable insight in having awoken to these two points at such an early stage.

Having made on-the-spot observations of the oil situation in America, he next conceived the idea of going to Mexico. He applied for expenses for the purpose, but his request was turned down because of "insufficient funds." Reluctant as ever to admit defeat, he suggested that he should make the trip at his own expense, and set off for Mexico armed with such dollars as he had saved himself plus a certain amount of money that a counselor at the embassy had lent him out of the kindness of his heart.

The military attaché at the Japanese embassy in Mexico was a man called Yamada Kenzo. He and Yamamoto discovered that they both came from Niigata Prefecture, and that Yamada had fought with Yamamoto's elder brother in the Russo-Japanese War. They had long, amiable talks, in the course of which Yamamoto realized that Yamada was in dire financial straits. In his biography of Yamamoto, Sorimachi writes, rather coyly: "Major Yamada threw himself into life with a careless abandon that finally brought him to a financial impasse." In plainer terms, he had gambled so heavily in Mexico that when the order to return home came, the funds for the purpose were already gone, leaving him in an awkward fix. Fortunately for him, Yamamoto not only liked helping others but was far more understanding than the average man of the gambler's psychology; and he gave Yamada the larger part of the money he was carrying, enabling him to return to Japan.

The result was that during his tour of the oil fields Yamamoto himself scarcely knew where his next meal was coming from. He even aroused the suspicion of the Mexican police, who sent the following inquiry to the Japanese embassy in Washington: "A man who claims to be Yamamoto Isoroku, a commander in the Japanese navy, is traveling around the country inspecting oil fields. He stays in the meanest attics in third-rate hotels and never eats the hotel food, subsisting instead on bread, water, and bananas. Please confirm his identity."

Despite such trials, the journey was a worthwhile one. In a letter that Yamamoto wrote to his brother Kihachi from Tampico on the east coast, he records his honest surprise at what he saw: "I am now in Tampico on a tour of the oil fields. Some wells are said to produce about twenty thousand gallons of oil per day, and some have apparently been yielding continuously for thirteen years. The current price of forty gallons of crude oil is one yen, and the tax is one yen, which must seem almost incredible back home in our part of the country."

In 1923, Yamamoto also visited the Texas oil fields, on his way home from a tour of Europe and America accompanying Admiral Ide. One reason why he was so quick to show an interest in oil was that his home district of Niigata was one of the few oil-producing areas in Japan, and he had been familiar with oil since he was a child. During his boyhood, Nagaoka had had hundreds of small factories producing oil for use in lamps. Fires were an almost everyday occurrence, and for a long time oil was, in both the good and the bad senses, a constant companion of Nagaoka's inhabitants in their daily lives.

Yamamoto's two-year stay in America and nine-month tour of Europe and America seem to have been, in all kinds of other ways too, an eye-opening experience. Not that he had ever been a stubborn,

Pacific as chief of staff of the First Air Fleet, he still went on writing. Then in June 1944, when he realized that Tinian's fate was sealed, he sent his notebooks to his wife Nagae—just as they were, with the last sentence breaking off at "a profoundly significant . . ."—by ordinary airmail. He was killed in action in Tinian shortly afterward.

The notebooks included Miwa's account of his first encounter with Yamamoto:

> I've forgotten the date, but after dinner one Sunday evening we took advantage of the holiday that had begun the previous afternoon to make a trip to Tokyo, and boarded a train for the return to base around dusk. There were eight or nine of my colleagues with me. The car was an old-fashioned second-class one with rows of seats across it, and apart from us the only other passenger was a middle-aged fellow in the corner seat at the front on the left. We took advantage of this to make ourselves at home, and moved about the car talking freely among ourselves. Glancing in the direction of the (as I thought) elderly gentleman, I noticed that he had us under observation all the time. His clothes and the suitcase he had with him suggested a recent return from the West, but his hair was short and the set of his eyes and mouth made me feel instinctively that he was a military man. The train arrived at our station. We tumbled out and were getting on the regular bus to take us to our unit when the man in question walked briskly up to us and asked if this was the bus for the Kasumigaura Aviation Corps. When we said yes, he got on without another word. Most of us, having no idea who he was, assumed he was someone—probably around the rank of lieutenant commander—who'd come on some special business. But it turned out that it was Captain Yamamoto, who'd come to join the corps.

Even if Yamamoto had identified himself, however, his name at the time was not yet particularly well known in the navy. And it seems that there was considerable antagonism within the Kasumigaura Aviation Corps toward the idea of someone who had so little connection with aircraft muscling his way into a position as one of the leading figures in the corps.

Miwa himself was then a young lieutenant straight from the flight cadet course; in his own words, he was "hotheaded and cocky, with the vigor of youth but otherwise, I must confess, unqualified in any way to be considered an 'outstanding young officer.' '' Shortly after this he was recommended as officer of the deck, but stubbornly refused to accept the job as being beneath the dignity of someone who hoped soon to be a flying instructor.

"If that's how you feel," he was told, "you'd better go to Captain Yamamoto and tell him directly." Miwa went—no doubt cockily prepared to give his refusal directly—but when he came face to face with Yamamoto he became oddly tongue-tied, overcome by the force of the other man's personality. In the end, he found himself completely cowed; he not only agreed to act as officer of the deck but even promised as he left to "do his very utmost" in the job.

From then on Miwa came into daily contact with Yamamoto, with ample opportunity to hear him talk and see him in action. In the end he was to develop an extraordinary affection and admiration for the other man. Although the relationship was particularly close in his case, the other flying officers all had more or less the same experience, objecting to Yamamoto at first, then gradually coming under his spell. Being fliers, a large number of them died during the war, and only a handful of members of the corps from that period still survive. One of them—Kuwabara Torao, flight commander when Yamamoto was second-in-command there—says of him, "He was usually taciturn and extremely uncommunicative, but he exerted a strange attraction over those under his command."

Although the navy's air arm was still in its infancy, its technology was of a relatively high level compared with that of Japan as a whole. Only the navy, for example, was studying oxygen masks for use at high altitudes, and a well-known mountain climber even made a special visit to Kasumigaura in order to have Yamamoto show him the masks for possible use in the Himalayas. Even so, Yamamoto was originally ill-informed where airplanes were concerned and, having asked for the posting himself, seems to have applied himself diligently to the study of what was actually involved in flying. According to Kuwabara, after the evening meal he would amuse himself playing billiards, *shogi*, or bridge with the younger officers until around ten. Even as he played, though, he kept an ear tuned to their conversation. Following this, the others all went to have a bath, then to bed, but it was only now that Yamamoto started his private studies. At least half his nights every month were spent at the corps, and Kuwabara says that the light in his room was never out before midnight.

It is not generally known that Yamamoto himself took training in flying. At an age when most flying officers were beginning to think of relinquishing the joystick to others, Yamamoto was training for several hours every day, and finally reached the point where he could fly a trainer solo. The fuselage of navy planes at the time was made of cloth over a wooden frame. They used a low horsepower engine, and the propeller was also made of wood. The corps usually followed the example of Britain's Royal Air Force, and it was laid down that all planes, even if in relatively good condition, should be scrapped after two hundred hours in the air. Honda Ikichi, however—an engineer who happened by strange coincidence to be posted to the same place as Yamamoto on the same day on three separate occasions—felt that this was a waste. Studying ways of prolonging the planes' life, he eventually developed aircraft that were safe for four hundred hours, then six hundred, and eventually eight hundred or even, in some cases, one thousand hours. It was laid down that while these attempts to lengthen the planes' life were being made, reports should be made to second-in-command Yamamoto and the chief maintenance officer after every hundred hours' extra flight. On one occasion Yamamoto encouraged Honda by saying, "If you develop a plane with a life so long that even you feel uneasy about it, I'll try it out for you myself." In the event, not a single accident was caused through prolonging the life of the planes.

Despite his flexibility on such matters, whenever it was necessary to put a firm foot down Yamamoto did it very firmly indeed. The navy's flying men in those days combined the pride of highly trained specialists with a kind of daredevilry fostered by the ever-present danger involved. There were many, even among the non-commissioned officers and men, who wore their hair long—an extreme rarity in the forces at the time—and reporting late for duty and breaking barracks were both common occurrences.

Yamamoto set himself to remedying this laxity, and would often poke fun at or scold his subordinates for considering themselves the cream of the navy. Flying officers, he declared, were "slobs." When one of them stood up to him and said that it couldn't be helped, since high altitudes had a physiologically muddling effect on the brain,

Yamamoto put him firmly in his place by saying, "I agree with you. So it's important, surely, to keep doubly alert and take the greatest care over one's preparations. As things are going now, I doubt very much whether the Aviation Corps will be able to keep going in the future."

It seems that besides being determined to restore good discipline in the corps, he was also genuinely afraid that the tendency of fliers to see themselves as specially gifted persons who could do anything by relying on intuition, without paying proper attention to logical method, together with the concomitant tendency to behave like hoodlums, would be bad for the future of naval aviation.

4

There is another interesting story about Yamamoto's period at Kasumigaura. On one occasion, a seaplane with two young cadet trainees on board made an emergency touchdown on Lake Kasumigaura. A rescue party was readied immediately, a special duties ensign with several petty officers and other men hastening to the scene in a rescue boat. They succeeded in getting a rope to the distressed aircraft, and made ready to tow it back to base. However, it was midwinter and the cold winds for which the area is famous were blowing. The surface of the lake was choppy, and the danger that the lightweight seaplane might ride up out of the water and overturn made operations extremely difficult.

The officer in charge and several other members of the rescue team transferred to the wings and floats of the distressed craft in an attempt to prevent it from overturning. Towing was progressing inch by inch, when a sudden blast of wind whisked the aircraft over, and the two crew members together with several members of the rescue team disappeared into the lake.

A search was launched immediately, with Yamamoto in charge. The search party assembled at 4:00 A.M. in front of headquarters and continued to search the lake for bodies until sunset that day and for several days afterward. The missing members of the rescue team were all discovered within two or three days, but there was no sign of the bodies of the two cadets who had formed the crew. Each morning at four, Yamamoto came out into the bitter wind to watch the search party set off. There was obviously no hope by now of finding any survivors, and the cold was so intense that on the fifth day Miwa suggested to Yamamoto that it might be time to call the search off. But Yamamoto insisted that he would continue for months if necessary. "They're somewhere in this lake," he said. "After all, it's not the middle of the Pacific Ocean. What would the men think if I called it off after only a week or so?"

So the search went on. One day, a holiday, trainees from the same class as the missing cadets asked for permission to carry on the search themselves, in their own way, without assistance from other units. The request was granted. As they were setting out, Yamamoto spoke to them: "You'll find them for sure today," he said, "so go hard at it. They were your comrades, and you're the ones who'll recover their remains for them." His tone, according to those present at the time, was extremely dogmatic. And, in fact, word that both bodies had been discovered reached headquarters from the search party around ten that morning.

My reason for retelling this story, a favorite with admirers, is the strange confidence with which he predicted that the search would succeed that day. When one considers this along with his abnormal success at gambling, the distress he showed while staying at Grosvenor House when Enomoto happened to relate his dream, and the intuitive sense he had that misfortune had befallen Hori, one cannot help wondering whether he did not possess, more than the average person, what is commonly referred to as prescience.

Miwa's notes relate all kinds of other episodes as well. Once, when Miwa asked him whether he had always been unable to take alcohol, Yamamoto said, "No, I used to drink occasionally until the time when I was an ensign, but the night we put in at Etajima to take cadets on board I visited a former classmate of mine who was an instructor at the Naval Academy, and got so drunk that I fell into a ditch on my way home and went to sleep there. It made me realize that I couldn't take it, and I stopped drinking from then on."

Shortly after Yamamoto's death, the Navy Club journal, *Suikosha Kiji*, published a special issue in memory of him in which it devoted a considerable amount of space to stories noted down by Miwa. The other pieces included in this special number are for the most part routine eulogies, and Miwa's piece stands out among them as unusual for its time. Even so, when one compares what is printed in *Suikosha*

Kiji with Miwa's original notes, one finds that the episode of his falling into a ditch is omitted from the account of how Yamamoto gave up drink. "No, I used to drink occasionally until the time when I was an ensign," he is quoted as saying, "but in the end I realized I couldn't take it and stopped." Somebody obviously cut the reference, considering it inappropriate to mention the hero's falling into a ditch, even if the hero had confessed to it himself.

This is no place to indulge in textual criticism, but it should be noticed that from then until the end of the war all other works used Miwa's account as published in the *Suikosha Kiji*. This does not matter much, of course, when the question is one of whether Yamamoto could take his drink or not; the danger is that a similar retouching of Yamamoto's remarks in more critical situations can easily give a false impression of the man. Such a case, in fact, was to occur during the war, when the publication of letters from Yamamoto with a number of totally unjustified cuts by various hands was seriously to distort the image of Yamamoto held by the Americans. More of this later, however.

5

In December 1925, after one year and three months in Kasumigaura, Yamamoto was once more to go to America, this time as naval attaché at the Japanese embassy. The appointment was announced on December 1, but he did not leave Japan until January 21 of the following year. There was such regret in the Kasumigaura Aviation Corps at seeing him go that as the *Tenyo-maru* with Yamamoto on board set sail from Yokohama a squadron of planes piloted by members of the corps appeared and dived low over the vessel in a farewell gesture to their former second-in-command.

This kind of thing was quite exceptional. Takagi Sokichi, at that time a lieutenant and navigation officer on board a survey ship, says that he began to hear rumors that Captain Yamamoto, the new naval attaché in America, was a man to take notice of: "Possibly," writes Takagi, "his reputation as second-in-command of the Aviation Corps at Kasumigaura was then gradually beginning to spread via the officers in the corps." It seems at least that Yamamoto had already established a firm position for himself in aviation circles within the navy.

Another man who was posted to America during Yamamoto's

spell as naval attaché was Ito Seiichi, a lieutenant commander at the time. Since Ito's position was the same as Yamamoto's had been during his previous stay in America, he consulted Yamamoto as to where he should stay. Yamamoto advised him to choose a place where he would be able to use Japanese as little as possible; ideally, it would be a good idea to stay in a university lodging house where he would have to share his life with American students. As a result, Ito entered Yale University at New Haven, and even when a training squadron visited New York he was forbidden to go down to the city, only a stone's throw away, in case he should use Japanese.

Yamamoto also told him that officers stationed in America should not expect always to eat three meals a day. So far as possible they should avoid such extravagances and save their money in order to visit places in other parts of the States.

It was July 1927 when Ito arrived in America, and it was during Yamamoto's period there that he became friendly with Matsudaira Tsuneo, then Japanese ambassador to the United States. Togo Shigenori, ambassador to the U.S. at the outbreak of the Pacific War, was a secretary in Washington at the time. The junior assistant to the naval attaché was Yamamoto Chikao, who relates his astonishment at the attaché's insistence on gambling on every possible occasion. Yamamoto was good at bowling, and on one occasion took Yamamoto Chikao and two others from the attaché's office to a bowling alley. When they got there, he wanted to bet as usual and proposed that if he lost he should buy each of them a gold watch, and that they should buy him a gold watch if they themselves lost. In the event, the three allies did in fact lose, and were relieved of a gold watch by Yamamoto.

According to Yamamoto's theory, betting was essentially a matter of putting down, say, a ten dollar note or a ten yen note as a token of responsibility for a certain statement. He often declared that he hadn't yet settled a bet that he had made with Hori when he was a young lieutenant. The bet in question, dating from the mid-1910s, had involved an argument as to whether or not the guns of the warships *Kongo* and *Hiei* would be able to sink the target vessel *Iki* during an experiment held in Ise Bay. Hori said they would, Yamamoto that they wouldn't, and the stake was a preposterous three thousand yen—enough at that time to buy quite a decent house. When the *Iki* in fact sank, Hori would rather have laughed the debt off, but Yamamoto insisted on paying it, and it was decided that the money should be contributed to the association of thirty-second-year graduates of the Naval Academy. It seems that he was still paying the money in monthly installments even after he became a captain.

Yamamoto's predecessor as naval attaché, Hasegawa Kiyoshi, had arranged to go sightseeing in Havana shortly after handing over to Yamamoto. Assistant Yamamoto Chikao was startled when, just as Hasegawa was leaving, Yamamoto announced that he was going with him. "You mean, sir, that you're going away on a trip when you've only just taken over?" he asked. "Right," replied Yamamoto. "I want to earn a bit at roulette. Don't look so worried—" he added, "I'll see I win enough to pay our hotel bills at least." And the two of them left New York by boat for Cuba. Some days later, Yamamoto returned to Washington with a miniature roulette wheel and a huge collection of Havana cigars. The latter he handed over to Yamamoto Chikao. "Here—I won all these in one night at the Havana casino," he said. "They'll do for visitors during the time I'm here."

In spite of his love of gambling, however, he seems to have felt bad if he won too much from the younger officers working under him in the attaché's office. Sometimes, apparently, he would produce checks they had given him six months or so earlier and say, "Look at all these I've accumulated. This won't do, will it?" and tear them up before their eyes.

A year or so later, Yamamoto Chikao was reposted to Japan, and his place as junior assistant in Washington was taken by Miwa Yoshitake. It was at this time that Yamamoto recommended he read a biography of Lincoln to help in his study of English. Yamamoto later asked Miwa if he'd read it. "Well?—" said Yamamoto, when Miwa said he had, "he was a great man, wasn't he? As a human being, he was the finest of all the American presidents. The last time I was here I read four or five biographies, and came to feel a great respect for him." And in detail he went into exactly why he felt this respect.

In a letter to his fiancée, Miwa recounts this exchange with Yamamoto in glowing terms. Testimony of this kind is valuable since— unlike, for example, the accounts in *Suikosha Kiji*—it is in no way touched up. The date, too—July 25, 1927—is quite certain.

One of the most interesting things in Miwa's account of the conversation is Yamamoto's description of the objectives for which Lincoln struggled from the days of his childhood in a poor family ("Born into poverty—there was a photo of his birthplace in Kentucky, wasn't there?—you wouldn't see many houses like that, even in Japan") until his assassination, by which time he had become "champion of the emancipation of the slaves, the emancipation of women—in short, human freedom."

"A man of real purpose," said Yamamoto, "puts his faith in himself always. Sometimes he refuses even to put his faith in the gods. So from time to time he falls into error. This was often true of Lincoln. But that doesn't detract from his greatness. A man isn't a god. Committing errors is part of his attraction as a human being; it inspires a feeling of warmth toward him, and so admiration and devotion are aroused. In this sense, Lincoln was a very human man. Without this quality, one can't lead others. Only if people have this quality can they forgive each other's mistakes and help each other."

Would one be wrong in detecting here a lingering trace of the boy who attended the church of the American missionary Newall?

All kinds of other anecdotes, far too many to relate here, are still told about Yamamoto during his spell as naval attaché. Hoketsu Kota, now president of the Kyokuyo Whaling Co., went to Washington as a probationary diplomat. When he went to introduce himself at the attaché's office in Massachusetts Avenue, Yamamoto startled him by asking, without warning, whether he gambled or not. Hoketsu, a serious young man barely out of college, had never gambled in his life. When he replied no, in some embarrassment, Yamamoto dismayed him still further by saying, "More's the pity. I don't set much store by a man who doesn't gamble." This could hardly have been very pleasant for Hoketsu, but—as he relates in a short piece entitled "Memories of Yamamoto Isoroku"—he applied himself to his "studies" with such zeal during his three years' tour in America, tackling not only poker and bridge but baccarat, roulette, and the like, that by the time Yamamoto became a vice-minister Hoketsu could take him on with some confidence.

Where *shogi* was concerned, he already had a certain amount of skill. A few days after his arrival, there was a dinner party at Ambassador Matsudaira's residence to which Hoketsu was invited as one of the humbler guests. After dinner, Yamamoto came up to him and asked him this time whether he played *shogi*. They agreed to a game immediately. Yamamoto launched an all-out attack and wiped the floor with Hoketsu before he realized what was happening. Hoketsu, however, was a clear-headed thinker, and watching Yamamoto's play soon realized that it depended rather too heavily on rush tactics. In the second game, Hoketsu was on his guard, and won. He also won the next three games straight off. Whether Yamamoto was piqued at this is not clear, but thereafter he never once suggested a game of *shogi* with the other man.

If only, Hoketsu says, America had gone into the character of the leader of the Japanese navy a little more carefully before the war started, it might well have guessed that Yamamoto's way of starting the war would be to launch a sudden assault—an assault on Hawaii, as it turned out.

6

Another quotation from Miwa Yoshitake's "Recollections of Fleet Admiral Yamamoto" reads:

> At this early stage, Yamamoto was already keeping a sharp eye on aviation in America. The great preoccupation in U.S. aeronautical circles at the time was the transatlantic flight. Eventually, Lindbergh brought it off and was followed by Byrd, even though the latter had to ditch his plane in the sea at the end. Aviation in Japan, unfortunately, could show nothing as yet to compare with this. Yamamoto told me to study these flights and give my views on them. Thus I came to realize that for long-distance flights over the sea, navigation using instruments or the stars was absolutely essential. America had already awoken to this fact and was using what were, for that period, excellent instruments, while Byrd had made use of astronomical observations during his flight. In Japan, on the other hand, even naval aviation remained stuck with the instruction given it by the British, with its overemphasis on intuition. . . . I drew up a report, which I presented to the attaché, arguing that naval aviation in Japan would find itself at a dead end unless it abandoned its reliance on the pilot's judgment and turned to instrumental flight, and I suggested various steps that should be taken to this

would plunge his hands into the tub of bran in search of any remaining pickles. Then, after a homely meal of salted salmon and boiled rice with hot tea poured over it, helped down with last year's pickles, he would go off satisfied.

A friend of Yamashita's son who was constantly in and out of the house says that his father, an old-style military man who had been principal of Toyama School, often told him that Yamamoto was one of the most brilliant men the navy had produced in recent years and that he would become well known before long. The young man had no idea of what was so outstanding about him, but was quite certain that he was unusual. He had never, for example, seen either his father or "Uncle Yamashita" rooting around in a pickle tub, much less taking a nap face down on the *tatami* matting in his uniform, with the Order of the Sacred Treasure, Second Class, still pinned to his chest. It was difficult to believe that Yamamoto was a rear admiral.

As such things may suggest, Yamamoto was more at home with Tokuko than with the admiral himself. For a long time before his death, Yamashita lay in critical condition. When he lapsed into semi-consciousness, he became reluctant to let Tokuko leave his side even for a moment. Yamamoto, who went every day to ask how the admiral was, saw that Tokuko could not possibly keep going much longer, so one evening he got her to lend him a dark blue kimono that she often wore about the house, together with a sash, and donning them himself went to sit by the admiral's bedside. Yamashita opened his eyes from time to time, but not being fully conscious did not realize that the familiar kimono was in fact Yamamoto, and, reassured, went off to sleep again. In this way, Yamamoto at last succeeded in getting Tokuko to take some needed rest.

Following his period as head of the Technical Division, Yamamoto, in October 1933, was appointed commander of the First Carrier Division. His flagship was the *Akagi*, on which he had already served once. During this period, from his late forties on into his fiftieth year, he seems to have studied a great deal concerning both aviation and military matters in general. But his reading was not confined to such subjects only. At one stage, there was an outbreak of dysentery on board the *Akagi*. The vessel was put into quarantine at Sasebo, and the headquarters of the First Carrier Division was shifted temporarily to the *Ryujo* whose captain was Kuwabara Torao. The C. in C.'s cabin and the captain's cabin shared a bathroom, which was situated between them. One night Kuwabara, summoned by nature in the small hours, rushed into the bathroom without knocking to find Yamamoto seated on the toilet reading a work by the ancient Chinese military tactician Sun-tzu.

Not that Yamamoto was ever completely serious-minded or completely studious; there was always something of the mischievous boy about him, some outlet for high spirits. Honda Ikichi, who was posted to the Technical Division of the Aeronautics Department on the same day that Yamamoto became its head, arrived in the office early one morning and found a book in a foreign language on Yamamoto's desk. "Hah, studying as usual," he thought—and opened the book to find that it was a pornographic novel in English.

A non-navy man who visited the *Akagi* while Yamamoto was commander of the First Carrier Division tells how he himself expressed admiration for two fighter pilots who were weaving in and out of each other's paths in a mock air battle over the vessel. Yamamoto's expression suddenly went serious. "You may think it's just a lot of fun and games," he said, "but to make sudden dives like that can cause hemorrhaging in the lungs and cut years off your life. That kind of training is impossible for men over thirty. Actually, I don't like having my boys do that kind of thing. But it can't be helped, it's for the country."

After eight months as commander of the First Carrier Division Yamamoto was posted ashore again, working with the Naval General Staff and Navy Ministry. This was in June 1934; shortly afterward, he was to be appointed Japanese delegate to the preliminary talks for the London Naval Conference, and go to London. What happened between then and his return to Japan in the following year has already been described above.

7

By the time he became chief of the Aeronautics Department, there was no doubt whatsoever in Yamamoto's mind that aircraft could play a leading role in naval warfare. The idea that the main role in any decisive battle on the seas would henceforth be played by aircraft and task forces based on aircraft carriers was already, for him, a self-evident proposition admitting of no argument. It would be wrong, however, to assume that this way of thinking was general among the upper echelons of the Japanese navy. In fact, just the reverse was true. The majority of senior naval officers still tended to put their faith in giant battleships and big guns, the classic concept of a Combined Fleet centered on its battleships. For them, aircraft were no more than a secondary weapon. If Yamamoto had had his way, the Naval Air Corps would have ended up as the "Air Naval Corps," and battleships would have become white elephants. Merely to conceive such an idea was held to constitute a kind of blasphemy against those glittering traditions of the imperial navy first established in the Battle of the Japan Sea.

On his return from London, Yamamoto apparently told Ito Masanori, "I had a personal talk with MacDonald and felt he was truly a great statesman. He talked to me almost like a kindly uncle; but I don't think we can expect anything of next year [the main conference]. The only thing we can do is consider what should be our second-best course."

In the new period facing Japan there would be no disarmament treaty, and unrestricted construction of warships would be the order of the day. Japan, indeed, was already going ahead with a top-secret construction program of its own, involving giant ships such as the *Yamato* and the *Musashi*. It seems to have had two main aims in turning to such preposterously large battleships. Experimental firing of 18.1-inch guns—far bigger than the main guns on the *Mutsu* and *Nagato*—had shown that their destructive power was enormous, and the question naturally arose as to whether it would be possible to construct battleships capable of carrying them.

The second aim centered around the fact that battleships of the class of the *Yamato* and *Musashi*, with a full load displacement of 72,000 tons, were too big to go through the Panama Canal. If, in any construction race, America wanted to have battleships in the same class, it would have to resign itself either to their being cooped up in the Pacific Ocean or to keeping vessels of the same class in both Pacific and Atlantic waters; this would give the Japanese navy an advantage in the race.

It was in October 1934—when Yamamoto had only just arrived in London—that the navy's Technical Department was asked by the Naval General Staff to study the possibility of such new battleships as part of the imperial navy's third supplementary program. When Yamamoto was put in charge of the Aeronautics Department, navy circles were trying to reach agreement as to whether, on the basis of their Technical Department's studies, such super battleships should actually be constructed. Yamamoto himself was strongly opposed to the plan. He sought to demonstrate, with detailed figures, that if only the amount of money and material required to construct the *Yamato* and *Musashi* were diverted to the improvement of Japan's naval aviation, the fighting power of the imperial navy could be improved immeasurably. But the advocates of construction were not to be dissuaded so easily.

The most vociferous advocate of positive construction policies at the time was Admiral Nakamura Ryozo, chief of the navy's Technical Department. Almost equally enthusiastic was Admiral Suetsugu Nobumasa, who was a leader of the "fleet faction" and one of the men among Yamamoto's seniors toward whom he felt the greatest natural antipathy.

Nakamura was opposed to Yamamoto's proposed emphasis on aircraft. He and Yamamoto had frequent, violent arguments concerning the construction of the *Yamato* and *Musashi*, and Navy Minister Osumi was obliged to bring in Prince Fushimi as mediator. The essence of Yamamoto's arguments was as follows: however big the battleship, it could never be unsinkable. The attacking power of the planes of the future would increase enormously, making it possible to destroy vessels from the sky before they ever fired a gun at each other. Thus super battleships would inevitably, sooner or later, become white elephants.

The trouble was that when asked for proof of his theory he could, of course, give none: so far, the history of naval warfare afforded not a single example of a battleship that had been sunk by aircraft. Yamamoto's theories may seem self-evident nowadays, but few felt them so at the time. To some people, they were little better than radical, unrealistic, undergraduate ravings. From the standpoint of our present knowledge, it is clear enough that the ones who were unrealistic, sentimental, and out of step with the times were the advocates of ever bigger battleships and guns, but the very presence of a considerable element of emotion gave their views a tenacity that enabled them to survive well past the outbreak of war.

92

It was far, far later—when Yamamoto was already dead and the whole situation was past retrieving—that these men first realized the truth of a saying going the rounds of the navy—that "the three great follies of the world were the Great Wall of China, the Pyramids, and the battleship *Yamato*"—and were finally obliged to awaken to reality. Not until one year before the defeat did the Japanese navy finally and unequivocally demote its battleship divisions to the level of "supporting forces."

The men responsible for designing the *Yamato* and *Musashi* were Hiraga Yuzuru and Fukuda Keiji, both authorities in the Japanese shipbuilding world. Yamamoto would often come into Rear Admiral Fukuda's room, put a hand on his shoulder, and say something on the lines of: "I don't like to be a wet blanket, and I know you're going all out at your job, but I'm afraid you'll be out of work before long. From now on, aircraft are going to be the most important thing in the navy; big ships and guns will become obsolete." Fukuda had long admired Yamamoto as a man. At the time, however, he was literally, as Yamamoto said, going all out, and his pride as a technician had fired him with the desire to produce the finest battleship in the world. So he replied, "No, I think you're wrong. We're going to produce a ship that's—I don't say absolutely impossible, but extremely difficult to sink. We're taking every eventuality into account in designing it."

As one of his counterarguments, he cited the new battleship's use of honeycomb armor plating. A type of armor riddled with apertures like a honeycomb, it had the advantage of being difficult to pierce with bombs dropped from a high altitude, and of being light as well. In the *Yamato* and *Musashi*, 11.7-inch-thick honeycomb plates, each pierced with one hundred and eighty holes seven inches in diameter, were to be used over the boiler room. When Yamamoto heard this, he reportedly said, "Yes, but—" and broke off as though still unconvinced.

Among the few men who enthusiastically supported Yamamoto's theories were Kuwabara Torao—who like Yamamoto before him was second-in-command at the Kasumigaura Aviation Corps at the time—together with Onishi Takijiro and other flying officers. As they saw it, the future of the Combined Fleet was above the clouds. They could not understand why it was necessary to invest such huge sums of money in building battleships when they, on the paltry budget allowed for

93

aviation, were using up a whole year's supply of fuel within the first six months. One day, after one of the series of top-level technological or administrative conferences, Kuwabara, who was in Tokyo at the time, dropped into Yamamoto's office in the Aeronautics Department and asked him how the conference had gone. "Badly," replied Yamamoto dejectedly. "It's a pity, but it wasn't in my power to do anything. They've decided to build both the *Yamato* and the *Musashi*. They're the kind of old men who believe there's only one way of doing things—the traditional way. There's nothing a younger man can do against them."

It seems likely that this conversation took place in July 1936, when it was formally decided to construct the two ships. Yamamoto, it is said, was prepared to risk his job in opposing the program, but in the end his objections were overruled.

As Yamamoto had predicted, both the *Yamato* and the *Musashi* were to be sunk by American aircraft—eight and nine years later, respectively—having made almost no effective use of their nine great 18.1-inch guns. It was shortly after the conversation just recorded that the keels of these ill-fated vessels were laid, under conditions of great secrecy, at the Kure naval station and the Mitsubishi shipyards in Nagasaki.

FIVE

1

In the early morning of February 26, 1936, some five months before the formal decision to construct the *Yamato* and the *Musashi*, and three months after Yamamoto Isoroku's appointment as chief of the Aeronautics Department, there occurred the celebrated "February 26 Incident."

Rebel military officers attacked the residences of Lord Privy Seal Saito Makoto, Finance Minister Takahashi Korekiyo, and Watanabe Jotaro, inspector general of military education, killing all three men on the spot. Lord Chamberlain Suzuki Kantaro was severely wounded.

The prime minister, Okada Keisuke, was asleep at his official residence when the rebels arrived, but his brother-in-law was mistaken for him and murdered in his place. Former Lord Privy Seal Makino Nobuaki, who was resting at the hot-spring resort of Yugawara, was saved by his granddaughter, who managed to get him to safety in the wooded hills when the raiders appeared.

The rebels were brought under control in four days, but it is generally agreed that the political dominance of the army was strengthened remarkably from then on. The prime movers behind the February 26 Incident were a handful of young army officers who dreamed of reforming the nation along nationalistic lines and of a "second Restoration." The men in the background, who fueled their ambitions, were to be found mostly among certain rightist elements and in the upper echelons of the army.

It would not be entirely correct to say that the navy was completely unconnected with the incident and had no hand in it all. Even setting aside the fact that Lord Chamberlain Suzuki, Prime Minister Okada, and Lord Privy Seal Saito were all Japanese navy veterans, it seems that in the course of the incident at least two separate camps appeared within the navy.

One, of course, involved a number of young naval officers who were for vigorous action in sympathy with their colleagues in the army. Immediately following the incident, a considerable number of young officers presented themselves in Yamamoto's office at the Aeronautics Department and announced that they could not stand by in silence while the army took such decisive action. Yamamoto, it is said, sent them packing in, for him, an unusually loud voice.

The second move was made by those who believed, on the contrary, that if necessary the navy should use its own resources to put down the army. For a day or two after the beginning of the incident on the twenty-sixth, the behavior of army leaders might have suggested that the young officers' dream of rebuilding the nation was on the verge of realization; War Minister Kawashima had a document in which the rebels set forth their views distributed throughout the army, while members of the Supreme War Council who interviewed the leaders of the rebelling units spoke with high praise of their action.

Two people, Furukawa Toshiko and Morimura Isamu (who was at Harvard with Yamamoto), were later to hear him say that if the army had gone too far the navy would have been prepared to trade blows with it. Almost certainly, however, this does not mean that Yamamoto was prepared to take action himself. In the end, both conflicting tendencies within the navy led to nothing, and Yamamoto himself took no overt action. Indeed, his position as head of the Aeronautics Department would not have permitted him to make any direct move or issue any directives.

Yamamoto happened to be staying at the Navy Ministry on the night of February 25, so he learned of the incident in official surroundings. According to Sorimachi Eiichi, the first practical steps that he took were to send a navy medical officer by car to Suzuki's residence to see whether he was badly hurt, and to call a surgeon at Tokyo Imperial University and request him to proceed to the Suzuki residence with all haste. These two purely personal acts seem, in fact, to have represented the whole extent of his reaction. And as chance would have it, none of four bullets that were fired into Suzuki's body proved fatal, and he lived to become the prime minister who, nine years later, wound up the war on Japan's behalf.

Suzuki showed a certain wiliness in hiding his true feelings, and it is far from clear just how strong was his opposition, during his period as Lord Chamberlain, to the advocates of a tough policy toward England and America, or toward the trend to the right within Japan. Whatever the case, Yamamoto had a particular respect for him. Yet for all the anger and concern that he felt as a result of the February 26 Incident, his position did not allow him to do anything in particular about it. However, there were two other naval officers in Yokosuka at the time who felt the same way about things as Yamamoto.

They were Yonai Mitsumasa, commander in chief of the Yokosuka naval station, and Inoue Shigeyoshi, the Yokosuka chief of staff. Shortly afterward, the three men—Yonai, Yamamoto, and Inoue— were to come together at the Navy Ministry as minister, vice-minister, and head of the Naval Affairs Bureau, respectively. They were to put up a stubborn resistance to the tyranny of the army and the right wing, and consistently oppose, in the name of the imperial navy, the con- clusion of a Tripartite Pact with Germany and Italy. The newspapermen of the Kokuchokai called them the navy's "left wing"; even those reporters who sided with the "fleet faction" were obliged to admit that they were the ablest trio to be found in the navy.

A record entitled *Things Remembered* was published, for the eyes of fellow graduates of the thirty-seventh year at the Naval Academy, by Inoue Shigeyoshi following his retirement to the country near Yokosuka after the war. Although it will mean digressing for a while, I will use it here to outline the activities of the navy's "left wing" in Yokosuka around the time of the February 26 Incident.

2

Everyone had been long aware, of course, of the ominous atmos- phere that was developing. A seemingly endless succession of inflam- matory documents and reports, of obscure origin, were being circulated at the time. A typical example was the following:

The True Nature of the Okada Government
Let Us Resolutely Smite the Anti-Patriotic Liberalist
Traitors Who Now Hold Sway!
The solidarity of the Empire is founded on the great principle of the identity of sovereign and people. The wily ministers

Makino, Suzuki, and the whole bloc of senior statesmen and ministers are now defiling this bright and shining principle. . . .

Makino has long been in league with the Freemasons and has by now become a pawn of the League of Nations, which has its hostile eye on the Fatherland; under cover of imperial authority, he is manipulating the Okada government just as he wishes in order to further his own ambitions.

We hereby draw attention to the true anti-patriotic nature of the Okada government, and call on all of like mind to rise against those who would betray the Empire.

Young Officers of the Army and Navy! Down with the Traitors Okada and Tokonami! The Righteous Cause of the Imperial Fatherland is Imperiled.

A copy of this document still survives, bearing the seal of the official of the Legal Bureau to whom it was delivered; the date is October 25, 1934—one year and four months before the February 26 Incident.

Another of many similar documents, "An Appeal to Young Officers of All the Imperial Forces," was issued just one year before the incident. It calls in vague, emotional terms for a "second Restoration" and suggests that its authors had some wishful notion that the emperor himself would support their cause. In fact, as accounts by those close to the emperor show, just the reverse was the case; but, as so often happens, dreams and wishful thinking were to become unshakable conviction, and conviction to give rise to still wilder ambitions.

Such documents turned out by men under the influence of some ideological kink or other all have a similar ring, but the sinister thing about those of this period is that the weapons at the disposal of their authors were not as restricted as they are with today's radicals.

Before becoming chief of staff at the Yokosuka station Inoue Shigeyoshi had been commander of the battleship *Hiei*, and before that head of the First Section of the Navy Ministry's Naval Affairs Bureau. While in the last-named post, he had already taken the precaution of arranging to have a tank stationed permanently at the Navy Ministry. Since it would not have done to say that this was for the navy to defend itself with should the worst come to the worst, the explanation given for its presence was, ironically, that it was "intended to help familiarize the general public with things military."

As commander of the *Hiei*, Inoue had forbidden the officers under his command to attend "meetings of young officers' groups" in restaurants ashore. Some people attacked him bitterly for this, but he always explained himself to his subordinates in the following fashion:

> The reason why military men are allowed to carry swords in peacetime and why we are proud to be seen so accoutered is that we are charged by the nation to use these weapons, should the occasion arise, in safeguarding the country. However, to determine whether the "occasion" has arisen or not is the job of the nation itself. In other words, it is only when the nation has decided on war and the supreme command has given the go-ahead that a military man is permitted to kill the enemy and destroy his possessions. When a military man takes advantage of the weapons he has always to hand in order to kill others unlawfully, of his own will and without word from the supreme command, his role is transformed immediately from an honorable one to that of the worst kind of criminal, and the sacred weapons are degraded into vile instruments of murder.

The point he makes is a perfectly obvious one, yet for some of the young officers such arguments were extremely difficult to swallow.

When Inoue became chief of staff in Yokosuka, he found that the front gate of his official residence lay just across the road from that of Captain Yamashita Tomohiko, head of the General Affairs Section of the Yokosuka naval station. Approximately once a week, a group of young naval officers would gather at Captain Yamashita's house, where they seemed to engage busily in debate. Yamashita explained to Inoue that these discussions were for the sake of the young men's "education," but the truth seemed to be that he was keeping them up to date with the latest information, gathered in Tokyo, on moves by army radicals. On their way home, the young officers would regularly stop in a row in front of Inoue's gate and, facing his residence, proceed to urinate.

"One suspects," writes Inoue, "that quite a lot of other such 'private academies' existed around that time." Elsewhere he writes: "Leaders of opinion seem to have been more interested in making a living than in what happened to the nation. There was a strong tendency to appease the right wing; hardly any writers openly and boldly put forward ideas of moderation.''

From his position as chief of staff, Inoue could clearly see the increasingly sinister turn that events were taking both inside and outside the navy. Even among naval officers themselves, people were so busy sounding each other out to find whether they belonged to the "fleet faction" or the "treaty faction" that it was impossible to talk frankly to any but one's closest acquaintances. Inoue began to feel the need to take precautions so that, should something happen, enough men could be sent from Yokosuka to guard the Navy Ministry. Whatever course the army chose to take, it had plenty of troops at its disposal in Tokyo, but the navy had no active units there at all.

He decided, with the approval of C. in C. Yonai, to take the following minimum measures:

1. To organize one special land unit and have it trained.

2. To arrange with the Naval Gunnery School to have twenty seamen gunners ready to gather at the station at any time so that they could be dispatched to the Navy Ministry to act as messengers and guards.

3. To give private orders to the commander of the light cruiser *Naka* to be ready, at any time of day and under any conditions, to proceed at top speed to Tokyo Bay.

The true purpose of all this, Inoue writes, was known only to the C. in C., Inoue himself, and senior staff officers. The warship *Naka* was kept standing by partly because of the danger that the army might interfere with the railway that would transport the navy's land unit to Tokyo, and partly so that the emperor could be transferred to the *Naka* should danger threaten the Imperial Palace.

3

C. in C. Yonai of the Yokosuka station had the nickname "*hiru andon*" (literally, a "bedside lamp in daylight"); later, after he became navy minister, he was to be known as the "goldfish minister," the implication in both cases being that he was there to be looked at rather than for practical use. An imprecisely defined character, he certainly lacked the incisiveness of a Yamamoto or an Inoue, but it has been suggested by various men who knew him that this quality went with a steady competence missing in the other two men.

One Sunday at the end of 1935 or in January 1936, the senior aide at the Yokosuka naval station, without consulting Chief of Staff Inoue, took a large group of young officers to the C. in C.'s official residence to meet Yonai. The latter had a dignity and bearing that went well with his position; in such situations he tended to say very little—which must have intimidated the young officers, or taken the wind out of their sails, for they soon retired again without having said or done anything menacing. There was a danger, nevertheless, that the incident would be falsely reported—that it would be claimed that the young officers had met Yonai, held forth at length on their views, and been personally commended by Yonai himself. Fearing just this, Inoue cabled various garrisons and stations in the name of the chief of staff of the Yokosuka station, informing them of the truth. Shortly afterward, the annual New Year get-together of army and navy leaders in Yokosuka was held at the restaurant Uokatsu. The geishas indispensable at such parties had arrived, and the sake was flowing freely, when a major called Hayashi, head of the Yokosuka military police, came over to Inoue and said sarcastically, "You were pretty nervous, weren't you, to send cables like that just because a few young officers had a talk with the C. in C.?" The contents of the cable sent in Inoue's name had apparently reached the ears of the military police with remarkable speed. Hayashi went on talking, addressing Inoue in extremely familiar terms. Finally Inoue became so irritated that he exploded: "Do you think that's the way for a major to address a rear admiral? I'll have you know that in the navy, even when the officers are having a drunken party on the afterdeck, the captain has only to appear and they're all on their feet saluting. We don't have louts in the navy! I've had enough of drinking with the likes of you." And he got up and went off to another room in a rage. A short while later, three or four geishas came rushing in to him, all agog, to announce that two of his friends were fighting with the head of the military police.

"Who's winning?" asked Inoue.

"The MP's getting the worst of it."

"In that case," said Inoue, "leave them to it."

In the main room, in fact, Hayashi was receiving a thorough thrashing at the hands of two rear admirals. But it was too late for any good to be done by beating the head of the Yokosuka military police.

About a month and a half later, Inoue was roused early in the morning by a phone call from his aide: "Report from a newspaperman, sir. Early this morning the army really put the fat in the fire. Some of them attacked the prime minister's official residence—"

"Right!" interrupted Inoue, "I'll hear the rest at the station. There's no time to lose. Have all the staff officers come in immediately."

He dressed hastily, but by the time he appeared at his office the whole of his staff was there waiting for him. The necessary measures were taken in rapid succession. A gunnery staff officer set off for Tokyo at once by car to find out exactly what was happening. The twenty seamen gunners were summoned, ready to be dispatched to the Navy Ministry. The special land unit was ordered to stand by. The *Naka* made ready to leave harbor at any time. It was close to nine when a call came from Yonai, who had been receiving telephone reports at the commander in chief's residence, inquiring in typically unhurried fashion whether they thought he too ought to put in an appearance.

He arrived before long, and the whole command of the Yokosuka station was to spend four days on duty not knowing whether the outcome would be peace or war. Concerning the departure of the light cruiser *Naka*, word came from the Naval General Staff that any dispatch of men to Tokyo as guards must follow proper procedure, and that the Yokosuka station must not send a vessel without awaiting orders. Thus it was not until the afternoon of that day that the special land unit boarded the *Naka* and set off for Tokyo, which seems to have displeased Inoue considerably.

The Combined Fleet at the time was engaged in exercises off Tosa. Orders came for the First and Second Fleets to enter Tokyo and Osaka bays immediately in order to stand guard there. The ships of the First Fleet secretly trained their main guns on the Diet building, which was under occupation by the rebels. According to Takahashi Sankichi, commander in chief of the Combined Fleet, the Diet building could have been destroyed with only three salvos if the army's actions had made it necessary.

Common sense tells one, of course, that there was one cause for thankfulness at least in the fact that the incident should have blown over without the navy's being obliged to open fire on the army. Yet one cannot help wondering how different Japanese history from 1936 on would have been if, instead of reversing course halfway, majority opinion within the army had been more sympathetic to the rebelling units and had pressed ahead with the establishment of a military cabinet and "reforming the nation," thus leading to a showdown between the armed services. But that is just another of those fascinating "ifs."

4

To return to Yamamoto in the Aeronautics Department, this department, though now separate, had originally been part of the navy's Technical Department, so that its chiefs had always tended to show deference to the latter and to be reticent in expressing their own views.

In the Technical Department, many men still viewed the Aeronautics Department's advocacy of increased air strength with a kind of amused contempt: what use in war was a machine that could be grounded by a little rain or inactivated by a rough sea? The Aeronautics Department, on the other hand, was equally convinced that it could work wonders if only it had an adequate budget—if only, for example, some of the funds that went into building warships were diverted to aircraft. In such clashes of views the Aeronautics Department had always tended to come off worst.

When Yamamoto became chief of the department, however, he proved himself to be an exception—positive, stubborn, and standing in no awe whatsoever of the Technical Department. Unlike previous department chiefs, moreover, he did not privately regard his new post as a mere step on the way up the promotional ladder. In practice, he occupied the position for a single year only, but—as already mentioned—many people heard him declare that he would be very happy to remain in the job indefinitely.

One reason for this was that he now found himself, as commander, in a position to reap the harvest of the seeds that he had taken so much trouble to sow during the three years, from the end of 1930, that he had spent in headquarters as head of the Technical Division. The good work he had done during the latter half of his period in the post was now—thanks to the understanding shown by Matsuyama Shigeru, then head of the Aeronautics Department—producing tangible results in the form of a first-rate, domestically produced plane.

A word should perhaps be said here concerning the naming of naval aircraft. Their dubbing with such nicknames as "Ginga," "Tenzan," and "Shiden" was a phenomenon that occurred chiefly after the outbreak of the Pacific War. At the time in question, they were identified by the year in which they first came into operational use—for example, "type-94 reconnaissance seaplane" or "type-97 carrier-based attack plane." The "year" was, of course, according to the prewar, nationalistic calendar which dated from the supposed accession of Jimmu, Japan's first emperor, in 660 B.C. Thus "type-94 reconnaissance seaplane" referred to the reconnaissance seaplane officially commissioned in 2594, or 1934 by the Western calendar, while the "type-97 carrier-based attack plane" was a plane adopted in 1937. The celebrated "Zero" fighter, officially the "type-0 carrier-based fighter," was so named since it first came into operational use in the year 2600 (1940).

Experimental aircraft were known according to the year of the Showa era (the present era, beginning in 1926) in which they appeared: "type-7 experimental reconnaissance seaplane," "type-9 carrier-based attack plane," and so on. The former was officially adopted in the year 2594, whereupon it became the "type-94 reconnaissance seaplane."

The planes that were coming into prominence while Yamamoto was head of the Aeronautics Department were those that had been experimental around the years 1932 and 1933 and in which he himself had had a hand as head of the Technical Division. Naval aviation in Japan modeled itself first on that of France, then on that of England, and also, following World War I, on that of Germany. Whenever an interesting aircraft was produced abroad, it would be purchased and dismantled for thorough study. Foreign manufacturers were known to remark sarcastically that they would be grateful if, for once, Japan would buy several at a time rather than just one; it is no wonder that the Japanese should have earned a bad name as a race of imitators.

This remained true until the beginning of the present Showa era, but once Yamamoto became head of the Technical Division, he stressed that Japan should learn to stand on its own feet and should produce its own domestically made aircraft. Everybody, of course, believed this in theory, but in deciding that the time had arrived Yamamoto seems to have been considerably ahead of general opinion in the navy. His ideas were, as goes without saying, backed up by his belief that the main strength of the navy in the future would shift from battleships to aircraft.

The most significant of the naval aircraft inspired by Yamamoto's ideas was doubtless the twin-engined long-range land-based aircraft known as the "type-8 special experimental reconnaissance plane." This was modified in 1934, the year after it first appeared, becoming the "type-9 experimental medium land-based attack plane." Then, in 1936—the year of the February 26 Incident, while Yamamoto was head of the Aeronautics Department—it went into mass production as the "type-96 land-based attack plane." This was the aircraft that astonished the world as a naval bomber capable of crossing oceans.

What was it that first interested Yamamoto in such a large, land-based aircraft? Though in name it was a "medium attack plane," it was in fact very large compared with the average naval aircraft of its day; apart from the unsuccessful type-7 experimental large attack plane (later the type-95 land-based attack plane), the navy at the time had, in fact, no plane referred to as "large." Should Japan and the U.S. go to war and the superior American fleet come sailing west across the Pacific, the imperial navy's only hope, being numerically inferior, was steadily to whittle down the enemy's strength so that by the time his forces were taken on in the seas near Japan they would at the very most be only equal to those of the imperial navy. Such a strategy must depend on submarines and aircraft, but where small carrier-based aircraft were concerned, at least, both sides were roughly equal in the ranges at which they could hunt out and attack the enemy; there was no guarantee, therefore, that Japan could deal a one-sided blow to the American fleet. Thus the necessity arose for some aircraft of long range and superior performance that could use the South Sea islands under Japanese mandate as "unsinkable carriers," and by shifting rapidly from one land base to another could hunt out and mount a preemptive attack on the American fleet.

It was Mitsubishi that undertook the design and manufacture of the plane that developed from the type-8 special experimental reconnaissance plane into the type-9 experimental medium land-based attack plane and so to the type-96 land-based attack plane. Combining know-how derived from Junkers and other foreign firms with their own theoretical designs, they succeeded in producing an aircraft that incorporated—for the first time in a Japanese military plane—twin engines and a retractable undercarriage with a sleek fuselage of an all-metal monocoque structure. In this type-96 land-based attack plane (the "Betty" torpedo bomber), a Japanese aircraft for the first time attained—and in some respects surpassed—the international level of the day.

The two airfields that came into being in order to carry out training with the new aircraft were those at Kisarazu and Kanoya. With the outbreak of the China Incident, the First Combined Air Force, made by amalgamating the Kisarazu and Kanoya Naval Air Flotillas, moved down to Taiwan; on August 14, 1937, a large formation set out from bases at Taipei and Kaohsiung and, crossing the East China Sea during a storm, made a dusk attack on the Chinese airfields at Kuangte and Hangchow. In this attack and others that took place on the two following days, the Chinese National Air Force was dealt an almost fatal blow. This, the first use of the type-96 land-based attack plane in actual combat, was to win it considerable fame. Experts everywhere were astonished that the Japanese navy, unnoticed by the outside world, should have been able to produce in large quantities and without foreign help an aircraft equipped with superior automatic pilot and radio equipment, and to succeed in making a return raid of one thousand two hundred miles across the ocean, under extremely unfavorable, low-pressure conditions. The groundwork, one might say, had already been laid for the subsequent sinking by Japanese naval air units of the mighty *Prince of Wales*.

This successful overseas sortie occurred when Yamamoto was no longer chief of the Aeronautics Department, but though he felt an extreme aversion to the China Incident set off by the army, he must surely have derived some private satisfaction from the part played by the type-96 land-based attack plane.

By the time this aircraft was due to be replaced by its successor, the type-1 land-based attack plane, and a halt was called to production, Mitsubishi had turned out 636 planes and Nakajima a further 412—a total of 1048 in all. The "Zero" fighter and the type-1 land-based attack plane were both in the trial stage in 1937, and as such came after Yamamoto's time as chief of the Aeronautics Department.

5

As head of the department, Yamamoto would invariably visit the

Mitsubishi Heavy Industries factory in Nagoya at least once or twice a month. Where aircraft were concerned, Mitsubishi at the time had the greatest productive capacity in Japan; even so, the figure still fell short of the navy's needs. Yamamoto tried to find out where the bottlenecks were, what materials were in short supply, and so on, and took steps to remedy matters in his own inimitably brisk way.

The aircraft industry in Japan made remarkable strides. At one period during the war, it was vying for second place in aircraft production among the countries of the world; and Yamamoto often dragged it along by the scruff of the neck. Some may wonder whether, as often happens in such cases, Yamamoto received anything in the way of kickbacks from financial and business circles. In all probability he did not; Yamamoto was little touched by the lust either for power or for material possessions.

The only evidence of any such dealing—though it is not connected with aircraft—occurred after the war, when what is now Yawata Steel supplied Yamamoto's widow on a number of occasions with a few tons of steel at the official price, as a "sign of gratitude for assistance given them by Admiral Yamamoto during the war." During the period of extreme hardship immediately following Japan's defeat, there was a considerable gap between the official price of steel and the actual market price, and Yawata Steel obviously intended that she should dispose of the metal as she saw fit, and that the difference in price should help keep her going.

Even today the details of this matter are still treated as confidential at Yawata Steel, but those in the know talk of it as something, rather, to be proud of. And in fact, once Yamamoto was dead and the imperial navy had ceased to exist, Yamamoto Reiko became a private citizen with nothing to offer that the company could possibly exploit.

Yamamoto's links with the world of business were not, of course, limited to Mitsubishi and Yawata. The value of aircraft in terms of national defense was obviously going to increase, and thanks to his untiring efforts people were steadily coming to realize the fact. Sooner or later, there would obviously be a major increase in demand, one which Mitsubishi and Nakajima would soon be unable to fulfill alone. If technicians were to be trained and broad foundations laid for the aircraft industry, it would be absolutely necessary to get such concerns as Mitsui, Sumitomo, and Hitachi also interested in the field. At one point, therefore, Yamamoto decided to ask Nanjo Kaneo, Ogura Masatsune, and Kodaira Namihei—presidents of Mitsui, Sumitomo, and Hitachi respectively—to meet him so that he could explain to them the situation as it affected naval aviation and seek their cooperation.

Since all three men were prominent figures in the Japanese business world, he gave his aide instructions to arrange the meeting in a way acceptable to them. His aide, however, decided off his own bat that, since Vice Admiral Yamamoto was himself an important figure, they could be asked to assemble in the office of the chief of the department. He was going to telephone them to that effect when Yamamoto stopped him and said, "That approach won't do. We're the ones who're asking a favor. It's not as though we're placing an order— we're merely explaining our position and asking for their understanding." In the end, a meeting was arranged at the Navy Club in Shiba, and it was there that, one day shortly afterward, Yamamoto met the three business leaders. One of the three, Nanjo, was on terms of considerable intimacy with Chiyoko (Umeryu), and though this fact could hardly have been the direct reason, his reply to Yamamoto's overtures was that he could not answer until he had discussed it with the others. Ogura, head of Sumitomo, replied in much the same way. Hitachi's Kodaira was the only one to promise unstinting cooperation on the spot. "Just one thing—" he added, "I don't want to make conditions, but the fact is we're suffering from a bad shortage of technicians. Our men are always being drafted or taken away to make munitions because of the 'national emergency.' This will be the first time that Hitachi has had anything to do with planes, so if we're going in, I'd like you somehow to arrange for us to have them back." Yamamoto agreed on the spot. He couldn't promise to get them all back, he said, but he would do what he could. And he apparently took immediate steps to carry out this promise. Hitachi fulfilled Kodaira's pledge by acquiring land for a factory in Chiba, and its new aircraft section became an independent company known as Hitachi Aircraft. Although it chiefly produced training craft, by the end of the war it had turned out a sizable number of engines and fuselages.

6

Besides frequent visits to the Mitsubishi and Nakajima factories,

Yamamoto also found time during his term as head of the Aeronautics Department to visit his old haunts at the Kasumigaura Aviation Corps. By now the corps had various front-line craft such as the type-96 land-based attack plane that Yamamoto had concerned himself with from the time of the first blueprints, and the type-96 carrier-based fighter—later to become famous when pilot Kashimura brought one home with a large part of one wing missing—and the purpose of Yamamoto's visits was to have himself taken up in these planes and see for himself how they performed and how easy they were to fly.

Neither Yoshida Zengo nor any of the other men who became C. in C. of the Combined Fleet ever flew, and it seems unlikely that any other naval leader of the day had so many flying hours to his credit as Yamamoto. Nevertheless, whenever there was an accident, the fleet and various air units did not hesitate to complain bitterly to Yamamoto, as chief of his department, about the poor performance or other inadequacies of his planes. Yamamoto took personal responsibility for these complaints, and though he must have got quite a kick out of being able to pit himself openly against well-entrenched highups in the Technical Department, his position could not have been an easy one. According to engineer Captain Nakamura, head of a section in the Technical Division of the Aeronautics Department under Yamamoto, if the number of complaints from operational units became too much for him to handle, Yamamoto would take himself off, without saying a word, to see Hori Teikichi. Since Hori had already retired from the navy by then, Yamamoto's purpose must have been simply to unburden himself to the one friend to whom he could talk quite freely.

Accidents involving naval aircraft were, in fact, so frequent around this time that the press was snidely suggesting that the army and navy must be competing to see who could produce the most; a crash one day at Omura would be followed the next by one at Kure, then two days later yet another at Oppama. Earlier on, when Yamamoto had been on the carrier *Akagi* as commander of the First Carrier Division, some flying officers who had just taken up their duties with his division came to the commander's wardroom to report to him. Yamamoto pointed to a list of men who had died in the course of their duties which he had posted in front of the table, and said: "The Naval Air Corps will probably never be really strong until the whole wardroom is plastered with names like these. I want you to be resigned to that idea in your work. The first thing I propose you do today is go up and do five or six loop-the-loops with your instructors; and when you've finished, you can come and report to me." Yet this was the same Yamamoto who, it is said, would often surreptitiously get out a notebook in which he had written the names of those killed, and gaze at it with tears in his eyes.

Various studies were made of the causes of the accidents; one of the thorniest problems of all was how to assess the suitability of potential air crews. Flight trainees and flight reserve cadets were all sifted very carefully before acceptance, being subjected to tests of scholastic ability and physical checkups, followed by a fairly strict testing of their suitability for the tasks involved; even so, many of them proved to be inadequate after the first six months or so. This would not have mattered so much if all that was involved in removing them from the flying course was the waste of money or the personal disgrace for those concerned. But in practice there were many cases where they caused accidents before they were removed. Precious lives were being lost, one or two at a time, and the destruction of expensive aircraft placed further strains on the limited budget available. Experts had been brought in from the psychology department of Tokyo Imperial University to give suitability tests. The men selected on this basis were all right at first, but later often failed to live up to their early promise. Experimental psychology, it seemed, was of little help in detecting this ability to live up to expectations, and the major question facing aviation in general still remained that of how to find suitable material. The head of the Education Division of the Aeronautics Department under Yamamoto at the time was Captain Onishi Takijiro (a devoted admirer of Yamamoto, he was to become known toward the end of the war as the "father" of the suicide squads and an increasingly fanatical advocate of fighting to the last man). One day, a telephone call came from this Onishi to Kuwabara, second-in-command of the Kasumigaura Aviation Corps. The gist of what he had to say was as follows:

"My wife's father, who is principal of the Juntendo Middle School, has a rather unusual young man called Mizuno among his former pupils. Mizuno studied history at university, and his graduation thesis dealt with ancient methods of divination. Even when he was a child he was fascinated by palmistry and physiognomy. When he read in the papers that the navy had been losing a lot of planes recently, he said it was because the navy used the wrong methods in selecting its pilots. I thought he must be rather conceited, but when I actually met him the other day, he told me that he believed that the kind of man who would be good at piloting a plane invariably showed it somewhere in his hand or his face, and that it was a mistake to take people 'by the gross.' Personally, I don't think the navy's method of choosing its fliers can be called 'taking them by the gross,' but I asked him anyway whether he himself could tell if they were suitable or not. 'Oh, yes,' he replied with all the confidence in the world. I'll send him to Kasumigaura with a letter of introduction to you, so why don't you hear what he has to say, if only for the fun of it, and let him try reading people's hands?"

Kuwabara, who by now was ready to clutch at any straw, agreed to meet the young man, and on the appointed day Mizuno Yoshito presented himself at the corps bearing Onishi's letter of introduction. It was lunchtime, and a stream of men in flying suits was arriving back from the airfield. Kuwabara suggested, therefore, that after lunch he should summon the instructors—about a hundred and twenty in all—and have Mizuno apply his methods to them, classifying them into three grades according to their suitability or otherwise for flying. He promised also to have on hand a list of all the instructors with marks for each indicating his skill as revealed over a long period of time.

Once they were all assembled, Mizuno stared intently at each of the men in turn for five or six seconds, then assigned him an A, B, or C. When Kuwabara and his aide compared these grades with the marks recorded in the list, they found to their astonishment that the grades and marks corresponded in eighty-three percent of all cases. That afternoon, the trainees were assembled and subjected to the same scrutiny; the correspondence this time was eighty-seven percent. Kuwabara and the others were astounded: this young man, utterly unconnected with the world of aircraft, had in the space of five or six seconds delivered judgments that corresponded in more than eighty percent of all cases to conclusions that it had taken themselves months or even years to arrive at. They had hoped for some "fun," but they found themselves obliged to take it all seriously.

Learning that Mizuno had not found a job yet and was free to come and go as he pleased, they got him to stay at Kasumigaura that night and talk with the officers. A certain lieutenant called Hanamoto was worrying at the time what to do about a marriage that was being arranged for him, so they got Mizuno to look at his hand. "I think you're in two minds about the question of your marriage, aren't you?" Mizuno said. "You should decide on the first one, after all." The "first one" was the girl whom Hanamoto himself fancied, as opposed to a match that was being pressed on him for reasons of family convenience.

Mizuno also declared his belief that war would break out within a year or so. Kuwabara objected that even should there be a war it wouldn't come as soon as that; but it was already the summer of 1936, just a year before the China Incident occurred. Later, when Mizuno's prophecy had come true, Kuwabara asked him what had led him to make it in the first place. "Back in my childhood, when I first got interested in palmistry and physiognomy," he said, "I noticed a lot of people walking around Tokyo with the mark of death on their faces. I thought it was odd, because I didn't see the same thing when I went to Osaka. Then came the Great Kanto Earthquake, and I understood. In the same way, I can't help noticing a lot of women in the streets of Tokyo nowadays whose faces show that they'll be widows in a year or two. So I've come to the conclusion that this time it won't be a natural disaster, but that they'll lose their husbands."

It is a fact that at the beginning of the incident the 101st Division, most of whose members hailed from Tokyo, suffered heavy losses in the fighting around Shanghai.

7

As soon as Mizuno had left, Kuwabara telephoned Onishi. "You know——" he said, "there's more to him than meets the eye. I'd like to consider whether there isn't some way of using his methods in selecting crews, and I'd like him to go into it a bit more deeply himself too. I wonder if it'd be possible to take him on as, say, adviser to the Aeronautics Department, so that he could have free

access to the navy's air units?"

Onishi obviously had no objections, having been responsible himself for the first initiative, so Kuwabara submitted a report in the name of the Kasumigaura Aviation Corps command, in which he argued that, as proved in the cases of moxibustion and acupuncture, ancient and apparently unscientific methods were not necessarily to be scorned; and he cited the view of applied statisticians that anything that showed a practical correspondence of sixty percent or more was worth taking into account.

Onishi's task now was to go around with the report, trying to persuade people to accept its recommendation. He took it to the Personnel and Naval Affairs bureaus of the Navy Ministry, and tried to convince them of the wisdom of taking on Mizuno as an adviser, but was met everywhere with skeptical smiles. "Come, now—you don't really think the navy . . ." people would murmur. "I mean, *physiognomy* . . ."

Kuwabara has ascribed his lack of success to the narrow "rationalism" of the people in the two naval bureaus concerned. To the Naval Affairs Bureau, it may well have seemed that the aviation people had finally taken leave of their senses. Either way, when it was apparent that he was getting nowhere, Kuwabara asked Onishi whether he had spoken to Yamamoto about it. Onishi had not, so one day they went together to call on Yamamoto in the latter's office. Begging him first not to laugh, they proceeded to explain about Mizuno in detail and requested Yamamoto's help in getting him taken on as an adviser. Yamamoto grinned as he listened, but when they had finished he said, "I see. I'll talk to him myself, so send him along."

They decided to summon Mizuno there and then by phone, while Yamamoto on his side telephoned to various sections of the Personnel and Naval Affairs bureaus and the Aeronautics Department, getting about twenty different people to assemble in his office. When Mizuno arrived, the first thing Yamamoto did was ask him how he would describe palmistry and physiognomy. As he had already explained to Kuwabara at the Kasumigaura Aviation Corps—Mizuno said—they were a kind of applied statistics. Popular folk beliefs, such as the Japanese belief that people with long, rabbitlike ears were careful and gentle by nature, or that a square chin meant such-and-such, were in fact based on empirical statistical observations.

Such beliefs might not be right in every case, but neither were the odds fifty-fifty. Intuition, too, gave an added accuracy to individual observations.

"Well, then," said Yamamoto, nodding, "there are twenty people here. Can you tell me which of them are flying officers?"

Mizuno scrutinized each of the naval officers' faces in turn. Eventually he pointed to one of them and said, "You're one, aren't you?" Then to another: "And you, too." The two men were Hoshi Kazuo and Miwa Yoshitake, both of them among the finest fighter pilots the navy had at the time. Hoshi and Miwa smiled sheepishly while the others glanced at each other in surprise.

"Is that all?" Yamamoto pressed.

"That's all," Mizuno replied.

At this point another of those present, a lieutenant commander from the Naval General Staff called Taguchi, spoke up: "I'm a pilot, too." Mizuno took his hand and gave it a close inspection. "You may be a pilot," he said, "but not a very good one." The others glanced at each other again, then burst out laughing. Taguchi, a graduate of Navy Staff College, was a seaplane pilot. He had an excellent brain, but as a flier his reactions were too slow. He would occasionally damage a seaplane in landing, and had been recently shifted to the Naval General Staff with a warning that he would smash himself up if he was not careful.

Several other demonstrations of Mizuno's uncanny ability followed. One man, a commander called Kida Tatsuhiko, had his hand examined. "You've taken somebody else's name, haven't you?" asked Mizuno. Kida was reluctant to reply, but when pressed he admitted with rueful admiration that he was, in fact, an adopted son.

Finally Yamamoto felt it was time to call it a day, and the assembly decided without further ado to take on Mizuno. Shortly after this, he was officially appointed adviser to the Aeronautics Department. As such, he was to be present at all examinations for trainees and reserve cadets at the Kasumigaura Aviation Corps, and was to scrutinize their hands and faces.

The navy made use of Mizuno's methods in combination with the conventional written and physical examinations; thus the most promising candidate of all was one who got good marks in these two examinations and also an OK from Mizuno. It was not entirely true,

therefore, to claim—as some quarters did during the war—that the Naval Air Corps was ruled by superstition.

Mizuno himself became increasingly busy thereafter. During the war, he brought in two assistants, and was so occupied visiting first one air unit then another that in the end they were showing him palm prints made with mimeographing ink. In all, he is said to have pronounced on the qualifications of over 230,000 men.

In 1941, in the presence of Kuwabara Torao, who trusted Mizuno entirely by now, he predicted that the war would start that year.

"And how will it go then?" Kuwabara asked.

"OK at first," answered Mizuno. "But after that I can't say."

"Why?"

"I don't like the look on the faces of the Naval General Staff people I see walking about the corridors with their papers. I'm worried about their future."

Four years later, in July 1945, Kuwabara—by then a vice admiral attached to the Military Procurement Ministry—asked Mizuno how he thought the war would go from then on.

"It will be over before the end of next month." Startled, Kuwabara asked him why he thought so. "I made a tour of the suicide squad bases recently, and I noticed that there are very few young officers and NCOs in the squads who have the mark of death on their faces. I take it as a sign that the war's going to end."

Following the war, Mizuno worked at Chofu penitentiary as an adviser to the Ministry of Justice, making studies of the physiognomy of criminals, but before long he was purged by order of SCAP, and today works as a consultant for the Komatsu Store in Tokyo's Ginza district, advising the store on the employment and stationing of personnel.

Mizuno, it seems, put a mark by the names of all those who were found suitable as pilots but prone to accidents, and kept the list in his safe. Two-thirds of them, he claims, were killed in mishaps. There is no means of telling to what extent Mizuno's methods were pure applied statistics, or whether they embodied parapsychological elements, or whether, even, they involved hypnotism or fakery of some kind. Nor is it relevant to our story here. What is rather interesting, however, is Yamamoto's attitude toward Mizuno. In one sense, this was a sign of his concern for the welfare of those under him, but in another it reflected his tendency to believe almost intuitively—or at least not to ignore—things that transcended the normally accepted limits of science and logic.

SIX

1

In the Hirota government that came into being following the February 26 Incident, Osumi Mineo was replaced as navy minister by Nagano Osami. It was Nagano who, as Japanese delegate to the London conference, had declared Japan's withdrawal; and he had returned home from England immediately after the incident. His vice-minister was Hasegawa Kiyoshi, but once the aftershocks of the incident had settled down, in a routine reshuffle made in December of that year, Hasegawa was appointed to the Third Fleet as its C. in C. As successor to the post of navy vice-minister, Nagano set his sights on the chief of the Aeronautics Department, Yamamoto Isoroku.

When he approached Yamamoto, however, the latter gave a flat refusal. Nagano was rather upset. "You turned me down in the same way last year," he said, "when I was appointed plenipotentiary to the disarmament talks and wanted you to go with me. Now you're refusing to become my vice-minister. Do you have some grudge against me?" The disarmament talks in question were, of course, the main 1935 London Naval Conference that followed the preliminary talks that Yamamoto himself had attended. Once Nagano put it like this, naval etiquette more or less obliged Yamamoto to accept. In his biography of Yamamoto, Sorimachi Eiichi writes: "Admiral Nagano was his senior, a man whom he respected highly. To refuse at this point would have given a very bad impression."

This, if not exactly a fiction, is at best a polite euphemism. There were very few signs that Yamamoto "highly respected" Nagano. Later on, when there was debate as to whether Nagano should be installed as chief of the Naval General Staff, an argument arose as to whether he would be popular with the navy or not. On this occasion, Yamamoto remarked scathingly that "he imagined Nagano would go down well, since he was the kind of man who was convinced that he was a genius, even though he wasn't." Takagi Sokichi, again, writes in his *Yamamoto Isoroku and Yonai Mitsumasa*: "Navy Minister Nagano was undoubtedly a courageous and able man, but he was given to impulsive action, and in many ways was temperamentally remote from Vice-Minister Yamamoto."

Furthermore, a mere week or two before asking Yamamoto to become his vice-minister Nagano had, in his capacity as navy minister, tacitly accepted—while not positively agreeing to—the Anti-Comintern Pact with Germany, a pact that was yet another product of the army's high-handedness. In the navy, the only person permitted to involve himself in politics was the minister himself, and the tradition of unquestioning obedience to the minister's political decisions was observed with relative faithfulness; in this respect the navy was very different from the army. Yamamoto himself was very correct on such matters, and as head of the Aeronautics Department did not see fit to object openly, whatever attitude the minister might take. Nevertheless, he could hardly have helped finding the prospect of becoming vice-minister under such a man extremely distasteful.

Those responsible for the February 26 Incident had been put down as rebels and their leaders court-martialed. The crisis had been contained, and a purge of the army carried out—on the surface, at least. The real truth, however, was very different from what it seemed. The incident marked a purge of the younger, more radical "Imperial Way faction" and the assumption of leadership by the "control faction," the army "Establishment," with a rapid strengthening of the army's say in politics. It was almost as though the seventeen men on whom the death sentence was pronounced, and the other young officers of the rebelling units, had been used as political pawns. With the "control faction" enjoying the upper hand in the army, the tendency for middle-ranking staff officers to dictate to their superiors became still more marked, and an unpleasant state of affairs gradually evolved in which, in order to get its own way, the army had only to announce petulantly that "it was afraid it could not provide a war minister for this cabinet." Army intransigence was to be a major factor in frequent political upheavals from now on.

Moreover, the "Bases of National Policy" announced by the Hirota Koki government, whose own makeup reflected many of the army's demands, struck a remarkably aggressive tone for a statement on national policy made by a country's prime minister in peacetime. It could hardly have been pleasant in such a situation for Yamamoto to give up his post as head of the Aeronautics Department—which he had hoped to fill indefinitely—and become a kind of political partner to Nagano Osami. But in the end he yielded to Nagano's request and on December 1, 1936, received the official cabinet order appointing him navy vice-minister.

The geishas of the Shimbashi quarter were unanimous in offering their congratulations, but he replied, with genuine anger, "What's there for a naval man to be pleased about in being suddenly shifted to political duties just when he's been trying his best to get naval aviation going?" And to Sorimachi Eiichi, who came up from Nagaoka specially to offer his congratulations, Yamamoto replied brusquely, "There's no cause for rejoicing."

Yamamoto was to stay in the post that he had taken over so reluctantly for two years and nine months, serving successively in the Hirota, Hayashi, first Konoe, and Hiranuma cabinets. The practical handing over of the reins of office took place unobtrusively in the vice-minister's office in the ministry, with no outsiders present. The former vice-minister, Hasegawa Kiyoshi, left most of the task of showing Yamamoto the ropes to Tayui Yuzuru, senior aide at the Navy Ministry, who had known Yamamoto for a long time. Yamamoto spent about two hours with Tayui, who told him the names of people on newspapers and magazines to whom he should be friendly, gave him lists of people at the Foreign Ministry and War Ministry with whom he should keep in contact, and so on. The whole procedure, however, was carried out on a purely businesslike level; whatever ideas each of them may have had about appointments within the ministry, there was absolutely no exchange of confidences.

Shortly after Yamamoto assumed his new position, Prince Takamatsu, younger brother of the emperor, joined the Navy Ministry as a staff officer of the Naval General Staff. The prince was still a young lieutenant commander, having graduated from Navy Staff College on November 26 that year. Senior aide Kondo, who had succeeded Tayui, inquired of the authorities concerned the exact day and hour at which he would take up his post, and made elaborate preparations to have everyone waiting at the front entrance of the ministry to greet him on his arrival. When Yamamoto—who seldom reprimanded a subordinate—heard about this, he summoned Kondo and inquired in unusually severe tones whether he thought the prince was coming to join them as a prince or as a lieutenant commander of the navy; if the latter, then he should be treated as such. As a result, all Kondo's plans were canceled and Prince Takamatsu arrived at the Navy Ministry as an ordinary naval officer, with no one to meet him or any other special arrangements. However, once he had taken up his post, Yamamoto, it is said, went personally to the prince's office to greet him, this time with the respect due to an imperial prince.

2

The year ended, and in January 1937 two political parties, the Seiyukai and Minseito, began openly to voice criticism of the military. The state of affairs that had been developing since the February 26 Incident was one that no party man with any moral fiber could possibly pass over in silence.

At question time on the first day of the newly convened seventieth Diet session, Hamada Kunimatsu of the Seiyukai made a speech criticizing the military which led to a sharp exchange with War Minister Terauchi. The army's attitude stiffened, and at government meetings Terauchi began to call for dissolution of the Diet in order to give the parties a chance—he claimed—to mend their ways. This was obvious nonsense to all concerned. It implied, in fact, that there should be an election just to single out those who objected to the army's methods.

Newly arrived as navy vice-minister though he was, Yamamoto provided a powerful backing for Nagano and opposed head-on the army's calls for dissolution. Nagano himself, it seems, was not as firm in his attitude as he might have been. Dissolution was, in fact, staved off thanks to opposition from the navy and party members within the cabinet such as Minister of Railways Maeda, Minister of Agriculture and Forestry Shimada, and Minister of Commerce and Industry Ogawa, but the army refused to have anything to do with the government and on January 23, only a few days after the exchange, the Hirota government collapsed.

One thing that suggests a weakness in Nagano's attitude is that although he went to call on the leaders of both the Seiyukai and

Minseito in an attempt by political maneuvering to mediate between the army and the political parties, he met with resounding failure. This failure was a leading factor in barring him from staying on in the next cabinet.

Ugaki Kazushige was commanded to form a new government to succeed Hirota's, but once again the army refused to cooperate, and Ugaki's attempts to form a cabinet proved abortive. There is no space to describe these unsuccessful attempts in detail, but it is significant that the men who visited his headquarters to explain how difficult it was to recommend a new candidate as war minister and to urge him to decline to form a government—among them Sugiyama Hajime, Tatekawa Yoshitsugu, and former war minister Terauchi Hisaichi—were all, seen in an army context, younger followers of Ugaki himself. Nothing could show more clearly how dominant was the influence in the army of relatively junior officers.

After some ten days of confused bargaining, General Hayashi Senjuro was finally appointed to head the next government. The new navy minister, who was brought in with a swiftness sufficient to arouse surprise even in those not normally interested in naval appointments, was Yonai Mitsumasa, who only shortly before had been shifted from the post of commander in chief of the Yokosuka station to that of commander in chief of the Combined Fleet. "Nothing could be worse," he announced as he left Yokosuka for Tokyo, "than to leave the fleet merely to become a civilian employee." He was replaced as C. in C. of the Combined Fleet by Nagano, on the latter's own recommendation. The strongest advocate of Yonai as head of the ministry had been the vice-minister, Yamamoto.

Having, like it or not, been given a hand in naval administration as vice-minister, Yamamoto could scarcely avoid giving some thought to his own political responsibilities and the role to be played in politics by the navy. Where the latter role was concerned, he saw clearly that if the situation progressed unchecked it would lead to war and eventual ruin, and that in practice the only possible check to the army's autocratic methods was the navy itself. To this end, it was necessary first to unify opinion within the navy—even if it meant getting rid of Admiral Suetsugu Nobumasa and other navy hawks inclined to sympathize with the army—and the only man who could manage this, as Yamamoto saw things, was Yonai.

Although the navy's household was smaller and relatively easier to keep in order than the army's, it was far from remaining totally uninfluenced by trends in the latter. In his *Life of a Naval Man*, dealing with Yonai Mitsumasa, Ogata Taketora writes: "The appointment of Yamamoto Isoroku as navy vice-minister to serve under Nagano was a genuine opportunity to set the navy on a new and firmer footing," and the appointment of Yonai as minister after Nagano had departed, leaving his second-in-command where he was, meant that the navy henceforth benefited for the first time from a leadership that could exert real control.

3

For all the pains attendant on its birth, the government of Hayashi Senjuro survived, from its formation on February 2 until its resignation on May 31, somewhat less than four months. Hayashi was followed by Konoe Fumimaro, in his first appearance as prime minister. According to Ogata Taketora, the twin slogans of the first Konoe government were "social justice at home, international justice abroad," and it set about its task with the proclaimed intention of removing the dissension and friction that had developed within the nation since the February 26 Incident. Konoe adopted a highly moral tone—so moral, in fact, that inevitably he gave the impression of believing that to be prime minister was not so much a matter of assuming responsibility for government as of training himself to serve one day as an elder statesman. It seems likely that this had been elder statesman Saionji's guiding motive in his political education of Konoe; nor would it have been entirely odd, in those days, if Konoe's aristocratic background had given him the same idea.

In Konoe's cabinet, Yonai and Yamamoto remained at the head of the Navy Ministry. Shortly after the government's inception, Yamamoto's elder brother Kihachi died at their home in Nagaoka.

Yamamoto's father Sadayoshi had married into the Takano family, which had adopted him. He and his wife had had four sons—Yuzuru, Noboru, Jozo, and Tomekichi. Following the death of his wife, he married her younger sister Mine and had three more children, Kazuko, Kihachi, and Isoroku. Isoroku, the last of them all, was more than thirty years younger than Yuzuru and the next eldest, Noboru; nor does he seem to have been particularly close to either Jozo or

Tomekichi. The two family members whom he loved most dearly were his elder brother Kihachi and his sister Kazuko. His parents had both died long previously, in 1913, and Kihachi's death meant that his only remaining full blood relative was his sister Kazuko.

On his return to Nagaoka after hearing of his brother's death, he placed in the coffin large quantities of the wild flowers that Kihachi had been so fond of, and stayed for a long time weeping by its side. Yamamoto seems to have shed tears very freely on such occasions; he even, as we shall see later, wept aloud by the coffin of a subordinate who had been killed in action.

Kihachi's death came on June 25. Yamamoto returned to Tokyo by night train on June 27, and soon afterward the China Incident began. Yonai's personal account of the events of these days includes the following passage:

> On July 7, 1937, the Marco Polo Bridge incident occurred. On the ninth, the war minister aired various views in a cabinet meeting and proposed the dispatch of troops. The navy minister opposed this, stressing that the incident should, as far as possible, be prevented from spreading and calling for efforts to achieve a rapid local solution. At a five-minister conference on the eleventh, the war minister put forward concrete proposals for the dispatch of troops. At the same conference the navy minister objected, in view of the situation as a whole, to the sending of troops, but the war minister requested so urgently that they be sent, claiming that not to do so would be to abandon to their fates the 5,500-strong Tientsin garrison and Japanese residents in the Pingtsin area, that he finally and very reluctantly agreed. . . .
>
> The war minister gave the impression of believing that the question could be solved instantly by the mere statement that troops would be sent, but the navy minister . . . declared his apprehension lest the sending of army units provoke general operations against the Chinese, and repeatedly urged that attempts be made to find a peaceful settlement.

In fact, thanks partly to the conciliatory attitude shown by the Chinese on the spot, a suggestion by the five-minister conference that the dispatch of troops from Japan should be postponed was put into effect for the time being, and the incident seemed to be moving toward a peaceful settlement. In its heart, however, the army had no real desire for a solution. As to what exactly "the army" means in this context, it is extraordinarily difficult to say. Perhaps the nearest approach to an answer is given by Ogata when he writes of "the lower-ranking officers whose wishes tended increasingly to overwhelm those of their superiors during the period following the Manchurian Incident."

Yonai had never been one to complain to others, but on coming back from these five-minister conferences he would regularly get hold of Yamamoto or senior aide Kondo and give vent to his grievances. "The five-minister conferences are a waste of time," he would say. "You think that the meeting has at last decided on something, or that the Foreign Ministry and the army have at least reached some kind of agreement, only to have a telephone call the next moment saying, 'Actually, when I got back to the War Ministry the General Staff Headquarters people were all very annoyed. It seems the army's policy has already been decided on; so I'd be grateful if you'd scrap what we agreed on a while ago.' There's just nothing you can do."

Just as Terauchi had been a puppet within the Hirota government, so War Minister Sugiyama, in the Konoe government, seems to have moved at the bidding of that strange entity known as "the army." Konoe, who had had the idea of dispatching Miyazaki Ryusuke, son of Miyazaki Toten (who had been active as a supporter of Sun Yat-sen), to meet Chiang Kai-shek in the hope of finding a solution to the incident, actually obtained Sugiyama's approval to the carrying out of his plan. However, just as Miyazaki was about to board a vessel at Kobe bound for Shanghai, the military police, without warning and without divulging on whose orders they were acting, arrested him and prevented him from going to China.

Thus by the end of July what was still in name an "incident" began to look increasingly like an all-out war between China and Japan. At this point, Yamamoto announced that he was going to give up smoking until the business came to an end. Although he did not drink, he was very fond of coffee and tobacco, and until then had been smoking a considerable number of the popular "Cherry" brand every day. Officially, he was giving it up "until we beat Chiang Kai-shek," but to Takei Daisuke and other intimate friends he declared, "Those damn fools in the army are at it again! It makes me so mad that I'm quitting smoking until it's all over. But when it *is* over, I'm going to smoke till the smoke comes out of my ass!" He gave away the expensive cigars that he had brought back from England, and even declined when Matsudaira Tsuneo—who was now imperial household minister, having being replaced as ambassador to England by Yoshida Shigeru the previous year—offered to let him have some of a good brand. "Keep them for me until the incident's over," he said.

4

One would have read the newspapers of the day in vain, however, for any suggestion of how strongly the navy disapproved of the extension of the incident. Not a single article so much as hinted at any disagreement. Just occasionally, tucked away in a corner beneath the headlines blaring "Major Resolve by Kwantung Army," one might find a brief mention of, for example, a "Navy Leaders Conference on Necessary Measures," but even with one's present knowledge it is impossible to detect any reference to the views of Yonai or Yamamoto. Nor was this confined to the occasion of the incident; at the time of the signing of the Tripartite Pact with Germany and Italy, and again on the outbreak of war with America and Britain, the public at large heard no more than vague, unconfirmable rumors of opposition from the navy, being completely cut off from any expressions of opinion by Yonai, Yamamoto, or other such men that might have been of use to it in forming its own judgment.

Some three years later, in a letter dated October 9, 1940, Yamamoto wrote to Sasakawa Ryoichi: "As you yourself say, one can gain absolutely no information from the press or other such publications as to the true state of the nation's affairs. Personally, I feel that the crisis threatening the nation could not be graver."

As we have seen before, Yamamoto—perhaps resentful of the way the public was kept in the dark concerning the true situation at home and abroad—always talked to press reporters with an astonishing frankness on any subject. Matsumoto Kentaro, who at the time was a political reporter for the Domei News Agency attached to the Kokuchokai, says, "Except in very extraordinary cases, Yamamoto seemed not to recognize the existence of military secrets. He talked completely frankly—you might say he was democratic, almost excessively so— and sometimes mentioned quite casually things that even we felt chary about divulging." Even as head of the Aeronautics Department, he had been criticized for revealing to the press things that should have been kept under wraps. But Yamamoto brushed such criticism aside. The result was that the reporters of the Kokuchokai always knew a lot about everything—though in practice they usually seem to have been at a loss as to what to do with their information.

Matsumoto Kentaro enjoyed a rather special position among the newspapermen attached to the Navy Ministry. He first came to know Yamamoto when the latter was a rear admiral, via personal introductions, and Yamamoto was later to take a fatherly interest not only in his work but even in his personal affairs. It was Matsumoto who, when Yamamoto came back from London, heard him say, "It's very regrettable that the Washington and London treaties should have to be done away with. I see nothing wrong with the 5–5–3 ratio. The point of those treaties was, after all, that they placed restrictions on the other two countries. . . ." It was he, too, who heard Yonai declare, in a rare expression of pessimism (this was around 1935–36), "The Japanese people, you see, have never yet been defeated in war; if they should be, the result could be chaos. That's the thing that I fear most of all." In practice, Matsumoto found himself unable to use such interesting quotes, and they were never printed.

Yonai had absolute faith in Yamamoto. The two had been instructors together at the Naval Gunnery School in the days when Yonai was a lieutenant and Yamamoto an ensign, and had lived together in the same lodgings. Thanks to this long-standing friendship, they had a close spiritual rapport. On one occasion, when Mizota Shuichi had an interview with the minister on some matter or other, he ended by thanking Yonai for sparing so much of his valuable time. "Not at all," replied Yonai. "Yamamoto's such a good right-hand man that I always have time to spare."

Whenever Yonai came back from a cabinet meeting, he would make a detailed report to Yamamoto, almost as though he were the subordinate and Yamamoto the superior. In private, Yamamoto would discuss Yonai's virtues and failings freely. "Most of the failings are all here and here [pointing to his head and mouth], but he's no problems here [pointing to his belly]. The minister may not be smart, but he has guts all right." On official occasions, however, he was correctness itself; he never allowed himself to sit down in front of the minister, and would listen to Yonai's reports standing stiffly upright, so that even Yonai felt uncomfortable at times. But once work was over and they ceased to be minister and vice-minister, they immediately reverted to their relationship of easy friendship.

Matsunaga Keisuke, who as a lieutenant commander was an aide and ministerial secretary at the time, has said that "where Yonai was an ax, Yamamoto was a spear." Of Yamamoto, he says, "I feel that he had a unique sensitivity toward the workings of each of his subordinate's minds. He would never bawl any of them out, but there was always an intimidating sense that he could read what one was thinking. You only had to be with him for a while to recognize that he was no ordinary person. People often ask me if it wasn't difficult to work under somebody as razor-sharp as he, but I never felt so in the slightest. At parties and so on, although he didn't touch alcohol himself, he would unbend even more than others who were drunk. His one fault, perhaps, is that he seems to have been what you might call very unsentimental, not to say harsh, where army people or personal rivals were concerned."

5

One thing on which, according to Matsumoto, Yamamoto spoke with particular feeling—though this was at a time when Yamamoto was already commander in chief of the Combined Fleet—was the horror of air raids. "Japanese cities, you see, being made mostly of wood and paper, would burn very easily. The army talks big, but if war came and there were large-scale air raids, there's no telling what would happen. Have you ever seen the sea on fire when a navy aircraft crashes and the gasoline starts burning on top of the water? It's hell, I can tell you—and that's on *water*!" He also said, "As I see it, naval operations in the future will consist of capturing an island, then building an airfield in as short a time as possible—within a week or so— moving up air units, and using them to gain air and surface control over the next stretch of ocean. Do you think that kind of thing is possible with Japan's present industrial capacity?" This was precisely the strategy that American forces in World War II used in their advance on Japan following Guadalcanal and their switch to the counteroffensive.

"Once, while Hokkaido was being opened up," said Yamamoto,

"somebody suggested mechanization of the civil engineering works involved, but nothing ever came of it because there was a depression at the time and it was cheaper to use human labor. Japan missed an important chance then. The navy's just beginning research into the development of civil engineering machinery, but the scale is too small to be of any use. The problem concerns everybody, and not just the navy."

Few armies can have compared with the Japanese army in placing emphasis on "spirit" at the expense of scientific know-how, mechanization, and modernization. A story is told, for example, of how the army opposed the paving of a road in Sendai City, the reason given being that "it would damage the horses' hooves." Open dislike for the army, says Matsumoto, frequently surfaced in Yamamoto's casual conversation. Another source tells how at a conference in which both the army and navy were involved, a high-ranking army officer sitting next to Yamamoto stood up and began to harangue those assembled at interminable length. Quietly, Yamamoto eased the man's chair away from him. Whether or not he did it as a deliberate joke, the result was that when the officer finally finished he missed his chair and plumped heavily onto the floor. Yamamoto neither laughed nor said a word of apology, but sat looking straight ahead of him as though nothing had happened.

Takagi Sokichi's book contains an account of how Yamamoto, during his period as navy vice-minister, poked fun at Tojo Hideki, his opposite number at the War Ministry. Even in those days, Tojo was an eloquent speaker and liked to have his own say, whatever the subject. One day, at a conference of vice-ministers, the subject of aviation came up, whereupon he benumbed those present with a lengthy account of the performance of the army's crack aircraft. Yamamoto listened in silence until Tojo drew breath, then commented with a perfectly straight face, "Well, isn't that's something! Your planes are actually flying, are they?" There was, in fact, a grain of truth in the familiar navy jibe about "navy eagles and army chickens," and the assembled vice-ministers burst out laughing; only Yamamoto and Tojo remained poker-faced.

Yamamoto disliked talkers. His own taciturnity was rivaled only by Yonai's, though he was in no way a difficult man to converse with. Other vice-ministers, self-conscious members of the Tokyo

Imperial University elite, more often than not showed surface respect for the press, which they professed to dread, while expressing contempt for it in private. Yamamoto, though, was genuinely considerate to newspapermen, cooperating actively in their work. Most of those concerned at the time agree that no other government official had ever enjoyed such a reputation with the Kokuchokai.

A cynic might say that Yamamoto was extremely clever at winning the press over to his own side. His undoubted skill may well have been unconscious. Either way, as he gradually got used to his job a situation of mutual trust developed where he had only to say, "This is between ourselves," and not a single member of the Kokuchokai would breathe a word of the matter.

The head of the Naval Affairs Bureau of the Navy Ministry under Yonai and Yamamoto was Toyoda Soemu. (It was Toyoda who, during the war, after Yamamoto's death and that of his successor Koga Mineichi, became the commander in chief of the Combined Fleet and served as the last chief of the Naval General Staff.) He had an extreme dislike for army people, whom he often dismissed as "horseshit" or "animals." When he in turn went off to another post, it was Inoue Shigeyoshi who replaced him as Yamamoto's second chief of the Naval Affairs Bureau.

Inoue, who has already been mentioned many times in these pages, was later to gain a reputation as the finest head of the Naval Affairs Bureau that the navy had ever had. If one may speak of a navy "left wing," then Inoue was probably farther to the left than either Yonai or Yamamoto. About five years earlier, when he was a captain and head of the Naval Affairs Bureau's First Section, the chief of the Naval General Staff had put forward a plan for administrative changes that would have vastly expanded the authority of the Naval General Staff, putting it on a level with the army's General Staff Headquarters; and this represented a kind of revolt against the navy minister. The chief of the Naval General Staff at the time was Prince Fushimi, and his second-in-command was Vice Admiral Takahashi Sankichi. Prince Fushimi is said to have been put up to making the demand by Takahashi in league with Admiral Kato Kanji, the power behind the "fleet faction."

Inoue opposed the move vehemently, assembling as much material as he could to demonstrate that such changes were not in the interest of effective control over the navy. Since his arguments, which he presented in a well-ordered fashion, were logically irrefutable, some members of the General Staff had recourse to threats of violence. At a garden party held at Prince Fushimi's residence, Nagumo Chuichi came up to Inoue and declared, "You're a fool! It would be the easiest thing in the world to get rid of you. One thrust with a dagger up under the ribs, and that would be it!" There seems to be a general belief that Nagumo and Yamamoto enjoyed a relationship of mutual trust, and that it was this that later enabled them to carry out the raid on Pearl Harbor together. In fact, Yamamoto, who thought along the same lines as Kato Tomosaburo, Yamanashi, Yonai, and Inoue, shared nothing with Nagumo—whose outlook was close to that of Kato Kanji and Suetsugu Nobumasa—apart from his high naval rank.

Inoue continued to oppose the planned changes, taking care to write his will first. After a few months, the head of the bureau, Terashima Takeshi, attempted to act as mediator. "The proposals may be stupid," he declared almost pleadingly, "but I'm the one who will be criticized for any changes they make in the system, so can't you somehow see your way to agreeing?"

Inoue was adamant. "I can't agree to something I don't feel is right," he said. "If I have any good point at all, it's that I stick to my principles, and so far the navy has been the kind of place where you could do that. That's the reason why I've enjoyed serving in it so far—and the reason, I believe, why the authorities have treated me so well. So to ask me now to agree to these proposals is asking me to prostitute myself. If you insist on passing the proposals, you should find another man to head the First Section, and bring in someone who could set his seal to them instead of me. If the navy has become the sort of outfit where you can get away with that kind of thing, I don't care whether I stay in it or not."

Despite this announced willingness to resign from the navy, Inoue was not fired but demoted to a post attached to the Yokosuka station, and the proposals were finally accepted as the General Staff had hoped. The exact importance of these revisions is difficult for the outsider to grasp, but a remark reportedly made to Inoue in private by a contemporary suggests that Inoue was justified in staking his job on the matter. "If this means that the General Staff's power is going to be increased, with a corresponding decrease in the power of the minister whose job it is to apply the brake of caution where matters affecting the welfare of the whole nation are concerned, then it's going to increase the danger of their starting a war."

History is said to repeat itself, and twice again—at the time of the signing of the Tripartite Pact with Germany and Italy, and when war was declared against America and Britain—a struggle similar to this was to occur within the navy, and men were to stake not only their jobs but their very lives on the attempt to stem the tide. In the event, however, reason was to be forced, little by little, to beat a retreat.

On September 20, 1937, the same Rear Admiral Inoue Shigeyoshi took office as head of the Naval Affairs Bureau in place of Toyoda Soemu. With Inoue as head of the bureau, the navy under Yonai and Yamamoto emerged with a far more united leadership. Around this same period, however, the China Incident had spread from north to central and southern China and was showing increasing signs of getting out of hand.

6

Yamamoto, nevertheless, showed no signs of dismay. As Matsunaga Keisuke says, "however difficult the question, he always appeared totally unperturbed." Takagi Sokichi, who worked under Yamamoto in a variety of posts, has written that "both physically and intellectually, he [Yamamoto during his period as vice-minister] seemed to be at the height of his powers."

One day, when Takagi met him in a committee room of the Diet, Yamamoto was in a state of high indignation, having got wind of the arrangements, which were secretly well advanced, for Admiral Suetsugu Nobumasa to join the newly planned Cabinet Council. The first idea for this council is usually ascribed to Konoe, but Ogata Taketora says that in fact "the only possible interpretation is that Konoe, who disliked displays of power, happened to be taken advantage of by ambitious men." The men scheduled for appointment as councillors included Ugaki Kazushige, Araki Sadao, Suetsugu Nobumasa, and Abo Kiyokazu, along with others such as Machida Chuji, Matsuoka Yosuke, Go Seinosuke, and Ikeda Seihin. Harada Kumao's *Prince Saionji and the Political Situation* contains many references to Admiral Suetsugu, recounting, for example, how he constantly advocated the occupation of Chinese territory, how even the army began to get fed up with the type of right-wing elements led by Suetsugu, and how Suetsugu invariably agreed with anything that Matsuoka cared to say. Nevertheless, it was agreed between Konoe and Suetsugu at an early stage that when the councillor system came into force Suetsugu should represent the navy, and Navy Minister Yonai only heard about it from the prime minister after it had become more or less a *fait accompli*.

"I have no objection," Yonai replied. "However," he added, "in the navy, no serving officer apart from the minister—not even the vice-minister—is allowed to play a part in politics. Since he will be taking office as a cabinet councillor, which is similar to minister without portfolio, Admiral Suetsugu will, of course, have to be placed on the reserve list."

This was something that Konoe—and possibly Suetsugu himself —had not foreseen. Konoe was rather taken aback, but Yonai simply presented him with the fact and refused to yield. For someone to be placed on the reserve list meant an end to his effective functioning as an officer.

With this removal from the active list of one of the chief figures in the "fleet faction," the leaders of the Navy Ministry, Yonai and Yamamoto, succeeded in imposing a strict if unspoken ban on politics in the ministry.

Konoe must have felt sorry for Suetsugu, for several months later he elevated him to the position of home minister. Yamamoto is said to have declared on this occasion, "Should Suetsugu start advocating hawkish, anti-British policies once he's in the cabinet, the navy will oppose him absolutely. The navy minister will tell him straight out that it's ridiculous to talk about fighting the British without considering Japan's present strength or the international situation as it affects Japan; it shows an utter lack of caution, and in no sense can be called loyalty to the nation. The result might well be the fall of the government."

On December 13, 1937, the day on which Suetsugu's appointment as home minister took official effect, Nanking fell. Newspaper extras proclaimed "Rising Sun Flags Flutter above Nanking Gateway," and the whole nation celebrated. On the same day, Suetsugu held a press conference at which he tried, rather defensively, to explain his transfer from the Cabinet Council to the government. And in the evening papers of that same day, there appeared in small type the following report, cabled from Shanghai, of an announcement made at 1:00 P.M. by the Information Section of the Third Fleet (later the China Area Fleet):

> On the evening of the eleventh, a naval air unit that had set out to bomb steamboats of the Chinese army reportedly escaping from Nanking and sailing upstream mistakenly bombed three steamboats of the Standard Company, sinking the vessels in question together with an American warship that happened to be in the vicinity. This unfortunate incident, involving as it does the American navy, is extremely regrettable, and Commander in Chief Hasegawa promptly began studying appropriate ways of making full amends.

The article, inconspicuously placed, probably attracted little attention at first, but the "American warship" in question was the U.S. navy gunboat *Panay*, and the *Panay* incident was to prove the first serious problem to arise between Japan and the United States since the outbreak of the China Incident.

The imperial navy's reaction to the incident, as is clear from the apologetic tone of the announcement, was one of consternation, and its unwillingness to get involved in trouble with America was obvious to everyone.

A warship of the Japanese navy promptly sailed upstream from Nanking to help in the rescue of survivors from the American vessels. At the same time, Rear Admiral Inoue Shigeyoshi called on the foreign vice-minister and expressed the navy's wish that he should send personal telegrams to the U.S. president and "British emperor," George V. The mention of the "British emperor" was occasioned by the fact that, almost simultaneously with the *Panay* incident, the army had fired on the British naval vessel *Ladybird* at Wuhu, upstream from Nanking. These steps taken by the navy, however, could hardly have been favorably received in some quarters.

Just at this point, Mizota Shuichi, who had been in Europe and America accompanying an economic mission as its interpreter, arrived home. Reaching Tokyo Station, he was met by Enomoto Shigeharu. "I'm sure you'd rather go straight home," said Enomoto, "but Yamamoto

specially asked if you could drop in at the Navy Ministry on your way."
When Mizota got there, he was asked to translate into English a pamphlet
that Yamamoto had written concerning the behavior of naval air units.
In the end, he sat up all night working on it. A day or two later it was
further decided, as a result of a strong request from Yamamoto, that he
should be sent to Shanghai. As Yamamoto put it : "So long as American
and British ships insist on using the international waterways of the
Yangtze River, another similar incident could well crop up at any
time. We can't afford to have any linguistic misunderstandings. You
need only be there for two or three months." Yamamoto asked him
whether he had any conditions to make on his side. "Yes," said
Mizota, "two : first, if any problem did arise, I would be dealing in the
negotiations with high-ranking officials. I couldn't talk with them on
equal terms if I was staying in some seedy little inn, so I'd like you to
put me in a decent hotel. Second, I don't like sitting in front of a
desk trying to look busy when there's nothing to do. I want permission
to do as I please at such times."

To "do as I please" meant golf. "I shall be only too happy," said
Yamamoto, agreeing to both terms, "if I hear you're playing golf.
If the younger officers have anything to say about it, tell them that
Yamamoto said it was OK."

The Japanese ambassador in America at the time was Saito Hiroshi,
who enjoyed a good reputation among the Americans. He was a native
of Nagaoka and an old acquaintance of Yamamoto's, so he was well
aware of how Yamamoto felt about the incident. Over the American
radio, he frankly admitted to the American public that Japan was in the
wrong, and offered its apologies. Yamamoto himself, as vice-minister,
made a frank statement in which he said "the navy can only hang its
head" and immediately replaced Rear Admiral Mitsunami Teizo, who
as commander of the Second Combined Air Force was responsible for
the incident. In dismissing him, he naturally assumed that the army on
its side would dismiss Colonel Hashimoto Kingoro, commander of
the Thirteenth Heavy Field Artillery Regiment which had fired on the
Ladybird, and that the requirements of international etiquette would thus
be satisfied. The army, however, did not dismiss Hashimoto, who was
later to become leader of the nationalistic Great Japan Youth Party.
Yamamoto, it is said, was incensed by the whole business, and remarked, "I'm always expecting someone to put a bullet through

Hashimoto, but it never seems to happen."

By now, Roosevelt was president in America, with Hull as his secretary of state. The Japanese foreign minister was Hirota Koki. For a while, the American stand stiffened considerably, and it is said that instructions came to the American embassy in Tokyo ordering it to take the matter directly to the emperor, but eventually Japan's intention to make amends was recognized, and a settlement in the *Panay* incident was reached after about two weeks. The following is the statement issued by Yamamoto, as navy vice-minister, to mark the end of the affair:

> With the reply sent today from the United States embassy in Japan to the Foreign Ministry, the *Panay* incident has come more or less to a close; the imperial navy, which bore responsibility for this incident, takes this opportunity to express its gratification at the fairness and perspicacity shown, despite a barrage of misunderstanding and propaganda, by the American public in appreciating the true facts of the incident and Japan's good faith in dealing with it. It also expresses its deep gratitude for the dispassionate and understanding attitude adopted by the Japanese public since the occurrence of the incident.
>
> The navy will, of course, take redoubled precautions henceforth to ensure the eradication of incidents of this type, but at the same time it earnestly hopes that the entire nation will help turn misfortune to good advantage by cooperating in the furthering of international understanding and friendship via the removal of the misapprehensions and suspicions that come between Japan and other nations concerned in the China Incident.

In this statement, Yamamoto succeeded in setting forth his own views just about as clearly as the times would allow.

SEVEN

1

By the end of 1937, therefore, Nanking had fallen and the *Panay* incident had occurred and been settled. The new year that now began, as a quick glance at a chronological list of its main events will show, was to see Japan swing still more sharply to the right.

On February 1, more than four hundred members of the Jimmin Sensenha (People's Front)—prominent among them a group of professors from the economics department of Tokyo Imperial University—were arrested. On the seventeenth of the same month, several hundred members of a right-wing organization known as the Bokyo Gokokudan (Association to Protect the Nation from Communism) occupied the headquarters of the Seiyukai and Minseito parties, where they chanted slogans and behaved like defenders of a beleaguered fortress. On March 3, Abe Isoo, the seventy-four-year-old leader of the Socialist People's Party, was attacked and seriously wounded at his apartment. And on the same day in the House of Representatives, at a meeting of the committee studying the National Mobilization Bill, there occurred the well-known incident in which Major Sato Kenryo, a member of the War Ministry's Military Affairs Bureau, bellowed "Shut up!" at members of the Diet. Sato at the time was engaged in replying to questions on the nature of the bill. "I am convinced, gentlemen," he declared pompously, "that what the nation looks for at a time of emergency such as this is not discussion of the relationship between parliament and government, legislature and administration, but swift and appropriate action by some powerful force. And at such a time of emergency it feels, I am sure, the urge to provide some demonstration of the traditional spirit of the Japanese people and to be of some use to the emperor. Yet it also feels that, since satisfactory results are not to be achieved by each individual's acting on his own, separately and without coordination, the War Ministry should give some command—that the government should give it orders of some kind—so that in demonstrating its loyalty it can have the satisfaction of knowing that its actions are really being of benefit to the state. The important thing is to appreciate this feeling among the public—for the government to take full and frank cognizance of the public's loyalty, allowing none of it to go to waste, and to appoint the public officially recognized tasks, so that the spiritual and material resources of the whole nation may be directed toward one single goal; it is the organization necessary to do this that is needed, and it is the National Mobilization Law that will . . ."

The speech was greeted by a storm of heckling, which finally prompted his angry "Shut up!" This in turn incensed committee members, who demanded an explanation and apology, and general uproar followed.

The atmosphere in Diet debates at the time was no pleasanter, it seems, than it is now. Even at the Navy Ministry, many of the more sensible members of the Naval Affairs Bureau asserted that Diet members were a pack of Jekyll and Hydes who behaved like gentlemen outside the House but were transformed, once they set foot inside it, into traders of downright nonsense and abuse. Yamamoto himself often declared that it "made him sick to think that such a pack of fools was being kept at the public expense." Yet, whatever the navy felt privately, there was no one in it who, in giving an explanation or making a reply to the men supposed to represent the whole nation, could have pushed his own claims so arrogantly and with such arbitrary logic as did Sato Kenryo.

The National Mobilization Bill in question—which had been drafted by the Cabinet Planning Board under the guidance of the army, with the paternalistic notion of (as Sato saw it) enabling the War Ministry and government to guide the public's patriotic urges into useful channels—provided that, should this become necessary in the interests of the pursuit of war, every aspect of the nation's freedom and rights, extending from the economy to education, research, the mass media, publishing, public assembly, and strikes, could be placed at any time, by a single imperial decree, under the direct control of the government.

An expression of regret by War Minister Sugiyama made the

following day put an end, more or less, to the "Shut up!" incident, and the bill in question became law three weeks later, on March 24.

In the meantime the China Incident, which the army had boasted would be over within three months, still showed no sign of abating, and on January 16 a statement by Prime Minister Konoe that the government would henceforth have no dealings with the Chinese Nationalist Government made it increasingly difficult to see ways of getting the situation under control. In fact, on two occasions—in December 1937, immediately following the fall of Nanking, and in May 1938, when a cabinet reshuffle replaced Foreign Minister Hirota and War Minister Sugiyama with Ugaki Kazushige and Itagaki Seishiro respectively—opportunities were presented for seeking a peaceful settlement of the incident; but in both cases, once as a result of the army's own pigheadedness and once because of Prime Minister Konoe's innate tendency to vacillation, the chance was let slip.

In a situation of this kind, many people find it easier to act than to think. "When a madman starts running," writes Ogata Taketora, "the sane run with him. Once the China Incident had really got going, the most unlikely people started scrambling to find reasons to approve of the war." It must, in fact, have been fairly difficult for a man in any position of importance to remain clearheaded and dispassionate, to stand in the midst of the torrent without being swept away by it. Yet it seems safe to say that Yonai, Yamamoto, and a few other navy officers who were close to them were among the handful of men who succeeded in doing so.

One day, newspaperman Matsumoto Sankichi was at the prime minister's official residence chatting with Miyagawa Tadamaro, Konoe's younger brother and secretary to the minister of finance in the Konoe government. Miyagawa remarked that there was a serious shortage of really able men in Japan at the time. Matsumoto, who had come increasingly to respect Yamamoto since first meeting him on the day he became vice-minister, named Yamamoto as one exception.

"Really?" said Miyagawa. "To tell the truth, my brother [the prime minister] has heard that Yamamoto's a man to be reckoned with, and I've been meaning to ask somebody about him. What would you say makes him so special?"

Matsumoto thought for a while, then replied to more or less the following effect:

"To put it in a nutshell, he's not a flatterer. In fact, he's forthright to the point of seeming rather eccentric. A military man, of course, can often get away with being brusque, but in his case he's far more consistent with it than other people. If you asked who, among the politicians, businessmen, military men, and bureaucrats I've had to do with, would tell you straight out what he was thinking without mincing matters, I could think of only two—Go Seinosuke in the business world, and Vice Admiral Yamamoto Isoroku in the navy. In Go's case, one should take his family background and career into account—he grew up in circumstances where he didn't need to bother about what people thought—but that doesn't apply to Yamamoto. I've no doubt he has lots of other good points too, but at the very least he's not a flatterer. Ogyu Sorai once said that 'a man of character means a man with a touch of eccentricity,' and Yamamoto's definitely an unusual man. . . . It seems to me, though, that the usual virtues people look for, such as keen intelligence, maturity, or the ability not to rub others up the wrong way, are just not enough to carry us through the present situation. I've a feeling that if one could get Yamamoto into politics, he'd prove to be at least as able as [former prime minister] Hara Kei was."

Several days later, when Matsumoto next met Yamamoto, he told him what he had told Miyagawa. "It seems Prince Konoe has got his eye on you," he said, "so I expect we'll see you in politics soon, won't we?" But Yamamoto listened with no more than the most perfunctory show of interest. "A military man in the political world is a complete innocent," he snapped dismissively. "A military man turned politician never achieves anything worthwhile. The more confidence he has, the less he can do." And that was the end of the conversation.

Both Yamamoto and Yonai refused to compromise with the trend of the time, remaining critical toward the army and the right wing, and extremely critical of the hawkish faction within the navy itself. They were different from the army, however, in that instead of trying to tell other people how to behave, they set about "minding their own business"—specifically, setting their own house in order—as an implied criticism of the way things were going. We have already seen how Yonai and Yamamoto largely succeeded in squashing the hawkish elements and asserting their control over the navy as a whole. At the time when

Suetsugu became a cabinet councillor and was placed on the reserve list, Yamamoto is said to have remarked with a mischievous smile that "Admiral Suetsugu's been driven up onto the roof, and the ladder taken away."

Nevertheless, to go one step further and deal with the army and the upper echelons of the political world was a rather more difficult matter. Obviously, this would never have been an easy task; but it is also a fact that the navy minded its own business rather too thoroughly— that it was too correct, lacking entirely the guile and obduracy needed to shout down the army and Konoe or employ tricks where necessary to swing things forcibly in its own direction. Admittedly, to criticize the navy for this is rather like complaining about the leopard's spots, yet from today's vantage point an ordinary citizen cannot help feeling critical of and dissatisfied with it.

The members of the navy's "left wing" were, beyond all doubt, critical—extremely critical, even—of Konoe himself. The general impression of Konoe, encouraged by his educational background, his social position as a member of one of the nation's noblest families, and his relative youthfulness, was of a man who would bring a breath of fresh air to the political scene. But none of these navy leaders cherished any such illusions. Rear Admiral Takagi Sokichi went so far as to describe him—admittedly this was after the defeat and Konoe's death—as "weak in spirit and vacillating in deed," while Rear Admiral Inoue Shigeyoshi writes scathingly, "I marveled that a man whose abilities in the army would have taken him no further than the rank of major should hold the post of prime minister."

"Konoe was the kind of man," he also writes, "who would try something and, if it did not turn out as he hoped, would withdraw and sulk. He evaded responsibility himself by setting people at each other's throats. In matters such as the signing of the Tripartite Pact and the declaration of war against America, he considered that so long as he got the navy to express its objections he could sit pretty himself, since any attacks would thus be diverted to the navy. It is Tojo's name that is always cited in connection with the responsibility for starting the war, and this is correct insofar as it goes, yet when one traces things back one finds that the seeds of everything were originally sown by Prince Konoe."

Nevertheless, questions such as the National Mobilization Law or the conflict between the parties and the right wing were still not a matter of direct and personal concern for the navy. Even the China Incident as such was hardly felt as being in the direct line of the navy's duties, although the navy played minor roles such as blockading the coast and sending bombers from Taiwan.

It was with the question of the Tripartite Pact with Germany and Italy that the swing to the right, the inability of the army leaders to control their subordinates, and the excesses to which this led first began to make things really uncomfortable for the navy itself. The reason was that, in the world situation of the time, the question of whether or not Japan concluded a military alliance with Germany and Italy would probably determine whether the navy should prepare for war with England and America. War with these two nations, and especially with America, would throw almost the entire responsibility on the navy. As such, the question called for something more positive than mere criticism.

"I have the feeling," writes Inoue Shigeyoshi in his *Recollections*, "that the larger part of my time and energies during the two years, extending from 1937 to 1939, in which I was head of the Naval Affairs Bureau, was devoted to the question of the Tripartite Pact." As a "feeling," this would no doubt have been shared by Yamamoto too. However, if one goes into the question more carefully, it is apparent that in actual fact it was not until the beginning of 1939 at the earliest—during the last eight months or so of Yonai's, Yamamoto's, and Inoue's terms as navy minister, navy vice-minister, and head of the Naval Affairs Bureau respectively—that the matter began to plague them day and night and they found themselves obliged to stake their very lives in dealing with it.

Sometime in 1938, it is true, the question of a tripartite alliance had apparently been put before the navy for the first time, albeit in vague terms. Precisely when this happened is not clear; what is beyond doubt, however, is that it represented a plot by the army, or a ruse adopted by it in its capacity as a tool of Germany.

Testimony given by Oshima Hiroshi at the Tokyo War Crimes Trials shows that the question of a possible military alliance was first raised between the two countries in January 1938. Lieutenant General

Oshima, who at the time was military attaché at the Japanese embassy in Berlin and who was later to become ambassador there, called on Foreign Minister Ribbentrop at his villa at Sonnenburg in early 1938, ostensibly to offer his New Year greetings. It was there that Ribbentrop asked him whether there was not some way of bringing Germany and Japan still closer together through the conclusion of some kind of treaty or other. It was three years since Ribbentrop—then in an unofficial capacity—had urged that Yamamoto visit Berlin on his way home from the preliminary disarmament talks in London, in the hope of arranging a meeting with Hitler. The discussion between Oshima and Ribbentrop was continued in rather more concrete form in both Tokyo and Berlin around June or July of the same year.

In late July, as a result of these exchanges, General Staff Headquarters and Berlin attaché Oshima decided to have Major General Kasahara, who worked under Oshima in Berlin, return to Japan. The ostensible reasons given were the necessity of seeking the views of the army and a special request from Ribbentrop that Kasahara should go personally in order to avoid security leaks. In fact, however, Kasahara was Ugaki's brother-in-law, and it seems that General Staff Headquarters and Oshima had privately arranged that he should be sent to Japan in an attempt to persuade the foreign minister, and via him the government as a whole, to take the first steps toward a new military alliance with Germany.

One day around that time, Sanematsu Yuzuru, who was serving as an aide and ministerial secretary under Yonai and Yamamoto, saw Major General Kasahara, who was said to be just back from Germany, come to call on the vice-minister carrying a bulky bag of papers, and disappear with Yamamoto into the minister's office. It was at this point, Sanematsu says, that he first became aware of the question of the Tripartite Pact. A cable sent from the War Ministry to military attaché Oshima and reading in part "Both the War and Navy ministries agreed to the main drift of the draft treaty brought by Major General Kasahara and reached accord concerning its adoption subject to the following conditions. . . ." is dated August 29, presumably in 1938, so it was probably around this time that Yamamoto too began to be aware of the question of the Tripartite Pact.

Following this, on September 30, Foreign Minister Ugaki resigned from the Konoe government, and Konoe took over the post himself for the time being. On October 8, Ambassador Togo Shigenori, who had been an obstacle to the furthering of the pact where Japan and Germany were concerned, was shifted from Berlin to Moscow, military attaché Oshima being promoted to take his place, and on October 30 Arita Hachiro was appointed Foreign Minister. Almost all these switches were carried out at the army's instigation.

Shortly after Oshima took over the ambassadorship in Berlin, the war minister requested a five-minister conference to discuss what he called the "Oshima-Ribbentrop plan." The plan seems still to have been vague—a kind of extension and reinforcing of the Anti-Comintern Pact, directed against the Soviet Union and hazy as to whether or not it was directed against the U.S., Britain, and France also. But from now on Yamamoto, along with Yonai and Inoue, was obliged to face up to the question.

This did not mean, even so, that within the navy they were constantly discussing the matter; during the long and wearying months to come before Yamamoto left the Navy Ministry and became C. in C. of the Combined Fleet, he, Yonai, and Inoue met only once or twice at the most to discuss this specific question. "All three of us were agreed as to the conclusion," writes Inoue, "so we never needed to argue about it."

The thing they were agreed on was, in short, that nothing was to be gained by concluding a military alliance with Germany. To join up with America's most hated foe would benefit the latter alone; Japan would merely increase the risk of a war with America, with no discernible advantage to itself. And such a war was the one thing that the navy wished most to avoid. Yamamoto, apparently, often declared gloomily, "The way things are going, we shall have war—war with the United States."

The minister, Yonai, had a temperamental aversion to the Germans. A stay of two and a half years in Germany had convinced him that it was excessively dangerous for any country to ally itself to that nation. A perusal of *Mein Kampf* had also brought home to him, he said, the threat presented by Germany, with its traditional strong-arm approach and its unrealistic dreams of establishing a new order in Europe.

The Yonai who so disliked Hitler's Germany also, naturally enough, detested controls, whether of the Nazi or the communist variety. Replying to a question by a member of the Socialist People's Party during

143

a meeting of the Navy Appropriations Subcommittee, he said in effect: "Armaments should be kept to a necessary minimum; I do not think one should demand the impossible. However adequate armaments may be, if other things are neglected the country will go to ruin. And there is a limit, too, to what can be done with controls. As I see things, it may be all right to control the distribution of production, but I don't think it is desirable to go as far as controlling consumption. If allowed to go that far, controls present serious problems of their own. I agree, of course, that all kinds of reforms are called for at this point, but I believe that they should be achieved through evolution, not revolution." It is said that this speech caused a ripple of excitement to run through the press gallery.

This kind of down-to-earth outlook was not limited to Yonai, but formed the mainstream of thinking in the navy, which had developed under the influence of its British counterpart. In this respect, the army was quite different. The latter's traditional admiration for and tendency to model itself on Germany was long established; but what is really odd is that even during World War I, when Japan threw its lot in with the Allies and Germany was theoretically its enemy, some officers in the Japanese army still continued almost overtly to favor Germany in their words and actions. The navy too, of course, was not without its quota of pro-Axis officers, and among their leaders were such immediate subordinates of Inoue as Oka Takazumi (then chief of the Naval Affairs Bureau's First Section), Kami Shigenori, and other members of the bureaus concerned. For men directly under him to hold such completely opposing views to his own must have made things very awkward for Inoue.

Looking back, after the war, on the efforts that he and his associates made at the time, Inoue laments that those efforts were in no way constructive, but were directed throughout at passively fending off the unanimous, powerful, and rash arguments of the army and the offensives of the young naval officers who sympathized with it. Nevertheless, they at least managed to keep the navy's middle-ranking officers—men like the Commander Kami just mentioned—from getting out of hand in the same way as their counterparts in the army.

3

In spite of what was going on around him, Yamamoto's daily routine was not, as yet, particularly pressing or fraught with any sense of peril. All the same, the vice-minister's job always kept him busy; moreover, he himself was extremely correct—not to say fussy—in the way he handled things. A former commander who knew him slightly at the time was later asked to give instructions on how to behave to an actor playing Yamamoto in a movie. "You shouldn't be too dignified and stately in the way you sit in your chair," he said. "You have to convey the impression of a rather restless man who was always ready to spring up and into action if the occasion arose. . . . You'd better move your eyes about a bit. Try to keep your chin well in, but not to concentrate your gaze on any one spot."

As the pressure of work increased, Yamamoto took to standing as he put his seal on the documents on his desk. These documents reached him via his aides; according to Matsunaga Keisuke, the job of stamping them was enough to give one a stiff shoulder by the evening. They omitted papers that were not important enough to show a vice-minister, but the volume was enormous even so. They could tell from the sound in the next room when Yamamoto had started on his task. With clockwork regularity the papers would fly from pending basket into outgoing basket. On one occasion, secretary Sanematsu remarked to Yamamoto with mild sarcasm that he must be putting his seal on a lot of them without even seeing them.

"That's right," admitted Yamamoto cheerfully. In fact, though, as Sanematsu realized when he watched carefully, a number of the documents to which Yamamoto set his seal with such apparent carelessness were set aside and comments later added. Sanematsu thought this odd, but the explanation, it seems, was that Yamamoto, as he stamped the documents, was keeping an eye on the names of those who had written them. He was well acquainted with the abilities and ideas of the men under him in the ministry, and he disposed of the documents according to what he felt the writer would be saying, and whether it would be reliable or not.

Whatever one thinks of such a method, it was very typical of Yamamoto. Equally typical was the conscientious way in which he replied to the many letters he received every day. He always wrote the replies with writing brush and Chinese ink rather than a pen. Whenever his secretary came to take away his papers, there would be several letters written in Chinese ink waiting to be posted. Among them, there was often one addressed to Kawai Chiyoko.

From the beginning of the China Incident, people at the Navy Ministry were supposed in principle to turn up on Sundays too, and on Sundays a servant often came from Chiyoko bringing cakes or *sushi* or a cold lunch in a double-decker, red-lacquered box; Yamamoto's letters were mostly notes of thanks written when he had not been able to see her personally. When Sanematsu expressed admiration for Yamamoto's diligence in writing replies, he answered: "But letters are a substitute for that person's coming to see me, aren't they? If somebody comes, it takes at least five or ten minutes of my time, so in view of the trouble they've taken to write, I can surely spend five or ten minutes on a reply. There's nothing to it."

In the morning, he was always early at the ministry. In the army, the war minister customarily dealt with official business at his official residence, while at other government offices it was very uncommon for bureau chiefs and above to show up earlier than ten. But Yamamoto turned up punctually at the fixed time. Shortly afterward, Minister Yonai would arrive. They would go into the minister's office, where they would spend a long time discussing the day's arrangements—Yonai seated and Yamamoto still standing. This meant that people like the aides had to arrive at the office still earlier, at least thirty minutes before Yamamoto.

On the other hand, Yamamoto was equally punctilious in leaving the ministry at the prescribed time in the early evening, taking himself off briskly without informing his secretaries where he was going. If they asked him, he would say, quite calmly, "I can't tell you." From that hour until the time, late at night, when the press caught up with him at his official residence, he presumably regarded his time as his and his alone.

Nevertheless, as the China Incident spread and problems such as the Tripartite Pact arose, there were often times when it was necessary to know where the vice-minister was. More than once, Sanematsu tried asking the driver of Yamamoto's car where Yamamoto had got off, then combed likely places in the area. But Yamamoto, with the cunning of a skylark, was never to be found at the spot where he had alighted, having taken adequate care to cover his tracks. On the rare occasions when he was traced—on account of some urgent cable, for instance, that people had felt he at least ought to see—he would show obvious displeasure: "Do you expect me to work even after I've left the office? Why can't the secretaries see to it?"

Sometimes, no doubt, he was playing *shogi* at the Navy Club or taking a nap, still in his uniform, upstairs at the minister's official residence. Even so, on most of the occasions when he went missing after leaving the ministry he was at some place or other associated with Chiyoko. It seems that most of his rendezvous with Chiyoko around this time took place at Nakamura-ya in Tokyo's Ginza district, but none of his aides had traced him this far. He took care, moreover, to see that when he went out for a meal or to see art exhibitions with Chiyoko he invited along Hori Teikichi or Yoshida Zengo, or another woman, so that the party never consisted too obviously of one man and one woman, or two men and two women. Yet despite all these precautions, somebody or other must have spotted him making a furtive visit to Nakamura-ya or somewhere similar, for a group of navy officers—quite probably young radicals who had long been dissatisfied with his way of doing things—requested an interview one day and complained to his face about his behavior.

"Don't you lot fart and shit like other people, then?" he demanded. "If any of you doesn't fart or shit, and has never screwed a woman, I'll willingly hear what he has to say!" And quite unperturbed, he sent them on their way. Although in something like the *Panay* affair Yamamoto could talk of the navy "hanging its head," where his own private affairs were concerned he never once promised to be more careful or showed any compunction. There is no doubt that this attitude did not help his reputation among certain sections of the navy.

Late in 1938, with assistance from the patron who, as we have already seen, knew of and accepted her relationship with Yamamoto, Chiyoko left her regular geisha house and set up her own establishment, which she named Umenojima, at the back of Nakamura-ya. From then on, Yamamoto naturally tended to visit Umenojima more frequently than Nakamura-ya, but he and Furukawa Toshiko of Nakamura-ya had a kind of temperamental affinity, and he continued to play flower cards and mahjongg with her as before.

Sometimes, Yamamoto would say jokingly, "Ah, me—I wish I could quit the navy and marry a masseuse or a hairdresser, then I could spend every day playing cards!" We have already seen how, not long after his return from the preliminary disarmament talks in London, he said that if he left the navy he would go to Monaco and become a gambler. We shall see later, too, how he said much the same kind of thing following the beginning of the war, when naval air units under his command sank the *Prince of Wales*, the flagship of the British Far Eastern Fleet. One could easily dismiss the talk of marrying a hairdresser as a bit of irresponsible nonsense tossed out in a moment of private relaxation; in fact, though, one suspects that with at least part of his mind Yamamoto really wished, not for the highest honors of the military life, but for release from the navy and a life of freedom away from all irksome responsibilities. Shinagawa Shukei, then an executive director of the *Yomiuri* newspaper, once asked a former high-ranking navy officer what kind of man Yamamoto Isoroku had been. "Yamamoto?" replied the officer, who admittedly may have had some personal prejudice against him. "He was a kind of navy hoodlum."

4

The New Year—1939—came round again for the third time since Yamamoto had become vice-minister. It was the custom in the navy at the New Year to lay on food and drink at the minister's official residence for members of the army and navy and associates from other walks of life who came to offer their New Year greetings. Among such visitors on January 2 or 3 of this year was a member of the House of Peers, Count Ichijo Sanetaka, a captain on the reserve list, who came shoving toward Yamamoto through the assembled throng and with great enthusiasm demanded to know if he had heard about a "scientist" who could change water into oil. "Actually, it's water from the area around the base of Mt. Fuji," he said with every sign of seriously believing the story. "I'm thinking of going to see for myself."

Since this happened in the middle of a party, his listeners murmured appropriate replies and thought no more of it. Oddly enough, though, Yamamoto suddenly brought up the subject again a few months later, speaking as though he really believed that oil could be got from water. When his secretary, Sanematsu, showed skepticism, Yamamoto brushed his objections aside as "shallow," and announced that he would fetch the self-styled "scientist" and have him perform his experiments at the Navy Ministry. He had apparently been prodded into it, as in the case of the young physiognomy expert, by Onishi Takijiro of the Aeronautics Department.

There were sour faces among the aides: Onishi's bit about physiognomy had been bad enough, but to talk of getting oil from water was going too far. . . . What was more, there had earlier been rumors of the same "scientist" with his magic tricks. Precisely where the deception lay wasn't clear, but deception it most certainly was. For a man like Vice-Minister Yamamoto to be taken in by a trickster was going to cause trouble. Sanematsu busily contacted people, asking them to try to bring Yamamoto to his senses, and even appealed to the chief of the Second Section of the Naval Procurement Bureau, as the man ultimately responsible for navy oil, to have a word with him. Whatever he did, however, Yamamoto continued to insist that their objections were "shallow."

A direct order from the vice-minister was not to be ignored. Even so, Sanematsu still objected to the use of a ministry car to transport the "scientist," so he had the anchor insignia taken off and civilian tag numbers substituted before letting it go. The same method was customarily used when navy cars were used to take people to geisha parties.

Another problem was whether the "scientist" should be put up at the Navy Club or not. In the end it was decided that the civilian inventor should come as guest of the vice-minister. A room was reserved for him at the club, and a ministry car provided, so that on the appointed day he could come and repeat his experiment in front of a large number of interested parties.

The place first designated for the purpose was the minister's official residence, but this was going too far for Sanematsu, and it was decided instead to use a medical clinic in the basement of the Aeronautics Department. The experiments, it was said, would take several days, and might possibly go on through the night—which would not have bothered Yamamoto much anyway. He showed great enthusiasm for the project, even ordering large trays of *sushi* for everyone's evening meal.

Despite appearances, it seems that Yamamoto did not necessarily place as much trust in this talk of the miraculous conversion of water into oil as his remarks to his aides might have suggested, for a few days before deciding to carry out the experiments, he had sent Onishi Takijiro to see Ishikawa Shingo—then head of a section in the Naval Procurement Department at the Yokosuka station—to ask him about similar odd experiments with which he had been concerned a few years previously.

"Yamamoto says he heard that you gave up the experiments half-way," said Onishi. "You normally like to carry things through to the end, and he wants to know why you quit. Was it because you saw through the deception?"

"I stopped because I was sure I was being had," replied Ishikawa, "though I couldn't tell just how. I'm sure it was all a trick, but neither I nor Morita Kan'ichi, who was present during the experiments, ever found out just what it was."

Morita was an expert in the field, but he had come back from half a day's experiments announcing excitedly to Ishikawa that "Archimedes' principle had been broken." The experiment, it seems, went through all kinds of processes, but the final stage involved heating in water a sealed glass bottle also containing water. By rights, no change should have occurred in the nature or quantity of the material inside the bottle, but suddenly the bottle rose to the surface and proved to contain oil. "There must be some trick somewhere," Ishikawa said, "but Morita insisted that if so he hadn't the faintest idea how it was done."

The experiments, their reliability still unproved, had been transferred from their original site to the navy's fuel depot at Tokuyama in Yamaguchi Prefecture, where they were carried out again in the presence of petroleum experts. According to reports from Tokuyama, the experiments were sometimes a success and sometimes a failure, and when they failed the "scientist" invariably fell down in an epileptic fit. This had been too much for Ishikawa, who instructed them to get rid of him, even though there was no proof of fraud, and the experiments had been abandoned forthwith.

"Right!" said Yamamoto when he heard all this from Onishi. "This time, then, we'll put it to a thorough test at our department. And we'll have Ishikawa come and sit in on it himself."

Thus it seems likely that Yamamoto had considerable doubts about the whole affair and was more interested in exposing the fraud, if fraud it was. His insistence that the aides' scientific thinking was too "shallow" was perhaps based on the realization that to dismiss the experiments as a kind of conjuring trick from the outset would make it difficult to hold them at all.

5

Nevertheless, it seems probable that at least with half his mind Yamamoto was prepared to believe. As we have already seen in the case of young Mizuno, Yamamoto had a fairly strong tendency to believe things that transcended what is normally considered scientific or rational. It is generally accepted, for example, that there is no infallible method of winning at roulette, but Yamamoto insisted that there was: so long as one used his twenty percent increase system dispassionately and without letting greed get the upper hand, one could always win. It is a fact, too, that time and again Yamamoto won large sums at Monte Carlo. He put his faith, it seems, in sound mathematical logic combined with a kind of special intuitive sense with which he happened to be endowed.

Nevertheless, the question arises—and it is one that later was to have a bearing on both his success at Pearl Harbor and his failure at Midway—as to whether this method, even pursued without "greed," always worked in Yamamoto's favor. In this matter of getting oil from water, for example, one has the feeling that what attracted him, rather, was the gambler's sense that there might just possibly be something in it.

One other factor was the strong preoccupation that he had always had with oil. At the period in question he was ready to clutch at anything that offered any prospects of obtaining it, and it is not surprising perhaps that when someone such as Onishi told him of an invention that produced oil from water, at least part of him should have been ready and willing to believe it.

The experiments in the basement of the Aeronautics Department finally began, attended by a large number of experts from the Navy Ministry, the Naval General Staff, and the Aeronautics Department itself. One hour passed, then another, but the water obstinately refused to turn to oil. On the evening of the second day, when word got about that results could at last be expected, those concerned assembled at the appointed time, but the inventor failed to materialize. They got the fellow who was his assistant to contact him, and were told that he had been relieving himself by the roadside on his way there, when a flying stone had struck him on the head. He had had a fit, vomited blood, and collapsed.

"It's all a lie," Ishikawa said to Yamamoto with some heat. "He played the same trick at Tokuyama. He wasn't hit by any stone. He does bring up blood, it seems, but according to the doctor there are a few people who can do so deliberately. When he sees he can't carry things off, he collapses in a 'fit.' Anyway, it's a fraud, so why don't you call off the experiments?"

But Yamamoto refused. "It doesn't matter if it *is* a trick. I'm determined to go ahead until I've found out just where the fraud lies." He had all the glass bottles used in the experiments collected, and detailed sketches made of them. The bottles were of the kind used at drugstores for keeping liquid medicines in, and the glass had a number of small bubbles in it. A careful note was taken, with sketches, of the location of these bubbles on each bottle. The inventor's "fit" soon passed off, and on the evening of the third day the experiment went on without a break. Sometime past midnight, when everyone there was getting bored and progressively sleepier, a tightly sealed bottle containing water which was being heated in a bath of hot water inside the apparatus suddenly "broke Archimedes' principle" by rising to the surface. The content of the bottle was oil.

However, when they compared the bottle that had risen to the surface with the one that had been handed over sealed and full of water, the placing of the bubbles showed that they were not the same. In short, the bottles had been switched: it was all an elaborate display of sleight of hand. The "scientists" were whisked off to the police station, and the experimental session broke up. Sanematsu and the other aides experienced a feeling of "What did I tell you?" mingled with relief, and the subject was the talk of the Navy Ministry for days afterward.

There was general admiration for the way in which Yamamoto carried a thing through to the bitter end, but there also seems to have been criticism. It was rather ridiculous, people said, for the vice-minister to install an unofficial inventor in the Navy Club and devote three whole days, with dinner for everybody laid on, to a sleight-of-hand show. Why couldn't he use some of the time and energy he spent on such experiments to establish closer relations with the army, devoting the same courage and doggedness to telling the army where it was going wrong? With the China Incident, for example, why couldn't he work harder to make the army change its mind and keep it in check? Yamamoto, they pointed out, was a man of strong emotions who, once he had taken a dislike to something, would hear nothing good of it. Thus ever since the February 26 Incident he had developed such a hatred of the army that the very sight of army men's faces, he said, made him want to throw up. Such an attitude might be all right for an individual, but a vice-minister's position called for something more. Granted that relations were not good between the army and navy, if the upper echelons avoided contact in this way, what could you expect of officers of the commander and lieutenant commander class in the Naval Affairs Bureau?

6

As these criticisms of Yamamoto may suggest, his character undoubtedly seems to have had, alongside the openness and the punctiliousness, an extremely emotional, and an extremely arbitrary, side as well. A good example of the emotional side is seen in the story of how he burst into tears and wept out loud on a visit to express his condolences to the family of a former subordinate who had been killed in action. Lieutenant Nango Shigeaki, an outstanding pilot and flight commander, was killed in action on July 18, 1938, in the skies over Nanchang in China. His father later described the visit Yamamoto paid to his home in the following terms:

> It comes back to me at all kinds of unexpected times—summer, one year ago, just after my eldest son Shigeaki was killed in action at Nanchang. Shigeaki had served in the carrier division that had once been led by Rear Admiral Yamamoto, and daily contact with that imposing character had fostered in him a truly heartfelt admiration and respect for his senior officer. . . .
> When my son was killed, Vice-Minister Yamamoto came at once to offer his condolences. I expressed my thanks for all the sincere guidance he had given my son while he was alive, and told him that I was genuinely content that he had been able to give his life for the sake of his job. . . .
> Vice-Minister Yamamoto stood perfectly still, listening with

downcast eyes, silent as though turned to stone. Then, quite suddenly, he crumpled up like a small child and, oblivious to the crowd of mourners about him, began to weep aloud, finally collapsing on the floor. I watched aghast, overcome by astonishment. After a short while Yamamoto got up, only to burst into violent sobs and collapse again. Those close to him helped him up, and finally, when he had recovered his composure, he took his leave. . . .

The young man's father, a rear admiral on the reserve list, was a member of the "fleet faction," temperamentally rather remote from Yamamoto, but Yamamoto seems to have been particularly fond of the son, for there is a poem by him entitled "To Nango, on Presenting Him with a Citation" which runs: "The warrior hero, / A flower sweeter / Smelling still / Than all the fragrant / Blossoms round about." The accuracy of the father's account is not entirely beyond doubt. Nevertheless, after all allowances have been made, there is something rather odd about Yamamoto's behavior. It is hardly normal for a naval officer of high rank, already in his fifties, to attend the funeral of a subordinate killed in action and twice collapse in tears like a child.

Ogata Taketora has described Yamamoto as a man "without the slightest trace of the theatrical." "Without the slightest trace" may possibly be going too far, but it is impossible to see his behavior at the Nango home as in any way an act for the benefit of those around him. One feels, rather, that he was a man unusually susceptible to emotion.

This extended to others who, unlike Nango, were not even his direct subordinates. It seems, for example, that he often went to offer up incense at the homes of ordinary petty officers and men who had been killed in the China Incident and whose families lived in Tokyo—going not officially as navy vice-minister, but almost furtively, without informing his secretaries. Similarly, during his period as commander of the *Isuzu* and *Akagi*, he often went to the naval hospital to see sailors under his command. "The normal thing," says Kondo Tamejiro, "was for the chief medical officer to report after a visit; no other commander went personally. I was impressed by his concern."

Shortly after the New Year of 1939, the first Konoe cabinet tendered its resignation. The ostensible reason for Konoe's handing over the reins of power was "disagreement within the government." At a five-minister conference held on November 11 the previous year, Foreign Minister Arita Hachiro, only recently appointed to the post, had asked to be allowed to give his views on the army proposal for a new treaty between Germany and Japan. "As I understand it," he said, "the treaty would be in the nature of an extension of the Anti-Comintern Pact, directed at the Soviet Union but not at Britain and France. Am I correct in this understanding?"

None of the other ministers, including War Minister Itagaki, objected to this interpretation—the most important question involved in the treaty—and a telegram to this effect was sent to Ambassador Oshima in Berlin. The reply from Oshima, however, disagreed strongly: "The passage contained in the five-minister conference's decisions on the eleventh, stating that the proposed treaty would not be aimed at Britain and France, seems to be greatly at variance with a cable that I received from the army during my period as military attaché."

Itagaki, who in theory had not objected to the November telegram, now flabbergasted his colleagues by announcing that "the idea behind the view expressed at the five-minister conference was that, although the Soviet Union would be the prime target, Britain and France would also be secondary targets."

This, it would seem, was what was referred to as "disagreement within the government." But even if the cabinet itself had agreed unanimously, there were outside forces not prepared to accept such agreement. It is said that Oshima in Berlin threw into the wastebasket any instructions from the Foreign Ministry that did not go along with the army's own schemes, refusing even to transmit them to the Germans. Basic policy in Japan's relations with Germany, and the orders for carrying it into effect, emanated neither from the foreign minister, nor from the war minister, nor from the prime minister, but from the ambassador on the spot, in league with certain men at General Staff Headquarters. A state of affairs seems to have been reached where it was impossible to get rid of Oshima even if he failed in his duties. Konoe, who by nature was irresponsible and easily discouraged, took a dislike to this situation and used "disagreement within the government" as an excuse for throwing in the sponge.

On January 5, Hiranuma Kiichiro formed a government to replace that of Konoe. Navy Minister Yonai, War Minister Itagaki, Foreign Minister Arita, and several other cabinet members retained their posts. So, under Yonai, did Vice-Minister Yamamoto and Inoue, chief of the Naval Affairs Bureau. Thus the new Hiranuma cabinet wrought no change in the navy's leadership.

Yonai's personal account notes: "January 5: first meeting of the Hiranuma cabinet. January 10: the question of reinforcing the Japanese-German-Italian Anti-Comintern Pact taken up for the first time at a five-minister conference." It is not clear whether the term "for the first time" here means "for the first time since Hiranuma came to power," or whether this was the first time that a five-minister conference formally discussed the question of a possible tripartite alliance.

On January 19, Foreign Minister Arita put forward the following compromise proposals concerning the question:

1. The pact should be aimed principally at the Soviet Union, but might also be directed at Britain, France, or another nation as circumstances required.

2. Military aid would of course be given in the case of involvement with the Soviet Union, but in the case of Britain, France, or another nation, whether or not to give such aid, and its extent if given, would depend entirely on circumstances.

3. Ostensibly, the pact would be an extension of the Anti-Comintern Pact. (Items 2 and 3 to be secret.)

This document, frustratingly inexplicit though it is, represented the maximum concession possible for Yonai and Arita. In short, if a treaty was concluded along these lines, Japan would promise military aid to Germany if it started a war with Russia; but if Germany went into action against Britain or France, Japan might give aid, or again it might not, and the use of the expression "Britain, France, or another nation" represents a careful avoidance of the word "America." Yonai and Yamamoto, it seems likely, were extremely reluctant to agree to a compromise proposal such as this. On the other hand, Ribbentrop, Oshima, and the army's General Staff Headquarters, as well as Foreign Minister Ciano and Ambassador Shiratori in Italy, must have been equally dissatisfied with the proposal's halfhearted-ness.

As a result, more than seventy five-minister conferences were held to discuss the subject during the Hiranuma government's period of office, which lasted until its resignation in late August. Things reached the point where people began to compose rhymes about it—such as the one whose sense is: "Hiranuma went to buy a bushel of rice, but couldn't bring himself to do so, so he bought half a bushel today, and will buy another half tomorrow." During this period, persistent efforts were made by Arita, with the backing of Yonai, supported in turn by Yamamoto, to tie down the tripartite military alliance to the level of an Anti-Comintern Pact. In other words, they wanted strictly to avoid putting into a treaty any promise that might involve Japan in a war with Britain and America.

In practice, nevertheless, the Japanese navy, albeit not explicitly, was treating America as its first "hypothetical enemy." The fleet was being trained chiefly with that in mind, and huge naval appro-priations were being granted on the same hypothesis. It is hardly to be wondered at that the right wing and some professional army men should eventually have started complaining that it was weak-kneed of the navy to set up America as the enemy when it wanted money, then to cry chicken when danger of an actual war with Britain and America threatened.

The most stubbornly "weak-kneed" figure of them all was, obvious-ly, Yamamoto Isoroku; and from now on right-wing harassment and threats against his person were to become increasingly frequent.

8

At the time of Japan's defeat, the army and navy—regrettably, it seems now—burned an enormous quantity of records and other docu-ments, but among those that were spared, or which they never got around to burning, and quite apart from those that were impounded by the U.S. forces as evidence in the Tokyo War Crimes Trials, there were some that in the general confusion were carried off by a person or persons unknown and thus scattered around the country. One of the more out-of-the-way of these documents is a "File on the Campaign Demanding the Conclusion of a Military Alliance between Japan, Germany, and Italy." Originally kept in the Legal Bureau of the Navy Ministry, the file is a record made, not by those responsible for the campaign, but by those at whom it was directed. In other words, it is a collection of contemporary documents showing how the right wing exerted pressure on the navy to agree to the conclusion of the Tripartite Pact, and the means it used in its attempts to black-mail Yonai and Yamamoto.

Despite his long spell in America, Yamamoto had relatively few American acquaintances—in which respect he differed from, say, diplomat Nomura Kichisaburo. Thus there was almost nobody among the American forces that occupied Japan following the defeat who had an accurate appreciation of Yamamoto's character, career, and way of thinking. For most of them, the name Yamamoto Isoroku signified the arch-culprit behind the Pearl Harbor attack, one of the most na-tionalistic of all Japanese military men. Most of them, it seems, were incredulous at first on being told that Yamamoto had been marked down by the right wing for his opposition to the Tripartite Pact, or that he had been a stubborn opponent of war with the U.S. and Brit-ain. Nevertheless, perusal of this file shows that this view of Yama-moto is neither exaggerated nor a fiction of the postwar years.

The file includes a large number of reports from various quarters, each labeled "SM Report," "S Report," "BS Report," and so on. The capital letters probably consist of "S" for spy—one of the in-formants used by the navy—plus the initial of his surname.

One of these reports says that a certain Diet member of the re-formist faction is highly incensed because Yamamoto, at a meeting of vice-ministers, countered talk of a "new order" by saying, "They talk of a new order, but what the hell do they mean by it?" Another relates that an organization under the aegis of the Great Japan Produc-tion Party is convinced that the imperial navy's attitude is mostly inspired by Vice-Minister Yamamoto, and has resolved that "informa-tion received shall be used to expose Vice-Minister Yamamoto's private life, i.e. the fact that a certain geisha from Shimbashi called Umeryu is his mistress, and to destroy him in the eyes of society." Yet another reports that the men plotting the assassination of the navy minister and vice-minister are a small group headed by a "former juvenile delinquent" living in ShibaWard, and that they are planning to do it for the notoriety, being resigned to sentences of five to six years. From the spring on into the summer of 1939, the reports become increasingly lurid: a store of dynamite is being maintained at a certain place; "the campaign to drive out Vice-Minister Yamamoto is particularly violent, and some are threatening that if he does not mend his ways he will be got rid of, with explosives or a bomb if necessary."

Besides these reports, the same file also includes "declarations," "demands," and "recommendations of resignation" that were brought directly to the Navy Ministry. There is even one entitled "Zankanjo"—the name of a document customarily written by an assassin in premodern times in order to explain and justify his deed.

Sawamoto Yorio, then attached to the Naval General Staff and later to be navy vice-minister at the outbreak of the war, said to Yamamoto, "I hear you're getting a lot of threatening letters."

"Yes," said Yamamoto, "some of the worst of them even announce that they're going to do me in the next day. But killing me isn't going to change the navy's way of thinking. I'm sure my successor would say just the same things. There could be five or ten new vice-ministers even, but the navy's ideas wouldn't change in the slightest." One suspects, however, that this statement of Yamamoto's represented not so much real conviction as a desire to influence; after only two changes of minister and vice-minister, the navy was, in fact, to shift its attitude and agree to the conclusion of the Tripartite Pact.

The "declarations" and "demands" were invariably written with brush and Chinese ink on handmade paper, and were delivered by men dressed in dark blue kimonos with *hakama* (formal skirts), who identified themselves as "a farmer from Ibaragi Prefecture," or "a writer," or the like. In a note in the margin of one such declaration—proclaiming, in the most high-flown language, the necessity of destroying England—secretary Sanematsu wrote: "This man persistently demanded an interview with the minister, but Sanematsu dealt with him instead. He questioned him on several points, and found him full of meaningless grievances and quite ignorant." A "demand" proclaiming that "a military alliance between Japan, Germany, and Italy is not only the destiny of the Empire but a matter of urgent policy necessitated by the objective situation in the world about us" still shows the signs of having been screwed up in anger by Inoue, head of the Naval Affairs Bureau, when he read it alone in his office. Some passages are heavily underlined in red pencil, with comments such as "Why?" "Not logical," "Bunch of fools," and "Insulting!"

As an example of the threatening letters, I will quote one of them calling on Yamamoto to resign:

> The next war will be a holy war aimed at the construction of a world order based on the Imperial Way, and will take the form of a conflict between Japan and England. Thus the severing of relations with England and the conclusion of a military alliance with Germany and Italy are urgent requirements of national policy. However, the nation's leaders—a latterday shogunate subservient to England—persist in obstructing these measures so as to maintain a status quo profitable to themselves. You, as a leader of the pro-British forces, and in league with Navy Minister Yonai, constantly obstruct the carrying through of policies based on the restoration of the national polity headed by the emperor, and are putting the glorious imperial navy in danger of becoming a private force of the senior statesmen and big business. The insult to Japan represented by the tripartite interference of England, America, and France, occurring the very day after you toasted Anglo-Japanese friendship at a banquet at the British embassy on May 17, was a divine warning sent down upon a vice-minister who has forgotten the sufferings of the tens of thousands of heroic spirits fallen in battle and the men and officers at the front; yet you remain stubborn, with no apparent sign of acknowledging your fault. To fulfill our duty as subjects of the Empire and to safeguard the Japanese Empire, we solemnly urge you to resign forthwith.
>
> The League for Carrying Through the Holy War
> July 14, 1939

On a piece of navy stationery attached to this document there is a note in Sanematsu's hand saying that the two men who brought it made further, verbal threats before leaving: "If Vice-Minister Yamamoto does not resign, the league intends to make a nationwide appeal that will put him to great disadvantage. We are also prepared to take other measures, so be forewarned."

It was the task of Sanematsu and his colleagues to act as doorkeepers, interviewing these visitors before they reached the minister's or vice-minister's office and deciding whether or not to let them see

Yonai or Yamamoto. The latter themselves would never refuse to see a visitor, but in most cases there was no point in letting him in, and the secretaries were obliged to hold out while he pressed for an interview, then finally to get him out somehow or other.

On one occasion, Sanematsu had to listen to a long harangue from a man who was outraged that Yamamoto should have attended a film-showing sponsored by the British embassy. The document quoted above also mentions Yamamoto's attendance at a dinner at the embassy, and he was in fact often invited to such gatherings, partly because of his long-standing acquaintance with Ambassador Craigie. He seems to have attended them without any particular qualms. The film-showing in question was also seen by Prince Takamatsu, the emperor's younger brother. When Sanematsu ventured to refer to this, the visitor bawled at him, "How dare you try to cover your own faults by referring to the personal affairs of a prince of the imperial blood!"

Such men would turn up, haul the secretaries to their feet, unroll the usual scroll of handmade paper, and read out some farrago of accusations or threats, the gist of which was that Heaven was going to punish Yamamoto Isoroku (via them). Anyone who tried to argue back was subject to such a flood of words that the secretaries were resigned to saying simply, "I'll take the message for him," and playing the part of butlers. Even so, they usually had to suffer a volley of abuse—"Cowards! The navy's a pack of cowards! Where's your Japanese spirit?"—before they could get the intruders to leave. When they had finally got rid of them, it was only to turn back to a formidable pile of documents waiting on their desks.

The secretaries' quarters were in the grounds of the Navy Ministry, and Sanematsu went to sleep every night with a sword by his bed. He confesses that he longed to be released from such an irksome post just as soon as possible.

9

As for Yamamoto personally around this period, he could not have been more relaxed—on the surface at least. Often, when word came that some suspicious character was approaching, he would change into civilian clothes, hail a taxi, and take refuge at the home of Enomoto Shigeharu in Shibuya Ward. Here, Hori Teikichi and two or three other trusted acquaintances would be waiting, and by the time

Yamamoto's secretaries at the Navy Ministry were listening to right-wingers pompously declaring that they had come "to punish Yamamoto Isoroku on Heaven's behalf," Yamamoto himself—whether one should call him fearless or happy-go-lucky is a moot point—would be plying the mahjongg tiles and singing one of his favorite hearty songs in a loud voice.

After the rightists began to step up their offensive, he would hole up every Saturday and Sunday, almost without exception, at Enomoto's house, where he helped himself freely to clean clothes from the closet and whiled away the time playing mahjongg. One reason was that he could no longer meet Chiyoko as freely as before; in any case, the only people who were informed of his hideout were his aides.

Gradually, the necessity of keeping a strict guard over his person became more and more apparent. However, the navy was loath to ask the military police to take the responsibility. As Yamamoto himself said, one of the navy's weaknesses was the lack of a military police of its own. The army's military police had policing rights over the navy as well, but it was quite obvious that its members often served as army spies, and there was no guarantee, even, that they might not turn assassins if so required. Whenever a navy minister or vice-minister was appointed, and on other occasions too, the army would offer to provide a military police escort, and the secretaries' list of instructions for incoming officials included one saying that all such offers were to be refused.

Sanematsu went to inspect the vice-minister's official residence, then called on the chief of the local police station and privately asked him to provide a guard for Yamamoto. When Yamamoto got wind of this, however, he was so angry that the watch over his residence was called off for a while; but eventually it was resumed, and a round-the-clock guard was stationed in the neighborhood of the house.

Ministers were always accorded special police protection, but vice-ministers normally were not. The present circumstances were exceptional, however, and an official of the local police station came and got Yamamoto's wife to show him the interior of the residence. He was discussing with her the possibility of stationing a policeman in a servant's room leading off the entrance hall, when Yamamoto himself arrived and told him, "I'm extremely grateful, but as a vice-minister on the active list I can't possibly accept protection."

The police were therefore obliged to rent a room in the head-quarters of a religious sect that stood opposite. There they installed an officer to keep contact with the janitor of the residence, so that when word came of Yamamoto's impending arrival or departure several policemen on their beat outside could keep an unobtrusive watch at strategic points on the road.

Eventually, Yamamoto was obliged to accept the protection of the military police that he disliked so much. "They say there's a price of a hundred thousand yen on my head," he told Furukawa Toshiko, with as little concern as if he were talking about a complete stranger. One day, he dropped in at the Kudanzaka Hospital to see a friend who was in for an appendicitis operation. While he was there he said to Furukawa Toshiko, who was also visiting, "Look down there," and pointed from the window at two plainclothes military policemen who were loitering outside the hospital.

"Are they guards?" she asked.

"Guards?" he laughed. "They're wolves in sheep's clothing!"

Simultaneously, the Navy Ministry as a whole was making prepara-tions for a possible siege, based on what had happened during the February 26 Incident. A detachment of the naval land unit was secretly dispatched from Yokosuka to Tokyo, to guard the ministry building. Emergency buzzers were installed between the secretaries' office and a room where members of the detachment, armed with pistols, were permanently stationed, and preparations were made for the building to supply itself with electricity and water in an emergency. It was around this time, too, that members of the ministry began to ex-change the half-serious warning: "Whatever you do, don't accept a lift in the vice-minister's car!"

It became more difficult than ever for Yamamoto to see Chiyoko, and sometimes he would not put in an appearance at Umenojima for more than a month. On the other hand, he would occasionally tele-phone from the official residence as late as two or three in the morning to ask her to listen to a few bars of some song that he had been practic-ing. According to Furukawa Toshiko, "he was a dreadful senti-mentalist, really. He was quite good at singing, with a rather deep voice, and not laying it on too thick. He was fond of the bit about 'with his head on a beautiful woman's lap'—he liked to think it was him-self. . . ."

In general, Yamamoto is said to have been more amiable to those below him than those above. He was always ready to do others a favor. On one occasion, he even wrote the characters to be used on a lantern hanging at the entrance of a newly opened teahouse, as well as on the boxes of matches provided by the house. The teahouse in question was called Wako; it stood near the Honganji Temple in the Tsukiji district, and its proprietress was Niwa Michi, known in the Shimbashi geisha district as Kosuga. For the matchboxes, Yamamoto, using Chinese ink on handmade paper, wrote three versions of the name of the teahouse, with the address and telephone number, and gave them to Michi, telling her to use whichever version she preferred. When she took them to the man who made the matchboxes, he was so impressed by the calligraphy that he asked her "if she couldn't get the man who'd done it to work for them regularly."

10

Yamamoto seems to have acutely disliked admitting defeat, and to have had little awareness of what fear was. In his days as a lieutenant, on a trip to the hot-spring resort of Yugawara with Hori Teikichi, he ate forty-seven mandarin oranges at one sitting, as a result of which he went down with appendicitis. When the time came for him to be operated on—or so the story goes—he requested that they do it without an anaesthetic. When someone later asked him why, he declared that it was because he "wanted to find out how much it hurt to commit harakiri." There is no telling how reliable the story is, but it has the ring of truth about it.

Another story maintains that when he was a child, the mother of a schoolmate once said to him, "Isoroku—you'll eat almost anything, but I'm sure even you couldn't eat that pencil," whereupon Yamamoto grabbed the pencil and without a word began to chew busily at it. On another occasion, Vice Admiral Tanimura Toyotaro made a bet with Vice-Minister Yamamoto in the officers' dining room of the Navy Ministry that he could not pass a lighted match through the hole in a nickel ten-sen piece without putting it out in the process. Yamamoto took him on at once, but however many times he tried, Tanimura always won. There was, in fact, a knack to it: the hole in a ten-sen piece varied somewhat in size, and Tanimura always kept one with a large hole in his pocket, giving Yamamoto one with a small hole.

Not knowing this, Yamamoto was very much put out, and persisted in trying until he finally succeeded in getting the match through the ten-sen piece with the small hole—something that Tanimura could not do. When Tanimura admitted defeat and revealed the secret, Yamamoto's mouth—as Tanimura himself wrote later—turned down at the corners, and he stared at the other man sourly.

Yonai would relate how Yamamoto remained quite unruffled in situations that would alarm most other people, whether in a speeding car, on the rim of a volcano, or climbing the mast of a warship. As vice-minister, his replies to questions in the Diet were always crisp and free of hesitation. Where naval operations were concerned, for example, it was usual to evade questions by evoking the need to protect military secrets, but Yamamoto—according to Takagi Sokichi—always replied directly and without equivocation. Even after he began to arouse the hostility of the rightists and found his person in danger, he seems to have felt little fear, and to have scorned any obviously cunning ruses in dealing with the adversary.

Threats from the right wing at the time could often be disposed of by giving the rightist agents money, but according to Sanematsu, Yamamoto never once gave them so much as a sen. Every day, he went on foot from the vice-minister's official residence behind the American embassy to the Navy Ministry in Kasumigaseki. Once, while talking to someone, he produced an object rather like a tube of toothpaste that apparently contained a chemical to induce tears or sneezing, and, showing it to the other man as though it were an interesting toy, said, "Look—they had this made for me. For my personal protection, they said!" But he obviously did not take it very seriously. One Saturday afternoon, another acquaintance bumped into Yamamoto in the Ginza district. Yamamoto was wearing a cotton summer kimono with a straw boater and was cheerfully strolling along, tapping with his stick and making a loud clatter with his wooden clogs. Nevertheless, however unconcerned he may have seemed to the outsider, it is unlikely that he was so casual about things in his own mind. Around May 1939, he seems to have resigned himself to the possibility of sudden death and gradually began to get rid of his personal effects. In the end, his office was almost empty of any belongings of his own.

After his death, in fact, a statement of beliefs was found which he had written and kept in the safe in the vice-minister's office:

To give up his life for his sovereign and country is the military man's most cherished wish: what difference whether he give it up at the front or behind the lines? To die valiantly and gloriously in the heat of battle is easy; yet who knows how hard it is to die for one's convictions, in the teeth of popular censure? Ah, how lofty is the sovereign's benevolence, how enduring his nation! All that matters is the Empire's far-ranging policies; personal glory or shame, death or survival, are of no import. As Confucius says: "One may crush cinnabar, yet not take away its color; one may burn the fragrant herb, yet not take away its scent." They may destroy my body, yet not take away my will.

The various documents of this nature written by Yamamoto, including those that he wrote later, during the war, all have in common a poetic or dramatic, somewhat self-conscious tone that might be found rather off-putting, but at least they make clear how he felt about things. As he once remarked, he wouldn't mind being assassinated if only it led the nation to reconsider the course it was taking.

As to the question of who, exactly, was aiming at Yamamoto's life, and for what purpose, there are still some areas that remain obscure, together with others that by now are perfectly clear. In many cases where a man entered—or seemed about to enter—the ministry bent on violence, his name and previous history were known, and some such men were taken into custody. There was a "stevedore of the right wing," for example, as well as the "former juvenile delinquent" of Shiba Ward, and the "farmer from Ibaragi Prefecture."

Concerning a certain member of the "League for Carrying Through the Holy War," an inquiry by the Navy Ministry's Legal Bureau uncovered all kinds of facts. His education, for example, had gone no further than first grade at primary school. In the mid-twenties, he had quarreled with the proprietor of a restaurant, inflicted fatal injuries on him, and been sentenced to hard labor. On leaving jail, he had joined a special service agency of the Kwantung Army and had later been involved in an abortive coup d'etat.

It seems impossible, however, that individuals such as these could, by themselves, have exerted such constant pressure on Yamamoto. In the background, as one might expect, there was the army. Even so, when one begins to inquire whether it was *only* the army that was pulling strings, the problem becomes obscure. What is certain is that the army had a hand in the business, at least as an intermediary.

As is clear from the threatening letter recommending that Yamamoto resign, the campaign for a tripartite alliance between Japan, Italy, and Germany and the anti-British campaign were the obverse and reverse sides of the same thing. To an inquiry from the emperor as to whether it would not be possible to clamp down on the anti-British campaign, Prime Minister Hiranuma had replied that to do so "would be difficult." As for why it should be so "difficult," Kido Koichi, minister of home affairs at the time, is recorded as having said, "The army provides the money and the military police take the lead, so we are almost powerless."

It goes without saying that Yamamoto himself hated the right wing. Around that time, the stevedore mentioned above as a probable tool of the rightists was arrested by the police with a large quantity of dynamite in his possession, and he confessed that he had intended to kill Yamamoto on the embankment of the Sumida River. But when the navy began to make its own investigations, it found that the army had got there first, and that it was impossible to elicit any further details. Yet at press conferences Yamamoto still spoke in the same confident—or perhaps one should say devil-may-care—tone as before. "Where the Tripartite Pact is concerned, the navy isn't going to yield another inch. No doubt there'll be a change of government before long. . . ."

11

In April 1939, Yamamoto had visited his old home in Nagaoka for the last time. His trip had a dual purpose: to attend, on behalf of the navy minister, the opening of a prefectural branch of the navy's Personnel Bureau, and to attend the inaugural meeting of the Nagaoka branch of the sea scouts.

The latter meeting was held in the open space behind the Nagaoka assembly hall, which stood on the site of the castle of the Nagaoka clan, whose forces had been branded only some seventy years earlier as "bandits." As a naval band played to welcome Yamamoto, entering the grounds as the navy minister's proxy, Yamamoto's elder sister Kazuko watched with tears in her eyes and said, "I only wish Mother and Father, or Kihachi at least, could have had a glimpse of Isoroku today."

In a speech that Yamamoto was asked to give at his old school, he spoke to the following effect:

> As your principal has just said, Japan today is facing an unprecedented crisis, as a result of which both the government and the people talk of nothing but "emergency" and the need for austerity. I myself, though, have serious doubts as to whether it is desirable that everybody in the nation, high and low, old and young alike, should be constantly strung up to such a pitch. If you pull a piece of elastic to the point where it will stretch no more, it loses its ability to function as elastic. Similarly, though it is important for the nation to be on its mettle, I believe that there should be enough free play for it to retain its elasticity.

The previous year, when he had been asked to talk to a Tokyo gathering of alumni from his old school, he had made no mention either of the political situation or of the war, but had talked to them of the fish of the South Pacific. It seems likely, in fact, that Yamamoto was getting rather tired of all the talk of "emergency," "new order," and "general mobilization of the national spirit." Since his family in Nagaoka had no bath of its own, he would drop in at the home of an old crony who ran a public bathhouse, where in the intervals of soaking in the tub he would sprawl on the tiles idly chatting with the other patrons. He seemed to enjoy this kind of thing more than anything else.

It is unlikely that Yamamoto was conscious of this as his last visit home, yet in fact his departure after a stay of three days—on the 11:35 express, on the evening of April 13, 1939—was to mark the last time he ever set eyes on his beloved Nagaoka.

The Hiranuma government in the meantime had held a full seventy meetings to discuss the question of the Tripartite Pact, but still failed to reach any conclusion, since the navy's leaders obstinately refused to agree to the signing of such a pact. On August 8 the newspapers carried bold headlines announcing "Five-Minister Conference Held on European Policy; Discussion Concentrated on the 'New Situation,'" but as usual the articles that followed conveyed no inkling of the actual nature of the deliberations. In fact, at the very outset of the five-minister conference in question, War Minister Itagaki made a statement in which he strongly advocated the speedy conclusion of a military alliance without reservations on Japan's part. Following this, each of the other ministers gave his own views. Ishiwata Sotaro, minister of finance, for example, spoke as follows:

> If we are going to sign this treaty, we must consider what would happen if Japan, Germany, and Italy were to go to war with Britain, France, America, and the Soviet Union. In such an eventuality, eighty percent of the burden of waging the war would almost certainly fall on the navy. In order to help us in making up our minds, therefore, I would like to ask the navy minister: would the Japanese, German, and Italian navies have an edge over the British, French, American, and Soviet navies in such a war?

Navy Minister Yonai was normally so taciturn that he was regarded in some quarters as ineffectual. On this occasion, however, the "goldfish minister" did not mince his words. Unhesitatingly and quite unequivocally, he replied: "We would have no chance of winning. In the first place, the Japanese navy is not constructed with a view to taking on the United States and Britain. And as for the German and Italian navies, they can be discounted."

Two weeks later—at 10:20 P.M. on August 21, by Berlin time—the Nazi government announced over the radio its decision to sign a treaty of non-aggression with the Soviet Union.

The Japanese government was thrown into confusion. It had shilly-shallied for so long that Germany, the country in which it had placed so much trust, had finally betrayed it for another. The question of the Tripartite Pact was shelved for the time being, and on August 29 the Hiranuma cabinet resigned, declaring that the situation in Europe had taken on a "new, complex, and bizarre aspect."

"In giving up the reins of power," Yonai wrote later, "Prime Minister Hiranuma is said to have confessed to the Lord Privy Seal of the time that naval opinion had been consistently correct in its estimate of the situation. But the admission came too late: the stable was already empty." Yonai's place as navy minister was taken by Vice Admiral Yoshida Zengo, a contemporary of Yamamoto's and C. in C. of the Combined Fleet. Yamamoto himself expressed his willingness to stay on as vice-minister under Yoshida, but he too was replaced, his successor being Sumiyama Tokutaro.

Vice Admiral Sumiyama had for long been a naval aide to the emperor, whose confidence he enjoyed. Takei Daisuke voiced doubts to Yamamoto as to whether Sumiyama would be up to the task facing him. "We shall have to show the army," Yamamoto declared, "that bringing in a mild, gentlemanly type like him doesn't mean that the navy's attitude will change." Even so, Yamamoto's own show of willingness to stay on as vice-minister suggests a definite change of attitude if one remembers his angry remark made three years earlier on first becoming vice-minister himself: "What's there for a naval man to be pleased about in being suddenly shifted to political duties? . . ." One suspects that, despite the difficulties and dangers, he had begun to feel a definite interest, even a sense of mission, in his work as navy vice-minister.

Much later, when someone asked Yonai if Fleet Admiral Yamamoto had had any interest in politics, Yonai thought for a while, then replied, "I think he had." This is backed up by an episode that occurred many years earlier, when Yamamoto was naval attaché in Washington. He was chatting in the attaché's office with his first assistant when the latter said, "It says in the Imperial Rescript that a military man should have nothing to do with politics, so I make a point of not taking much interest in political affairs. I hardly ever look at the political columns in the newspapers, even."

"Nonsense," retorted Yamamoto angrily. "Not to take any part in politics doesn't mean you should be ignorant of them."

There seems to have been a considerable body of opinion within the navy in favor of making Yamamoto navy minister in Yonai's place, but Yonai would not give his approval. When Takei asked why Yamamoto was not brought in as his successor, he replied, "Because Yoshida's approach will be just the same." Then he reflected a moment and added, "You see, if we'd shoved Yamamoto in willy-nilly, there'd have been a danger of his being killed." It seems likely, in short, that Yonai could not face the idea of the possible tragedy that might occur if Yamamoto were left in such a conspicuous and vulnerable position.

A well-known anecdote tells how Yamamoto, one day around this time, noticed another man sitting in the minister's office while he himself was talking to the minister. "I didn't introduce you," said Yonai afterward, "but he's a famous fortune-teller. He came again

170

later and said you should take great care, since you had the mark of assassination on your face." No one, however, knows who the "famous fortune-teller" was, and some people claim that Yonai, knowing that Yamamoto had an inordinate interest in things such as physiognomy, getting oil from water, and so on, told him a deliberate lie as a way of getting him to agree to being shunted back to sea and comparative safety.

Early one morning, the journalist Matsumoto Sankichi called on Yamamoto at the Navy Ministry. The bookshelves and tables in the vice-minister's office were all bare, and Yamamoto had the drawers of his desk open and was going through them as he waited for Sumiyama, his successor, to come and have the everyday business of the post explained to him.

"So you're going back to sea at last," remarked Matsumoto.

"Yes, at last," said Yamamoto. He was obviously relieved and cheerful, according to Matsumoto.

Conversation turned to Hitler's most recent and sensational move, the non-aggression pact with the Soviet Union. "That's why I don't like dictators," said Matsumoto. "I'm sure the German public is completely appalled."

"I'm sure it is," said Yamamoto with a sardonic grin, "but not half so much as the Japanese army, if you ask me!" He paused, then added: "The man who's replacing me is quite a different type—he's so courteous and good-natured they call him the 'saint' of the navy. So from now on you and your people had better not come barging in here any more."

Matsumoto, however—convinced that one day, inevitably, Yamamoto would become navy minister—went on: "But surely you'll be back here yourself sooner or later, won't you?"

"No," declared Yamamoto. "I shall never come back here. Never!" He repeated the word as though for his own benefit.

Thus Yamamoto finally left his job as navy vice-minister and took up the post of commander in chief of the Combined Fleet and the First Fleet in succession to Yoshida Zengo.

171

EIGHT

1

After a very long digression, our story has arrived back at the point where the Combined Fleet sailed from Wakanoura Bay with its new commander in chief, Vice Admiral Yamamoto Isoroku, on board the flagship.

Sanematsu Yuzuru and the other Navy Ministry aides who went to Tokyo Station to see Yamamoto off on August 31 admit to having felt a sense of relief as they watched the limited express with Yamamoto on board draw out of the station without any untoward incident having occurred. Almost certainly Yamamoto himself felt a similar emotion once he found himself safely installed in the C. in C.'s cabin of the flagship *Nagato*. In place of the murky office overlooking the courtyard of the Navy Ministry, he had all around him the glittering, sunlit ocean. In contrast to his life in Tokyo—where, in the third year of the China Incident, shortages of materials and foodstuffs were beginning to make themselves felt—he could, as commander in chief, wine and dine in style. The air was sweet. In place of the rightists who had watched his every movement, thirsting after his blood, he found himself in the midst of forty thousand officers and men all concerned for his safety. Indeed, he himself, as we have already seen, remarked to his aide Fujita that he "rather liked being commander in chief. One's popular. A navy vice-minister's just a high-grade office boy."

Nevertheless, it would be wrong to assume that all the forty thousand officers and men of the Combined Fleet were equally impressed by, and equally willing to place their trust in, their new chief. Many of the wilder, more headstrong members of the air corps were fond of Hitler-style heroics, and some of the younger fliers who had been too young to know Yamamoto during his days as second-in-command of the Kasumigaura Aviation Corps and commander of the *Akagi*, as well as others whose appointments had kept them out of contact with him, seem to have had considerable doubts about the newly appointed commander in chief. Lieutenant Commander Fuchida Mitsuo, flight commander on the *Akagi* and a hothead among hotheads, openly declared, "Yamamoto's got no guts. He's too fond of England and America. Something of a coward, I'd say."

One might naturally assume that, having weighed anchor and left the shelter of harbor, the world's third largest navy would sail freely over the vast tracts of the Pacific Ocean in the course of its maneuvers, but in fact this was not so. In reality, it was constantly haunted by the specter of an oil shortage. The quantity of fuel available was limited, and any waste out of the question; as a result, the fleet's training grounds were restricted almost entirely to the waters off the Pacific shores of Japan.

The areas where specific types of training were carried out were also, for the most part, laid down: gunnery practice was carried out off Sukumo or Cape Ashizuri, and other types of training in the area from the Kii Channel to Ise Bay, while winter training in torpedo firing was done at Hashirajima in the Inland Sea. Similarly, as the fleet proceeded, for example, from Beppu Bay in Kyushu to Yokosuka, an intense program of training—daylight training, twilight training, night training, dawn training—was carried out right up to the point where they entered harbor, so that precious fuel should not be wasted. So fierce was training in the imperial navy that its week was popularly said to include an extra Monday and Friday instead of a Saturday and Sunday.

This did not mean, though, that the fleet was given no holidays at all. Generally speaking, statistics showed that if training went on for more than four weeks without shore leave, accidents became more frequent. Fights would start over the most trivial matters, increasing still further the possibility of other accidents. Thus the Combined Fleet's exercises were usually planned on a four-week basis, punctuated by spells of rest and recuperation in Kure, Sasebo, or Beppu. Since such occasions involved thousands—or tens of thousands—of men giving vent to the frustrations of a whole month, the smaller, remoter ports were not suitable for the purpose; where the population was too small, there were undesirable incidents on shore. Thus places such as Beppu—a large hot-spring resort with plenty of recreational facilities—were considered best suited as ports.

The staff officers and the C. in C. himself were no different from those under them in beginning to long for the shore lights after several weeks at sea. Whenever their vessels docked at the home port of Yokosuka, they would go back to their respective homes in nearby Tokyo, Kamakura, Zushi, or Hayama. When the fleet called at some other port, some of them would arrange to have their wives come to see them there. The inns officially designated for navy use in Kure and Sasebo often had their rooms arranged to create a newly-wed or small-family atmosphere.

When the *Nagato* entered harbor, Yamamoto almost always went ashore and stayed at an inn. When the fleet entered Yokosuka harbor and he went up to Tokyo, he usually stayed at the Navy Club in Shiba at first. After that—though this is partly conjecture—he seems to have spent more time in secret meetings with Chiyoko than at his own home.

A geisha called Koume, who worked in the Shimbashi quarter at the time and was the mistress of a prominent businessman, had a house in Kamiya-cho, in the same district as the Navy Club. Obliged for personal reasons to move out of it, she suggested to Umeryu—Chiyoko—that it would be ideal for her meetings with Yamamoto. Chiyoko went to see it, took a fancy to it, and, approximately one year after Yamamoto left to become C. in C., established her own private home in Kamiya-cho while continuing as before to run Umenojima. Koume still owned the house, which Chiyoko merely rented, but from then on it was to be the site of rendezvous between herself and Yamamoto whenever the latter came up to Tokyo.

2

When Yamamoto came to the Combined Fleet, former Navy Ministry senior aide Tayui, who had since risen to the rank of rear admiral and was now commander of the Sixth Cruiser Division headed by the *Kako* and *Furutaka*, found himself under his direct command. According to Tayui, an extremely tense atmosphere prevailed in the Combined Fleet around the period 1938–40. Its maneuvers, for example, were not normal peacetime exercises, but were as intensive as though a major war were in progress. One manifestation of this was a new type of training being adopted for entering harbor. Entering and leaving harbor by night was an extremely tricky and dangerous operation for the fleet; there was even the risk, should a blunder result in one of "His Imperial Majesty's" vessels being damaged, of the officer in charge being obliged to commit ritual suicide. Thus in normal times it was usual practice to employ distinguishing lights of different colors and to maintain radio communication among the vessels concerned. Now, however, the whole fleet was required to douse its lights and follow the flagships in silence, since in wartime it would be impossible either to use colored lights or to send out even the weakest radio signals. The most nerve-racking business of all was leaving harbor. Since it took time for a vessel displacing thousands or tens of thousands of tons to develop its own momentum, it was very difficult to handle in darkness; even if the vessel in front became invisible, it was necessary to keep it at a certain distance since, should something go wrong, one's own ship would not respond at once.

Tayui himself and naval men in general, not to mention many others outside the navy, seem to have been impressed, despite themselves, by the degree of readiness that the Japanese navy had reached immediately prior to the outbreak of the Pacific War. "All the same," Tayui says, "not a single naval officer with any sense actually wanted war."

On the *Akagi*—the carrier on which Lieutenant Commander Fuchida Mitsuo was serving—extremely rigorous training was being given under orders from command. It involved, for instance, training in emergency deck landings, and in taking off and landing by night; all fliers took part, irrespective of their ability or technical level. Initially, this caused considerable muttering among those concerned.

The *Akagi*'s captain was Kusaka Ryunosuke, and the commander of the First Carrier Division, to which the *Akagi* belonged, was Ozawa Jisaburo. Fuchida Mitsuo was a far younger man, a graduate of the fifty-second year at the Naval Academy and just at the peak of his vigor and ability.

Fuchida was preoccupied with the question of increasing accuracy in night bombing. Since there were of course no missiles or radar at the time, it was usual, in giving training in night bombing, for the "defending force" to search out the planes of the "attacking force" with searchlights, then take aim with anti-aircraft guns and fire. Unfortunately, frequent crashes were caused by the searchlights, which dazzled the pilots, and their use was abandoned at one stage. But Fuchida objected. "This is training for *war*," he declared. "Put the lights on—I'll do it myself!" Donning sunglasses, he began training in flying right through the dazzling light, thanks to which he and his fellow pilots gradually got used to the searchlights.

In October 1939, one month after Yamamoto became C. in C., it was decided to hold maneuvers—to be known as "Operation 123"—in Hyuga Bay. The battle force was to leave Ariake Bay and proceed northward up the east coast of Kyushu toward Saeki. Air units were to search it out and make an attack on it as it sailed by night.

The twenty-seven torpedo planes led by Lieutenant Commander Fuchida kept close on the tail of the flagship *Nagato* carrying Yamamoto. In the dark and despite the ship's searchlights and the barrage of anti-aircraft fire that it put up in a desperate attempt to escape, they scored "hits" with all the training torpedoes that they fired.

Yamamoto, who was watching from the combat bridge of the *Nagato*, asked the air staff officer for the name of the man responsible, and after completion of the exercises sent a message to the commander of the First Carrier Division declaring, "Operation 123 splendid."

This was the occasion on which Yamamoto first became aware of Fuchida's existence, and Fuchida on his side—possibly because of his pleasure at being praised—began to revise somewhat his earlier, derogatory view of the C. in C. It still remains rather doubtful, even so, whether a hotheaded flier like Fuchida could really have been classified at the time among the naval officers "with any sense" of whom Tayui had spoken—nor, in fact, would it have been a very good thing for the forces if, when war was announced, the young men had all lapsed into despondency without any of the necessary will to fight. There was one thing, even so, that Yamamoto often warned his young officers about:

You can tell a man's character by the way he makes advances to a woman. Men like you, for example—when the fleet's in port and you go off to have a good time, you seem to have only two ways of going about things. First, you put it straight to the woman: "Hey, how about a lay?" Now, any woman, even the lowest whore, is going to put up at least a show of refusing if she's asked like that. So what do you do next? You either act insulted and get rough, or you give up immediately and go off to try the same thing on the next woman. That's all you're capable of. But take a look at Western men—they're quite different. Once they've set their sights on a woman, they invite her out for a drink, or to dinner, or to go dancing. In that way they gradually break down her defenses until, in the end, they get what they want, and in style at that. Where achieving a particular aim is concerned, that's surely a far wiser way of going about things. At any rate, they're the kind of men you'd be dealing with if there were a war, so you'd better give it some thought.

3

Sometime around this period, Yamamoto was visited on board the *Nagato* in Yokosuka harbor by friends who had been in the same "English E" class at Harvard. They included Keio University graduates such as Oguma Shin'ichiro and Morimura Isamu, who were leading figures in the business world by now but who, twenty years earlier, had been on extremely easygoing terms with Yamamoto. This was from 1919 through 1921, when he had been a lieutenant commander, then commander, but even after his return to Japan he had kept up his acquaintance with the friends of those days. With them, and with other prominent figures of the business and academic worlds whom he got to know through them, he enjoyed an easy, informal relationship not above a certain amount of schoolboyish ragging and horseplay. Such being the case, their approach to the visit was quite different from, say, countryfolk from Nagaoka, who were overcome by the honor of being allowed to inspect the *Nagato*. They were more than half inclined, in fact, to poke fun at Yamamoto in the dignity of his new position.

When Yamamoto agreed to their request to be allowed to come and give the Combined Fleet a lookover, Morimura announced that they were thinking of bringing along some geishas: would it be all right? "Of course," said Yamamoto, so they decided to board the *Nagato* with a large party of the girls, just to see how Yamamoto would react.

The group consisted of four or five men and around ten Shimbashi geishas. Arriving at Yokosuka Station on the appointed day, they were surprised to bump into Yamamoto himself. It is not clear whether he had come to the station on some other business, or whether he happened to have taken the same train as them on his way back from a stay in Tokyo; either way, he greeted them with apparent pleasure and shepherded them through the gate leading to the Hemmi Pier. From there on, they were in a different world, a world where the navy and naval discipline dominated everything.

Seeing that the man coming through the gate at the head of a bevy of geishas was the commander in chief, the guard on duty in his box bellowed the crisp command "Attention!" and the young ensign in charge of the C. in C.'s launch stood rigidly at the salute. The party boarded the launch according to prescribed etiquette and, to a series of snappy commands from the ensign, the boat shot away from the quay leaving a flurry of foam in its wake.

The floor of Yamamoto's cabin on the launch was covered with a black woolen carpet bordered with yellow and with two cherry-blossom emblems indicating his rank, and the women, accustomed to addressing Yamamoto informally, gradually fell silent, oppressed by the unfamiliar surroundings. Yamamoto himself, however, was no different from usual. He did not, of course, behave as he would have done at a party, but he showed no inclination to walk apart from the geishas, or to avoid sitting next to them, or any other sign of embarrassment, but chatted completely naturally and with every sign of enjoyment—so much so that those present began to suspect that this was not, after all, the first time such a thing had happened.

Not long after arriving on board the *Nagato*, they sat down to lunch, at which they were joined by those staff officers who had remained on board. The luncheon menu for command usually proceeded from soup, through fish and entrée with salad, to fruit and coffee, but when there were guests there was usually an additional course as well. When the meal was ready, an orderly would call out to the bandmaster of the naval band waiting on the afterdeck, "I'm going to fetch the C. in C.," and would run off to the C. in C.'s private cabin. In this way, at approximately the same moment that the commander in chief opened the door of his cabin, the bandmaster's baton would descend, and the march that always accompanied his progress along the passage to the wardroom would begin.

In the same way, therefore, Morimura, Oguma, and their party of geishas lunched with Yamamoto on board the *Nagato* to the accompaniment of a naval band. As Oguma remembers it, the meal was "quite good." Even so, it must have been a remarkable sight to see a dozen or so geishas, all of them rather subdued, earnestly plying their knives and forks on either side of Yamamoto as he sat in state in the C. in C.'s wardroom.

Chiyoko, who had not been invited on this occasion, immediately decided she would not be outdone. First she suggested to Furukawa Toshiko that they should go and see the *Nagato* for themselves sometime, then she roped in Toshiko's sister and another ten or so fellow geishas, and a few days later they all descended on Yokosuka. The *Nagato* thus welcomed on board in rapid succession two different parties of some of the most attractive women from the Shimbashi quarter. The story was later to snowball, until the legend grew up that Yamamoto had taken large numbers of geishas on board the Combined Fleet flagship, where he held wild drinking and singing parties. The reality, in fact, seems to have been much tamer.

4

Chiyoko personally, however, would always visit Yamamoto at least once whenever the *Nagato* entered harbor at Yokosuka. She would come bearing underwear, socks, even presents for his aides and their wives, and would busily set about tidying up the wardrobe, bed, and so on in his cabin. On one occasion, even, she reportedly scolded him—when he offered to give the wife of one of his officers some good Hokkaido salmon, and proceeded to produce a bulky package containing salted salmon from amongst the uniforms in his closet.

The training year in the navy ended in December. There would be a memorial service at sea for any men who had died during training, then the fleet would return to its home port and the crews disperse. The end of the year was always marked by the announcement of the regular repostings. This year (1939), there was also a general reshuffle of the whole Combined Fleet command.

Staff officers from the days when Yoshida had been C. in C.—men such as the chief of staff, Rear Admiral Takahashi Ibo, and senior staff officer Captain Kono—were retired, and a new lineup took over, including Chief of Staff Fukudome Shigeru, senior staff officer Kuro-shima Kameto, torpedo staff officer Arima Takayasu, and admini-strative staff officer Watanabe Yasuji.

One of these, Chief of Staff Fukudome, left to become head of the First Division of the Naval General Staff in April 1941, eight months before the beginning of the war; he was replaced by Rear Admiral Ito Seiichi, who stayed for only four months, then in August the post was taken over by Rear Admiral Ugaki Matome. Again, just before the outbreak of the war, Captain Miwa Yoshitake and Commander Fujii Shigeru joined command as air "A" staff officer and liaison staff officer respectively. Three or four such changes apart, however, Yamamoto was to maintain the same basic team until the beginning of the war.

The term "Yamamoto's team" does not of course imply that he had authority to make appointments himself; this rested with the Personnel Bureau of the Navy Ministry. The post of political affairs staff officer (also known as "liaison staff officer") was created for the first time under Yamamoto.

New Year's Day, 1940, found Yamamoto and his new staff at sea. He composed the following poem to mark the occasion:

> Today, as chief
> Of the guardians of the seas
> Of the land of the dawn,
> I gaze up with awe
> At the rising sun!

Possibly because he found himself in different surroundings from when he was vice-minister, Yamamoto gradually came to compose more poems, and he was to turn out a considerable number between then and the time of his death in action. During the war, and par-ticularly after his death, these short, thirty-one-syllable poems were treated almost as though they were an indispensable element in the nation's education, and some of them were even set to music. They were treated, in short, as though Yamamoto could be regarded as a poet in his own right, so it might be as well to say something about them at this point.

To put conclusions first, it seems likely that he wrote them far more casually—and with his tongue more firmly in his cheek—than was generally supposed. Yonai, who ought to know, said that Yamamoto's taste for turning out poems was "another case of not wanting to be outdone; for him, they were a kind of contest." He was quite capable of setting out to see how many he could turn out in an hour, and the results as poetry could, with the best will in the world, scarcely be called outstanding.

Much later, Rear Admiral Ozawa Jisaburo was to risk grumbling to Yamamoto's face, "It seems you're fond of writing mock-classical poems and giving them to subordinates who're off to the front, but I don't think much of it. You've had plenty of first-rate poets in your own part of the country—men like Ryokan—so why don't you study a bit more and turn out something rather better?"

One should not, perhaps, be too hard on the indiscretions of Yamamoto's youth. There was a poem, for example, that he wrote while in the naval hospital at Yokosuka after being wounded in the Russo-Japanese War, in July 1905:

> I will not staunch it:
> The bloodstains on
> The handkerchief
> Are the signs of
> My true devotion.

And there was another, written in his own cabin on board the warship *Soya* on January 1, 1910, which he sent home to his father:

> Being my own,
> It seems large—
> This tiny cabin;
> I yawn, I sprawl,
> I do as I please.

But what of those written somewhat later? There is one composed in 1919 during his first stay in America and entitled "Washington by Night":

> Tonight again
> The moonlight is pure
> And pellucid:
> It calls to mind

My distant home.

And another headed "In America, February 1920":

> Forlornly gazing
> At the scene outside
> In the blizzard,
> I long for you
> Far away back home.

Both of these, as poetry, are crude and sentimental. After becoming a senior officer, he stopped writing poetry as juvenile as this. The New Year composition beginning "Today, as chief / Of the guardians of the seas" at least does not disgrace its author's rank and is one of the better efforts among a poor lot.

On one occasion, when Yamamoto was still a rear admiral and head of the Technical Division of the Aeronautics Department, he went on a trip to Kishu with Hori Teikichi, then head of the Naval Affairs Bureau. In a letter to Takei Daisuke, a true poet and a friend of Yamamoto's since the latter's first stay in America, he sent a poem that had a more professional air than Yamamoto's usual efforts, so, when Yamamoto came back to Tokyo, Takei said to him, "I got your letter, but you pinched the poem from somewhere, didn't you?"

"Can you really tell, then?" said Yamamoto, looking at Hori in dismay.

"Of course I can," Takei replied, laughing. "Think of when I play *shogi* with you. You can tell exactly what I'm up to. Well, with poetry it's the same in reverse. So don't think you can fool me!"

Pressed to divulge the source, Yamamoto confessed that another poet, Ishikure Chimata, a friend of Hori's, had accompanied them on the journey. At the inn at Shingu, Ishikure had tossed off a whole string of quite passable poems and Yamamoto, impressed, had begged the "loan" of one of them. So he had been given the poem and had sent it to Takei as a kind of joke. Although it is doubtful that he ever lifted another's poem outright, a surprising number of the poems published during the war as the work of Yamamoto Isoroku, commander in chief of the Combined Fleet, depended in part on "loans" from various sources. Thus a poem written on a visit to the Grand Shrines of Ise in the fall of 1941, and another written to mark

Yamamoto, a formal portrait.

Yamamoto's birthplace in Nagaoka.

Yamamoto just before going into action in the Russo-Japanese War.

The *Nisshin* after one of its guns burst during the Battle of the Japan Sea (May 1905).

The carrier *Akagi* during official trials in 1927.

Yamamoto as a captain (second from right in second row from front), with former Naval Academy classmates.

Yamamoto (center) on arrival in Southampton, England, to participate in preliminary talks for the London Naval Conference, 1934.

米内光政　　　山本五十六

As navy vice-minister, with Minister Yonai.

Yamamoto at Tokyo Station on his way to join the Combined Fleet as its C. in C., August 1939.

The *Nagato*, Combined Fleet flagship.

As C. in C. on board the *Nagato* (from left, Chief of Staff Ugaki, Yamamoto, liaison staff officer Fujii, and administrative staff officer Watanabe).

A dive-bomber setting off for Pearl Harbor.

The end of the *Zuikaku* (1944), one of the Japanese carriers involved in the Pearl Harbor raid.

The battleships *Yamato* and *Musashi* in the Truk anchorage.

Yamamoto seeing off fliers of the Rabaul naval air unit as they go into action in April 1943.

Yamamoto (extreme left) at Rabaul, April 1943.

Inspecting submarine *I-33*, raised after accidentally sinking, at Truk.

The tail of Yamamoto's plane after the crash.

Yamamoto's ashes leaving the *Musashi* on their way to Tokyo (off Kisarazu, May 23, 1943).

During Yonai's term of office there was, in fact, no further attempt to bring up the subject of the Tripartite Pact—or if there was he refused to have anything to do with it. He also, as prime minister, made remarks with profound implications concerning the National Mobilization Law and the question of controls. Newspapers of the day report him as saying, in reply to a press conference question concerning wartime economic controls, "Where a controlled economy is concerned, I shall do what has to be done. However, if the adverse effects of controls prove to be greater than the beneficial effects, then we shall have to do some rethinking." This reply, which tallies well with answers he gave in the Diet as navy minister in the Hiranuma government, reveals a consistent underlying outlook. He was, accordingly, anathema to the army. As he later said, "With me as prime minister, they saw there was going to be no Tripartite Pact and no 'reform' at home, which is why they decided that the government should be overthrown."

From the very outset, violent dissatisfaction with the new government was smoldering within the army and certain sections of the right wing. Even among the cabinet councillors, there were three—Suetsugu Nobumasa, Matsui Iwane, and Matsuoka Yosuke—who resigned in defiance of Yonai's request that they stay in office. Thus right from the time of its inception there were ominous signs that this government would not last long.

Some army and rightist circles saw the emergence of a Yonai government as "a plot by the emperor's advisers," and many of the young officers bore a grudge against the Lord Privy Seal for his part in the emperor's request that the war minister should cooperate with the new government. Around this time, Matsumoto Sankichi wrote a letter to Yamamoto on board the *Nagato* in which he gave details of Yonai's efforts to form a government. Yonai was doing his best, he declared, but the government's future would be beset with difficulties, and it was to be hoped that Yamamoto himself would go into politics. It is said even that the hope was being expressed in some quarters of the political world that Yamamoto would himself head a government. But on February 18 Yamamoto wrote a reply to Matsumoto's letter in which he said: "Many thanks for your letter. I have now been at sea for half a year. A navy man's place is, after all, on board a ship. There is still more than enough for me to do here at sea, and anyway I believe that a sailor's business is to be an expert in maritime affairs; it is a fatal mistake for him to meddle in unfamiliar political matters."

In July 1940, scarcely half a year after its inauguration, the Yonai government resigned, to be replaced by a second Konoe government. With barely concealed impatience, the new government at once took up the question of the Tripartite Pact again, and two months later, on September 27, the new military alliance was brought into being with an unexpected lack of fuss (though the navy minister, Yoshida Zengo, had resigned a few weeks earlier).

Yoshida, who had stayed on in the second Konoe government, found himself caught between, on the one hand, the army and reformists both inside and outside the navy, and, on the other, the demands of men like Yamamoto. As a result, he developed what would nowadays be called a severe neurosis. Before long, he was ordered into hospital for a rest, and he resigned as minister three weeks before the signing of the Tripartite Pact. His disappearance from the scene, together with the appointments of Matsuoka as foreign minister and Tojo as war minister, was one of the three most significant personnel changes in the second Konoe government.

Somewhat earlier, Yamamoto had presented another statement of views from the fleet concerning the question of the alliance:

A war between Japan and the United States would be a major calamity for the world, and for Japan it would mean, after several years of war already, acquiring yet another powerful enemy— an extremely perilous matter for the nation. If, after Japan and America had inflicted serious wounds on each other, the Soviet Union or Germany should step in with an eye to world hegemony, what country would be able to check it? If Germany should prove victorious [in the war with Britain] Japan might look to its goodwill as a friendly nation, but if Japan at the time happened to be in a wounded state, its advances would carry no weight; a friendly nation can only look for friendly treatment so long as it has powerful forces of its own. The reason why Japan is respected and its hand frequently sought in alliance is that it has actual power in the shape of its naval and other forces. It is necessary therefore that both Japan and America should seek every means to avoid a direct clash, and Japan should under no circumstances conclude an alliance with Germany.

Only the main substance of this statement survives, and it is not known to whom it was submitted, but the minister, Yoshida, must certainly have read it. He would undoubtedly have sympathized, but for the most part such opinions did not find much general favor at a time when Germany had just startled the world with its military feats (it had, for example, brought the whole of Denmark under its control in the space of three and a half hours).

As navy minister, Yoshida was succeeded by Admiral Oikawa Koshiro, known as a mild, scholarly man. Such qualities, however, were scarcely enough for a navy minister at such a time of crisis. The general trend at the higher levels of the navy was to concentrate on handling things as skillfully and smoothly as possible, but even in such circles Oikawa was notorious for his attempts to please everybody at the same time.

Inoue Shigeyoshi is scathing about him: "What an unwise appointment! One wonders who was responsible for bringing in a man like Oikawa at a time when he would have to deal with the Japanese army—an army that was fond of setting itself above the state itself. One can only assume that the army, aware of his impotence and lack of any decisive views of his own, recommended him to Konoe."

The vice-minister under Oikawa was Toyoda Teijiro, another naval leader who by normal Japanese standards would be considered a "well-rounded" character. Unlike Yamamoto, he had early on conceived the ambition of becoming first vice-minister, then minister—an ambition that was later fulfilled when he became foreign minister in the third Konoe government. In early 1939, however, when Yamamoto was vice-minister, he was still commander of the Sasebo naval station.

Ogata Taketora quotes the following passage from a personal reminiscence by Konoe Fumimaro entitled "Lost Government":

> I was sure from the start that the navy would not lightly agree to the signing of a Tripartite Pact. . . . However, once Admiral Oikawa became navy minister, the navy soon gave its consent. Feeling the capitulation to be almost too sudden, I summoned Navy Vice-Minister Toyoda and asked him what lay behind it. The navy, he declared, was in fact privately opposed to the

Tripartite Pact. Nevertheless, the domestic political situation no longer permitted it to object, and it had been obliged to give its agreement. The navy was acquiescing for political reasons: but from a military viewpoint, it was still not confident of its ability to take on America. . . .

In all the memoirs of the Pacific War that he had read, Ogata comments, he had seen nothing so depressing as this exchange. . . .

6

Oikawa replaced Yoshida as minister and Toyoda replaced Sumiyama as vice-minister on September 5 and 6, 1940. During the three weeks between this and the signing of the treaty, Oikawa, as navy minister, summoned a conference of naval leaders in Tokyo. The aim was to decide on the navy's final attitude toward the Tripartite Pact; it seems likely, however, that it was already decided in advance that the navy should give its consent.

The flagship of the Combined Fleet was at anchor at Hashirajima in the Inland Sea, and Yamamoto came up from Hashirajima in order to participate, bringing with him a large quantity of reference materials. It was only about a year since he himself had been vice-minister, and it seemed unlikely to him that Japan had armed itself adequately in the meantime.

At the conference, Navy Minister Oikawa asserted that if the navy opposed the pact at this point, the second Konoe government would be obliged to resign. The navy could hardly allow itself to be responsible for bringing down the government, and he asked them to give their consent to the signing of the treaty. Neither Prince Fushimi, chief of the Naval General Staff, nor any of the military councillors and commanders of fleets and naval stations who were present had anything to say.

Yamamoto got to his feet.

"I accept the minister's authority implicitly," he said. "I haven't the slightest intention of raising any objections to steps on which the minister has already decided. However, there is one point that worries me greatly and on which I would like to ask your opinion. According to the Cabinet Planning Board's blueprint for the mobilization of material resources—as it was until August last year when I was vice-minister—eighty percent of all materials were due to be supplied from areas under the control of Britain or America. The signing of the Tripartite Pact will inevitably mean losing these, and I would like you to tell us quite clearly—since I wish to be able to carry out my duties as commander in chief of the Combined Fleet with an easy mind—what switches have been made in the materials program in order to make up for the resulting inadequacies."

Oikawa made no direct reply at all, merely repeating what he had already said: "I'm sure each of you has his own views, but the situation is as I have already described it, and I would ask you at this juncture to give your approval to the Tripartite Pact."

At this, senior military councillor Admiral Osumi Mineo chimed in with "I agree," and a general murmur of assent went around the table.

Yamamoto was enraged. In a letter written to his contemporary Shimada Shigetaro, then C. in C. of the China Area Fleet, he complains angrily: "What happened around the time of the Tripartite Pact, and what has happened since then where the materials program is concerned, demonstrates the utter inconsistency of the present government's methods. At this stage, to profess shock and indignation at American economic pressure is either childishly impetuous or suggests an extraordinary inattentiveness to recent events."

Another passage in the same letter reads: "The other day I got word through an intermediary that Prince Konoe was anxious to meet me. I declined two or three times, but he was so pressing that eventually, with the minister's agreement, I met him for about two hours."

This meeting took place during Yamamoto's visit to Tokyo for the naval conference just mentioned. He called on Konoe at his private residence, and was questioned by the prime minister concerning the navy's prospects in the event of a war with America.

"If we are ordered to do it," said Yamamoto, "then I can guarantee to put up a tough fight for the first six months, but I have absolutely no confidence as to what would happen if it went on for two or three years. It's too late to do anything about the Tripartite Pact now, but I hope at least that you'll make every effort to avoid war with America."

Concerning the Tripartite Pact, Konoe told Yamamoto that he had thought it odd that the navy should agree with so little objection; however, the vice-minister had subsequently explained that the prospect for materials was rather bleak, that the navy itself was not ready for war, and that though politically it had agreed to the treaty, the situation was deplorable in terms of national defense. This, Konoe said, had disappointed him considerably. The navy should have taken its own position fully into account in giving its views; the domestic political situation was his own affair as prime minister, for him to deal with as he saw fit.

In his letter to Shimada, Yamamoto wrote: "He must take me for a fool, the way he complained to me. Yet it's not really surprising, since Prince Konoe always talks in that way. In fact, it is excessively dangerous for the navy to act lightly on the basis of anything he, Foreign Minister Matsuoka, or the like have to say. I felt a strong sense of guilt toward His Majesty." In fact, Yamamoto also disliked Shimada, whom he mistrusted and described as a typical "blarney merchant." He could not have known, of course, that Shimada was later to join the Tojo government as navy minister, becoming so close to his boss that he was referred to as "Tojo's lackey," yet Yamamoto's letters to Shimada, unlike those written to another classmate, Hori, always had the air of conveying a veiled warning.

Thus Yamamoto was still nursing his grievances as he returned to the *Nagato* at Hashirajima. However, as commander in chief, he was no longer in a position to disassociate himself from any war that might break out between Japan and America. If one were to indulge in hypotheses, there are, admittedly, a number of "ifs" that one could introduce at this point concerning what he should have said or done in the intervening period before the outbreak of war. For example, although his post as such did not qualify him to do so, he could have staked his position as C. in C. of the Combined Fleet on continued opposition to the Tripartite Pact. If he had been in the position of vice-minister or minister, he would almost certainly have risked his job—not to say his life—on such opposition. The reason for his reluctant withdrawal seems to have been fear of damaging the good old naval tradition— which he himself had had a hand in reaffirming—that only the navy minister himself should have any hand in politics and that everyone else should submit to his authority.

The navy's "left wing" thus behaved with almost excessive correctness. In this respect, it somewhat resembled the correctness of the emperor's attitude to politics—a difficult question, but one that those who suffered so much on account of it cannot dismiss lightly.

Yonai had been put on the reserve list when he formed his government. Following his resignation six months later, he is said to have refrained entirely, even on visits to the Navy Ministry, from any public pronouncements as an admiral. As he observed to Harada Kumao around that time, "The life I lead nowadays is almost entirely divorced from the affairs of the world."

"This might have been all right in normal times," observes Takei Daisuke, "but at that particular moment one wishes that Yonai had talked rather more. . . . ."

What would have happened if Yamamoto had ignored navy traditions and tried a little insubordination, going against his seniors' wishes just as his counterparts in the army did, but in a different direction? When Yonai, in near seclusion, heard the news of the signing of the Tripartite Pact, he said of his own period as navy minister: "Looking back on it, our opposition to the Tripartite Pact was a waste of effort, rather like rowing a boat against the current a hundred yards or so above the Niagara Falls." Hearing this, Ogata asked him whether they would have persisted in opposition to the bitter end if he and Yamamoto had continued to head the navy.

"Of course," replied Yonai; then, after thinking for a moment, he added with signs of considerable emotion: "But I imagine we would both have been killed."

It was not only the navy, of course, and not only Yonai and Yamamoto who were inclined to oppose the Tripartite Pact. On hearing the news of the pact's signing, elder statesman Saionji, at his home in the country, remarked to the women attendant on him: "So even you probably won't be able to die in your beds!"

Somewhat earlier, when the alliance was being considered in a plenary session of the Privy Council, adviser Ishii Kikujiro issued the following warning: "It is a striking fact that of the countries that have signed alliances with Germany, or with its predecessor Prussia, none has ever reaped any benefit from that alliance. On the contrary, there have been some that suffered disaster as a result and have lost their sovereignty. German Chancellor Bismarck once said that every alliance between nations required a knight on horseback and a mule, and that Germany must make sure that it was always the knight on horseback." But in the end no one had the power to check the trend of the times, or to open the eyes of the stupid mule.

Some two weeks after the signing of the pact, in the course of a meal with Harada Kumao, Yamamoto spoke as though he had made up his mind once and for all:

"It's an impossible state of affairs," he said. "The one thing the navy must do now is see that it gets everything that it considers necessary in making proper preparations. Personally, I feel that if we're going to war with America we must accept the idea that we're taking on almost the whole of the rest of the world. Even if we sign a non-aggression pact with the Soviet Union, it won't mean much—the Soviet Union can't be relied on; what guarantee is there that such a treaty would stop it from stabbing us in the back while we were at war with America? Anyhow, now that things have come to this pass I'll throw everything I have into the fight. I expect to die in battle on board the *Nagato*. By that time, I imagine, Tokyo will have been set on fire at least three times and Japan reduced to a pitiful state. I shouldn't be surprised if Konoe and the rest—though I don't like to say it—end up by being set on and torn to pieces by the public. I don't like it, but there's no going back now."

The "non-aggression pact with the Soviet Union" was, of course, the Soviet-Japanese treaty of neutrality that was being prepared at the time and which was signed by Foreign Minister Matsuoka in Moscow in April of the following year, 1941. It was this treaty that the Soviet Union broke when it joined in the Pacific War just before its end.

If Yamamoto had carried opposition to the Tripartite Pact to the point of threatening to resign his post as commander in chief, the result might well have been a domestic upheaval more serious, even, than the celebrated February 26 Incident. It was Yamamoto's oft-stated opinion that domestic revolution would not in itself ruin the country, and would be better at least than a war against America. But he might well have been killed. Or his threat to resign might have been welcomed in some quarters and accepted without demur, in which case he could have been put on the reserve list and obliged to remain inactive while the storm swept over his head. Either way, such questions can never leave the realm of speculation.

In practice, Yamamoto remained in his post as commander in chief of the Combined Fleet and thus found himself obliged to consider how the navy should wage the war with America that was now so fast becoming a real threat. If such a war came, there would be little hope of victory, or even of a favorable and early peace, unless some quite extraordinary measures were resorted to.

It was considerations such as these, it should always be remembered, that lay behind the gradual birth in Yamamoto's mind of the idea of a sudden onslaught on Hawaii at the very start of hostilities.

7

It is not certain just when Yamamoto began to toy with the idea of an attack on Hawaii. We know a certain amount about the timing of the draft plan for the Hawaiian operation—the time when the fleet submitted it to those responsible, and when the Naval General Staff, after much hesitation and many objections, finally gave its formal approval. What is not at all clear is when the idea first evolved in Yamamoto's own brain. Fukudome Shigeru sets the date at around April or May in 1940—at a point, that is, before the signing of the Tripartite Pact, when the Yonai government was still in power.

Far earlier, however—around 1927–28—Kusaka Ryunosuke had committed to writing a plan for attacking Pearl Harbor from the air. Kusaka at the time was a lieutenant commander just out of Navy Staff College, working simultaneously as an instructor at the Kasumigaura Aviation Corps and at the college itself. His field was aerial tactics, but having no clear idea of what he should lecture about, he used the time to put forward all kinds of personal theories; his students would sometimes joke that his lectures were "not aerial tactics but aerial philosophy."

Not long afterward, it was decided that a group of ten important people including Nagano Osami, Terashima Takeshi, and other men far senior to Kusaka himself should come to spend a week at Kasumigaura for an on-the-spot course on aviation, and Kusaka, who was put in charge of the course, had to think of something to talk to them about. The result was the document in question.

The gist of it was as follows. Ever since the end of World War I, the time had gradually been approaching when the airplane would become the main protagonist in warfare. Should war come, Japan would have to make use of aircraft in skillful conjunction with its mandated territories in the South Pacific. The basis of the imperial navy's American strategy was that it should lure the U.S. fleet from San Diego, on the West Coast, out into the West Pacific and take it on in a battle similar to the Battle of the Japan Sea. But what should be done if the enemy refused to be lured out? In such an event, it would be necessary for Japan to take the lead and strike at America's most vulnerable spot, Hawaii. And the only possible way to strike at the naval base at Pearl Harbor would be to use aircraft.

Thirty copies of this document were printed and, with the blunt references to "America" deleted, distributed to naval personnel.

On his return from his appointment in America, Yamamoto probably saw Kusaka's document. It was not, of course, a plan for a preemptive strike against Pearl Harbor, but it seems perfectly possible that, if Yamamoto in fact saw it, it should have lingered as an interesting possibility in some corner of his mind, ready to put forth fresh buds after a dozen years or so had passed.

Nevertheless, when Yamamoto's plan for a raid on Pearl Harbor was given rather more concrete shape and shown for the first time to the staff officers of the Combined Fleet, they were dismayed by the unconventional strategy involved and opposed it almost to a man. Before discussing this plan, however, we should glance perhaps at the Japanese navy's traditional, "orthodox" plans for operations against the United States.

By April 1 every year, it was the custom for the Naval General Staff to draw up, in consultation with the army's General Staff Headquarters, a "Plan of Operations for the Coming Year" covering the period until March 31 the following year. This was submitted to the emperor for approval, then shown as a secret military document to the minister and commanders in chief. It was a kind of blueprint, outlining the way in which the navy would react should a war occur during the period in question.

The task of drawing it up was undertaken by some ten staff officers of the First Section, First Division, of the Naval General Staff. Despite the heavy responsibility involved, it had become the custom each year to base the plan largely on the previous year's, with a few new touches. There were three hypothetical enemies—the United States of America, the Soviet Union, and the Republic of China. Where China was concerned, however, the plan of operations each year consisted of little more than a single page. The reason was that the navy's role in such a case would be very minor, and that little importance was attached strategically to China anyway, which was seen less as a modern state than as a conglomeration of rival warlords; in the event of war, it was believed, Japan would need only to lift a little finger for China to fall (in practice, the Naval General Staff was obliged to revise this view following the outbreak of the China Incident).

In the case of the Soviet Union, any war would undoubtedly be a major one for Japan, but the emphasis would be on land forces, and the navy's role would not be so great. The question, thus, resolved itself into that of operations against America. To sum it up very briefly, the orthodox plan of operations called for the navy to throw its strength first into an attack on the Philippines. Then, when the U.S. fleet came to the rescue and launched the inevitable counterattack, the Marshalls, Marianas, Carolines, Palaus, and other Japanese mandates in the South Pacific would be used as bases for whittling down the strength of the attacking American forces with submarines and aircraft so that finally, when they had been reduced to parity with the Japanese forces or even less, they could be engaged in a decisive battle in the seas near Japan and destroyed. This was much the same concept as underlay the Battle of the Japan Sea in which, in 1905, Japan had taken on and annihilated the Russian Baltic Fleet off Tsushima.

There were certain changes in this plan each year, but the name Hawaii had never once put in an appearance; it was unthinkable that the Japanese navy, of its own free will, should sail to the attack as far as Hawaii. Nor was any very practical consideration given to the question of what would happen should the war prove protracted or come to involve the resources of the whole nation. There was, it is true, an institution called the "Total War Research Institute," but its function was academic.

What was worse, even the islands of the inner South Seas—whose value as "unsinkable carriers" or "unsinkable submarine tenders" in any attempt to bring the Japanese and enemy fleets to parity was officially recognized—were in fact extremely inadequately equipped as military bases. Around the beginning of 1937, the American naval attaché in Tokyo had sought permission for a trip to Japanese mandated islands in the South Pacific, but the Japanese navy, after much hemming and hawing, refused to grant it. The reason, it is said, was not that it did not want him to see installations being built in that area, but that it was afraid he might find out that there were no decent military installations at all; it wanted to leave him with the impression that some did, in fact, exist.

The Naval General Staff's plan of operations against America was clearly full of wishful thinking. As a piece of prose it was superficially convincing, but nobody believed that if war actually occurred things would—unless Japan was extremely lucky—go according to plan. Yamamoto himself was highly skeptical about the formalistic view of tactics against America that prevailed in the Naval General Staff and Navy Staff College. A hitherto unpublished work entitled *Gohoroku* (Records of Isoroku and Mineichi; the title is derived from one ideograph of each name, given a different reading, plus *roku*, "records") is relevant here. A compilation in two parts of letters written by Yamamoto, memoranda, letters from Koga Mineichi to Hori Teikichi, and other similar documents, it was put together by Hori seven years after the end of the war with the idea that the time might come when it should be made available to the public as reference material. Hori's intention was to let people know what his bosom friend Yamamoto had really been like, but there are parts where both Yamamoto and Koga express themselves in fairly vehement terms, and Hori was fearful on two scores: that to publish it without warning might hurt people still living; and that as things were in 1952 there was no telling what undesirable use, contrary to his real intentions, the work might be put to. Thus he left it, without showing it to anyone, in the care of two personally selected trustees.

Gohoroku has a kind of commentary, written by Hori himself. According to this, the map maneuvers and plan of operations against America drawn up at Navy Staff College and the Naval General Staff were both products of a kind of self-deluding formalism which assumed that the enemy would act according to predetermined conventions. They were an intellectual game based on the assumptions already mentioned, i.e., that (1) Japan would attack the Philippines; (2) the U.S. fleet would sail to the aid of the Philippines; (3) Japan would wage a campaign of attrition on the Marianas front; and (4) that there would be a great sea battle between the two fleets in which the American fleet would be destroyed.

"This kind of creeping formalism spread until it became a kind of strategic orthodoxy," Hori writes, "and [the navy] ended up as a smug little society which insisted that all ideas on strategy should conform to this orthodoxy and in which anyone who tried to embark on a new and different course was promptly branded a heretic ignorant of tactics."

"The type of military thinking fostered under such circumstances," he also writes, "eventually acquired a political coloring. . . . There was an increasing trend in society at large to make forceful and exaggerated statements in front of others and to shun any effort to think things over calmly."

He cites three examples of this trend which he personally experienced. I will quote two of them in brief here. One year, the usual map maneuvers simulating war against America were held, and during the ensuing seminar an officer got up and said something to the following effect: "Since it's quite possible that the enemy would not go to the aid of the Philippines, and that he would come immediately and launch an attack against the Japanese mainland, I wonder if it's wise to spend so much energy in this way, studying operations against the Philippines only. Surely we should also study different eventualities?"

An officer from the Naval General Staff who was present as one of the supervisors of the maneuvers replied: "The campaign against the Philippines has already been decided on as operational policy by the imperial navy, and as such is under study in collaboration with the army. It is highly regrettable that one should hear arguments rejecting it. We must not forget that to coordinate ideas on strategy is one of the aims of these exercises."

During map maneuvers another year, a certain unit was advancing carefully, with one eye on the level of remaining fuel and the time at which it was due to contact the enemy. It was criticized, however, as "lacking alacrity." Too much worry about fuel, it was said, made "proper"—which is to say, convenient for those in charge—maneuvers impossible. The outcome of such maneuvers was judged with reference to the navigational charts of the various units of "Blue" and "Red" forces, and calculations occasionally showed that the fleet in question would, in practice, have been brought to a standstill by running out of fuel. In such cases, the special hypothesis was allowed that it had been refueled at sea, and the fleet set sail once more. If things got too awkward, those in charge would usually not press the matter, but solve things by announcing that exercises had been called off. (A letter to Hori written by Yamamoto on board the *Musashi* at Truk says, "The trouble is not the enemy but our own side," and in view of the above, his disgust seems quite natural.)

"Talk about war with America should not have been undertaken lightly in the first place," Hori writes in his commentary. "Some people talked about 'staking the fate of the nation' on such a war if necessary, but to use such a phrase was wrong to begin with; it implied a readiness to gamble on the nation's welfare or ruin, and to consider the latter as a legitimate possibility. . . . When one considers the real sense of the words, they obviously represent ideas that should never have been entertained. It is intolerable that nebulous concepts such as 'a new order in the Far East' or the 'building of a co-prosperity sphere' should lead people to put the fate of the whole nation in the balance."

This does not mean, of course, that everybody in the Naval General Staff was a self-opinionated formalist, much less that everybody wanted to "stake the fate of the nation" on a war with America. Moreover, the plans of operations in question, whether the hypothetical foe was America, the Soviet Union, or China, all envisaged the war as being waged against one nation alone. Following the outbreak of the China Incident, those responsible were obliged to change their strategy to account for two enemy countries, either America and China or the Soviet Union and China. In the latter case, the scheme envisaged by the First Section, First Division, of the Naval General Staff was that the navy should transfer the whole of its air strength to Manchuria.

By 1938, however, the situation at home and abroad made it evident that the possibility of operations against Britain would also have to be taken into account in the "Plan of Operations for the Coming Year." Thus there was talk of attacking the Malay Peninsula in support of landing operations at Singora and Kota Bharu, and discussion of how the British Far Eastern Fleet could be destroyed; even so, the plans went no further than operations against Britain alone or, at most, against Britain and China.

By 1939, the possibility had become strong that, should war with the U.S. or Britain occur, operations would have to be waged against three countries—the U.S., Britain, and China—all at once. In view of the difficulty of working out any convincing plan for tackling

America alone, it was obvious that Japan should avoid such operations from the start. As Yonai stated clearly during his term as minister, the Japanese navy was not constructed with this in mind, and there was no chance of its being able to win.

Nevertheless, there was still the possibility that the other side would start the war, and since Japan could hardly act on the assumption that it would capitulate immediately on being attacked, some plan or other, if only on paper, must be drawn up for operations against the three powers. At this point, however, the possibility arose that Holland might join the enemy as well—not to mention the Soviet Union. What should be done in such an eventuality? The basic question of how to divide up Japan's forces was headache enough; and talk of transferring the air force to Manchuria was obviously out of the question.

In short, the idea of operations against five nations simultaneously was one that must, and yet could not, be entertained. The more one contemplated it, the more one went round in futile circles, and the more clearly the same conclusion emerged: Japan could not under any circumstances afford to go to war with America.

It is usually said that naval men associated with the Naval General Staff tended to be more bellicose than the administrative people. This was of course true in some respects, yet for anyone actually involved in the responsibility of drawing up a plan of operations it was quite impossible to carry heroic talk beyond a certain point. Neither Minister Oikawa nor Vice-Minister Toyoda, despite their approval of the Tripartite Pact, was really convinced that Japan should wage war with America. It seems possible that, lacking courage, they merely allowed fear of political friction at home to lead them into wishful thinking.

8

Once a series of maneuvers was over and the fleet was back at anchor, a study meeting would be held. An awning would be stretched over the afterdeck of the flagship, and a crowd that included commanders in chief, staff officers, captains, and others concerned would gather from the other vessels and units. A flock of launches would be moored on both sides of the *Nagato*—the usual sign that an operational conference at sea was in progress. It was usual at such study meetings for those present to indulge in fierce arguments without regard to rank. The gunners, for example, would insist that all planes had been shot down, while the aviators would assert equally heatedly that anti-aircraft fire of the kind they'd had wouldn't have downed a single aircraft. Yamamoto would sit silent in the center, occasionally adding a comment of his own.

Arguments about whether aircraft had been shot down or not were necessarily inconclusive, but in practice attacks by torpedo planes on capital ships, real torpedoes were used, though of course they contained no explosives. The depth was adjusted so that a torpedo passed beneath the hull of the target, but it was no problem to tell whether it had scored a "hit" or not.

During war games in 1940, the planes taking part succeeded in tracking down and hitting the battleships despite all evasive tactics—just as in the "Operation 123" already mentioned—and Yamamoto, who had watched appreciatively, remarked to Chief of Staff Fukudome at the study meeting afterward, "It makes me wonder if they couldn't get Pearl Harbor."

After another study meeting, he said to Fukudome and Rear Admiral Ozawa, who was commander of the First Carrier Division at the time, "Don't you think the Naval General Staff's idea of attritional operations relying fifty percent on submarines is a bit risky? I can't really believe that the idea of bringing them out to fight would work."

It seems, therefore, that sometime in 1940 the idea—if war came—of making a long-range preemptive strike against the American fleet in Hawaii was already taking gradual shape somewhere in Yamamoto's mind.

Nineteen forty was the year celebrated in Japan as the 2,600th anniversary of the accession of the emperor Jimmu, the nation's first emperor. Among the many rites marking the occasion there was an imperial review, held off Yokohama on October 11, which was to be the last time that the Combined Fleet ever showed itself officially to the public.

That morning Yamamoto, who had been placed in charge of the review, welcomed the emperor on board the *Hiei*, from which His Majesty was to inspect his fleet. Then he explained things to the emperor as, with the cruiser *Takao* leading the way and the cruisers *Kako* and *Furutaka* escorting it, the imperial vessel passed among the ships of the Combined Fleet, which were strung out in five lines across Tokyo Bay with the *Nagato*—its entire crew manning the sides—at their head.

The crown prince and other princes of the blood were also present, and the review could be clearly seen from vantage points in Yokohama such as Nogeyama Park, the roofs of commercial offices, and the windows of foreign legations and trading houses. The total displacement of the naval vessels taking part was 596,060 tons, and the number of aircraft 527—a Combined Fleet, third largest in the world, that was to be almost totally destroyed in the war that began one year and two months later. As the *Hiei* sailed proudly through the assembled lines of warships, squadrons of attack planes, bombers, fighters, reconnaissance seaplanes, and flying boats of the Naval Air Corps under the command of Rear Admiral Ozawa Jisaburo flew over the fleet in rapid succession, dipped in salute off the port side of the emperor's ship, then made off to the west into the skies over Tokyo and disappeared from sight. None of those who witnessed the review could have dreamed that four years and eleven months later, at almost the same spot in Tokyo Bay, the instruments of Japan's unconditional surrender were to be signed on board the U.S. battleship *Missouri*.

That night, it seems, Yamamoto made one of his rare visits to his home in Tokyo. Legend has it that since his family was not expecting him he found the gate locked, and that in the end the man who that day had directed a special imperial review was obliged to get in by climbing over his own garden wall like a common thief.

One month later, on November 11, another ceremony celebrating the anniversary of Jimmu's accession was held in the plaza before the Nijubashi entrance to the Imperial Palace. It was one of the most impressive occasions of the age; the emperor and empress were there, with national leaders both civilian and military and representatives from every walk of life in attendance, not to mention four hundred men and women students from the Tokyo Academy of Music who, to the accompaniment of army and navy bands, sang an ode composed for the occasion. But Yamamoto, though invited, did not attend. When someone asked him why, he replied, "Japan is at war with China. If I were Chiang Kai-shek, I would have used all the planes I had in a raid on the Imperial Palace plaza, wiping out all Japan's most important leaders in one fell swoop. So I declined the imperial invitation and spent two days at sea instead, keeping an eye on the skies."

For the C. in C. of the Combined Fleet not to attend such an important ceremony on such an auspicious national occasion seems ungracious, to say the least. The explanation given makes sense; but if Yamamoto were still alive one would be tempted to ask him whether it should really be taken at its face value. It seems unlikely that Yamamoto had any particularly negative views concerning the myths of the nation's founding or the 2,600th anniversary celebrations as such, but he disliked dragging the gods into what should be practical matters. A former rear admiral says, though not with direct reference to Yamamoto: "With the arms race, for example, it was obvious in terms of figures which side would have the advantage if Japan and America were to indulge in unrestricted competition, but that didn't matter to people infatuated with the 'Way of the Gods.' You could quote them figures till you were blue in the face, but they'd have none of it."

The same individual (who asked that his name not be used, having severed all connection with public life since the defeat as a mark of his own responsibility for the war) also had the following to say:

It was the same with the race to build warships, and the question of operations against the U.S. and Britain. If one worked out the figures—for example, the number of men in the total population, the percentage of people who could be put to work in industry, the maximum number of men who could be drafted for the navy, the number of men needed to man a warship, and so on—it was perfectly clear that there was no point in Japan's killing itself to construct warships, since it would be obliged to keep them tied up in harbor, without the fuel to move them or the men to man them. Armament under such conditions was the height of folly; but if you said such a thing in those days you were berated as "pro-Western." People got away with the most irrational nonsense so long as it was in the name of the "Way of the Gods." I often used to think how difficult it must be to teach history in the nation's schools. In the navy, those men with any sense who couldn't go along with all this god stuff came to dislike any noisy expression of views, and tended to keep quiet."

Yamamoto had already had a hard enough time with rightist clap-trap, and he may well have resented the way the nation was getting carried away by the idea of the anniversary. But there may have been more personal motives, too, for his refusal.

One of the slogans of those who aimed to overthrow the Yonai government was, "We must not let the 2,600th anniversary rites be held under the auspices of a prime minister from the navy." Again, on February 11 that same year, Yamamoto had been due to take the Combined Fleet into Osaka Bay so that all the forty thousand officers and men under his command could visit, over a period of four days, such sacred sites as the Grand Shrine of Kashiwara and the imperial mausoleums at Unebi and Momoyama. On this occasion administrative staff officer Watanabe, who had been sent to Osaka in advance to prepare for the visit, reported to Yamamoto that the navy was surprisingly unpopular in that city and that during Yamamoto's period as vice-minister there had been a lecture meeting calling for his impeachment. Yamamoto peevishly threatened to take the fleet to the area off Nishinomiya instead of Osaka Bay (Nishinomiya, though not far away, was in another prefecture). The officials of Osaka City and Osaka Urban Prefecture were half annoyed and half dismayed when they heard of the threat, and a protest came pointing out, among other things, that souvenirs had already been prepared as gifts for the sailors. But Yamamoto was adamant. "If they want to give us presents, they can bring them to Nishinomiya," he declared. In fact, it is far from certain that the city and urban prefectural authorities had had anything to do with the lecture meeting in question, and the affair is a good example of the more high-handed aspect of Yamamoto's character. One cannot help suspecting that it was pique about something equally trivial that led Yamamoto to absent himself from the 2,600th anniversary ceremony in front of the Imperial Palace.

9

On November 15, 1940, a few days after the ceremony, Yamamoto was promoted to the rank of full admiral. Two other admirals were also created on the same day—Yoshida Zengo and Shimada Shigetaro, both former classmates of his.

Whether or not there were, as Inoue Shigeyoshi suggested, "first-grade" and "second-grade" admirals, the fact remained that for a navy man the rank represented the pinnacle of his career. The appointment was naturally gratifying to Yamamoto himself, but there was also a woman who, in her own way, had been privately looking forward to this day for the past thirty years.

Where Yamamoto's relationship with women are concerned, I have so far mentioned only his wife and Kawai Chiyoko, yet in fact there was another woman in Kyushu—a woman who, though she played a less prominent part in his life, had known him longer than any of the others and who was possibly the most single-minded of all in her affection for him.

All the letters from Yamamoto in her possession—enough to fill a suitcase—were destroyed in the air raids. After the end of the war, she lived in ill health and poverty in Kyushu, anxious only that there should be no public fuss about her relationship with Yamamoto and hoping that she herself might die on the same day of the year as he. In fact, she died on the morning of November 11, 1968, her death unnoticed by any of the former naval men who had known Yamamoto.

In accordance with her wishes, nothing concerning her relationship with Yamamoto was made public during her lifetime. In a work entitled *Eagle of the Pacific: Yamamoto Isoroku*, Matsushima Keizo, a former head of the navy's Information Division, briefly introduces a woman who may correspond to her, but—either because he did not know enough or because he wished to spare her—ninety percent of the facts are wrong.

Her name was Tsurushima Tsuru, but she was usually known as Tsurushima Masako. She was born in Isahaya, in Nagasaki Prefecture, and to a tiny handful of people close to Yamamoto she was for long known as "Yamamoto Isoroku's first love."

Her first encounter with him occurred shortly after she started working at a Sasebo restaurant, Takara-ya, under the name Kotaro, along with her sister, who was known as Umechiyo. This, it seems, was not long after Yamamoto's appointment, on December 1, 1912, as staff officer with the Sasebo station's reserve squadron.

Yamamoto, in his fourth year as a lieutenant, was twenty-eight and still unmarried. Masako, sixteen years his junior, was twelve. Where Yamamoto might already have been considered rather old for a "first love," Masako was literally a "fledgling" geisha, still no more than a child. Even so, her manner was mature for her age, and her looks and liveliness made her popular with the naval officers.

The two first met at a formal party, at which Kotaro—Masako—got herself scolded by the daughter of the restaurant for putting Yamamoto's glove on the hand with two fingers missing and exclaiming in mock dismay to her sister, "Oh dear, it won't go on!" She and Yamamoto were soon on friendly terms, and Yamamoto acquired the habit of summoning her and her colleagues to a large teahouse in Sasebo where they performed dances for him as he sprawled on the *tatami* watching. On her side, Masako often got him to give her piggybacks, and to take her to buy candy and fruit.

The lively, intelligent little girl grew fond of Yamamoto and, perhaps sensing something that distinguished him from the rank and file of naval officers, was convinced that he would one day become an admiral. But her age, if nothing else, forbade the relationship from going any further for the moment.

Eventually she was brought to Tokyo by the daughter of the proprietor of Takara-ya, the purpose being to train her properly as a geisha. The daughter wanted her to stay on in her household in the capital, but Masako preferred the country and returned alone to Sasebo after less than a year. Shortly afterward she became a full-fledged geisha, retaining Kotaro as her professional name.

She was no longer the child who had so charmed the young naval officers, but an attractive young woman whose photograph appeared on the cover of a popular magazine in the mid-1910s. The popular magazines of the day often carried pictures of geishas on their covers or in their photogravure sections, much as the weeklies of today use photos of movie stars and popular singers. Masako's picture bore the caption "The Flower of Kyushu."

One day—it was probably shortly before Yamamoto's marriage in 1918—Masako was buying something at a stall in a Sasebo street when a bus stopped close by and a man got off. It was Yamamoto. Startled, she called out to him. It was the beginning of what rapidly became, this time, an intimate relationship. He had seen the photo in the magazine, and during the days to come would often address her teasingly as "Flower of Kyushu." They were in each other's company whenever circumstances allowed, and stayed together at a hot-spring resort before his departure for America. The words "I long for you" in the poem already quoted, written "In America, February 1920," are probably a reference to Masako.

In the years to come they sometimes did not see each other for three, four—once, even, close to ten—years, but they continued to write to each other. Although Masako was a geisha, she stayed single, and for thirty years, from the time Yamamoto was a lieutenant until he became an admiral, her feelings did not change. It was almost— she said—as though, having no other talents, she had been born solely to love him.

Yamamoto, on his side, invariably wrote her letters on his journeys, and sent her presents from the ports at which his ship called; he seems never to have refused her any request. Even when he was vice-minister and his life was in danger on account of opposition to the Tripartite Pact, he would sometimes go to department stores, his bodyguard trailing in his wake, to buy things for her. It is true, however, that at least in his later years, he was more strongly drawn to Chiyoko. Masako, essentially the "faithful" type, was probably less exciting than Chiyoko, who had enough of the "bitch" in her to make Hori declare that he couldn't understand what drew Yamamoto to her: "after all, it wasn't as though she was someone he'd just picked up on shore leave."

In late 1940, shortly after Masako's dream was realized and Yamamoto became a full admiral, the Nagato entered Beppu harbor. Masako, who was forty by then and owned a small teahouse called Togo in Sasebo, came up to Beppu to see him.

At first that evening he talked and laughed pleasantly enough with the staff officers accompanying him, but a telephone call from Saeki, possibly on the subject of aircraft, plunged him into morose taciturnity. When Masako, waking the next morning before it was light, asked what time it was, the only reply was a surly, "I don't know—I'm not a clock." There was a naval air base at Saeki, and the timing suggests that Yamamoto's mind was preoccupied with matters connected with Pearl Harbor.

Masako next met Yamamoto in February the following year, 1941, when the Combined Fleet entered Sasebo harbor. This time he was in high spirits, and one night after dinner at an eel restaurant insisted on walking all the way back to Togo—a distance of four or five hundred yards—in the bowlegged style of Charlie Chaplin. Sasebo at the time was overflowing with petty officers and men on shore leave, and Masako had to stifle her amusement, mixed with a kind of proprietary satisfaction, on hearing one sailor mutter to another on a street corner, "Hey, look—that's the C. in C.!" "Come off it," said the other, "you don't think the C. in C. would go about like that, do you?"

Togo was a small establishment, standing back somewhat from the main street, and there were only two or three maids; and during the four or five days that the fleet was in port, Masako would not let anyone else attend to Yamamoto's needs. The short time that she spent waiting hand and foot on the man she had loved ever since she was twelve was the happiest in her whole life.

NINE

1

At the beginning of 1941, around the time that the concept of a raid on Pearl Harbor was taking definite shape in Yamamoto's mind, one part of him was also beginning to toy once more with the idea of retirement. In August of that year, he would have been C. in C. for two years. Few of the men who, since the Meiji Restoration of 1868, had held the same post had served longer than that. From Togo Heihachiro (the hero of the Russo-Japanese War) to Yoshida Zengo, they had handed over to others after periods ranging from a few months to two years and three months.

So it was quite natural that with the beginning of the new year Yamamoto should begin to think of being relieved of his duties. But he also seems to have realized that, the times being what they were, this would not be easy to arrange. A letter that he wrote on January 23, 1941, to Koga Mineichi, C. in C. of the Second Fleet on board the *Takao*, is one of the most important of all his communications, dealing as it does with the use of naval appointments as a means of avoiding war, and with the question of his own future:

On returning to my ship from Tokyo following indications of a forthcoming Tripartite Pact in August or September last year, I felt extremely uneasy and wrote asking [Minister] Oikawa his view of future prospects. He told me that there was a definite possibility that we might have to pull Germany's chestnuts out of the fire, but that America would be reluctant to enter the war, so that it would probably be all right. I seemed to remember that His Highness [Prince Fushimi, chief of the Naval General Staff] had said something to the effect that "things having come to this pass, there is no alternative for us but to do what has to be done." Feeling that this was very dangerous, I decided that the only possible solution was to bring in Yonai as soon as possible. In order to effect this, I felt the proper procedure would be to have him appointed first as commander in chief. There are signs that Oikawa is gradually coming to appreciate the danger. . . . He said that the vice-minister was too much of a schemer and had better be replaced as soon as possible. The Naval General Staff also needed to close its ranks, he said, and he asked if I couldn't let him have Fukudome as head of the First Division.

I told him therefore that: (1) now that the Tripartite Pact had been signed, to prevent Japan's joining in the war would require an unusual degree of determination, and was unlikely to be achieved simply by replacing a divisional chief or installing a new vice-minister.

First of all, then, I would either install Yonai as chief of the Naval General Staff or appoint Yoshida or Koga as vice-chief (both would be difficult in practice), with Fukudome as assistant and Inoue as navy vice-minister. I believe this aligning of like minds that could work together to be a minimum requirement if the navy's position is to be strengthened. If the changes he had in mind were sweeping enough to achieve this difficult feat, and a real effort was made to "grasp the nettle," the fleet on its side would be willing to make the hard but necessary sacrifices and refrain from opposing the personnel changes. To these suggestions, Oikawa made no reply either affirmative or negative.

(2) Quite apart from the foregoing, Oikawa asked my opinion concerning my successor as commander in chief; there was no hurry, he said, but who did I think would be suitable? I avoided any immediate answer, telling him that I needed time to think carefully about it, and around December 25 last year I replied by letter to the following effect:

"I have already submitted this opinion, and His Highness does not agree, but I still think that the best plan would to be to appoint Admiral Yonai [C. in C.] at the time of the April repostings. If that is done, I have a feeling that His Highness too would come round to the idea of Yonai [as chief of the Naval General Staff] within 1941 or next year at the latest.

"If one sets aside the possibility of appointing Yonai, the four logically possible choices would seem to be Shimada, the two

Toyodas, and Koga, but of these I think we can dispense with the two Toyodas. ....

"To sum up, my first proposal is that Yonai should be appointed immediately, and if this seems impossible then—in the sense of successors to myself—I think the only two possibilities are Koga and Shimada.

"I also feel that if His Highness is not to be replaced for the time being, the best thing would be to appoint Koga—though it would be a burden for him—as vice-chief.

"As for myself, my honest feeling is, seeing that I am already pushing Yonai as hard as I can, I have no objection either to being retired or to staying on in the First Fleet. Not that I want to shirk the heavy responsibilities involved; if it should be decided, for example, that Koga should come to the Combined Fleet only after one year ashore, I would have no objection to carrying on for a third year.

"And if it seems from the international and domestic situation that Japan might in certain circumstances be obliged to go to war, it would be a mistake to replace either the commander in chief of the Second Fleet or the chief of staff of the Combined Fleet."

It is very regrettable, but since the loss of Yoshida it does not seem that there is anyone suitable at top levels, and things are likely to prove very difficult unless Yonai, you, and Inoue are willing to step into the breach. Should Japan go to war, one would have to resign oneself to it as unavoidable and throw oneself wholeheartedly into the fight, yet I believe it should be delayed just as long as possible so as to allow Japan all available time to concentrate on preparing itself.

Oikawa should be well aware that, as I have written above, important conditions attach to any change in the posts of C. in C. of the Second Fleet or chief of staff of the Combined Fleet, but I think I had better advise him so once more by letter.

The two Toyodas referred to are Toyoda Teijiro and Toyoda Soemu. The reference to the possibility of Prince Fushimi "coming round to the idea of Yonai" implies that the prince, who had been in the post of chief of the Naval General Staff for nine years, ever since

1932, might take it upon himself to suggest that Yonai should take his place.

The letter, though a private communication, had a considerable official importance. The request for Fukudome was conveyed by Nakahara Yoshimasa, head of the Personnel Bureau, who personally came to the fleet to see Yamamoto. Yamamoto, it seems, questioned him bluntly as to its significance: "Is the minister so firmly convinced that we should not go to war that he wants to strengthen his lineup at the ministry as a way of ensuring this? Or does he want Fukudome out of a vague idea that his present staff is somehow inadequate? Did he say anything to you on that point?"

"The minister does seem to be worried in all kinds of ways about the international situation," replied Nakahara, "but he didn't give me any message, so I'm not sure how strongly he feels on the subject."

Yamamoto therefore entrusted Nakahara with the following message for Navy Minister Oikawa:

> It has been a foregone conclusion ever since last autumn that relations with the U.S. would reach their present pass. If your request is based on the idea that in view of the armament program and the resources necessary to realize it the navy should put its foot down at this point, and that in order to do this it is necessary to have a really reliable staff at the ministry, then I believe that your wishes should be given all possible attention.
>
> However, if the idea is that it is already too late, and that in all probability Japan will have to go to war, then as commander in chief of the Combined Fleet I believe that the present commander in chief [of the Second Fleet] and chief of staff, in whom I have the greatest confidence, should be retained. . . . To replace these two officers at the present moment—irrespective of the abilities of their successors—would not only be unsettling for myself, but would inevitably have an undesirable effect on the officers and men of the fleet. In this case, therefore, I would prefer to leave things as they are.

In dealing with Koga, a mild tone was quite enough to get his meaning across, but with Oikawa he apparently felt the need for a considerably more forceful style.

Although in his letter to Koga he makes the semiofficial statement that if circumstances required he would not object to spending three years at sea, his true feelings still seem to have inclined toward retirement. To Sorimachi Eiichi, during a visit by the latter to Tokyo, he said in effect: "This year I'll have served in the navy for thirty-six years. Of the two hundred-odd men who entered the Naval Academy along with me, only four—Shiozawa, Yoshida, Shimada, and myself—are still left on the active list. I imagine that this autumn I, too, shall be handing over to my juniors and leaving the navy. If so, I look forward to going back home to Nagaoka and spending my time reading the books my father and my ancestors wrote, scratching about in the fields out back, looking after the chestnut and persimmon trees, and making friends with the young people of the town."

In a letter dated April 14, addressed to his friend with the bathhouse in Nagaoka, he wrote: "Another year spent defending the seas, and if nothing untoward happens I hope to have done with service in the navy. Then I look forward to taking it easy back home in the country—where I'm sure there'll be time to show off my skill at *shogi*, so tell everybody to brush up their games by then! On the other hand, if by any chance there should be a war between Japan and America within the year, I'm ready to carry out my duties in a way that'll have you all saying 'Good old Iso!' . . . The fleet at the moment is in harbor preparing to sail, and at the end of the month I'll be setting forth over the mighty deep."

One thing that made Yamamoto talk and write in this way was, undoubtedly, nostalgia for his home in the country, from which he had been absent so long. Another was the navy's unwritten rule that a C. in C. of the Combined Fleet normally held his post for no more than two years. Yet it could not have failed to occur to him that, even should he leave the fleet that autumn, after just over two years at its head, he might not be able to return to Nagaoka immediately—in other words, that the post of navy minister might be awaiting him. If there was any idea of reinforcing the close communication between senior and junior ranks traditional to the navy and its acknowledged reluctance to go to war, then what more natural than that Inoue should be vice-minister with Yamamoto over him as minister? But even in his letters to Koga, Yamamoto makes no mention of such a possibility.

At one stage, it seems, moves were begun in Tokyo by Hori, backed up by Okada Keisuke, Yonai Mitsumasa, and Yamanashi Katsunoshin, to bring Yamamoto back to the ministry. These moves seem to have become fairly explicit in autumn that year, when the third Konoe government gave way to the Tojo government; but Shimada Shigetaro, who became Tojo's navy minister, insisted—possibly out of concern for his own position—that Yamamoto was the only man for the post of C. in C. of the Combined Fleet.

Once again, Yamamoto himself showed no sign whatsoever of desiring a government post, whether as minister or in any other important capacity. Though doubtless a fine example of the traditional indifference to preferment, his diffidence was in practice regrettable. As Takei Daisuke has said, if only Yamamoto had been back at the ministry by autumn 1941, the declaration of war would have been postponed at the very least. Yamamoto would have been assailed from various quarters as a coward and a pawn of the U.S. and Britain; but while this was happening, Germany's failing strength would gradually have become apparent, and Japan could have taken advantage of the general upheaval to pursue some course more beneficial to itself.

In the April reshuffle that had inspired Yamamoto's letter to Koga, Fukudome was switched from chief of staff of the Combined Fleet to head of the First Division of the Naval General Staff, as Oikawa had wished. Prince Fushimi resigned as chief of the Naval General Staff for health reasons. But none of the other appointments that Yamamoto had proposed as a means of avoiding war was made.

After Prince Fushimi's retirement, his successor as chief of the Naval General Staff was not, as Yamamoto had hoped, a Yonai brought back off the reserve list, but Nagano Osami. It was on this occasion that Yamamoto said, "I expect Nagano will go down well, since he's the kind of man who thinks he's a genius, even though he's not."

Few people in the navy seem to have regretted the disappearance of Prince Fushimi, who had originally been appointed chief of the Naval General Staff to counterbalance the appointment of Prince Kan'in as chief of the army's General Staff Headquarters. It is doubtful, even so, if Nagano was much of an improvement. The "Sugiyama Memorandum," published as part of a multivolume *History of the Hundred Years since the Restoration* series, contains the gist of an exchange between the emperor and Nagano that took place on November 3, one month before the opening of hostilities, when Chief of General Staff Headquarters Sugiyama Hajime went with Nagano to report to the emperor concerning operational plans:

EMPEROR: On what day does the navy intend to move?
NAGANO: The eighth, according to our schedule.
EMPEROR: That is a Monday, is it not?
NAGANO: We thought the day after a holiday, when they were all tired, would be best. . . .

As hardly needs pointing out, the International Date Line runs between Tokyo and Hawaii, and Monday, December 8, scheduled for the commencement of hostilities, was of course Sunday, December 7, in Hawaii. It should be added that the *Hawaiian Operation* volume in the Defense Agency's *History of the War* records the content of another report made to the emperor by Nagano on December 2, immediately before the beginning of the Pacific War. This time most of it makes good sense:

In order to make the first attacks by the army, navy, and air units as easy and effective as possible, we consider the best time to be a moonlit night, with the moon around twenty days old, sometime between midnight and dawn.

We also consider that it would be advantageous to carry out the Hawaii raid by the naval task force on a Sunday, a holiday there, when the number of ships at anchor in Pearl Harbor would be relatively large. We have therefore chosen December 8, when the moon will be nineteen days old, and which is a Sunday in the Hawaii area.

The eighth is, of course, a Monday in the Far East, but we have given prior importance to the raid by the task force in our choice of day.

The last couple of lines, even so, are nonsensical, and the use of "of course" betrays Nagano's acute embarrassment at his error of a month earlier. The whole episode is a good illustration of the sloppiness of some of the men who were in key positions governing army and navy operations.

2

Previous to this, as we have seen from Yamamoto's letter to Koga, Yamamoto had been seriously thinking, in view of the danger of war, of strengthening the fleet by stepping down to the position of C. in C. of the First Fleet and restoring Yonai to the active list as commander in chief of the Combined Fleet.

When a friend of Yamamoto's from Nagaoka, visiting him on board the *Nagato*, asked him whether, in the event of war with America, there wasn't some way of managing things as skillfully as in the Battle of the Japan Sea, Yamamoto replied that it might be possible if only the enemy brought all his forces out to do battle at once, but that in practice such a thing would never happen. Around this time, he also said to Oguma Shin'ichiro: "If there's a war, it won't be the kind where battleships sally forth in leisurely fashion as in the past, and the proper thing for the C. in C. of the Combined Fleet would be, I think, to sit tight in the Inland Sea, keeping an eye on the situation as a whole. But I can't see myself doing anything so boring, and I'd like to get Yonai to take over, so that if the need arose I could play a more active role. . . ."

In February 1941, when Inoue Shigeyoshi, as chief of the Aeronautics Department, came to the *Nagato* to watch some war games, Yamamoto once more aired his idea of having Yonai as C. in C. of the Combined Fleet and himself as C. in C. of the First Fleet. Inoue, however, opposed the idea. "The thing I feel doubtful about," he said, "is that it would discredit all the dozen or so admirals on the active list. If I were the minister, I'd never make such a change."

"Yes," said Yamamoto, looking rather disappointed. "I suppose some people might see it like that."

In the event, his plan bore no fruit, and the desire to resign that he privately cherished was frustrated; time marched steadily on to the point where war came and found him still in charge of the Combined Fleet.

On April 17 of that year, a party of a dozen scholars made a tour of the naval harbor at Yokosuka, the Naval Air Corps, and the *Nagato*, which was then in port. They were shown around by Captain Takagi Sokichi, accompanied by members of his section and naval professor Enomoto Shigeharu. With one or two exceptions, the group was made up of university professors of liberal, pacifist tendencies, and was an indication of how the navy was trying to use the ministry's Research Section as a way of keeping in contact with liberal intellectuals. The navy had a number of groups organized to study political ideas, foreign relations, and so on. These groups, in the nature of advisory bodies to the Research Section, had a variety of ostensible aims but in fact were devoted to seeking ways of staving off war with the United States, or of bringing about a rapid peace should war break out.

At the outset, it seems, the navy had no very definite aim in creating this "brain trust." However, the navy kept a compact household compared with the army, and traditionally lacked political influence; if it was to exert a restraining influence on the army, it could no longer afford to remain isolated, and must ally itself with a broad spectrum of the public as well; but as things were in Japan the only possible ways to reach it were via the major newspapers or via members of the business and intellectual worlds. Thus it arranged gatherings of businessmen at which Ikeda Seihin and Go Seinosuke acted as intermediaries in sounding out their views. Where the intellectual world was concerned, it sponsored occasional meetings of between thirty and forty scholars from various fields in the hope of letting them know what the navy was thinking, what its special difficulties were, and what kind of support it looked to the public to provide.

However, by the time this task of creating a "brain trust" for the navy had got under way, war was already imminent. When it actually broke out, the outlooks of the scholars concerned were largely focused on the idea that unless some settlement were reached quickly, Japan would soon find itself in dire straits. One of them, Nishida Kitaro, is said to have demanded: "Do they really think that Japan can make war with the countries of the West at its present level of modernization?" Naturally enough, hopes came to be pinned on such groups as a means of seeking some way to an early settlement, and the twelve intellectuals who went to visit the *Nagato* were all associated in some form or other with them.

On the day in question, it was stated that C. in C. Yamamoto would be away from the fleet. He was, in fact, absent when the party arrived on board the *Nagato*; but when they arrived back on the afterdeck, having spent an hour or so inspecting the interior of the vessel, they were informed that the C. in C. had just turned up on board. Takagi promptly went to thank Yamamoto, and introduced the party he had brought with him. Yamamoto, however, looked displeased, and reproached Takagi for not having let him know before. "What a wasted opportunity!" he complained. When Captain Takagi told him that they

216

had been invited to lunch at the Yokosuka Navy Club by Admiral Shiozawa, C. in C. of the naval station, he looked still more disgruntled. Thus the party left the *Nagato* having exchanged no more than a few cursory remarks with Yamamoto. In the military world, where material power and courage were all that mattered, and even in the navy's own Information Division, intellectuals tended to be dismissed contemptuously as a pack of talkative cowards, but Yamamoto, according to Takagi, was an exception.

To Takagi, meeting Yamamoto for the first time after a long interval, the C. in C. looked bronzed and healthy, but he was stouter than during his vice-ministerial days and was acquiring a paunch. Even when the war was at its height, most things were still available in the Combined Fleet command's galleys. The *Nagato* had its own bakery, which turned out such things as Western-style cakes, bread, caramel creams, and the like. These, together with the local products sent to the vessel as gifts whenever it entered harbor, ensured that Yamamoto's sweet tooth never went unsatisfied. At a meeting with Prince Konoe, when Yamamoto was asked for any political advice he might have, he suggested the prime minister do something to improve supplies of everyday necessities. "I don't know much about politics," he said, "but I was somewhat surprised to hear about the general shortage of food when my officers and men got back from leave a while ago." This was in 1941, when the food shortage was already becoming a serious topic of conversation in homes throughout Japan, and one cannot help feeling that the amenities of life in Combined Fleet command must have left Yamamoto rather out of touch with the times for him to be "somewhat surprised" at this late stage.

Nevertheless, it was not only high living that was making Yamamoto fat. Another obvious reason was lack of exercise. He had always insisted that "a man who couldn't stay healthy without exercise wasn't qualified to be a naval officer," since the crew of a submarine or destroyer could hardly expect to take adequate exercise. It was also essential, according to Yamamoto's theory, to give oneself a change from time to time, both to maintain one's health and to keep one's flexibility of body and mind. In fact, this was an excuse that Yamamoto used for spending so much of his spare time gambling. (Chief orderly Omi recalls that Yamamoto would often call for the *shogi* board even when the ship was in port.)

It goes without saying that performing handstands, or doing a few exercises, or even walking on the deck of a large ship like the *Nagato*—much less "giving oneself a change" by playing *shogi*—were not going to ward off obesity, and it seems unlikely that Yamamoto's growing stoutness went with tip-top physical condition.

3

From 1937 to 1939, Yamamoto Chikao (who had been Yamamoto Isoroku's first assistant while the latter was naval attaché in the United States) had been in the First Section, First Division, of the Naval General Staff, where he took a hand in writing the "Plan of Operations for the Coming Year," but early in the summer of 1941 he had joined the fleet as commander of the seaplane tender *Chitose*. One day in June, he came on board the *Nagato* in order to take part in map maneuvers against the Americans held by Combined Fleet command. He found, however, that command proposed to make no use whatsoever of ordinary carriers in the assault on the Philippines, devoting only one small training carrier, the *Hosho*, to the task. This was very different from the idea of throwing everything into an assault on the Philippines right at the start that he had always had in mind while concerned with operations at the Naval General Staff.

Puzzled and disturbed, he summoned air staff officer Sasaki Akira and demanded to know the reason for this seemingly dangerous procedure. Sasaki looked embarrassed. "Just a moment," he said, and led Yamamoto off to another cabin. Then, lowering his voice, he went on, "It doesn't matter if *you* know, I suppose. The *Akagi*, *Kaga*, and other carriers—the whole lot of them, in fact—can't be sent to the Philippines because they're due to head for Hawaii at the outset of hostilities."

This was a possibility that the *Chitose*'s commander had never dreamed of. "That sounds a damned risky undertaking to me," he said in astonishment. "Whose idea was it?"

"The C. in C.'s, of course."

"And did you go along with it?"

"No. At first, almost all the staff officers were opposed to it, but the C. in C. insisted. . . ."

It was a gamble truly worthy of Yamamoto Isoroku, the other Yamamoto thought to himself. Questioning Sasaki further, he learned that since the range of the "Zero" fighters had been extended, it would be possible for them to reach the Philippines from the south of Taiwan if so required. Onishi Takijiro, chief of staff of the Eleventh Air Fleet, was making a study of whether it would be possible to direct the whole carrier fleet to the raid on Hawaii if necessary. "But remember—" Sasaki told him, "this is all ultra top secret." Yamamoto returned to the *Chitose* with very mixed feelings.

Nevertheless—according to Chihaya Masataka, who after the war wrote *The Curse on the "Awa-maru"*—quite a few people both in the navy and outside had got wind of the C. in C.'s plan by around the middle of 1941. Chihaya also says that members of the Naval General Staff and the Personnel Bureau were the most uncommunicative of all, and that the proportion of people who had not got wind of what was up was probably highest in the heart of the Naval General Staff itself. Chihaya was on board the *Nagato* as anti-aircraft officer from late 1940 until September 1941. Lieutenant Takahashi Yoshio, chief codes officer, was a former classmate of his, and he relates how he suddenly put two and two together when he dropped into the staff wardroom one·day and found his friend studying a chart of the North Pacific.

There were plenty of people on the American side, too, who voiced warnings of the possibility of a Japanese surprise raid on Pearl Harbor. These warnings seem to have been based on something more than mere imagination; as early as the beginning of 1941, American Ambassador Joseph Grew sent a secret cable to the State Department which ran as follows: "The Peruvian minister has informed a member of my staff that he has heard from many sources, including a Japanese source, that in the event of trouble breaking out between the U.S. and Japan the Japanese intend to make a surprise attack against Pearl Harbor with all their strength and employing all their equipment. The Peruvian minister considered the rumors fantastic but he considered them of sufficient importance to convey all this." The date of this cable is believed to have been January 28, 1941.

It was on January 7 of the same year that Yamamoto wrote a document entitled "Views on Preparations for War" on nine sheets of naval stationery and sent it to Navy Minister Oikawa. This document for the first time set forth officially the idea of an assault on Hawaii. "No one can make any definite predictions concerning the international situation," it began, "but it seems obvious that the time has come for the navy, and the Combined Fleet in particular, to go ahead with arming and training itself, and possibly drawing up a plan of operations, on the assumption that war with America and England cannot be avoided.

"I take the liberty, therefore, of submitting for your consideration an outline of my personal convictions as to what should be done (it corresponds for the most part with the recommendations I made verbally in late November last year)."

While his ship was at anchor at Yokosuka in November the previous year, Yamamoto had visited the Navy Ministry on a number of occasions for talks with Minister Oikawa, in the course of which, it seems, he had outlined his views. Written in red in the margin of the document in question is the warning, "For the eyes of the minister alone: to be burned without showing to anyone else." Nevertheless, liaison staff officer Fujii had a copy of it in his possession which survived the end of the war. It is divided into four sections: "preparations for war," "training," "operational policy," and a fourth section in which Yamamoto sets forth in detail a "plan of operations to be followed at the outset of hostilities." According to this fourth section, the entire air strength of the First and Second Carrier Divisions was to be thrown into a raid, to be carried out on a moonlit night or at dawn, on the American fleet in Pearl Harbor, with the aim of "annihilating" it. A destroyer squadron was to be detailed to rescue crew members of any Japanese carriers that might be sunk. Submarines were if possible to sink at the entrance to Pearl Harbor any enemy vessels that came out, so as to block the entrance to the harbor.

This plan, with its strong flavor of "do-or-die," was based on the realization that, as Yamamoto wrote, "the outcome must be decided on the first day." Another man would replace him as commander in chief of the Combined Fleet; he himself "earnestly desired that he should be appointed C. in C. of an air fleet so that he would have direct control of the attacking units." Another passage in the same document says, "When one considers what will happen if Japan goes to war with America and England, it seems quite possible that throughout the war there will be no practical opportunity for spectacular operations pitting the whole fleet against the enemy's in an all-out onslaught with guns and torpedoes."

Following the beginning of the war, when the Pearl Harbor raid had in fact succeeded and the *Prince of Wales* and *Repulse* had been sunk off Malaya, Prince Takamatsu is said to have remarked to Fukudome Shigeru, head of the First Division of the Naval General Staff, "Things have gone just as C. in C. Yamamoto said, both at Hawaii and off Malaya. . . ." A survey of the subsequent course of hostilities would reveal that Yamamoto was right there, too.

Simultaneously with the submission of his official statement, Yamamoto set down on three sheets of writing paper an outline of his idea for the attack on Pearl Harbor and handed it to Onishi Takijiro, chief of staff of the Eleventh Air Fleet, requesting him to study the idea and draw up a plan.

If one examines the dates of these events, it is apparent that the American embassy in Tokyo, at least, had got wind of the plan for a raid on Pearl Harbor within three weeks of Yamamoto's outlining his ideas on paper. Yet the leaders of the U.S. government and navy showed little serious interest in Ambassador Grew's warning. In a cable sent to the C. in C. of the Pacific Fleet by Chief of U.S. Naval Operations Stark on February 1, 1941, Stark declared that U.S. naval intelligence considered this rumor to be incredible. Why they should have remained indifferent to such a valuable piece of information remains something of a mystery even today.

Onishi Takijiro seems personally to have had objections to an operation that he felt to be excessively unconventional. Nevertheless, he showed the plans to senior staff officer Maeda of the Eleventh Air Fleet, then, summoning Commander Genda Minoru, air staff officer of the First Carrier Division, to Kanoya, showed him Yamamoto's letter and asked him to study the question. The Eleventh Air Fleet, in which Onishi served, was a shore unit based at Kanoya. The First Carrier Division was a sea unit consisting of the *Akagi* and *Kaga*, and Genda at the time was on board the *Kaga*. He had returned from England not long before, and had earned the name "madman Genda" at Navy Staff College on account of his radical advocacy of priority for aircraft. He was the man who, on behalf of Onishi and thus on behalf of Yamamoto himself, drafted the first detailed plan for an attack on Hawaii.

One of the ideas contained in the draft was that all the fleet's main carriers, in the First and Second Carrier Divisions, should be thrown into the raid; that repeated raids should be carried out in order to achieve certain and thorough results; and that the point of departure should be Chichijima in the Ogasawaras or Atsukeshi in Hokkaido.

Onishi's report based on this draft was submitted to Yamamoto at the beginning of April. Yamamoto made a few amendments, then ordered Onishi to take it to the Naval General Staff. At this stage, it seems, it did not extend to much concrete detail.

The Combined Fleet, in the meantime, was making its own independent study, parallel with those of Genda and Onishi, of the proposed Hawaiian operation. In the course of a conversation between the C. in C. and his staff officers, Yamamoto apparently asked whether it wouldn't be feasible to make landings in Hawaii at the same time as the air strike. If only it were possible to take prisoner in one fell swoop all the U.S. naval officers on Hawaii, America would find it difficult to recover in terms of personnel, since there was no shortcut to training a naval officer.

Four preliminary study groups were established in Combined Fleet command, and senior staff officer Captain Kuroshima Kameto set about drawing up a plan of operations. Kuroshima was the most eccentric of all the Combined Fleet's staff officers. Once inspiration came to him, he shut himself up in his cabin, closed the deadlights of the portholes, and seating himself stark naked at his desk (since the *Nagato* had no air conditioning), worked day and night as though possessed. He burned incense and smoked continuously, crushing one cigarette out almost as soon as he had lit it and lighting another immediately. All kinds of legends grew up about him—that if called out on some business he would calmly walk about the ship without a stitch on; that he had never once eaten a meal with the C. in C.; or that however many documents piled up on his desk he never so much as glanced at them. Yet "the plan of operations for the first stage of the war, including the raid on Hawaii, would have been quite impossible," says one observer, "with strict reference to figures alone. The whole thing was dragged out of Kuroshima's abnormal brain and drawn up against all nature."

At the end of April, on Yamamoto's orders, he went to Tokyo to explain the Combined Fleet's strategy for the raid on Pearl Harbor as he himself had drawn it up. The head of the First Division of the Naval General Staff at the time was Rear Admiral Fukudome; the head of the First Section was Captain Tomioka Sadatoshi; and the air staff officer was Commander Miyo Tatsukichi. All three of them were opposed to the plan.

On August 7, Captain Kuroshima went to Tokyo to discuss the question again, this time taking the torpedo staff officer with him. The operations division persisted in its strong attitude, and a violent argument developed between Kuroshima and Tomioka. According to Tomioka, everyone at the Naval General Staff was always on his guard to make sure that the operations division kept control over the Combined Fleet. It was the General Staff that had to strike a balance with the claims of the army in allotting forces to particular operations, as well as arranging supplies of the necessary matériel and weapons. Should war break out, moreover, they would be faced with the task of getting as far as Java so as to gain control of the oil fields of the South Pacific. Thus they could not—as Kuroshima or Yamamoto did—think solely in terms of Pearl Harbor.

But one of the main reasons why they were reluctant to accept the Combined Fleet's plan was that the operation was too much of a gamble. Even if the raid itself were successful, what guarantee was there that the American fleet would be in Pearl Harbor at that hour on that particular day? Kuroshima vehemently stressed the absolute necessity of an attack on Hawaii, promoting Yamamoto's pessimistic view that, if war was unavoidable, the only possible tactics would be to annihilate the enemy's main strength at the outset, thus destroying the balance of power and putting America at a disadvantage. A strike against Pearl Harbor was essential to operations against the U.S.; no strike meant no operations.

The "Views on Preparations for War" quoted above contains the following sentence: "Success in this would not be easy to achieve, but if all officers and men concerned were united in truly selfless determination, then success might, with Heaven's aid, be possible."

Either way, Kuroshima requested that the map maneuvers normally held every year in November or December at Navy Staff College should be advanced to September, and a special room set aside for study of the plan, and First Section chief Tomioka promised to consider this suggestion if nothing else.

4

Somewhat earlier than this, in July 1941, Yamamoto himself went to Tokyo. Japan had decided it would send forces into southern French Indochina, and Navy Minister Oikawa had summoned Yamamoto and Koga Mineichi, C. in C. of the Second Fleet, so that they could be put into the picture.

The site of the meeting was the navy minister's official residence, and others present included Chief of the Naval General Staff Nagano Osami and Inoue Shigeyoshi, chief of the Aeronautics Department. Japan's progress toward war from the time of the February 26 Incident on was marked by a number of episodes in which the gradual downward slope made, as it were, a sudden, vertical plunge. The sending of Japanese forces into southern Indochina was to be one of the most significant of these "plunges."

At the very start, Yamamoto asked: "How's our air strength?"

"Just as it was when you were vice-minister," replied Inoue. "To make matters worse, a lot of skilled workers have been drafted as a result of the Indochina venture."

As an opponent of war with the United States, Inoue was even more dogmatic than Yamamoto himself. At the New Year, the draft armament plan for the coming year given him by the Naval General Staff had impressed him as "armament for the 1940s as conceived by late nineteenth-century minds," and he had drafted a lengthy memorandum entitled "A New Theory on the Armament Plan" and formally submitted it to the navy minister on January 30. Some of its statements were fairly hard-hitting: "It is deplorably obvious that if Japan persists in a race to build warships with England and the U.S., it will eventually be obliged to yield the palm." And at greater length:

> When one considers the actual course of any hostilities between Japan and the United States, it is clear that, given the right kind of armaments, it would be possible for Japan to avoid defeat by America, and one naturally hopes that this is what would happen. But it would be impossible, on the other hand, for Japan to defeat America and bring about its capitulation. The reason is unmistakable. . . . American operations against Japan would be on the same footing as Japanese operations against America in this one respect, that Japan lies at a vast distance from the United States; but in other respects they would differ greatly since: (1) it would be possible for America to occupy the

224

whole of Japanese territory; (2) it would be possible for America to occupy the Japanese capital; (3) it would be possible for America to wipe out Japanese forces in the field.

The point of Inoue's "new theory" was that if Japan did not want to lose the war against America, it should greatly increase its air strength; if it embarked on war with America in its present state, the imperial army and navy would be annihilated and all Japanese territory might well fall under U.S. occupation. Since the end of the war and the fulfillment of all Inoue's predictions, the points he made have seemed glaringly obvious, yet to state the situation so clearly in the atmosphere prevailing at that time must have required an unusual degree of perspicacity and courage.

The memorandum in question is included, in summarized form, in the *Hawaiian Operation* volume of the *History of the War*—which also records that Inoue's ideas on tactics were so far removed from those of the men responsible at the Naval General Staff that nobody would have anything to do with them. It is also said that his being sent to sea as C. in C. of the Fourth Fleet four months before the beginning of the war represented a virtual demotion due to this memorandum.

At the July meeting, after Inoue had had his say, Koga got up and tackled the minister. "Why was such an important decision taken one-sidedly, without even consulting the C. in C. of the fleet?" he asked. "Do they think that if they start a war we'll fight for them just like that?" He also questioned Nagano concerning the ideas of the Naval General Staff authorities on the government agreement with France.

"Well," replied Nagano vaguely, "seeing that the government's made up its mind, I suppose we'll have to go along with it." Both in these conversations and at the time of the signing of the Tripartite Pact, it seems that Oikawa's method was, so far as possible, to steer clear of people likely to raise objections, then to summon them to Tokyo and bludgeon them into acceptance once a *fait accompli* had more or less been achieved.

After a meal at the minister's official residence, the meeting broke up, and Yamamoto appeared in Inoue's room in a black mood and announced: "Nagano's a dead loss. There's nothing we can do now. Here—" he went on, "have you got anything sweet to eat?" When Inoue produced some chocolate, he bit off a piece and complained peevishly, "Is this stuff the best you can manage?"

On July 26 it was announced that complete agreement had been reached between the Japanese and French governments concerning the "joint defense of French Indochina." Japan, taking advantage of France's weak position in Europe, had already had troops in northern Indochina for the past year; on July 29, a Franco-Japanese document ratifying the agreement on joint defense was signed in Vichy, and within the same day Japan began sending units of its army and navy into the southern part of French Indochina (later to become South Vietnam).

There was a swift reaction from the American government, which was getting nervous about the Japanese advance to the south. It froze Japanese assets in the States as a form of retaliation, and on August 1 enforced a ban on a broad range of exports to Japan. This ban amounted to a refusal to allow the loading of any goods for Japan, including oil, with the exception of cotton and foodstuffs.

It was the general view, though not openly expressed at the time, that in view of figures for reserves, production, and consumption of liquid fuels, if oil stopped coming from America Japan would be obliged within four months either to move to secure supplies in South Asia or to capitulate.

Inexorably, the navy was being obliged to make up its mind to war. At the beginning of August, Tomioka Sadatoshi, head of the First Section, First Division, of the Naval General Staff, instructed members of his section to start preparing for hostilities. When Commander Miyo complained that he had no confidence about their chances in a war with America, Tomioka flared with anger. "Nonsense!" he said. "One doesn't go to war because one has or doesn't have confidence. The decision is one for the government to make. What kind of a navy would we be if the government said, 'It's war!' and we replied, 'Sorry, but we didn't have confidence, so we haven't made any preparations'?"

In the fleet, fierce training under near-combat conditions was in progress. Particularly where the projected assault on Hawaii was concerned, "near-combat conditions" was taking on an ever more detailed and concrete significance. The air unit of the carrier *Akagi*, which was in Yokosuka at the time, had gone south to Kagoshima for training. The real significance of this—known only to a select few at the time—was that the topography of Kagoshima harbor, with the volcanic island of Sakurajima just across the bay, closely resembled that of Pearl Harbor.

Lieutenant Commander Fuchida, who until spring that year had been flight commander on the *Akagi*, had transferred to the staff of the Third Carrier Division, but in August there came without warning a mysterious order for him to transfer back to the post of flight commander on the *Akagi*. Fuchida was due for promotion soon, moreover, and to appoint a commander as flight commander was unprecedented. The switch felt like a demotion, yet he had no idea of anything he might have done wrong, and it was with mixed feelings that he flew his plane to Kagoshima to take up the post. Shortly afterward, however, he was summoned to the office of Chief of Staff Kusaka and given a general outline of the plan for the raid on Pearl Harbor. He was also informed that C. in C. Yamamoto had asked who was to be put in charge of the attack force, and had given an approving smile when told it was Fuchida.

Fuchida himself is said to have opposed the idea of a surprise raid at first, but whether he agreed or not in principle, the plan was the kind to have him—a man always ready for a fight—raring to go. The one thing, though, that proved particularly difficult was to train the attacking force without letting it know what the real target would be. The attack on Pearl Harbor would, of course, be directed at ships at anchor, but when attack on ships at anchor was included in the training schedule, the crews—all of them veterans—began muttering that they were being "treated like kids."

Fuchida was given the task of training crews not only on the *Akagi*, but on all the carriers in the First Air Fleet newly organized that April. From then on, unrelenting training began under his command, with the Kagoshima Bay area playing the role of Pearl Harbor.

5

The main forces of the U.S. Pacific Fleet around this time were already geared for action, and at Pearl Harbor preparations for sailing into battle were already more advanced than those of the Combined Fleet. This seemed to strengthen still further Yamamoto's determination to attack Hawaii first of all in the event of war. "The fact that the other side has brought a great fleet to Hawaii to show us that it's within striking distance of Japan," he said, "means, conversely, that *we're* within striking distance too. In trying to intimidate us, America has put itself in a vulnerable position. If you ask me, they're just that bit too confident."

He was well aware of the strong opposition to his views both at the Naval General Staff and within the fleet under his command. Sometimes he would be irritated by this opposition and declare to his administrative staff officer Watanabe, "If they're going to make so many objections, I've a good mind to give it all up." To "give it up" did not refer to the Hawaiian operation, but to his post as C. in C.

Thanks to a concession on the part of the Naval General Staff, the map maneuvers at Navy Staff College were held for ten days beginning on September 11, just as Kuroshima had requested. (Chief orderly Omi went up to Tokyo in attendance on Yamamoto. He had already been warned by a command aide that he was the only enlisted man who knew of the plan, and that he must not mention it to anyone. At the end of August he had been given leave, and after going home to Akita, where he had visited the family grave and bade a silent farewell to his unsuspecting mother, who was ailing at the time, he had come back ready to go into battle.) Of the ten days devoted to war games, two—September 16 and 17—were allotted to exercises simulating the Hawaiian operation, and a special room, different from those used for the other exercises and seminars, was set aside for the purpose. Entry was strictly limited to some thirty carefully selected personnel. These were divided into a "Blue" (Japanese) force and a "Red" (U.S.) force, the two sides engaging in a tabletop battle.

Battle was supposedly joined on November 16, and as a result it was judged that four of the enemy's capital ships had been sunk and one badly damaged, two carriers sunk and one damaged, 180 aircraft shot down, and six cruisers sunk or damaged. The losses suffered on the Japanese side were also great: on the first day, two carriers were sunk and two slightly damaged, and 127 aircraft shot down. Whatever the outcome, though, the Combined Fleet command remained obstinate, the Naval General Staff cautious, and the leaders of the task force detailed to go to Hawaii negative in their attitude to the plan. Few among the opponents of the plan dared declare their opposition to Yamamoto's face, but Kusaka Ryunosuke and Onishi Takijiro, chiefs of staff of the First and Eleventh Air Fleets respectively, were exceptions. Despite his respect for Yamamoto, Kusaka was a man of unbending principles. "I disliked games of chance such as mahjongg and poker," he declared afterward. "I never joined in the gambling, nor was I invited to. Lots of people would go to ask Yamamoto to write something [do a piece of calligraphy] for them, but not me; it smacked too much of bootlicking." He was "strongly opposed to the Pearl Harbor plan. It was like putting one's head in the lion's mouth. It was a mistake to engage in such a gamble in the first battle of a major war on which the nation's future depended."

He frequently engaged Onishi in argument, gradually winning him over to his own view. As a result, Onishi too had come down firmly on the side of the opposition by the time the map maneuvers at Navy Staff College were over. At a discussion held by the chiefs of the First and Eleventh Air Fleets at the Kanoya base at the end of September, he said: "It would be impossible in any war with the U.S. for Japan to bring the other side to its knees. Going into a war with America without this ability means that we must consider ways to bring it to an early end, which means in turn that at some point we'll have to reach a compromise. For that reason, whether we land in the Philippines or anywhere else, we should avoid anything like the Hawaiian operation that would put America's back up too badly."

C. in C. Nagumo was also in opposition, and so was almost everyone else, but no one set forth such a clear justification for his stand as Onishi. Eventually, it was decided to make a written request that the plan for a raid on Hawaii be abandoned. The document was signed by the commanders of the two air fleets, and on October 3 Kusaka and Onishi visited Yamamoto on board the *Mutsu* (the Combined Fleet command having transferred its flag temporarily from the *Nagato* to this ship). Yamamoto heard them out in silence, then said: "But what would you do if, while we were engaged in the South Pacific, the U.S. fleet launched air raids on Japan from the east? Are you suggesting that it's all right for Tokyo and Osaka to be burned to the ground so long as we get hold of oil? Still, the fact is I'm determined that so long as I'm C. in C. we shall go ahead with the Hawaiian raid. I'm sure there'll be many things that are difficult for you, or go against the grain, but I'm asking you to proceed with preparations on the positive assumption that the raid is on." Then he added, in a mildly joshing tone, "I may be fond of bridge and poker, but I wish to hell you'd stop calling it a gamble!"

Gradually Onishi found himself coming round to Yamamoto's side; eventually, he helped in trying to win Kusaka over, but the latter refused to have anything to do with the plan. However, as the two of them were leaving the flagship, Yamamoto, who had broken custom by coming to the gangway to see them off, put a hand on Kusaka's shoulder and said with an air of utter sincerity, "Kusaka—I understand just how you feel. But the Pearl Harbor raid has become an article of faith for me. How about cutting down on the vocal opposition and trying to help me put that article of faith into practice? Where the actual operation is concerned I guarantee I'll do my best to meet any requests you may have."

This finally broke down Kusaka's resistance. "Very well, sir," he said. "I won't say anything more against it. I'll do all I can to help you bring it off."

This episode inevitably recalls, on a more serious level, the time at the Kasumigaura Aviation Corps when young Lieutenant Miwa, having sworn never to serve as officer of the deck, was no sooner in Yamamoto's presence than he was eating out of his hand and promising to "do his very utmost."

Although there was, of course, no guarantee that if Japan went to war without the attack on Pearl Harbor at the outset it would have the option of an early and favorable peace settlement, the opposition expressed by Onishi and Kusaka—headstrong and stubborn though they undoubtedly were—still sounds quite reasonable even today. That their opposition should have melted away so rapidly in the face of talk of "articles of faith" plus an unusually warm send-off at the gangway points up not only a peculiarity of the Japanese military man but also the strange fascination that Yamamoto exerted over other people.

From October 9, five days of map maneuvers were held on board the *Nagato*, which was once again the Combined Fleet flagship. Now that the fleets under Yamamoto's command had completed preparations for war and assembled in the west of the Inland Sea, the aim was to get together commanding officers at various levels and thoroughly acquaint them with the plan of operations; among them, there were some who were hearing about the planned attack on Hawaii for the first time.

"Some of you may have objections," declared Yamamoto, "but so long as I'm C. in C. I'm intent on going through with the raid on

my own studies have shown—Japan would only last for a year and a half."

Yamamoto continued to have *Life* magazine sent to him until immediately before the outbreak of war. He would circle in red any articles worthy of attention, then leave the magazine lying around in the staff officers' wardroom. It was on "studies" such as these that his reply to Konoe had been based. Inoue Shigeyoshi, despite his admiration for Yamamoto, considers this reply to constitute a serious black mark against him: "It should have been obvious," Inoue says, "that to talk like that would leave a man like Prince Konoe—who was a novice in military matters and vacillating by nature—with the vague but encouraging idea that Japan could keep going for a year and a half. Why didn't Yamamoto come out and say that the navy wasn't able to take on America, that it would be defeated if it did, and that if such a view disqualified him as commander in chief, he was willing to leave his post? No doubt he would have found it hard to stand up and say he couldn't fight in front of the forty thousand men under his command, but he should have overcome such scruples and stated forthrightly what he felt."

In his *Last Days of the Combined Fleet*, Ito Masanori, while not blaming Yamamoto directly, expressed similar thoughts in his own rather florid style: "The navy should have insisted straightforwardly that it could not agree to the war with America. Alas, its lack of the courage to say a simple 'no' was to lead to its being dragged into a rash conflict and, after many a vain battle, going down to annihilation. No, indeed—the Combined Fleet will never be seen again!"

As to why Yamamoto should have told Konoe that he could "give them hell for a year or a year and a half," Inoue sees this as consideration for his subordinates, but one cannot help suspecting that Yamamoto was influenced to some degree by the psychology, characteristic of military men, that longs to test the results of training in actual battle. One suspects, too, a touch of resentment at having been labeled "weak-kneed" for so long, and a desire to impress the folks back home and the women. One might, even, wonder whether the childish streak in him did not give him the feeling "If they want me to, then I'll let them see what I can do," so that he had actually come to look forward to war; but that would probably be going too far.

In the letter to Hori Teikichi written on October 11 and quoted above, Yamamoto had commented, "As things are . . . the only possibility left is that the emperor should make a personal decision." A couple of weeks later, when the third Konoe government resigned, to be replaced by a Tojo government with Shimada Shigetaro as its navy minister, he wrote a long letter to Shimada in which he says: "When one views the situation as a whole, it is obvious that a collision between Japan and America should be avoided if at all possible and that the important thing at the moment is to show patience, circumspection, and a willingness to put up with any unpleasantness for the sake of the final goal—but that is something that will require an extraordinary amount of courage, and now that Japan has been driven into its present situation one wonders whether such a changeover is feasible. The only course left, although I say this with the utmost trepidation, is for there to be a gracious decision from His Imperial Majesty." This would seem to suggest that Yamamoto was privately hoping for some precedent-breaking decision such as the emperor was to make later, at the end of the war.

Following Toyoda Teijiro's promotion to the Ministry of Trade and Industry in the April reshuffle of the cabinet, it was Sawamoto Yorio who served as navy vice-minister in the second and third Konoe cabinets and the Tojo cabinet that followed. Around the time under discussion, the same Sawamoto called on Yonai Mitsumasa and Okada Keisuke in the hope of getting advice on the crisis from senior statesmen associated with the navy.

A theory prevalent at the time among advocates of war held that if things continued as they were, Japan's strength would be slowly sapped until none was left. Yonai, according to notes taken by Sawamoto, did not agree. It was a mistake, he said, to decide everything in terms of that theory; the situation in Europe must be taken into consideration, and time would undeniably solve quite a few problems.

"They talk a lot about sapping Japan's strength," said Okada, "but a slow sapping is at least better than having it destroyed all at once. . . . There's a danger that the army will use the talk of oil only lasting for one year as an excuse for demanding some from the navy. Japan should be very careful about launching a war at this point in time. Given the resolve, domestic questions can somehow be handled. To blunder in foreign relations would be to cause the nation untold

234

suffering over a long period." Nevertheless, there was by now quite a strong current of feeling within the navy itself, especially among the younger officers, in favor of opening hostilities.

It is interesting to note, incidentally, that the yearly amount of oil required by Japan in peacetime in those days was 3,500,000 tons, of which two million tons went to the navy, 500,000 tons to the army, and one million tons to satisfy civilian needs. Thus the question of whether Japan went to war with America depended directly on a quantity of fuel equivalent to 1/35 of the 120 million tons of crude oil imported and used every year by Japan today (1969).

"A navy cannot make war without oil," said Tomioka Sadatoshi after the war. "The imperial navy furiously built up its reserves so that just prior to the outbreak of war it had 5,500,000 tons in hand. Without it, we couldn't have gone to war; like it or not, we should have had to go along with what America said. In a sense, those carefully hoarded reserves were to prove a curse for Japan."

7

In his long letter written to Shimada Shigetaro toward the end of October, Yamamoto also says:

> If the situation is going to force us into action, I feel, as officer in command of the fleet, that there will be little prospect of success if we employ the normal type of operations. . . . There are some people, it seems, who have considerable doubts about my own character and abilities as commander. In an extreme emergency such as the nation now faces, one cannot take personal considerations into account, nor have I ever seen myself as fitted for the post of commander in chief of the Combined Fleet. . . . In short, my plan is one conceived in desperation, on account of my own imperfectly developed abilities, from lack of confidence in a perfectly safe, properly ordered frontal attack; if there is some other suitable person to take over, I am ready to withdraw, gladly and without hesitation.

However, there was, by now, no one who would have let Yamamoto "withdraw gladly." Five days before this letter was written, the Naval General Staff had given its formal approval to the Hawaiian operation in more or less the precise form that the Combined Fleet had wished.

In the meantime, the training of the entire fleet was going ahead as planned.

One day, Fuchida asked Combined Fleet air staff officer Sasaki whether the C. in C. was satisfied with the results of training so far in Kagoshima Bay and elsewhere.

"No," said Sasaki. "He's still rather worried, judging from the way he talks. Only the other day, he said that the attacks were still being made from too far off and that I was to tell them to get closer."

"That's bad," said Fuchida. "If the C. in C. still feels uneasy, the men on the job aren't going to be happy. I'll go to the *Nagato* and have a talk with the C. in C. myself." It was customary in the navy, particularly among officers in the aviation branch, to express one's opinions quite freely, whatever the other man's rank.

Going on board the *Nagato*, he requested an interview with Yamamoto. "I hear you're not completely happy about the attack force, sir," he said. "If so, I'd like you to put out another fleet order for maneuvers. Please put all six carriers on the job. We'll assume that Saeki Bay is Pearl Harbor, and make contact with the enemy somewhere around Cape Ashizuri, finishing up by bombing Saeki itself."

With the date of departure not far distant, the fleet was extremely busy, but Yamamoto agreed. The order for these final special exercises went out after midnight on November 3, and on the morning of the fourth, half an hour before sunrise—as was due to happen in actuality—the first attack force took off from the carriers. In four groups—horizontal bombers, dive-bombers, torpedo bombers, and escort fighters—it converged on Saeki Bay, then carried out the prescribed operations and returned to the carriers. The exercises, which spanned three days, were for the most part successful.

"Well, sir—" said Fuchida once everything was over, "were you satisfied?"

"Yes," replied Yamamoto encouragingly. "I'm sure you can do it."

By now, war was virtually unavoidable, and December 8 had already been fixed on for the start of hostilities. In the diary kept by Rear Admiral Ugaki Matome, chief of staff of the Combined Fleet—later published under the title *Sensoroku*—the entry for November 3 contains the following haiku: "Do they come to gaze up / At the fleet in full dress— / This shoal of horse mackerel?" together with the note "Am informed that the date for the signing of an agreement with the army has been fixed for somewhere between the eighth and the tenth. Everything is OK. Die, die all of you! I will die too, for my country!" On November 5, the second day of the Combined Fleet's special exercises, "Imperial HQ Navy Section Order No. 1" was issued by Nagano Osami, chief of the Naval General Staff, in the emperor's name:

To Commander in Chief Yamamoto of the Combined Fleet:

1. In the interest of self-defense and survival, the Empire is due to open hostilities with the United States, Britain, and Holland in the first ten days of December. Preparations are to be completed for the various operations involved.

2. The commander in chief of the Combined Fleet is to carry out preparations for the operations under his command.

3. Details will be as laid down by the chief of the Naval General Staff.

In accordance with this, a long and detailed "Combined Fleet Secret Operational Order No. 1" bearing the same date was issued by Yamamoto. It began: "The Combined Fleet's operations in the war against the United States, Britain, and Holland will be put into effect as detailed in the accompanying booklet." However, although the date and provenance of this document are given in writing as November 5, 1941, on board the flagship *Nagato* in Saeki Bay, it was not until November 8, in Tokyo, that the last amendments were made and steps taken to have it distributed to the units destined to carry out its directives.

On November 6, Yamamoto, accompanied by Chief of Staff Ugaki and other staff officers, left by plane for discussions in Tokyo, and on the afternoon of November 11, having finished his business in the capital—the issuing of Combined Fleet Secret Operational Order No. 1, followed by No. 2, and the signing of an operations agreement with the army at their Military Staff College—he took a transport plane back to Iwakuni, and thence returned to the *Nagato*. Two days later, on November 13, he summoned to Iwakuni naval air base the commanders in chief, chiefs of staff, and senior staff officers of all the fleets except the Hawaii-bound fleet for an explanation and discussion of the operational order. In the course of this conference he informed them that the date more or less decided on for the opening of hostilities was December 8, and that the main task force would assemble in Hitokappu Bay off Etorofu, in the Kuriles, then set sail from Hitokappu in late November and take the northern route to Hawaii. "However," Yamamoto added, "should the negotiations with the U.S. now in progress in Washington be successful, we shall order our forces to withdraw. If such an order is received, you are to turn about and come back to base, even if the attack force has already taken off from the carriers."

This last statement prompted objections. First, Vice Admiral Nagumo, commander of the task force, got to his feet. "Turn back once we'd started out?" he demanded. "It couldn't be done. It would damage morale, and just wouldn't be practicable." Several other commanders backed him up, some of them talking as though to turn back would be a kind of physiological impossibility.

Yamamoto got up with a grim expression. "Just why do you think we spend so much time training military men?" he asked. "If there's any commander here who doesn't think he could come back if he got the order, I forbid him here and now to go; he can hand in his resignation forthwith." No one, it seems, raised further objections.

This conference was the first occasion on which Rear Admiral Inoue, who had switched from command of the Aeronautics Department to commander in chief of the Fourth Fleet, put in an appearance at an operations conference of the Combined Fleet. After the meeting had wound up with the drinking of toasts and the taking of a commemorative photograph, Inoue went into the office of the Iwakuni command to discover Yamamoto sitting all alone on a sofa.

"Yamamoto," said Inoue arousing him from his reverie, "this is one hell of a mess, isn't it? Hasegawa [Kiyoshi] was saying that we'd suffer for this—their industrial capacity is ten times our own. As for the minister, I just can't make him out. Before I left, I went to say good-bye and tell him I was coming to Iwakuni, and I found him all smiles, as though everything in the world was wonderful."

"I'm sure you did," said Yamamoto gloomily. "Shimada lives in a fool's paradise."

Nevertheless, this was the last time, to Inoue's knowledge, that Yamamoto said anything suggesting that he opposed the war. The "imperial decision" had been made (though Yamamoto knew well what the emperor's private feelings were), and from that day on he refrained, publicly at least, from all such pronouncements.

8

On the afternoon of the following day, November 14, the liner *Tatsuta-maru*, on the North American route, arrived in Yokohama carrying a large number of Japanese repatriates from various countries, including between seven and eight hundred who had gone to California as immigrants. Also among them was Rear Admiral Kondo Yasuichiro, who had been naval attaché in England. Kondo was the man who, as senior aide at the Navy Ministry when Yamamoto was viceminister, had been told off by Yamamoto for making too much fuss about the arrival of Prince Takamatsu. He had been in many of the London raids, and knew that England was taking things better than was generally believed in Japan. He could not believe that air raids alone would ever bring England to its knees; invasion was the only possible way to make it capitulate, but he doubted that Germany would have the necessary strength. Moreover, the rate at which British merchant vessels were being knocked out by German submarines was tending to slow down. If Japan's policies were based on wishful thinking—on the idea that England was on the verge of collapse—it would surely suffer for it. He had sent the ministry frequent cables to that effect from London, but the cables coming from his counterpart in Berlin had conveyed a totally different message.

Those responsible at the Navy Ministry and Naval General Staff ought, quite obviously, to have attached equal weight to these two sets of reports. By now, however, they were inclined to give eighty percent credence to the attaché in Berlin and only twenty percent to their man in London, and they had even sent a message to Kondo—much to Kondo's indignation and that of the military attaché, who shared his ideas—asking him to stop sending so many cables in the same vein.

Eventually, the order came for him to return home. Since he had about a week's wait in Lisbon on the way home via America, he sent word asking naval attachés in other European countries to join him there for an exchange of information and discussion on the world situation. On this occasion too, Yokoi Tadao, attaché in Berlin, and Mitsunobu Motohiro, attaché in Rome, both voiced views very different from Kondo's.

He arrived in Japan determined at least to let people know directly what he thought. But even this proved to be harder than he expected. A naval attaché who had lived abroad for nearly three years and been promoted to rear admiral during that time would normally have been welcomed back with a lavish geisha party at a good restaurant, and a meeting would promptly have been held at the ministry to enable him to make his report and answer questions. But with Kondo, at first, there was no move to do anything.

After about four or five days, when it could not decently be postponed any longer, a meeting was held in the minister's office so that he could make his report. For about an hour he talked to those assembled—among them Minister Shimada, Vice-Minister Sawamoto, Chief of the Naval General Staff Nagano, and Vice-Chief Ito—about his experience of the raids in London, the daily lives of the inhabitants, and (with figures and plenty of detail) military questions. He concluded that England would be a tough nut to crack, and begged them to take this into account in drawing up the imperial navy's policies. They heard him out in utter silence, and there were no questions.

Following the meeting, Kondo went into Ito's office and found him sitting silent on a sofa with his head between his hands. After a while, Ito said quite simply and with a look of utter despondency, "I heard you. It's like that, is it?"

By this time, the vessels that were to take part in the attack on Hawaii had already finished putting ashore inflammables, personal possessions, and all unnecessary paraphernalia, and taking on weapons, ammunition, and foodstuffs. The air squadrons that had been training so strenuously at shore bases had all gone on board. Since they were to take the northern route, the flaps and rudders of the planes had all been treated with anti-freeze grease.

In theory, no one below the vice-chief knew exactly where the fleet was heading. The men, who found themselves issued with both winter woollies and tropical wear, could only scratch their heads in bewilderment.

Eventually, the vessels concerned set sail, each separately and in secret, for their rendezvous at Hitokappu Bay. On November 17, the day before they left, the *Nagato* with the C. in C. on board was diverted to Saeki, and Yamamoto took part in a send-off party for C. in C. Nagumo and his men on board the *Akagi*, the flagship of the task force.

The episode is recorded in Ugaki Matome's *Sensoroku*: "C. in C. Yamamoto gave an address on the flight deck. The commander's words sank deep into the hearts of all present. The expressions of the officers and men were grim, yet the general atmosphere was of calm confidence."

As Yamamoto raised his sake cup in a toast, all he said, quite brusquely, was, "I wish you Godspeed and pray for your success." His expression, according to those present, was somber, almost gloomy.

It was at 9:00 A.M. on the morning of November 18 that the *Akagi* left Saeki Bay. As soon as the vessels left harbor, they clamped down completely on radio communications. For the receipt of information and orders, they had to rely henceforth on the Tokyo Signals Unit's No. 1 station; even the *Akagi* severed all contact from its own side with Combined Fleet command and with land.

On the afternoon of the nineteenth, the *Akagi* passed far to the south of Tokyo and three days later, on the morning of the twenty-second, entered Hitokappu Bay. The long, narrow island of Etorofu lies next to Kunashiri in the southern Kuriles, and Hitokappu (Tankan) Bay is situated on its south side, in the very center of the island. Mt. Tankan, which is visible to the west of the bay, was covered from summit to foot in snow.

Some ships had arrived before the *Akagi*, but others came in later. With the arrival of the *Kaga*, which sailed into harbor one day later, loaded with a large number of shallow-depth torpedoes, the main elements of the task force were ready, at anchor in their prearranged positions. Sometime earlier, all transport and communications between the small fishing villages on Etorofu and the outside world had been closed down.

Masuda Shogo, a flight officer on the *Akagi*, wrote in his diary that the waters of the bay were black, and occasional cold rain came interspersed with snow flurries; he felt, he said, like one of the forty-seven masterless samurai in the celebrated *Chushingura* story, gathered on the second floor of the noodles shop before sallying forth to take their revenge.

TEN

1

On the evening of the twenty-fifth at Tokyo Station, Kawai Chiyoko boarded the 10:10 express for Shimonoseki en route for Miyajima, where she was to meet Yamamoto by previous arrangement. She had obtained a berth on the sleeping car—no mean feat in those days. Yamamoto, in civilian clothes, was on hand at Miyajima-guchi Station to meet her. The two of them took the ferry to Itsukushima, an island not far from Iwakuni, off the southwest coast of the mainland; and there they registered at an elegant old inn. They were shown to a pleasant but unpretentious room beside a small red bridge over a stream, and spent the night there alone together.

Yamamoto seems not to have entered his real name and profession in the register—partly, presumably, because he was with a woman, but also because of the need for security at such a time. Some years before, in the register of a hotel at a hot-spring resort in Niigata Prefecture, he had given an address in Nagaoka City and described himself as "Yamamoto Choryo, 52, seaman." He may well have employed the same pseudonym this time; "Choryo," written with two Chinese characters that can also be read "Nagaoka," was a pen name that he was fond of using when he wrote verse.

As a result, no one at the inn paid any particular attention to the latest guest for a while. Even when the proprietor and one or two others realized the truth, they agreed that there must be some very special reason for the commander in chief of the Combined Fleet to come to their island incognito at such a time, and decided to keep the matter strictly to themselves. Someone who went to Yamamoto's room to welcome him to the inn found him sitting opposite Chiyoko in silence, playing a game of flower cards.

It was on the morning of November 26 that the task force under

Nagumo Chuichi weighed anchor and set sail from its rallying point at Etorofu. As the bows of the vessels began slowly to slice through the waves and the anchors rose into sight, still covered with mud from the bottom of Hitokappu Bay, the officers and men on board may well have reflected with emotion that this might be their last sight of Japanese soil.

The task force, thirty-one vessels in all, took up a "ring" formation, spreading out until eventually the distance between the front and the rear was roughly fifty miles. On December 1, the sixth day out of Hitokappu Bay on the way to Hawaii, the task force crossed the International Date Line. At 2:00 P.M. on that day, in the Imperial Palace in Tokyo, a final imperial conference was held, attended by the entire Tojo cabinet, President Hara of the Privy Council, Chief of the Naval General Staff Nagano, and Chief of General Staff Headquarters Sugiyama. Tojo Hideki took charge of the proceedings and outlined his views as prime minister. Nagano Osami, representing the operations staff of the army and navy, reviewed the plan of operations. President Hara of the Privy Council asked a number of questions, to which the government and Imperial Headquarters replied. Thus the formal decision to declare war on the United States, Britain, and Holland was taken. The emperor himself seems to have remained silent throughout the meeting.

On the same day, Yamamoto received a cable from the Navy Ministry summoning him to Tokyo and, leaving his flagship at anchor at Hashirajima in the Inland Sea, took a train for Tokyo via Iwakuni. The following day (December 2), he called at the Navy Ministry for discussions. His business finished, he looked in on Accounting Bureau chief Takei Daisuke in his office. Takei had heard Yamamoto say on several occasions that it would be crazy to embark on a war that could not be won, and was himself of like mind.

"What are you going to do now?" he asked Yamamoto.

"Lock the door," said Yamamoto. Then, when they were alone, he went on. "Considering how I opposed the war, I ought, properly speaking, to have resigned, but it wasn't possible. One thing we could do now is disperse as many submarines as possible around the South Pacific so as to make the other side feel they've been set on by a swarm of hornets. If the hornets around it buzz loudly enough, even a hefty animal like a horse or cow will get worried, at least. American public opinion has always been very changeable, so the only hope is to make them feel as soon as possible that it's no use tackling a swarm of lethal stingers." Events were to show clearly that this "hornet" theory of Yamamoto's represented a gross overestimation of the fighting power of Japan's submarines. He also added, in what seems to have been a hint at the raid on Pearl Harbor, "And the one other thing we can do is take bold risks, resigned from the start to losing up to half our own forces."

At 5:30 P.M. that day, the various units of the Combined Fleet received a message in Yamamoto's name: "*Niitaka-yama nobore* [Climb Mt. Niitaka] 1208."

Most people are now aware that this meant "Operations will commence on the day beginning at 0000 hours, December 8," but the message itself was not, as is generally believed, sent letter by letter in morse. In order to doubly safeguard secrets, a fleet normally had a book of code phrases covering every aspect of operations, and "*Niitaka-yama nobore*," which happened, in much the same way as a telegraphic abbreviation, to signify the opening of hostilities, was sent, syllable by syllable, using a five-digit, random numbers code. However sophisticated the code, of course, any signal sent made it possible to pin down the location of the vessel by means of direction finders. With call signs too, there was always a strong possibility, despite various methods adopted to disguise them, that the other side had realized their significance. Even should the other side be ignorant of the call sign and unable to decipher the code, so long as it caught the signal and worked out the position of the vessel transmitting the signal, it had only to put it through an oscillograph to be able to distinguish between, say, the *Nagato* and *Akagi* by the characteristic shape of the waves put out by their transmitters.

One word, in short, would have been enough to give the task force away, so on every vessel under Nagumo the key of the radio transmitter was sealed or removed so as to keep the ships dumb—but not deaf—as they proceeded toward Hawaii. All they had to rely on was transmissions of the No. 1 station of the Tokyo Signals Unit—a somewhat disquieting state of affairs.

To forestall any failure to catch the signal through some human or technical lapse, the station sent out the same coded message on four different wavelengths simultaneously—three shortwaves in the

10,000, 8,000, and 4,000 kilocycle ranges respectively, and one ultra-longwave signal that could be picked up by a submarine with only its periscope above water.

On the night of December 2, the task force received from Tokyo a short numerical message with the designation "urgent operational message." The codes officer deciphered it, filled in the message "*Niitaka-yama nobore* 1208" on the usual form, and delivered it to the chief codes officer, who passed it on to the communications staff. In this way, C. in C. Nagumo and those under him learned that the die had finally been cast.

The entry for this day in a diary kept by flight commander Masuda of the *Akagi* reads: "Everything is decided; there is neither here nor there, neither sorrow nor rejoicing."

2

Around the time that the task force received and was digesting his message, Yamamoto went privately to call on Chiyoko at Umenojima. Umeryu, as Chiyoko was known there, was out, and a geisha told him that she had gone to a Mr. Yamashita's residence in the company of Mr. Hori. A party was in progress at the home of an influential businessman, with Marquis Kido, Hara Yoshimichi, and Hori Teikichi among the guests and Chiyoko with one other geisha from the Shimbashi geisha quarter in attendance. The day before, Hori had taken up a new post as president of the Uraga Shipyards, and the gathering was probably to celebrate his appointment.

Yamamoto called Yamashita's residence, had Chiyoko brought to the phone, and told her that he had come to Tokyo in strict secrecy and wished to meet Hori sometime that evening. Around eight, Hori, unobtrusively informed by Chiyoko, went to Nakamura-ya. He has related how he found Yamamoto lying on the *tatami*, an unmistakable look of gloom on his face.

"What's up?" Hori began.

"They've finally decided. He flew out on the twenty-sixth, apparently." "He" was General Terauchi Hisaichi, supreme commander of the army. "Okada had a lot to say, it seems, but . . ."

"No use. The fat's in the fire, eh?" said Hori.

"Right. In the fire. Admittedly, arrangements have been made to recall the force should the negotiations get anywhere, but . . ."

"When do you see the emperor?"

"Tomorrow. I leave by plane the morning of the day after tomorrow."

"I'll see you off."

"I'm officially leaving from the minister's official residence, remember."

The next day, December 3, Yamamoto called at the palace for an audience with the emperor, from whom he received the following injunction: "In commanding our forces into action we entrust to you the command of the Combined Fleet. The task facing the Combined Fleet is of the utmost importance, and the whole fate of our nation will depend on the outcome. . . ."

The message that Yamamoto later radioed to the whole fleet quotes his reply, that he "reverently accepted the imperial command and assured His Imperial Majesty that all the officers and men of the Combined Fleet would devote themselves unsparingly to the achievement of their mission, to satisfy His Imperial Majesty's wishes."

One can only speculate as to the complex emotions of the two men —the ruler who did not like war, and the subject who, better than anyone, realized its inadvisability—as they went through this ritual exchange. Yamamoto's reply had been drafted by Chief of Staff Ugaki. The day before, Yamamoto had submitted it to Takei Daisuke, head of the Accounting Bureau, for his opinion.

"I wouldn't have put it like that myself," said Takei.

"Nor would I," replied Yamamoto.

Takei had the impression, he says, that after reading aloud his formal reply, Yamamoto would have liked to tell the emperor something more of his true feelings.

That evening, for the first time in months, Yamamoto put in a sudden appearance at his home in Tokyo. His wife Reiko and the four children were all surprised at this visit. Despite her plump, solid build, Reiko tended to poor health and had been in bed that day, but she got up at once. All six ate dinner together that night, and—an equally rare event—Yamamoto spent the night under the same roof as his wife.

From nine on the morning of the fourth, a send-off party for Yamamoto was held secretly at the official residence of the navy minister. Those present included the emperor's aide Vice Admiral Samejima Tomoshige, Prince Takamatsu, Captain Hosoya (aide to Fleet Admiral

Prince Fushimi), the minister, the chief of the Naval General Staff, and officials from the ministry, as well as Hori Teikichi, representing Yamamoto's personal circle. Hori's attendance had been approved by the navy vice-minister, but the navy tended to be unfriendly toward officers once they had been put on the reserve list, and some eyebrows were raised when he appeared.

Wine specially sent by the emperor was poured, and the company raised their glasses in response to a toast by the minister: "To the success of Commander in Chief Yamamoto's mission!"

Yamamoto was to have left by plane, but this was changed to a 3:00 P.M. limited express, so after the party Yamamoto went to see Chiyoko at Umenojima. That day her friend Toshiko had been to buy some Chinese drawing paper that Yamamoto had asked her to get, and she was surprised on arriving at Umenojima to find Yamamoto himself sitting opposite Chiyoko, eating a late lunch. A vase was full of roses that Yamamoto had bought for Chiyoko.

After a while, Toshiko got a maid to call a taxi, and left with Yamamoto. The latter was wearing a gauze mask—of the kind that the Japanese still sometimes wear when they have a cold—in order to escape notice, and carried a bundle wrapped in purple crepe. From the care with which he held it, refusing to let her carry it, she guessed that it contained an imperial message or the like.

They parted in the Ginza district, and Yamamoto took a passing taxi to Tokyo Station.

Strict restrictions on seeing people off at stations were in force, so Hori Teikichi had gone on to Yokohama Station, where he had got the stationmaster specially to sell him a platform ticket, and was on the platform awaiting the arrival of Yamamoto's train—the "Fuji," bound for Shimonoseki—when it drew in on time at 3:26. Yamamoto was already out on the deck of the observation car. The one-minute stop allowed only a few brief exchanges. No sooner had the train arrived than the bell announcing its departure began to ring. Hori took Yamamoto's hand.

"Well," he said, "look after yourself."

"Thank you," Yamamoto replied. "I don't imagine I shall be back." And as the train began to draw out he called from the deck: "Take care of Chiyoko." The "Chiyoko" in this case was Hori's wife, who happened to be ill.

247

Compared with the time, two years and four months previously, when Yamamoto had left to take up his post as C. in C. of the Combined Fleet, this was a sad little leave-taking. It was the last time that Hori was to see his lifelong friend Isoroku.

The younger brother of Yamamoto's Nagaoka bathhouse friend happened to be on the same train. An army doctor, he was on his way to Peking to serve as head of the army medical corps in northern China. Just past Hamamatsu, Yamamoto came along to his sleeper and chatted with him for more than an hour about Nagaoka and the like, in a manner no different from usual. The media at the time knew nothing, of course, of Pearl Harbor or the war about to begin; and it was only after his arrival in Peking that, finally hearing the news, he realized what had been up.

The "Fuji" arrived at Miyajima-guchi at 6:09 the following morning. Ugaki's *Sensoroku* has an entry that reads: "December 5, Friday; fine. C. in C. comes back on board at 8:30 A.M."

Hearing from Yamamoto about the latter's audience with the emperor, Ugaki wrote in his journal: "His Majesty, I have been told confidentially, has been extremely cheerful ever since he made up his mind that war was inevitable, and at the final imperial conference on the first of this month he immediately gave his consent to the decision. Beneath a wise ruler there are no cowardly troops." Nevertheless, it is doubtful whether the emperor was in fact so "cheerful." *The Hawaiian Operation* compiled by the Defense Agency's War History Office states that in the late afternoon of the day before this last imperial conference, Nagano and Navy Minister Shimada were suddenly summoned to the palace and questioned concerning the navy's attitude. "It seems the arrow is finally to be loosed," said the emperor. "If it is loosed, I am sure that it will mean a protracted war. Can you manage things as planned?" And he asked what would happen if Germany withdrew from the war. This suggests that he was still deeply concerned about the course Japan was taking.

"Everything and everybody is ready," replied Shimada, "and awaiting the imperial command. . . . I believe that we must win this war, whatever hardships we have to put up with. As for Germany, we are not pinning too many hopes on that nation. I am sure we can manage somehow, even if it pulls out of the conflict." Shimada's explanation of this reply was that he was reluctant to disturb the emperor's mind the day before he was due to make his final decision. One wonders, however, why—if Germany was not to be depended on—it was necessary to conclude the Tripartite Pact in the first place. And it seems far more disrespectful to tell the emperor half-truths in case he should be "disturbed." One can understand why Yamamoto dismissed his old classmate Shimada as a "blarney merchant."

There was a considerable gap, too, between the outlook of an Ugaki who could write "Beneath a wise ruler there are no cowardly troops" and a Yamamoto who wrote that "the only possibility left is that the emperor should make a personal decision," and who—as shown by his order that the planes due to attack Pearl Harbor should return to their carriers in the event of an agreement in the Washington talks—continued to cherish some faint hope of evading war right up to the end.

In a letter to Hori Teikichi dated February 6, 1941, Yamamoto had expressed disagreement with the appointment of Ugaki as chief of staff of the Combined Fleet, and he also expressed his views concerning appointments on various other occasions. Yet as fate would have it, he found himself at the crucial time with very few men, even among his trusted subordinates, who really understood how he felt about things. He must, secretly, have felt forlorn; on the same day that he got back to the *Nagato* from Tokyo, he wrote a letter to Chiyoko:

> I was disappointed that this time I had only three days, and was so busy into the bargain that I couldn't see much of you or even stay one night. Forgive me! Even so, I'm happy that we could meet every day, if only for a brief while. I hoped when I left to be able to do it quietly, in a settled frame of mind, and I was sorry that we couldn't even go together as far as Owari-cho. . . . Are the roses completely out by now? By the time the first petal falls . . .
>
> Take care of yourself, and my regards to everybody. Hurry up and send the photo. Bye-bye.

The last few lines sound more like a lovelorn schoolboy than a full admiral; they show how strong must have been the urge to unburden his loneliness, without worrying about appearances, to this woman whom he had known for so long.

Steaming out from the Kuriles, the Nagumo fleet had set its course at 97° and proceeded more or less due east; at longitude 165° west and latitude 43° north, it changed its course to 145° and was now advancing on Hawaii from the north in what, seen on the charts, was a precipitous downward swoop. The crews were chilled to the bone by successive days of heavy mist without a glimpse of the sun, but on December 5 they left the cold, dark waters of the northern Pacific for calmer seas and gradually rising temperatures. One of the innumerable sources of worry where the proposed raid was concerned, affecting the task force command, Combined Fleet headquarters in the Inland Sea, and the Naval General Staff in Tokyo alike, was the question of the weather. Statistics for the previous ten years showed that December in northern Pacific waters, through which the force was obliged to sail, offered only seven days of calm as against twenty-four days of stormy weather. Possibilities for refueling smoothly at sea were rated at a fifty-fifty chance by Tomioka, head of an operations section at the Naval General Staff. Fortunately, the fleet was accompanied on its advance eastward by a high pressure front that came bulging out over the ocean from Siberia, and was little troubled by rough seas until December 3. "A high pressure front from Heaven!" remarked Yamamoto more than once as he eyed weather conditions.

On December 6 the *Toho-maru*, *Toei-maru*, and *Nippon-maru* of the Second Supply Unit, their mission completed, signaled "We pray for your success," and escorted by the destroyer *Kasumi* turned westward and set sail for home.

Another worry was the possibility of encountering vessels of other nations. One reason why the northerly route had been chosen despite the difficulty of refueling at sea was that American patrol planes from Oahu were not making flights over the northern part of the island, which thus offered a convenient hole in the net. At the beginning of the year, when it seemed that word of the Hawaiian operation had leaked to the Americans, American patrols had started keeping a watch on the whole periphery of Oahu, but in April or May, for some unexplained reason, they relaxed their watch over the northern half. (An extremely cynical observer might jump to the conclusion that this was a trap devised by America in order to lure on the Japanese fleet; but this would be absurd.)

Another reason was that this route was the farthest from those normally followed by merchant vessels in the Pacific. Even so, the Naval General Staff still considered that there was a fifty-fifty chance of their being discovered. If this should happen, the point of the raid would be lost and there was even a possibility that a free-for-all on the high seas would occur before "X" Day, with the task force on the defensive.

Yamamoto's orders for such an eventuality were fairly strict: only the unit subjected to attack would be allowed to counterattack; other units must not allow themselves to be drawn into the hostilities. In fact, on December 6 the Nagumo force did catch sight of one passing vessel of a third nation. Those in command of the task force watched the progress of the ship in question, a merchantman, with an extraordinary degree of tension. Had it shown any signs of radioing a report on the movements of the task force to anyone else, it would probably have found itself at the bottom of the sea within a few minutes. The vessel, however, must have thought that the Nagumo force was a fleet engaged in exercises—or possibly it made a correct guess as to its purpose and was too scared to signal its find—for it soon disappeared from sight without anything happening.

The third source of worry was whether the main body of the American fleet would, in fact, be at anchor in Pearl Harbor on "X" Day, December 8. The only guarantee here was that it was customary for the American fleet to be in harbor from Saturday through Sunday for rest and recuperation. Everything depended here on the other side—which is the main reason why critics of the operation have labeled it "a gamble." Information about the American fleet was absolutely essential, and informants' reports were reaching the Nagumo fleet every day from the Japanese consulate in Honolulu via Tokyo.

The leading figure among Japanese spies in Honolulu was a Foreign Ministry clerk called Morimura Tadashi. Morimura, whose real name was Yoshikawa Takeo, had been an ensign in the navy, but had quit the service on account of illness and had been taking things easy at his home in Matsuyama when he was summoned to Tokyo to serve as a part-time employee in the Third Division (in charge of intelligence) of the Naval General Staff. In March of that year, his name changed to Morimura Tadashi, he had been "posted" to the consulate in Hawaii.

Yoshikawa has published his own detailed account of his espionage activities. They involved, among other things, dish-washing at officers' clubs in the guise of an unemployed Filipino; taking a sightseeing flight over the island with a geisha in order to get a look at Pearl Harbor from the air; and lurking hidden in fields of sugarcane. As a result, the information he sent was highly accurate, and included the precise positions, and methods of anchorage, of American vessels within the harbor. Besides these reports from "Morimura" which came through the No. 1 station of the Tokyo Signals Unit, the task force command was in constant receipt of reports direct from private commercial stations in Honolulu.

The personal advertisements that were broadcast after dinner often included such apparently harmless messages as "lost German police dog with name Mayer. . . ." or "Chinese rug, almost new. . . ." The German dogs, Chinese rugs, and so on were references to aircraft carriers and warships in Pearl Harbor, and the broadcasts were arranged and paid for by the consul general in Honolulu.

On December 7, the *Kyokuto-maru*, *Tenyo-maru*, *Kokuyo-maru*, and *Shinkoku-maru*—the First Supply Unit—took leave of the fleet, having fulfilled their mission where the voyage out was concerned. The other vessels of the task force, which had been matching their pace to the leisurely progress of the tankers, now increased speed. They changed course to due south, and had switched to readiness "Condition One" and battle rations when another report came from Hawaii via Tokyo. "*Nevada* and *Oklahoma* entered harbor on fifth," it began; "*Lexington* and five heavy cruisers have left harbor. Vessels now at anchor in Pearl Harbor consist of eight battleships and two heavy cruisers. A-zone: battleships *Pennsylvania*, *Arizona*, *California*, *Tennessee*. . . ." This made it more or less certain that on "X" Day all the battleships of the U.S. Pacific Fleet would be in Pearl Harbor.

The *Lexington*'s leaving harbor, however, also made it certain that not a single aircraft carrier would be left at anchor—to the obvious frustration of those crews who were to have been responsible for attacking the carriers. Of more practical importance, though, was the doubt this raised: was it mere coincidence that had taken both American carriers, the *Lexington* and the *Enterprise*, out of harbor at the same time, in defiance of normal custom at weekends?

Nevertheless, the worries facing the Japanese navy melted away one after the other in a way that, after the event, gave rise to talk of "divine aid." Whether it was divine aid or not would require more careful analysis, but the fact remains that—as Yamamoto, with his love of gambling, would have put it—Japan's "luck was in" in every respect. A message from the commander in chief was sent from the flagship of the Combined Fleet. "The fate of the Empire rests on this enterprise," it said. "Every man must devote himself totally to the task in hand." The message is very similar to one issued in the name of Admiral Togo at the time of the Battle of the Japan Sea. According to administrative staff officer Watanabe, the idea for it occurred to Chief of Staff Ugaki while he was in the toilet; he insisted, Watanabe says, that his predecessor had said all that it was possible to say in such circumstances.

Next, a "DG" signal flag was raised on the mast of the task force flagship. Its meaning was the same as the "Z" flag flown on the *Mikasa* thirty-six years previously, and Vice Admiral Nagumo's message was precisely the same as that issued at the time of the Battle of the Japan Sea: "The future of the Empire depends on this battle. All men must give their utmost."

Nagumo had graduated from the Naval Academy four years after Yamamoto. Originally a torpedo expert, he had little experience in the field of aviation. In a sense, it was perhaps expecting too much of his capacities to put him, as commander of the First Air Fleet, in command of the task force due to attack Hawaii. During his days as a section chief of the Naval General Staff, he had come into collision with Inoue Shigeyoshi of the Naval Affairs Bureau concerning the revision of Naval General Staff orders. As we have seen earlier, he had called Inoue a fool and more or less threatened him with a knife in the belly. Such big talk, however, was mere bravado, and Nagumo was essentially weak by nature.

It was only in April that year that he had been put in charge of the First Air Fleet; a mere eight months later, he found himself involved in the Hawaiian operation in a position of immense responsibility. The strain kept him awake at nights, and he would often summon his subordinates to his cabin in the small hours in order to ask their opinion about some trifling matter that was bothering him.

One of those who suffered through Nagumo's nervousness was Fuchida, who was awakened in the middle of the night by an orderly who announced that the C. in C. wished to see him. Entering the dimly lit commander's cabin, he was told by Nagumo, who seemed to be in an acute state of anxiety, that there were indications that the destroyer at the rear was being trailed by an American submarine. What did he think they should do?

"If it was true," Fuchida complains irritably, "he should have taken appropriate measures. One could understand if he'd consulted the chief of staff, but for a C. in C. to summon his flight commander and ask him a thing like that was plain stupid. . . ."

According to Chief of Staff Kusaka in his work *Combined Fleet*, Nagumo said to him: "What about it, Kusaka?—this is a fine job I've taken on, isn't it? I should've stood up for myself, and refused on the spot. As it is, I'm here, but I wonder whether I can manage. What do you think?"

It was not until later that he became overconfident; at the period in question, Nagumo was still the man who reportedly went into battle reluctantly and timidly, as one about to "tread on the tiger's tail."

4

Nevertheless, on the night of the seventh, Nagumo and the other officers and men of the task force acquired that special type of calm that so often precedes a major enterprise. The weather was rather cloudy, and a strong northeast wind was blowing. As the fleet sped southward beneath the fitful light of the moon breaking through the clouds, the aircraft carriers listed to an angle of fifteen degrees. Every time the flight deck lurched, the tires of the planes with their full tanks and their excess loads of bombs bulged almost to bursting point. Scrawled in chalk on a bomb already loaded onto one of the planes were the words "First bomb in the war on America."

The final intelligence cabled from Tokyo contained the following news: "*Utah* and seaplane tender entered harbor at dusk on fifth. Vessels at anchor on sixth included nine battleships, three light cruisers, three seaplane tenders, and seventeen destroyers. In dock, four light cruisers and two destroyers. All heavy cruisers and aircraft carriers are out. No signs of anything unusual in fleet. Telephone communication with Japanese resident on Oahu between 1330 and 1400 today December 7 confirmed all normal, no blackout. Imperial HQ Navy Section convinced operation will succeed." The final sentence was added by Tomioka Sadatoshi to bolster the morale of the officers and men on the eve of war.

It was 12:40 A.M. on December 8 (Japan time) when the first attack force took up its stations on the *Akagi*. Throughout the voyage, the task force had stuck to Tokyo time, without altering its clocks, and the daily lives of the crews had gradually got out of phase. Thus it was still the middle of the night according to the clocks when the crews had their breakfast of "red rice" with *okashiratsuki* (sea bream cooked with the head and tail on) and *kachiguri* ("victory chestnuts") and with a satisfying sense of finality went up on deck.

Dawn was near on the seas to the north of Hawaii as the order went out for all planes to take off, and their propellers began to turn in unison. The order came at 1:30 A.M. The six aircraft carriers turned into the wind. As the takeoff controllers waved their green lamps, the first plane on each carrier slipped its rings and took off from the flight deck with a blast of hot air that beat down on the prostrate mechanics.

The first to leave the *Akagi* was a "Zero," piloted by Itaya Shigeru, commander of the first wave. His and all the other aircraft were so overloaded at takeoff that on leaving the end of the flight deck they sank perceptibly, as though they might drop into the sea, before beginning to climb. Those left behind on the ships watched them go, waving their caps and with tears in their eyes. The first attack force, made up of a total of 183 aircraft—189, less six that could not take off because of accidents or engine trouble—took off from six aircraft carriers in the space of fifteen minutes. Commanding officer Fuchida's plane had distinctive yellow and red markings on the tail. Thirty minutes after takeoff, as the 183 planes were switching off their formation lights, a great sun began to show over the eastern horizon. The aircraft flew on toward Pearl Harbor, some two hundred miles south.

After the intensive training they had undergone in Kagoshima Bay since summer, Fuchida had few worries concerning the technical prowess of his team. What concerned him more was to observe Yamamoto's strict instructions as to the timing of the attack—that the first bomb should be dropped at precisely 3:30, thirty minutes after Japan's final ultimatum was due to be handed to the American government in Washington. The first plane to arrive over Pearl Harbor was a reconnaissance seaplane from the *Chikuma*, a cruiser sent on ahead of the task force. About an hour and a half after takeoff, as Fuchida was peering ahead for the first signs of the island of Oahu, his radio operator received a report from the *Chikuma*'s seaplane.

Reporting on the vessels at anchor in Pearl Harbor and their disposition, it also gave such meteorological details as "wind direction 80°, speed forty-three feet, seventy percent cloud, cloud altitude 5,500 feet." Shortly afterward, through a break in the clouds, Fuchida saw, directly below, a long line of white breakers—Kahuku Point, at the northern extremity of Oahu. He made a right turn.

One of his most important duties as commander of the force was to decide at this point whether to make a surprise attack or a frontal assault. If the other side still suspected nothing and a surprise attack was possible, then the torpedo bombers were first of all to swoop down to an altitude of thirty feet and fire torpedoes at the anchored American fleet. If the other side were ready and waiting for them, so that a frontal assault became necessary, Lieutenant Commander Takahashi's dive-bombers were to take the lead and put aircraft on the ground and anti-aircraft batteries out of action before the other units moved in.

With a frontal assault, smoke from the explosions might obscure the vessels in the harbor, making it difficult for the torpedo bombers and horizontal bombers to operate. A surprise attack was therefore preferable, if at all possible.

The signal was to be given with Fuchida's Verey pistol: one shot for a surprise attack, two for a frontal assault. As he led the entire force over to the west coast of the island, he called over the tube to his pilot in the front seat, Lieutenant Matsuzaki:

"Matsuzaki, keep a close watch on the sky over Pearl Harbor, to the left. Enemy fighters might appear."

The sky was clear over Pearl Harbor, with haze rising over the naval harbor—a peaceful Sunday morning scene. Fuchida kept watch with binoculars on the scene over ten thousand feet below, but all he could see were the masts of first one, then another, then another American warship; neither on the ships themselves nor on land were there any signs of alertness. Fuchida grinned. "Right—a surprise attack it is!" He took the pistol in his right hand, held it high above his head, and with a single shot gave the order. It was nine minutes past three.

At this point, the various squadrons should have spread out from the normal formation in which they had been flying and taken up battle formation so as to be in position for the order to attack. Lieutenant Commander Murata's torpedo squadron got the signal and began to descend. Takahashi's dive-bombing squadron also got the signal and began to climb. They were to climb to thirteen thousand feet in

readiness for their subsequent swift descent. However, the escort fighters led by Lieutenant Commander Itaya failed to see the signal; the "Zeros," being faster than the other planes, found it hard to fly at the 125 knots of the other formations, and for this reason—as well as to keep a lookout—they had been sweeping the sky from right to left and flying around the others from front to back.

It happened that just at the time of the signal the fighters were two or three miles away from and almost two thousand feet higher than Fuchida's plane. "What the hell are they playing at?" Fuchida thought to himself. He fired another shot, for the fighters' benefit. Seeing the black trail of smoke in the air, the Itaya squadron finally realized that they were to take up their positions.

Unfortunately, however, Takahashi of the dive-bombing squadron —as Fuchida puts it, "that fool Takahashi, he was a bit soft in the head"—promptly saw this as the second of two shots intended to signal a frontal assault. Assuming that he had thereby been singled out to lead the attack, Takahashi, without climbing to the predetermined height, abruptly led the fifty-odd bombers under his command into a dive. This seems in turn to have flustered Murata of the torpedo squadron. Determined, it seems, not to wait till the dive-bombers got in the way, he, too, hurriedly led the carrier-based attack planes under his command in swooping down to a low altitude. Seeing them go, Fuchida was obliged at 3:19—five minutes before schedule—to turn to his radio operator in the back seat and give the order "*To-renso.*"

"*To-renso,*" a repetition of the single syllable *to*, was the signal for the whole force to launch its attack. Grasping the key of his communications panel, the operator began to tap out the same syllable over and over again: *to, to, to, to, to, to.* . . .

Thus at 3:25 A.M. on December 8, Japan time, with the first 550-pound bomb dropped on Wheeler Field by Takahashi's dive-bombers, the one-sided Hawaiian battle began.

5

On board the flagship *Nagato* in the anchorage at Hashirajima, the evening of December 7 found Yamamoto, as usual, playing *shogi* with staff officer Watanabe. These games between Yamamoto and Watanabe usually came to an end after Yamamoto had won four times in succession, but very occasionally Watanabe instead would wi

several games in a row. This invariably happened when a low-pressure front was approaching; possibly Yamamoto was the type that is allergic to changes in the weather. That particular evening, however, it was fine, and Yamamoto won. They finished playing rather earlier than usual, then Yamamoto and his staff officers bathed and retired temporarily to their own cabins.

Some of them slept for two or three hours, others could not sleep at all, but not long after midnight most of the staff officers were once again assembled in small groups in the operations room. The officer on duty was air "B" staff officer Sasaki Akira.

The four walls of the operations room were plastered with large maps of the entire Pacific area and charts of various zones of Southeast Asian waters. On the table were a large globe and still more charts, and on a smaller table files of operational orders and radio messages.

Yamamoto was sitting quite still, eyes shut, in a folding chair in front of the big table at the back.

News came in of the army's landing at Kota Bharu, then of the successful landing at Bataan in the Philippines. There followed a long and trying period of waiting. Time seemed to drag interminably. An uneasy silence prevailed in the operations room. No one spoke; the only sounds were the rustle of messages being flipped over in their files and the occasional scratching of a pencil.

Across the passage lay the radio room, from which a cord led to a receiver standing on the table in the operations room, so that those present could hear directly any messages that came in. Eventually, senior staff officer Kuroshima said in a quiet voice, "It should begin any moment now."

He glanced up at the clock on the bulkhead, and a stir ran through the room. At that moment, the radio operator came running in and shouted at the staff officer on duty: "Sir—the repeated *to* signal!"

Sasaki turned to the commander in chief. "As you hear, sir," he reported. "The message was sent at 0319 hours."

Yamamoto opened his eyes wide and nodded. His mouth turned down grimly at the corners. "Did you get that message direct from the plane?" he asked the operator. The *Nagato*'s radio room had, in fact, received the "*to, to, to, to* . . ." direct from the skies over Oahu.

"Direct reception?" said Ugaki. "Good work!" The young operator looked pleased, saluted, and rushed out of the room again.

There followed a succession of reports from the attacking units:
"Surprise attack successful."
"Enemy warships torpedoed; outstanding results."
"Hickam Field attacked; outstanding results."

At the same time, the radio in the operations room was picking up directly a great number of uncoded radio messages from the American side. From what Ugaki says in his *Sensoroku*, the messages tended to be broken and jerky: "SOS—attacked by Jap bombers here. . . ." or "Oahu attacked by Jap dive-bombers from carrier. . . ." When Yamamoto heard one of them—"Jap—this is the real thing"—a brief grin seemed to pass over his face.

Exactly one hour after the first assault, the second attack force led by Lieutenant Commander Shimazaki Shigekazu, 170 planes in all, swept into the skies over Pearl Harbor and also achieved considerable results before withdrawing. By the time dawn broke over Hiroshima Bay, the number of messages being received in the operations room of the *Nagato* was dwindling steadily.

From any point of view, the raid had been an outstanding success, and the staff officers could not conceal their jubilation; Yamamoto alone, apparently, remained sunk in apparent depression. The day was fine, calm, and warm. That morning the commander in chief and his officers sat down to breakfast together. There was laughter among the staff officers, and an unusual amount of talk. But as he was leaving the table at the end of the meal, Yamamoto called Fujii Shigeru to his side.

"As you know," he said, "the government says that it cut the time between handing over the final ultimatum and launching the attack to thirty minutes. I suppose the Foreign Ministry's arrangements are all right, are they? From the cables that have come in so far, it looks as though the attack force has kept its side of the bargain. But there'd be trouble if someone slipped up and people said it was a sneak attack. There's no hurry, but bear it in mind, would you, and make a thorough check."

"I'm sure it's all right," Fujii replied. "But I'll check carefully."

At 8:00 A.M., the commanders and chiefs of staff of the units remaining in Hashirajima assembled on board the *Nagato* for an account of the situation and an assessment of results achieved. Taken together, the reports so far received seemed to suggest that all the warships at anchor in Pearl Harbor had been put out of action. However, to allow for cases where the same damage had been sighted and reported by more than one plane, the staff officers present reduced the numbers to what seemed a more probable figure and asked Yamamoto for his opinion. Yamamoto advised them to take a still more conservative view of the losses inflicted. They accordingly cut the figure to approximately sixty percent; the result was the announcement made by Imperial Headquarters Navy Section at 8:45 that evening: "Two battleships sunk; four battleships seriously damaged; approximately four large cruisers seriously damaged. The above confirmed."

In fact, four American battleships had been sunk and three seriously damaged, while another had suffered medium damage, and the main strength of the Pacific Fleet in Pearl Harbor had been wiped out. Thus on December 18, ten days later, Imperial Headquarters issued a supplementary announcement concerning losses inflicted in the Hawaiian operation. At this stage, announcements by Imperial Headquarters Navy Section were believed even on the American side.

NHK's Station One began its broadcasting on December 8 with a special news bulletin at 6:00 A.M. Over and over again the joint communiqué by the navy and army sections of Imperial Headquarters was repeated: "Before dawn today, December 8, the imperial army and navy entered upon a state of hostilities with British and American forces in the West Pacific."

At 11:45, the Imperial Rescript declaring war was broadcast, and at 1:00 P.M. came the first report on hostilities from the navy, a four-item announcement beginning: "Before dawn on December 8 the imperial navy carried out a crippling raid on U.S. naval and air forces in the Hawaii area. . . ."

The man handling the morning news broadcasts that day was Tateno Morio, whose name became well known when he took charge of the imperial broadcast announcing the end of the war on August 15, 1945. So far as he remembers, the news that day did not mention the name of the commander in chief of the Combined Fleet. Nor is Yamamoto's name to be found in the announcement by Imperial Headquarters. However, no attempt had been made to conceal the fact that he was commander, and most Japanese were aware of it. There is little doubt, indeed, that both the imperial navy itself and the name of Yamamoto suddenly acquired a new importance in the minds of the public on that day.

The vast majority of the public heard the news broadcast with an extraordinary degree of excitement and emotion. It was the same with most intellectuals, too; writers such as Tokuda Shusei, Takamura Kotaro, Mushanokoji Saneatsu, Nagayo Yoshiro, Muro Saisei, Ito Shizuo, and Ito Sei—men generally considered to be the farthest removed from run-of-the-mill "patriots"—all expressed emotion in terms not necessarily dictated by mere timeserving. Some, admittedly, adopted an attitude of more or less complete indifference—among them Nagai Kafu, who wrote in his *Danchotei Nichijo*: "December 8. Drafted first installment of novel *Ukishizumi*. At dusk went as far as Doshubashi. Newspaper extras announcing war between Japan and the United States. Eating in a restaurant in Ginza on my way home when blackout announced and all street lamps and shop signs went out one after the other; but streetcars and automobiles kept their lights on. Scramble among passengers to get on streetcar for Roppongi; among them a patriot, who made a speech in a shrill voice."

An entry for December 11 in the same work includes the following passage: ". . . in the afternoon went to Asakusa to see how things were there. The Rokku was as crowded as ever, and talk in the green room of the Opera-kan went as usual, with absolutely no signs of apprehension or intense excitement. To a nervous person like myself, the inhabitants of Asakusa are the personification of imperturbability. . . ."

In its recorded music program on December 8, NHK broadcast Beethoven's Fifth Symphony, interspersing it with repeated announcements proclaiming, "The imperial navy has finally gone into action!" Such announcements must have been particularly repugnant to men like Kafu; yet the choice of music, and the use of the expression "finally," might suggest that at NHK someone, at least, had a fair idea of the anguish with which the navy had embarked on hostilities with the United States.

6

Seeing that the war was going more or less as planned, the main body of the fleet in the Inland Sea severed the telephone link that had connected it, via Kure, with Tokyo and on the afternoon of the eighth sailed out from its anchorage at Hashirajima.

After dark that day, the fleet of some thirty vessels—the flagship

Nagato followed by battleships *Mutsu*, *Fuso*, *Yamashiro*, *Ise*, and *Hyuga*, the carrier *Hosho*, and a group of destroyers of the Fourth Destroyer Squadron—passed through the east mine-free fairway of Bungo Channel and sailed south with the ostensible aim of picking up and protecting the task force.

In practice, it was to prove a rather odd voyage. The great fleet wasted a large deal of precious fuel in advancing as far as the line of the Bonins, during which time the *Hosho* and three destroyers became temporarily separated from the rest, and there was a near miss with an American submarine; then finally, without having achieved anything in particular, it returned to its anchorage in the Inland Sea on the morning of the fifth day, December 13.

It seems that the talk of picking up and giving protection to the task force was merely a cover; what was really at stake was, to put it nicely, morale—or, to put it more bluntly, medals. For Yamamoto and his staff officers, merely to be at Hashirajima constituted a "Distinguished Service," but for ordinary crew members to hang around in the Inland Sea without sailing into action at all meant no merit at all. Whoever took the first initiative, it seems that this was another case where Yamamoto's heart—his concern for his men—got the better of his head.

Around the time that the main force left Hashirajima, Nagumo's task force had completed its attack on Hawaii and was already on the way home. The task with which Fuchida had been entrusted was to make it impossible for the U.S. Pacific Fleet to leave Pearl Harbor for six months, by which time Japan hoped to have secured for itself oil in Southeast Asia, and it was his duty to take note with his own eyes of the overall results achieved by the attack. Even after most of the aircraft of the first and second attack forces had returned to their carriers, he remained in the sky over Oahu, slipping back and forth behind the clouds in his lone plane, observing what was happening below.

The pall of black smoke hanging over everything made it difficult to obtain a precise picture, but the only ship that had quite obviously sunk was one battleship of the *Arizona* class; the rest seemed to be staying afloat at least, though the shallowness of the water made it difficult to tell whether a vessel was still in fact afloat or not.

Fuchida was in constant apprehension lest he encounter American fighters, which would have meant the end for him, but none appeared.

His aircraft had a large hole in the rear of the fuselage caused by shrapnel from ground fire, and two-thirds of the control cable had been torn off, but he hung on for some three hours in the sky over Pearl Harbor, finally deciding that four battleships had in fact been sunk and four severely damaged. Then, taking with him the remaining fighters from the second wave of attackers, he returned to the carrier *Akagi*.

On his return, air staff officer Genda and those of Fuchida's subordinates who had got back before him rushed up and started to report to or question him, but an immediate summons from the bridge gave him no time to reply. On the bridge, he found C. in C. Nagumo waiting impatiently, and was met with a volley of questions. How did things go? Did he encounter any fighters? Did he think the enemy's planes had the ability to make a counterattack?

Fuchida, as flight commander on the *Akagi*, felt that his first report should go to the captain of that vessel, but the captain was motioning with his eyes in Nagumo's direction, so he turned to the latter and gave his account.

Four battleships had been sunk and four more severely damaged at the very least; it seemed likely that these eight vessels would be out of action for at least six months. They had missed the aircraft carriers, so the possibility of an enemy counterattack should not be ruled out, but the ground bases on Oahu—though raging fires in the hangars made it difficult to tell—would seem to have lost most of their effectiveness, since he had not encountered a single fighter during the three hours he had been circling the area.

Nagumo was so gratified by this that he seemed to have very little interest in anything further.

"Supposing we were to launch another attack," Chief of Staff Kusaka asked Fuchida, "—what do you think its objectives should be?"

"The enemy's battleships may have been sunk," replied Fuchida, "but they're only resting on the shallow bed of the bay, and I'm sure they'll start work salvaging them immediately. I think our next objectives should be arsenals, the American forces' repair facilities, and heavy-oil tanks."

This view tallies closely with that of someone associated with the the U.S. navy who came to Japan after the war: "I don't understand," he said, "why Japan didn't take the opportunity to destroy military factories and fuel tanks on Hawaii. The Pearl Harbor base, being on a remote island, always had difficulty with supplies of oil and other materials. Because those facilities were left intact, America was able to make an extremely swift recovery."

Yamamoto, the staff officers of the Combined Fleet, and the Nagumo fleet itself were all resigned at the outset to losing at least half the carriers taking part in the Hawaiian operation. But in fact they had lost a mere twenty-nine aircraft with fifty-five men on board; the fleet itself had suffered not so much as a scratch. If the six carriers were brought as close to Oahu as possible without running them aground and a fresh attack launched, the fighters would be able to protect both attacking units and carriers at the same time, and the U.S. Pacific Fleet could be more or less put out of action.

Fuchida put forward this suggestion himself, but neither the C. in C. nor the chief of staff gave any clear answer. They thanked him for his good work, and told him to take a rest, whereupon he left the bridge.

Rear Admiral Yamaguchi, commander of the Second Carrier Division, who was on board the *Hiryu*, sent a signal saying, "Have completed preparations for second attack." This was of course an indirect invitation to action, and Fuchida likewise assumed automatically that the order would be given for a second attack. But though he had taken the necessary steps and was eating in the wardroom, an order came over the shipboard intercom: "All aircraft except fighters to be stowed in hangars." Thinking this odd, he went up on deck and looked at the flag. The fleet was already headed north. Once again, he relates, he thought, "What the hell are they playing at?"

For the immediate cause of this failure to act one would probably have to look to Nagumo's and Kusaka's personalities. If one probes a little deeper, however, the reason would seem to lie, rather, in the nature of the Japanese navy as a whole. There was a tendency among experienced navy men, especially those serving with the fleet—a tendency, in fact, that may not have been limited to Japan alone—to harbor a dislike, albeit unconscious, for action on land and action against fuel supplies. There was a tendency, too, to dislike approaching land except when entering harbor. The navy's fighting spirit was prone to be directed, to a disproportionate degree, against the enemy fleet alone. Just as in his message to the fleet Ugaki could not get away from Admiral Togo's words, so the ghost of the man who destroyed the Russian fleet in the Battle of the Japan Sea always stood before him, blocking his way. Even Yamamoto was not necessarily an exception to the rule, since it was he, ultimately, who rejected the Combined Fleet command's proposal that a second attack on Hawaii should be ordered.

A furious argument, in fact, developed among the staff officers on the *Nagato* concerning the news that the Nagumo force was on its way home. Unexpectedly great results had been achieved, and the enemy was in confusion. Since the operation had aimed at "annihilation," and at determining the outcome "on the first day," it seemed reasonable to follow up the first attack in order to achieve still more decisive results. Almost all the staff officers with the exception of air staff officer Sasaki were unanimous in deciding to propose a second attack.

"No, wait," Yamamoto is said to have told them. "It would be fine, of course, if it were successful. But even a burglar hesitates to go back for more. I'd rather leave it to the commander of the task force. A man who wants to do a thing," he went on, "will do it without being told. He isn't going to do it just because he's prodded from a distance. I imagine Nagumo doesn't want to."

The proposal for a second attack, in short, was not adopted. One explanation, of course, is that Yamamoto—as his devoted staff officers would often relate in tones of reverence in later days—was very sensitive to the psychology of his subordinates in the battle line. There were two targets for a second attack: the ground facilities on Hawaii and the aircraft carriers that escaped destruction because their whereabouts was not known. The latter were, without doubt, dangerous to have around, but it is highly unlikely that Yamamoto, who had been thinking in terms of "annihilation," should have feared them at this stage. However, at least where the former objective was concerned—which involved action against oil storage tanks—one suspects that he was not as concerned with it as he might have been. Thus the orders radioed from Combined Fleet command said merely: "On the way home the task force, if circumstances permit, is to raid Midway and try to put it out of action once and for all."

This order was ignored by the Nagumo fleet on the grounds of bad weather. A separate force charged with the task of putting Midway out of action and consisting of the destroyers *Ushio* and *Sazanami* had left Tateyama, quite independently of the Pearl Harbor task force, on November 28, and was proceeding to the attack; nor was there any objective at the time requiring a force larger than that to dispose of it thoroughly. According to Yoshida Toshio, a former intelligence officer on the Naval General Staff, Nagumo was incensed by the signal. "It's like asking a junior sumo wrestler who's just beaten a grand champion if he'd mind buying some vegetables for dinner on the way home," he said.

Another participant in the Hawaiian operation beside Nagumo's task force was a group of submarines that had been dispatched in advance to take up secret stations in the vicinity of Oahu by the evening of the seventh. Amongst these, the five midget submarines which were released from the *I-16* and four similar submarines were to attract a particular degree of attention in countries on both sides. The nine men who were killed in them were awarded a special promotion of two ranks, their names being officially announced by the Navy Ministry on March 6 the following year.

The subject of these midget submarines has been dealt with in a literary work entitled *Navy* by Iwata Toyoo, published during the war, and in the war memoirs of Sakamaki Kazuo, whose midget submarine ran ashore on Oahu owing to gyroscope failure, and who thus became the first Japanese prisoner of war. At first, Yamamoto would not sanction their use at Hawaii on the grounds that they were not recoverable. However, at the earnest request of the crews themselves, the submarines were modified in order to increase their range, thus making recovery at least a theoretical possibility, whereupon it was decided to use them. In fact, however, none of the five returned to their parent submarines, and their mission achieved almost no practical results. When Yamamoto heard that none of their crews had come back he reportedly looked grave and said: "I would never have sent them if I'd known we'd achieve so much with air units alone."

7

On December 9, on board the *Nagato* sailing south off the coast of Shikoku, Yamamoto heard the news of the British and American declarations of war against Japan. On the afternoon of the same day, the *Nagato* command received a report saying that a submarine had sighted two British warships sailing north at a speed of fourteen knots in the South China Sea at a point midway between the islands of Poulo Condore and Anambas.

Once again the atmosphere in the operations room was tense with excitement. It had been known for some time that the two battleships that England had dispatched to the Far East were operating from Singapore, but the Naval General Staff and the fleet itself were both still firmly wedded to the traditional idea that no decisive results could be achieved against battleships in battle order on the high seas unless other battleships were pitted against them. Yamamoto, however, took the view that—to take a metaphor from chess—it was not necessary to be drawn into using one's own queen just because the enemy used his; having taken on America and England, Japan could not afford such extravagance: it must learn instead to use its pawns. And he planned to take on the two vessels using only air units from land bases.

Thus the battle against the two ships became a chance to put to the test Yamamoto's theories on the obsolescence of large battleships and the need to give priority to aircraft. A squadron of thirty type-96 and type-1 land-based attack planes took off from an airfield near Saigon loaded with 1,100-pound bombs (no torpedoes were available in time), but they were unable to spot the enemy, and the attack was called off when night fell. On the morning of the next day, the tenth, as the *Nagato* and other vessels of the fleet were passing between Hahajima and Kita-Iwojima in the Bonins, another attack force of eighty-four planes took off from bases in south Indochina. It would be some time before the enemy could be spotted again and an attack launched, and the staff officers in the *Nagato*'s operations room were speculating idly on the outcome when Yamamoto turned to air "A" staff officer Miwa Yoshitake—a subordinate of many years and a veteran aviator—and said, "How about it? Do you think we can sink both the *Renown* and the *King George V*? Personally, I think we can sink the *Renown*, but as for the *King George V*, I'd say we should be content if we can badly damage it." (The two battleships of the British Far Eastern Fleet were, in fact, the *Repulse* and the *Prince of Wales*, but at this stage the Japanese still believed them to be the *Renown* and the *King George V*.)

"No, sir." replied Miwa. "I'm sure we can sink them both."

"Right," said Yamamoto, taking him on at once. "Let's make a bet on it." They agreed that if Yamamoto lost he should give Miwa ten dozen bottles of beer, and if Miwa lost he should give the C. in C. a dozen bottles.

Unlike carrier-based planes, there was plenty of room on board the type-96 and type-1 land-based planes, and Lieutenant Commander Miyauchi Shichizo and his men were able to fortify themselves on the way to the attack with canned "red rice," hot pork-and-vegetable soup, and other such delicacies. Spotting the Anambas Islands below them to the right, they continued south, and had arrived at a point at which, if no report of sighting the enemy had come within thirty minutes, they would have reached the limit of that day's activities, when a scout plane flying ahead radioed the bomber squadron: "Enemy capital ships sighted. Latitude 4° north, longitude 103°55′ east. 1145."

The point indicated was off Kuantan on the Malayan peninsula, and it was 1:40 P.M. when the planes arrived on the scene. According to an account by a pilot in the first group of torpedo bombers, the two battleships, cruising with their escort of three destroyers, were a surprisingly drab, muddy color, probably on account of their camouflage. As he flew in over the *Repulse* to launch his torpedoes, he could see an Englishman, red-faced and helmeted, furiously operating a machine gun on the deck.

Several columns of water shot up, showing where torpedoes had gone home. His plane climbed again, and the ships were already dwindling into the distance when, quite suddenly, the *Repulse* belched black smoke and without warning disappeared beneath the waves.

The staff officers in the operations room of the *Nagato* were overjoyed on receiving the report of the sinking of the *Repulse*, but thirty or forty minutes later they heard over the intercom the voice of Lieutenant Shingu, codes officer, announcing in a tone shrill with excitement, "Another battleship sunk!" The *Prince of Wales*, the latest word in battleships and the pride of the British navy, had also met its fate.

At the time of the Pearl Harbor attack Yamamoto had seemed almost depressed, but this time, according to those who were there, he was smiling gleefully, his cheeks flushed with excitement. Even so, he was being rather inconsistent: if battleships were in fact as obsolete as he said, there was no particular cause for rejoicing in having sunk two of them; at least, there was more cause for rejoicing in Pearl Harbor, where four had been sunk. In all probability, Yamamoto was uncomfortable at having caught the enemy asleep in Hawaii, whereas in the present case land-based bombers—whose development he himself had furthered—had launched a frontal attack on the open seas, thus bearing out his long-held theories on the superiority of air power. In all probability, too, even he had not—for all his theories concerning battleships and air power—shaken off completely the feeling that battleships somehow symbolized the might of the country possessing them.

"I hope you won't forget those ten dozen bottles, sir," Miwa reminded him.

"Of course, of course—you can have fifty dozen if you like. Get an aide to see to it, will you?"

"I wouldn't be surprised if they make you a baron or a fleet admiral for this, sir," Miwa went on.

"Not me, thank you," replied Yamamoto. "If they were going to reward me, I wouldn't mind them buying some land in Singapore or somewhere and setting me up in my own casino. I'd earn a hell of a lot of money for Japan!" As mentioned often above, Yamamoto was inordinately fond of gambling. This taste of his, however, did not always find favor with those about him; it is said that among the things of which the Navy Ministry was to forbid public mention during the war was "the fact that the commander in chief of the Combined Fleet is skilled at games of chance."

8

At noon on December 21, shortly after the Japanese navy had twice demonstrated so decisively to the world the superiority of aircraft over battleships, the battleship *Yamato*, whose construction Yamamoto had vehemently opposed five years earlier, put in its first appearance at the Hashirajima anchorage.

Although details were veiled in secrecy at the time, the *Yamato* was literally the world's largest battleship. Fully loaded, it displaced 72,800 tons, it had three triple gun turrets, and a maximum speed of twenty-seven knots. Set beside the *Nagato* and the *Mutsu*, it made them look like cruisers. (Later, in fact, an American patrol plane that spotted the *Yamato* and *Mutsu* sailing together was to radio: "One enemy battleship and one cruiser sighted"!)

Two months later, the Combined Fleet command was to shift its flag to the *Yamato*; and the next day but one after the *Yamato* anchored at Hashirajima the Nagumo fleet passed through the Bungo Channel and returned to Japan for the first time in a month. It was already dark when the flagship dropped anchor in Hashirajima Sound, but Ugaki and other members of the Combined Fleet staff went out to the *Akagi* to express their thanks and congratulations. The report that Nagumo made in response was brimming with confidence; and concerning the order to raid Midway on the way home, he could scarcely veil his scorn. He would be grateful—he said in effect—if people sitting at home, unacquainted with the situation on the spot, would not interfere. The order, he said, had annoyed him considerably.

At the entrance to the Bungo Channel it was decided to send the majority of the aircraft on the carriers back to land bases. Thus flight commander Fuchida soon found himself flying back down the east coast of Kyushu, and by the afternoon was back home at the Kamoike base in Kagoshima. That night, he stayed up drinking and making merry with his companions until one in the morning, but in the course of the party a message came from the *Nagato* saying that Yamamoto wanted to see him, and that he was to fly to Iwakuni, leave his plane there, and return to the *Akagi* by steam launch.

On the morning of December 24, bleary from lack of sleep and with a pounding headache, Fuchida let a fellow pilot fly him to Iwakuni. On board the *Akagi*, Yamamoto was waiting for him together with Chief of the Naval General Staff Nagano, who was on a visit from Tokyo.

Yamamoto shook him by the hand and told him he had done a good job. Following this, however, Yamamoto gave an official address in his capacity as commander in chief to all commanding officers of the task force. Its content was completely at variance with the attitude he had shown toward Fuchida. In essence, it said: "The real fighting is yet to come. The success of one surprise attack must not lead to any slackening-off. Never was the saying 'winning, one should tighten the cords of one's helmet' more appropriate than now. You are far from having conquered. You have come home only temporarily, to prepare for the next battle; from now on, you must be even more on your mettle."

Miwa Yoshitake, who was present at the time, had the feeling, almost, that the officers in question were being reprimanded. When he suggested to Yamamoto in a low voice that he should perhaps praise them just a little more—for example, during the toasts that were to follow—Yamamoto grunted and made no reply. With Yamamoto, an emotional nature gave a peculiar intensity to his likes and dislikes of others. Nagumo, commanding officer of the force, at whom the message was largely directed, belonged to the "fleet faction"; it was he, for example, who had earlier worked to have Hori Teikichi dismissed. One cannot help wondering whether Yamamoto's grunt did not sum up long years of suppressed resentment against Vice Admiral Nagumo.

Following Yamamoto's address, Chief of the Naval General Staff Nagano made a speech. Then a commemorative photograph was taken, and toasts were drunk in the wardroom, in cold sake accompanied by "victory chestnuts" and dried squid.

Yamamoto questioned Fuchida about the precise timing of the attack, and Fuchida explained how it came to be launched five minutes early. "I suppose one shouldn't complain about a mere five minutes," said Yamamoto. But America was already publicizing the view of the raid as a "treacherous sneak attack," and using the phrase "Remember Pearl Harbor," and the matter seems to have bothered Yamamoto for the rest of his life.

If one inquires into the circumstances leading up to the "sneak attack" that bothered Yamamoto so much, it is obvious, on the surface at least, that bungling on the Japanese side was to blame. Nevertheless, if one delves a little further, one encounters a number of riddles whose answer is not clear even today, and one begins to wonder how much the success of the Hawaiian operation was really due to "divine aid" alone.

On November 5 that year Kurusu Saburo, special envoy to the U.S., had left Tokyo in a great hurry, having the departure of the "China Clipper" from Hong Kong delayed for two days so that he could board it. One theory concerning the dispatch of Kurusu is that the aim was not to bring negotiations with the U.S. to a successful conclusion, but to restrain Ambassador Nomura Kichisaburo, who was pursuing the talks in all good faith. However, Kurusu's own diplomatic memoirs make such an interpretation almost impossible. Kurusu himself, at least, had no such intentions.

On his arrival in Washington, Kurusu joined Nomura in sincere efforts to arrive at some settlement. Both President Roosevelt and Secretary of State Hull were at first extremely friendly, even jovial. Despite the friendly atmosphere, however, the Americans made a number of important points in the course of the talks. The Tripartite Pact with Germany and Italy was the chief stumbling block in the negotiations; for Japan to seek an agreement with the U.S. while maintaining the Tripartite Pact intact, though understandable possibly to the secretary of state, would be difficult to square with domestic opinion in America. The Nazis were insatiable; eventually, in all probability, they would turn their eyes on America. Then, if Hitler were victorious, he would naturally advance into East Asia and bring pressure to bear on Japan; it was difficult to understand why Japan failed to perceive this. The occupation of southern French Indochina by the Japanese army, coming after the opening of negotiations between Japan and the U.S., had been a great shock to America; moreover, the latest intelligence reports suggested that there was a danger of America's being shocked yet again. Nevertheless, there was never a "last word" between friends (this phrase was used by Roosevelt himself); and America finally agreed to Kurusu's suggestion that the only possibility of avoiding war was to have the president send a personal cable to His Majesty the Emperor.

This proposal was in fact put into practice. The cable was obstructed on its way by a number of persons, and did not reach the emperor himself until 3:00 A.M. on December 8, nineteen minutes before Fuchida ordered the "repeated to" signal to go out over Oahu Island. The direct cause of the obstruction, it is said, was a lieutenant colonel named Tomura in the Signals Division of General Staff Headquarters, who that day had given instructions that all foreign cables, including personal cables from the U.S. president, were to be automatically delayed for ten hours.

Kurusu's intentions, therefore, were frustrated, but it is interesting to note that the points that Roosevelt and Hull stressed were almost completely identical with the views that Yamamoto, along with Yonai, had been putting forward consistently ever since his days as vice-minister.

Hull had at first been very affable with Kurusu. However, beginning with the talks on November 22, his manner suddenly became chillier and his attitude toughened. When Nomura and Kurusu received the Hull note of November 26, their reaction—Kurusu has written—was of utter consternation and despair. The only possible interpretation was that Hull had found out something and made up his mind in some way or other.

The Hull note, later to become so famous, included demands—among them Japan's complete withdrawal from China and French Indochina, the non-recognition of the Wang Ching-wei regime, and the dissolution of the Tripartite Pact—that were hardly likely to be acceptable to Japan, much less the Japanese army.

The journals of Henry Stimson, secretary of war at the time, record that Stimson spoke to Hull by telephone early on the morning of November 27, when Hull said, "I have washed my hands of it, it is in the hands of you and Knox, the army and the navy."

The long, coded cable containing Japan's ultimatum to the U.S. was delivered, split into fourteen separate sections, to the Japanese embassy in Washington during the night of December 6 and the early morning of December 7. Besides the fourteen cables in question, a pilot message announcing the imminent sending of the ultimatum and the cable specifying the time when it was to be handed over arrived around the same time.

December 7 was a Sunday. Although the embassy staff worked even on holidays, in practice they did not arrive in their offices until later than usual. Thus although the telegrams were delivered, they lay idle in the embassy's mailbox. A little after nine, when Sanematsu Yuzuru, now assistant naval attaché in Washington, reached the door of his office, he saw at the top of the stairs several bottles of milk and a bulky bundle of Sunday papers; there was no one about, but the mailbox was overflowing with cables and letters. Muttering to himself over the slackness of the embassy staff, he divided the bottles, the newspapers, and the cables into those intended for the embassy and those intended for the naval attaché's office. Even he was not aware that the war was to begin that day.

If there was no particular business in the naval attaché's office, they were due to play golf that afternoon. He glanced quickly through the newspapers, but there were no articles of special interest, nor any matters worth reporting to Tokyo. He went out briefly to have a meal. When he got back, the atmosphere in the office had changed. The embassy staff had arrived and decoded the pilot message, according to which the final notice was to be handed over at 1:00 P.M. on the seventh, Washington time, or 3:00 A.M. on the eighth, Tokyo time. The pilot message included a single sentence from Foreign Minister Togo to Ambassador Nomura saying: "I hardly need ask you to take every possible precaution to maintain secrecy in the preparation of this memorandum, and under no circumstances to employ typists or the like.''

Unfortunately, however, almost none of the leading members of the staff could type. Private secretary Okumura was one of the few who knew how, but he was no match for a professional typist. While he was at work, a colleague stood expectantly by his desk, but the more pressed Okumura felt the more he made mistakes or missed out lines. By the time the translation of the final section of the long, coded telegram was ready, it was already close to the appointed hour, one o'clock.

Secretary of State Hull received a telephone message requesting him to postpone the time of their appointment until 1:45, since the documents were not yet ready. And by the time a clean copy was at last complete and Nomura and Kurusu, driving at top speed, arrived with it at the State Department, it was already five minutes past two. They were not admitted to see Hull until 2:20. Secretary Hull glanced at the big clock in the room, announced the time, then without offering the two envoys a seat, began to read the memorandum they had handed him. Before long, his hands began to shake, and as he finished reading the last page he declared, in a voice quivering with suppressed emotion, that in fifty years of public service he had ''never seen a document that was more crowded with infamous falsehoods and distortions.''

Without saying a word, Nomura and Kurusu exchanged frigid handshakes with Hull, then left the State Department. Japan's attack on Pearl Harbor had begun fifty-five minutes earlier.

9

It is difficult to believe that Hull's reaction, which is described both in Kurusu's diplomatic memoirs and in Nomura's biography, was a piece of playacting. Nevertheless, it later became evident that Hull at the time was already aware of the whole content of the final notice that the Japanese envoys brought him. Ever since the ''Black Chamber'' period, America had had a long and distinguished tradition of deciphering the codes of other nations. Japanese codes, of course, were no longer as unsophisticated as they had been at the time of the Washington Conference in the early 1920s. Moreover, the Foreign Ministry, suspecting that the codes that it used were still being read by the other side, had decided, as relations with the United States became more tense, to install a new code machine known as the ''type-97 *injiki*" at Japanese embassies in leading countries and in the Foreign Ministry itself.

The code this produced was still more sophisticated than previous mechanical codes or codes such as the navy "*ro*" code, and the "*ha*" code. The navy used a machine called the "type-97 *hobun injiki*," the code being known as "navy J," while the Foreign Ministry used a machine known as the "type-97 *obun injiki*." The former used the Japanese *katakana* syllabary, the latter the Roman alphabet.

A coded text was first drawn up making use of a two-volume code-book arranged in alphabetical order, whereby a word such as "Japan" might be converted into, say, "KXLL." This was then put through the machine, whereupon, in accordance with the way the electronic plugs were arranged, it automatically emerged as a completely random, doubly coded string of Roman letters. The machine itself occupied about as much space as two old-fashioned Underwood typewriters set side by side.

The machine was constructed so that if anyone tried to force the lid off and take a look inside, the electronic plugs would fly out and scatter. In ordinary codes, if the original text uses, say, the word "Japan" five times, then the same letters "KXLL" appear five times in the coded message also. This type of repetition, if left as it stands, invariably makes it possible to decipher the code. However, in messages codified by the type-97 *injiki*, the probability of such a repetition occurring was estimated at one in approximately two hundred million.

It was generally agreed among experts at the time that this type of code was impossible to decipher (things would be different, of course, using the highly sophisticated computers of today), but American cryptanalysts cracked it just the same.

For a long time after the war, little was known as to how this was achieved, apart from fragmentary rumors saying, for example, that several hundred decoding experts along with early, vacuum-tube computers had been mobilized for the task, and that the man chiefly responsible had had a nervous breakdown after he had finished and had subsequently been awarded $100,000 for his pains. In 1967, however, Macmillan of New York published a book by David Kahn entitled *The Codebreakers*, which apparently lifted the veil from most of the remaining secrets.

According to this, most of the credit for cracking the Japanese diplomatic code based on the type-97 *obun injiki* must go to a man called William Friedman. The American army's "Black Chamber" was disbanded in 1929 under Secretary of State Stimson, in accordance with Stimson's view that "a gentleman does not read other people's private correspondence." However, it made a new start before long under the name SIS (Signal Intelligence Service), and it was Friedman who, joining the service from the start, became a second Herbert Yardley.

The Americans referred to the code in question as "Purple." The very latest in modern mathematics was applied to its deciphering, and every effective weapon in the cryptanalyst's armory was brought into play. As a result, after approximately a year and a half of "sweating blood," in August 1940 they finally succeeded, apparently using only paper and pencil, imagination and deduction, in producing a first copy of the type-97 *obun injiki*.

Shortly after this, Friedman fell sick and was admitted to the psychiatric ward of an army hospital, but after three and a half months' rest made his comeback at SIS. One year after the completion of the first model—in the summer of the year in which war broke out—America found itself able to read all Japan's principal diplomatic cables coded on this machine. So far as is apparent from David Kahn's work, William Friedman and the other code officers of SIS seem to have cracked the "Purple" code purely by means of a head-on assault. This may in fact have been so, but one cannot help having certain doubts.

In the first place, there is the question of whether, however superior the brains they brought to bear on the question, they could really have produced a copy of the type-97 *obun injiki* within as little as a year and a half, using only paper and pencil. "Though the Americans never saw the type-97 *obun injiki*," says Kahn, "their contraption bore a surprising physical resemblance to it, and of course duplicated it exactly cryptographically." One cannot help wondering whether he is not here condemning his argument in his own words.

Secondly, the cover of the basic codebook containing Japan's diplomatic codes is said to have been purple in color. If the Americans cracked the code using only means such as deduction and calculation, they presumably never saw the book—in which case, why should they have hit on the name "Purple" for it?

Thirdly, there is the fact that Kahn's work met with prepublication difficulties in connection with the protection of state secrets. Although it was published in the end, the manuscript was subjected to censorship by the Defense Department. It has been said that the only parts affected were those having a bearing on present-day communication and intelligence activities concerning the Soviet Union and China; but one wonders if this was really all.

In practice, the quickest way of learning to read another country's code is to steal it. Of course, to steal an actual object is to give the game away immediately, so that the other side promptly changes its code. But to make, unobserved, a copy of someone else's machine— or codebook, as the case may be—is common practice in international intelligence, and no one is likely to claim that neither Japan nor America had given any thought to such methods at that time. The only way of distributing the type-97 *obun injiki* and the basic codebook to embassies and legations abroad was to make use of couriers with diplomatic privileges, and there is no way of knowing what eyes were watching to take advantage of one brief, unwary moment in the course of a long voyage. It is possible, also, that a spy in Tokyo could have secured a copy of the blueprints of the machine and taken them to Shanghai, whence they would have gone to America.

The information obtained through the deciphering of "Purple" was labeled "Magic" by the Americans. Its distribution was limited to less than a dozen persons including the president, the secretary of war, navy secretary, secretary of state, the chief of Naval Operations, and his army counterpart. This fact, again, gives rise to all kinds of speculations.

A book entitled *The Final Secret of Pearl Harbor*, published in America after the war, states that the American decoding team first got hold of the ultimatum on the morning of the sixth, and that all fourteen sections of the main text had been deciphered somewhere between 4:00 A.M. and 6:00 A.M. on the seventh, U.S. Eastern Standard Time. The author of the book was Rear Admiral Theobald, commanding destroyers in the Pacific Fleet at the time.

America kept listening posts at various places in readiness for possible intelligence warfare, but it was a naval radio station on Bainbridge Island, opposite Seattle, that picked up Japanese diplomatic cables relating to the U.S.-Japanese negotiations. Japan's ultimatum was directly intercepted by the same station and relayed immediately by Teletype to Washington; the cable received by the Japanese embassy was—in contrast to practice nowadays—delivered by a private telegraph company. It is natural, perhaps, that there should have been a difference in the speed with which they arrived, yet one feels that the Americans were almost too quick in getting hold of the text, deciphering it, and translating it, while the Japanese embassy was almost too slow in doing the same thing.

The cable as deciphered by the team of cryptanalysts was delivered bit by bit to the president, so that Roosevelt and Hull knew the content of Japan's final notice, and that Japan was going to make war, several—possibly more than a dozen—hours before the launching of the attack on Pearl Harbor.

The Americans had also deciphered the message "easterly wind, rain," which NHK's shortwave foreign station sent out repeatedly just before the opening of hostilities, and knew that it was a warning to all diplomatic agencies on American soil that they were to burn their codebooks on account of impending hostilities. This "wind message" is mentioned in Kahn's book, while a similar message instructing diplomatic agencies on British territory to burn their codebooks, which was also broadcast by NHK—"We interrupt the news today to bring you a special weather report: westerly winds, fair; westerly winds, fair. . . ."—is mentioned in *The Final Secret of Pearl Harbor* as being quoted in American government records.

It is of course an incontrovertible fact that the handing-over of the communication—the proper diplomatic process—took place after the launching of the attack, and Japan cannot escape the charge of having committed a cowardly and treacherous act. However, if Americans are to continue to refer to Pearl Harbor as a "sneak attack," there are a number of awkward questions that need to be answered.

One major question is whether the same nation that succeeded in deciphering coded telegrams from the Japanese Foreign Ministry using the type-97 *obun injiki* was unable to decipher the navy's codes—whether, in short, it was really unaware in advance of the Japanese attack on Pearl Harbor.

Concerning the position of Japan's aircraft carriers, the U.S. navy's operational intelligence had concluded that as of December 1 the *Akagi* and *Kaga* were in southern Kyushu and the *Soryu*, *Hiryu*, *Zuikaku*, and *Shokaku* in the western Inland Sea. This was probably a result of spurious messages sent since late November on the orders of Combined Fleet command as a means of concealing the movements of the task force; and it suggests that Japanese naval codes were not, in fact, being deciphered at the time of the outbreak of the war.

No attack on Hawaii would have been possible if all six carriers forming the main air attack force had in fact been off the Japanese coast. Yet even though operational intelligence came to such a mistaken conclusion, and even assuming Japan's naval codes had not been cracked, it should still have been perfectly possible, at a somewhat higher level, to divine that Pearl Harbor was in danger.

Any number of persons besides Ambassador Grew had issued warnings as to the possibility of a surprise attack by Japan on Hawaii; they included Navy Secretary Knox and Admiral Richardson, chief of Naval Operations before Stark. Moreover, the FBI had for some time been keeping an eye on the espionage activities of embassy official "Morimura"—Yoshikawa Takeo—in Honolulu; the early intelligence messages he had transmitted to Tokyo had been deciphered, and it was known in Washington that Japan was showing an unusual interest in the number and position of naval vessels at anchor in Pearl Harbor.

Any synthesis and analysis of the various intelligence reports coming into the White House should have prompted the issuance of a strict alert in Hawaii. Despite this, on November 27, when Chief of Naval Operations Stark finally issued a war alert in answer to the growing urgency of the situation, he made no mention whatsoever of a possible Japanese attack on Pearl Harbor.

The night before war began, President Roosevelt was talking to political adviser Harry Hopkins in the study of the White House. The decoded version of Japan's final notice was coming through, and as the thirteenth section arrived and he finished reading it, he looked up and said, "This means war." But he made no move to issue any warning to the Pacific Fleet in Hawaii. The next morning, Stark, having looked through all fourteen sections, is said to have twice refused to let his subordinates pass the information on to Hawaii.

Both Admirals Stark and Halsey state in their memoirs that the president held up the report for some reason or other. Thus the morning of the seventh found the local commander, Admiral Kimmel, totally unaware of what Roosevelt, Stark, and Hull already knew, and the Pacific Fleet sleeping peacefully, totally off its guard, in Pearl Harbor.

It may have been coincidence that the vessels drawn up there were, if anything, old-fashioned battleships; the two aircraft carriers were out of harbor, and there is evidence suggesting that one of the two, the *Enterprise*, was already operating on a war footing by the end of November. Items 1, 2, and 3 of "Battle Order No. 1" issued on "November 28, 1941, at sea," in the name of G. D. Murray, captain of the *Enterprise*, read as follows:

1. The *Enterprise* is now operating under war conditions.
2. At any time, day and night, we must be ready for instant action.
3. Hostile submarines may be encountered.

It may be another coincidence that the patrol line on the northern half of Oahu remained open almost as though to invite attack. In this connection, there is the story of the strange voyage of the American gunboat *Lanikai*.

"Gunboat" is something of an exaggeration; the *Lanikai* was a two-masted 85-ton sailing vessel manned by six U.S. navy officers and men, together with twelve hired Filipinos dressed up as sailors. The duty of this odd gunboat, which only just qualified as an "American warship," was to keep an eye on the movements of the Japanese fleet in the South China Sea. At dusk on November 12, it left Manila harbor in order to sweep a specified area of sea between Hainan Island and Da Nang in what is now South Vietnam.

Two other sailing vessels flying the Stars and Stripes were due to be sent into other areas of the South China Sea under personal, secret orders from the president, but as soon as the news of the Japanese attack on Pearl Harbor came through, the *Lanikai* was ordered to return immediately to Manila. If the *Lanikai*'s task had really been to spy on the movements of the Japanese fleet, then its role should have been still more important after the outbreak of hostilities. In fact, it looks as though it was a decoy; it would seem that its purpose was somehow to provoke Japan into an attack on an "American warship," thereby giving America a chance to act "in self-defense."

The captain of the *Lanikai*, who after the war, as a rear admiral, was commander of the Yokosuka base in Japan for a while, told the story in an American navy magazine in September 1962. In his article, he writes of the order for him to return to Manila: "That saved our lives. The Japanese attack on Pearl Harbor must have satisfied the president better than anything the *Lanikai* could do."

According to Secretary of War Stimson, the subject of a conference of American government leaders held at the White House on November 25, the day before the Hull note was handed to Japan, was "how we should maneuver them into the position of firing the first shot without allowing too much danger to ourselves."

Again, a work by Omae Toshikazu, a member of the Naval Affairs Bureau at the outbreak of the war, quotes Oliver Lyttleton, who as British minister of production had a great deal of contact with America, as saying in 1944 that Japan was provoked into attacking America at Pearl Harbor. "It is a travesty on history ever to say that America was forced into the war."

American public opinion was not in favor of joining in the war in Europe, and there was a very strong isolationist trend in Congress, but President Roosevelt doubtless felt that America should not stand by and watch Hitler having everything his own way. Though America may have felt it should, given some pretext, go to the aid of England, and despite studied violations of neutrality and frequent flouting of diplomatic convention, Germany refused to rise to the bait. Yet, even though Germany did not fire any guns at America, there remained what was, in a sense, the very convenient fact of the Tripartite Pact: if Japan could be provoked into firing first, Germany would automatically enter into hostilities with America, and the president would be able to send troops into Europe with the official backing of American public opinion.

The question resolves itself into one of whether America genuinely did not know that Japan intended to attack Pearl Harbor. Even today, no really clear-cut answer is forthcoming. The findings of the Pearl Harbor inquiry commission, which met on a number of occasions during the war, and of the postwar joint investigating committee of both Houses of Congress are that, through neglect of their duties, Pacific Fleet commander Admiral Kimmel, General Short, army commanding officer in the Hawaii area, and Chief of Naval Operations Stark bore responsibility for Pearl Harbor. However, this verdict has encountered many objections, and still seems to be a source of controversy, even within America itself.

One thing that seems certain, however, is that even if it knew of the impending attack in advance, America did not expect to suffer such devastating losses; the reason was its gross underestimation of Japanese air power. Likewise, according to Inoue Shigeyoshi, "Japanese politicians and army men both underestimated America's natural strength and the spiritual strength of its people, particularly its women. They had a childish notion that, since women had such a powerful say there, it wouldn't be long before they started objecting to the war. . . ." Similarly, a majority of Americans at the time quite seriously accepted the cartoon view of the Japanese as a pack of funny little men with buckteeth, horn-rimmed spectacles, and inscrutable smiles on their faces, who were no good at piloting planes because of the unusual structure of their eyes. One thing that is certain at least is that mutual ignorance and contempt worked to both sides' disadvantage.

Fuchida Mitsuo survived the war, having been grounded by a leg broken in the Battle of Midway; following the war, he became a Christian minister and now spends the greater part of each year in America. From his own experiences, he concludes that many American intellectuals assume that U.S. government leaders knew of Japan's surprise attack on Pearl Harbor before the event. Rear Admiral Theobald's work is written from a similar point of view. In the preface, William F. Halsey says that Kimmel and Short were "our outstanding military martyrs," cast to the wolves for the sake of something about which they themselves could do absolutely nothing.

Nevertheless, as Nakano Goro points out in a postscript to the Japanese translation, there have been strong arguments against Theobald's theories within America, and quite a few people in Japan have also expressed opposing points of view. According to Tomioka Sadatoshi: "Even supposing America wanted Japan to fire the first shot, it had no need to have it fired in Hawaii, and in such a drastic way. It is being over-cynical to suggest that America knew of the Pearl Harbor plan before the event."

Takagi Sokichi also takes the view that America knew nothing, while Kusaka Ryunosuke declares: "I know from my own experience at the front that the Americans' eagerness to save human life supercedes anything we could imagine, and it is unthinkable that they should have consciously provoked the attack on Hawaii at the expense of thousands of men."

Particularly worthy of credence is the view of Tsunoda Jun, who is engaged in research on contemporary history at the National Diet Library. According to Dr. Tsunoda, no final conclusion has yet been reached on the question, yet the theory that America had knowledge before the event is propounded chiefly by a group of historians from Chicago and other universities who are looked on in America as a revisionist minority. The most detailed summing-up of the facts concerning Pearl Harbor, a book entitled *Pearl Harbor: Warning and Decision*, written by Roberta Wohlstetter and published by Stanford University Press, contains nothing at all to bear out the theory that America willingly lured Japan into Pearl Harbor.

A majority of scholars today, says Tsunoda, are inclined to deny such prior knowledge, and he himself concurs. The trouble, he says, is that those made to shoulder responsibility for Pearl Harbor still feel indignant that information in the hands of government leaders was kept from them, and feel resentment at the mere idea of having been used as decoys; thus their views are necessarily one-sided. Their claims, however, along with other theories that America knew beforehand, are not necessarily displeasing to Japanese ears; thus, Tsunoda says, what is in fact a minority opinion in America is reported in Japan as a majority view on its way to general acceptance among scholars and intellectuals. The Japanese public, he warns, should beware of such a view.

Today, more than thirty years after Japan's attack on Pearl Harbor, the question is passing out of the hands of those directly concerned and into those of the historian. It seems likely that the view that America did not know of the attack in advance will gradually find general acceptance. If, by any chance, hitherto unpublished government documents now lying in the darkest recesses of some State Department or Defense Department storeroom should come to light to upset the view of a majority of historians, then Yamamoto Isoroku's spirit will doubtless grin ruefully at his naiveté in continuing, right up until his death, to feel guilty about the "sneak attack." But despite a number of still unexplained points, it now seems unlikely that that day will ever come.

ELEVEN

1

Following the beginning of the war, large numbers of letters from all over the country began to descend on Yamamoto on board the *Yamato* every day. Yamamoto himself wrote that he "felt intolerably embarrassed at the way the achievements in battle of those under me and of the young rank and file have made me a star overnight."

Chief orderly Omi says that even after the excitement aroused by Pearl Harbor at home seemed more or less to have subsided, a pile of letters about eight inches thick would arrive for Yamamoto every day. They came from elderly generals and right-wingers who had once hated him, from the families of men serving under him, and even from elementary school children, and ranged from simple eulogies to a rather impertinent request from the principal of a country middle school for a specimen of his calligraphy to be used as a prize for the best school in the prefecture. And Yamamoto, with a naive sense of duty, personally wrote a reply with writing brush and Chinese ink to every one of them. Thus it is very common to hear that someone or other in some part of the country still has a letter written by Admiral Yamamoto; any collection of his letters would almost certainly reach vast proportions. Most of them, however, are almost certainly perfunctory replies and letters of thanks, with little value apart from being in Yamamoto's own hand; where the letters were something more than perfunctory, they have often not survived.

The total number of letters, whether official or private, from which one can judge Yamamoto's true feelings is not large, but I will select two or three, written in the early days following the outbreak of war, from among those quoted in various records or of whose originals I have copies to hand.

Early in 1942, on January 9, Yamamoto sent a reply to a letter of thanks from Ogata Taketora in which he wrote:

Thank you for your kind letter of New Year's Day. A military man can scarcely pride himself on having "smitten a sleeping enemy"; it is more a matter of shame, simply, for the one smitten. I would rather you made your appraisal after seeing what the enemy does, since it is certain that, angered and outraged, he will soon launch a determined counterattack, whether it be a full-scale engagement on the sea, air raids on Japan itself, or a strong attack against the main units of our fleet. Either way, my one desire is to carry through the first stage of operations before the enemy can recover, and, on the surface at least, achieve some basis for a protracted war. . . .

A passage in a letter to Harada Kumao dated December 19, 1941, reads: "The favorable results achieved at the commencement of hostilities would suggest that Lady Luck is still watching over the nation. . . ."

Anyone who gave such passages more than a perfunctory reading could not help but be brought up short by phrases such as "Lady Luck is still watching over the nation," or "on the surface at least . . . some basis for a protracted war." At the time, of course, these letters were not made public.

To his sister Kazuko in the country, Yamamoto wrote, on December 18:

The war has begun at last, but there's no point in feeling pressed, since it's almost certain to go on for decades. The public seems to be kicking up a great deal of fuss over nothing. But I don't think it will be very good either for education, for the public morale, or in increasing production. . . . I don't see what there is to get so excited about in somebody's sinking a handful of warships.

The following is a letter to Koga Mineichi, who was in Shanghai as C. in C. of the China Area Fleet:

I received your letter of December 15 on the second of this month (they say that a hundred thousand letters are piled up at Kure, and it's impossible to cope with them). Many thanks for your congratulations. I on my side must congratulate you on the fall of Hong Kong somewhat earlier than planned. Now that Hong Kong has been taken I feel that if we strike a bit harder at Burma, Chiang [Kai-shek] will feel the pinch. Couldn't something be managed?

Britain and America may have underestimated Japan somewhat, but from their point of view it's like having one's hand bitten rather badly by a dog one was feeding. It seems that America in particular is determined before long to embark on full-scale operations against Japan. The mindless rejoicing at home is really deplorable; it makes me fear that the first blow at Tokyo will make them wilt on the spot. . . . We are far from being able to relax at this stage. I only wish that they had had, say, three carriers at Hawaii as well. Things may be different in your part of the world since you're near the enemy on land, but here, apart from occasional submarine scares since December 14, we're just staring idly at the sea as usual. Hardly a festive New Year! Take care of yourself in this cold weather. . . .

There were considerable objections to the idea of a raid on Hawaii, both at the ministry and in the units actually concerned (not among the fliers). Even if it were successful, they argued, it would be no more than a showpiece operation, while if it failed it would be disastrous for Japan. So I had a lot of unpleasantness at the time. Now, however, they're very pleased with themselves and talk as though the outcome of the war was already settled. To tell the truth, the question of the ability and insight of the top leaders of the navy causes me more worry than all the public hullabaloo.

It was impossible for Yamamoto to let himself go and join in the national euphoria, and he seems to have exerted strict control to prevent himself from being carried away. Not that he always showed what he was truly feeling in his letters to prominent figures; with the exception of a few friends such as Hori Teikichi and Enomoto Shigeharu, it was only to Chiyoko and one or two other women that he really unburdened himself.

The command orderlies had a fairly good idea of Yamamoto's private affairs. When Omi sorted Yamamoto's mail, he would always put any letter from Chiyoko on the very top of the tall pile before delivering it all to Yamamoto. On days when there was a letter addressed in her writing, Yamamoto would go out of his way to thank Omi as he handed the letters over; on other days he said not a word. A letter to Chiyoko written by Yamamoto on December 28 includes the passage: "I get piles of letters and the like from all over the place, but the only ones I'm always eagerly waiting for are from you. Aren't the photos ready yet? . . ."

Letters from his family were comparatively infrequent, and the orderlies would privately accuse his wife of being indifferent. But this was, in fact, nothing new, and there is no way of telling which of the couple it was that was "indifferent." According to Yamamoto Chikao, Isoroku had been an indefatigable letter writer ever since his days as naval attaché in America. But "not to his family." It was usual for people in the naval attaché's office to use the pouch that regularly went, with diplomatic immunity, from the embassy in Washington to the Foreign Ministry in Tokyo, in order to send small presents or private letters to their families. But when Yamamoto Chikao once suggested that Isoroku might want to send something to his wife and children, the brusque reply was, "No. Not necessary." The cause may, of course, have been his customary embarrassment at mentioning any personal matters or feelings in front of others, but on the surface, at least, he was soft toward women and children outside his own family and extremely tough toward those inside it.

A similar embarrassment was typical of Yamamoto in many other situations too. It was decided on one occasion to ask the well-known painter Yasuda Yukihiko—a traditional artist in the Japanese style— to paint Yamamoto's portrait, and a friend who got wind of the matter asked him about it in a letter. In his reply he said, "As far as the talk of a portrait by Yasuda is concerned, there is no basis in fact. . . . Anyway, as I see it portraits are vulgarities to be shunned only less rigorously than bronze statues."

In the end, Yasuda was not able to paint Yamamoto from life and was obliged to refer to photographs in executing his *Fleet Admiral Yamamoto Isoroku on December 8*, which was shown in 1944 at a "Special Wartime Art Exhibition" sponsored by the Ministry of Education. The work, regarded as one of Yasuda's finest efforts, disappeared after the war and was said to have been carried off to Washington by the U.S. navy, but no one was able to verify its whereabouts until finally, in 1966, it transpired that it was in a private collection in Japan.

2

Yamamoto also seems to have disliked the Imperial Headquarters announcements over the radio, with their musical accompaniment of stirring military pieces such as the well-known "Battleship March." Early in 1942, when conversation in the staff officers' recreation room happened to turn to these radio announcements, Yamamoto said with a look of disgust: "All they need do really is quietly let people know the truth. There's no need to bang the big drum. Official reports should stick to the absolute truth—once you start lying, the war's as good as lost. Information Division's outlook is all wrong. All this talk of guiding public opinion and maintaining the national morale is so much empty puff."

When it was decided to erect a stone engraved with the words of the "Battleship March" in Hibiya Park in central Tokyo, Yamamoto was asked to write the original calligraphy for the carved inscription. He discussed it with staff officer Fujii, dwelt on the matter overnight— then wrote a letter of refusal.

The Japanese navy, in the same tradition as its then leader, had long been known as "the silent navy," but from the time of Pearl Harbor on it became remarkably prone to blow its own trumpet. Not that the general public minded, for the navy at the time was extremely popular: thanks in large measure to the navy, the war at the time was going favorably, not to say one-sidedly. On January 11, the first paratroop units in the history of the Japanese navy landed on the Celebes. Manila fell on January 4, and Singapore on February 15.

At 1:00 P.M. on February 27, off the coast of Java, four cruisers— the *Nachi*, *Haguro*, *Jintsu*, and *Naka*—and fourteen destroyers belonging to the Fifth Fleet under the command of Rear Admiral Takagi Takeo encountered an enemy fleet of roughly the same strength— five cruisers and nine destroyers. An Allied fleet combining U.S., British, Dutch, and Australian vessels, it was commanded by Rear Admiral Doorman of the Dutch navy. Seen through a telescope, the

Dutch, British, and American flags could be clearly seen fluttering over the first, second, and third vessels respectively.

Unlike the dark waters of the North Pacific, the seas here were dazzling with sunlight, yet at a speed of thirty-two knots the wind was like a typhoon met head-on.

The guns of the *Nachi* and other vessels of the Fifth Fleet engaged in a lengthy exchange with the enemy ships, in the course of which the Allied forces lost two destroyers and started to flee in disorder. At nightfall, the Japanese fleet gave up the pursuit and withdrew to the north, but battle was joined again at 1:00 A.M. the next morning, and the latest-model Japanese torpedoes proved so effective that the leading Allied vessel, the Dutch cruiser *De Ruyter*, was soon sunk, followed by the fourth vessel—another Dutch cruiser, the *Java*. The remaining ships were caught the next day by the cruisers *Ashigara* and *Maya* and other vessels of the Third Fleet under Vice Admiral Takahashi Ibo. They clinched Japan's victory by sinking the British cruiser *Exeter* and two destroyers.

The Dutch admiral on board the *De Ruyter* refused to be rescued and, like Sir Thomas Phillips on the *Prince of Wales*, went down with his ship. There were no losses on the Japanese side. This is what is known as the Battle of the Java Sea. Approximately one week later, the Allied forces on Java surrendered. This battle, together with the Battle of Sunda Strait in which the U.S. cruiser *Houston* and the British cruiser *Perth* were sunk, has been seen as marking the end of "premodern sea warfare."

Hori Teikichi, as we have seen, abhorred the phrase "invincible navy" then current within the navy itself, but when Pearl Harbor was followed by a succession of one-sided victories off Malaya, Surabaya, and Batavia, the younger officers began to ignore the navy's "silent" tradition and the warnings of their superiors, and to use it freely. Public opinion, as we have seen, was quite willing to go along with them.

Yamamoto, as ever, seems to have found such unqualified complacency distasteful. "The first stage of operations had gone so smoothly," says liaison staff officer Fujii Shigeru, "that there was, conversely, an unmistakable sense of letdown. It was around this time that an occasional trace of impatience began to be discernible in the C. in C., whose surface normally resembled calm water with suggestions of unexpected depths. . . . At times he gave vent to irritation at the authorities' failure to take the steps that ought to be taken. . . . To end a war while it's going favorably for one's own side requires a special, different kind of effort. Even the Russo-Japanese War was only brought to a favorable conclusion with great difficulty." Most of the staff officers who had come under Yamamoto's personal influence seem to have shared the same feelings.

Even Chief of Staff Ugaki wrote in his *Sensoroku*: "A month has passed since the opening of hostilities . . . the imperial forces have carried all before them; yet however much one praises their magnificent achievements, unless there is the farsighted statesmanship to go with them, all those lives have, in the end, been staked for nothing."

Admittedly, the Ugaki revealed in his *Sensoroku* gives one some doubts as to the profundity of his thinking. In both the good and bad senses, he was more impetuous than Yamamoto, and one sometimes has the feeling that he was being restrained by the other man.

One interesting fact to note in passing is that, of all the forty thousand officers and men in the Combined Fleet at the time, Yamamoto was the only one who also had experience of actual fighting in the Russo-Japanese War.

3

On February 12 of that year, the Combined Fleet command moved to the newly built *Yamato*. The *Yamato* was far more comfortable than the twenty-three-year-old *Nagato*, and the staff officers were all delighted with their new quarters.

It was three days later that Singapore fell.

A "limited" war implies starting moves, at some point, aimed at a compromise that will bring peace. An "unlimited" war means slaughtering indiscriminately the population of the other country and fighting on until it capitulates. In the event, Japan found itself more or less obliged to fight an unlimited war, but—whatever the case with the army—there was probably not a single professional navy man who believed that Japan could successfully carry through such a war with America.

Ten and a half months before the beginning of the war, Yamamoto wrote a celebrated letter to his rightist acquaintance Sasakawa Ryoichi.

The full text is as follows:

> I hope that you are in good health, and am happy about the tour of the South Pacific that I hear you made recently on the *Uranami*. I am most deeply impressed by the sincerity with which you try faithfully to embody your own views in deeds at a time when most people are juggling with abstract, unrealistic policies. The one thing that embarrasses me deeply is your idea that, with me in charge on the seas, there is no need to worry. All I am doing is concentrate day and night on painstakingly building up our strength, inspired by the imperial injunction that "the weakest enemy should not be made light of, nor the mightiest feared." My whole reliance is on the loyalty of the thousands of officers and men who remain modest despite their brilliant successes. However, if there should be a war between Japan and America, then our aim, of course, ought not to be Guam or the Philippines, nor Hawaii or Hong Kong, but a capitulation at the White House, in Washington itself. I wonder whether the politicians of the day really have the willingness to make sacrifices, and the confidence, that this would entail?

The letter was a reply to some message from Sasakawa, who had been on a tour of the islands of the South Pacific on a flying boat. The letter's celebrity is due to the fact that it was published during the war —with the flying boat's name suppressed and the omission of the sentence beginning "I wonder whether the politicians . . ."—as a means of "raising the nation's morale."

The letter reached America via the Domei News Agency, with the result that the Americans came to view Yamamoto as a fanatical warmonger bent on personally leading the Japanese forces into Washington—an enemy leader worthy of the same loathing as Tojo himself. In fact, the letter was, indirectly, an expression of Yamamoto's strong dissatisfaction with Konoe and Navy Minister Oikawa, men who seemed to have no clear idea of what kind of war or what kind of negotiations they should engage in with the U.S. even though they ought to have known that an unlimited war with the latter was impossible.

Once the war began, therefore, Yamamoto's constant preoccupation was the question of an early peace and how to create a favorable situation for such a peace. The period immediately following the fall of Singapore can be seen as having presented one such situation.

As we have seen above, Sasakawa was the only man in Japan's right wing who stood up in defense of the "cowardly, pro-British, pro-American" Yamamoto. The things that attracted Yamamoto to Sasakawa, apparently, were a certain decisiveness of outlook and a willingness to tell everybody just what he felt, plus a strong interest in aviation. One day in September, three months before the beginning of the war, on a trip to Tokyo from Hashirajima, he summoned Sasakawa to the Navy Club in Shiba, where he told him that the situation had developed to the point where war was inevitable. "For a while," he said, "we'll have everything our own way, stretching out in every direction like an octopus spreading its tentacles. But it'll last for a year and a half at the most. We've just got to get a peace agreement by then. The right timing would be when Singapore falls. If it does fall, it will unsettle Burma and India. Unrest in India would be the hardest thing for Britain to put up with—to lose it, for Britain, would be like an old man being deprived of his foot warmer. But is there any politician with the sense to see that and act accordingly? I think Singapore can be captured within six months, and when it is, I look to you. . . ."

What kind of peace settlement, then, did Yamamoto personally hope for? Although they may not have gone as far as the Potsdam Declaration later produced by the Allies, his ideas seem to have been quite drastic, coming as they did out of a Japan then at the height of its victories.

Kuwabara Torao, the man who had introduced Mizuno, the physiognomy expert, to Yamamoto, was now a rear admiral commanding the Fourth Carrier Division. He came to see Yamamoto one day on his way to take up a new post, and in the course of conversation ventured to ask Yamamoto what he felt about possible terms for peace.

Yamamoto reflected for a moment. "I'd say that now is the government's only—and ideal—chance for making peace. If it were to offer peace terms, it would have to be prepared to stress that it wasn't interested in territorial expansion, and to return the lands it has occupied so far: it wouldn't be easy, but there'd be a possibility of an armistice. But then, the government's in a seventh heaven at the moment. . . ." And in fact the moment was rapidly passing without the chance being seized.

There is no telling just how far Yamamoto considered Sasakawa a politician with the sense to act properly, but Sasakawa, who stood for election as a candidate without official recommendation in Tojo's "Imperial Rule Assistance" election and became a member of the Lower House, apparently went around expounding Yamamoto's views to those in authority in the army—though without awakening any response.

If there was no hope of obtaining a peace settlement, then as C. in C. of the Combined Fleet it was Yamamoto's business to set about preparing the next operation. In a letter written to his nephew at the end of December the previous year, Yamamoto said: "The first stage of operations—i.e., the assaults on the Philippines, Hong Kong, Malaya, and the Dutch East Indies—will, I'm sure, prove no trouble; the real outcome will be determined after that, in the second stage, and we should be making our mental and physical preparations accordingly. . . . However, operations from then on will need to be based on a perfect blending of the administrative and the strategic, and I wonder whether we have the men of ability required to carry this through. . . ."

Nevertheless, it was not until January 5, 1942, that Yamamoto's staff officers were ordered to start studying the second stage of operations. In *Sensoroku*, under the heading "Sunday, January 5; fine and cold," Ugaki writes: "The first stage of operations, at least as far as the forward thrust is concerned, should be more or less completed by the middle of March. The question is what our next move should be after that: whether we should press on to Australia, or to India, or launch an attack on Hawaii, or possibly make a preemptory strike against the Soviet Union. Either course, however, will require that some plan should be drawn up by around the middle of February, and for this reason the staff officers have been set to work studying the question."

This again, though, ranges very widely and vaguely over the possibilities; although admittedly it was written before the fall of Singapore, it was late in the day to start such studies. Yamamoto, of course, had drawn up thorough, detailed plans for the Hawaiian operation with which hostilities began, and seeing that his idea was to stake everything on this first move, and that he was even ready to abandon all subsequent operations in the event of its failure, he may well have been reluctant

293

to think about the second stage until he had seen how things went in practice. In a letter replying to a New Year's card from Hori Teikichi, he says:

". . . since things are going to get tough in the future at any rate, one might as well be a bit cheerful while one can.

The planes have suffered less from wear than we thought, so I've given orders to start training again while the going's good. We're also going to feel the need badly for more small warships and cheap cargo vessels, and I think preparations should be made.

I've been doing nothing for a month, ever since the thirteenth of last month. It gets pretty boring—know any good books?"

Of the four possible plans of operation mentioned in Ugaki's journal, the idea of taking on the Soviet Union can be set aside; of the rest, it was the first—the attack on Australia—that was most enthusiastically advocated by the operations division of the Naval General Staff. As the latter saw things, the Allied counteroffensive would almost certainly be launched with Australia as its base. The timing of such a counteroffensive would not be earlier than the spring of 1943, so before that Japan should advance from the Solomons to New Caledonia, Fiji, and Samoa, preventing the enemy from deploying its air forces to Australia, and if possible isolating the latter so that it dropped out of the war. The Naval General Staff's idea, in short, was to cut Australia and America off from each other.

The second operational plan—that Japan should carry the attack into the Indian Ocean—was the first to be put forward by Combined Fleet command; the idea was that Japan should deal a blow at England and India by attacking Ceylon with a force of some five army divisions, lure out and destroy Britain's Far Eastern Fleet, then link up with German forces as they advanced from the Caucasus into the Middle East.

To this plan, however, the army itself was opposed head-on. It has been said that the Pacific War was begun by men who did not know the sea and fought by men who did not know the sky; and the army in general had little enthusiasm for, nor had it devoted study to, island-hopping operations in Southeast Asia. The enemy toward whom it felt most belligerent—and which it most feared—was the Soviet Union, and General Staff Headquarters was unlikely to agree to sparing five more divisions for operations in the Indian Ocean at a time when, the first stage of the advance on Southeast Asia having been completed, it would be thinking of withdrawing most of the forces it had used there to Manchuria and China.

Following the abandoning of this plan on account of the army's opposition, Combined Fleet command decided to adopt the third plan, for an advance into the central Pacific. At the time in question, the only force with the capability of delivering an air raid on Tokyo was the American strike force. And the idea of a raid on the imperial capital had a psychological importance difficult to imagine in retrospect, after most of Japan's major cities were laid waste; it involved the pride of the imperial navy and of the whole nation.

Thus the plan—as a plan, the grandest of them all—was to advance from Midway, if possible striking at Hawaii again and at the same time occupying vital points in the Aleutians, thus expanding Japan's sea and air defenses two thousand nautical miles to the east—and, concurrently, to lure the U.S. Pacific Fleet out onto the ocean and destroy it.

Another factor influencing the choice of strategy was that the navy—in contrast to the army's innate hankering for the grim, footslogging kind of campaign—had, as we have already seen, a kind of nostalgia for the old-fashioned, spectacular confrontation of fleets on the high seas.

In this way, the hitherto almost invincible Japanese navy was to set a course directly leading to the Midway disaster. The army, in the meantime, had already been responsible for a large number of shameful episodes in the occupied areas of Southeast Asia. Toward the end of a letter written by Yamamoto to Koga Mineichi on March 7, there occurs the following passage: "I hear, now that the first stage of the fighting is coming to an end, the army [he uses a more contemptuous term common in the navy] is showing or seems likely to show itself in its true light in Hong Kong as well as French Indochina, Singapore, and elsewhere. There is a real danger that this may eventually cause disruption behind the lines." "In its true light" would seem to refer to incidents of rape and plunder committed by the army, and the massacre of Chinese in Singapore that came to light after the war.

4

It was on April 2 that Watanabe Yasuji went to Tokyo bearing the Combined Fleet's more or less completed plan for the MI (Midway) and AL (Aleutians) operations. Once more, the Naval General Staff showed extremely strong opposition to the plan. The opposition centered around Captain Tomioka Sadatoshi, chief of the First Section, First Division, and Commander Miyo Tatsukichi, a member of his section.

After the war, Miyo, using the name Kazunari, was to write a personal account entitled "The MI Operation Controversy." According to this, he and Watanabe, who had been contemporaries at both the Naval Academy and Navy Staff College, found themselves on this occasion on opposite sides of the fence and engaged in a violent exchange. There is no space here to go into details of the arguments, but Miyo writes: "One wonders whether C. in C. Yamamoto appreciated just how ineffective aerial reconnaissance using Midway as a base would be. Had he really taken into thorough account the enormous drain on resources and difficulty in maintaining supplies on such an isolated island, or the reduction in air strength necessary in other areas in order to keep it up, and the influence on the fleet's operational activities?" Tomioka has expressed the similar view that where Midway is concerned he feels that Yamamoto was ignorant of the larger workings of strategy. He still believes, even now, that the second stage of operations should have given priority to cutting off Australia from America.

Compared with Tomioka and Miyo, the opposition put up by the rest of the Naval General Staff—by Vice-Chief Ito and First Division chief Fukudome, for example—seems to have been rather ineffectual. This was natural enough perhaps, since Tomioka and Miyo had had little personal contact with Yamamoto, while Fukudome had been commander of the *Nagato* when Yamamoto came to take over the Combined Fleet in 1939, then later, when promoted to Combined Fleet command, had served as Yamamoto's chief of staff. Ito, too, had been stationed in America when Yamamoto was naval attaché there, and had been given all kinds of advice, even on personal matters, by him. He too, moreover, though only for a short period, had served as chief of staff of the Combined Fleet, after Fukudome and before Ugaki. And, just as Miwa Yoshitake and Watanabe Yasuji had been completely captivated by Yamamoto's personal charm, Ito and Fukudome seem to have been led by their personal contact with him into taking a favorable view of almost everything he advocated.

The opposition of the First Section was not merely stubborn, but was well organized logically as well. Watanabe, though hesitant, eventually began to say that their opposition was not enough to justify withdrawing a plan that the C. in C. was determined on, and that he could not leave without hearing the views of those at the top. The argument was accordingly laid before Fukudome in the First Division chief's office. Fukudome heard Watanabe through to the end, but interrupted Miyo's counterarguments in mid-flow. "Come, come," he said soothingly, "don't get too excited. Since the Combined Fleet's so set on the plan, why don't we study it to see if we can't accept it?"

On April 5, in the operations room at the Naval General Staff, the results of this "study" gave rise to another heated argument, in the presence of Vice-Chief Ito. Halfway through, Watanabe Yasuji left the room and telephoned to the *Yamato* to tell Yamamoto how the people at the Naval General Staff felt and to sound out his own reactions. Coming back, he informed those present that the C. in C.'s mind was firmly made up, and that there had been no change in his views.

Rear Admiral Fukudome turned to Ito. "If the C. in C.'s so set on it, shall we leave it to him?" he asked. Ito nodded without speaking. Miyo, it is said, merely bent his head, fighting back his tears. Chief of the Naval General Staff Nagano had no objections.

Incidentally, the day before this meeting—April 4—had been Yamamoto's fifty-eighth birthday, and an official from the Navy Ministry's Personnel Bureau had visited the *Yamato* at Hashirajima bringing two decorations for the C. in C. Yamamoto, apparently, was very doubtful about accepting them. "I could never wear them," he said. "I'd be ashamed." Nor, one feels, was this assumed modesty: the fact was that since the beginning of the war he had yet to see an enemy warship or an enemy plane with his own eyes. On the same day, he wrote the following letter to Hori Teikichi in Tokyo:

Dear Hori:

I was disappointed that Takei came all the way to Kure but was kept from visiting the fleet by a cold. The things I have asked him to put in the safe in the vice-chief's room—nothing very much—are as follows: a kind of memorandum, written on January 7, 1941, of what I told Oikawa about the Hawaii operation and the replacement of the C. in C. of the Combined Fleet; a thing I wrote around May 1939, when I was being followed by the military police; a very simple note written on December 8, 1941 (nothing here about family matters etc.); and an envelope containing a certain amount of money.

I put all of these in a large envelope with the request that if necessary they should be handed over to Vice Admiral Hori. I was taken aback today when a messenger came from Tokyo with decorations. I wonder how the men who've seen action in the front line would feel about it? It's most distressing. I can hardly, like Prince Takamatsu, summon the head of the Decorations Bureau and chew him out. . . .

Yamamoto Isoroku

April 4

Takei Daisuke, head of the Accounting Bureau, had come on business to Kure, but a feverish cold had prevented him from visiting the *Yamato*, so Yamamoto had had the envelope delivered to Kure for him to take back to Tokyo, where it was to be placed in the security of the Navy Ministry safe. The first part of the letter, for all its casual air, is a kind of will, and "if necessary" refers of course to the possibility of his own death. As for the envelope's contents, some of them have already been mentioned; I will leave discussion of the rest until the point at which, after Yamamoto's death, the safe is opened by Vice-Minister Sawamoto Yorio and Hori inspects them.

Watanabe returned to the *Yamato* from Tokyo two or three days later. On the afternoon of April 18, 1942, just two weeks after Yamamoto's birthday, Tokyo was quite unexpectedly raided by American bombers. A letter from Yamamoto to Niwa Michi at her geisha house in Shimbashi includes the following passage:

The thing that worries me slightly is that, although the war's only been going for something over three months, a lot of people are feeling relieved, or saying they're "grateful to Admiral Yamamoto" because there hasn't been a single air raid. They're very wrong: the fact that the enemy hasn't come is no thanks to Admiral Yamamoto, but to the enemy himself. So if they want to express gratitude to somebody, I wish they'd express it to America. If the latter really made up its mind to wade in on us, there'd

298

be no way of defending a city like Tokyo. If that happens, I shall hardly be indifferent, but I only hope they won't start trying to put the blame on the navy, complaining that the navy's doing nothing. Anyway, my advice is that it would be safer, if only it were possible, to keep half one's property and half oneself somewhere outside the city.

The "first stage of operations" has been a kind of children's hour, and will soon be over; now comes the adults' hour, so perhaps I'd better stop dozing and bestir myself. . . .

The thing that "slightly worried" Yamamoto had now happened. The force responsible was an American task force led by Vice Admiral William F. Halsey and consisting of two carriers—the *Enterprise* and *Hornet*—four cruisers, and eight destroyers. The raid itself was carried out by sixteen B-25s from the *Hornet* under the command of James Doolittle.

The B-25, a twin-engined medium bomber of the U.S. army, could just manage to take off from a carrier, but could not land there, so after the bombing the aircraft were scheduled to make for mainland China and land at an airfield under the control of Chiang Kai-shek's forces. The idea of putting army men and large army bombers on an aircraft carrier in order to carry out a raid had never even occurred to anyone else, at least in Japan. For the American task force itself, it was a stratagem born of strict necessity: at this stage, it could not do anything with impunity—unlike the latter stages of the war—and this was the one way of launching aircraft over the sea at a distance great enough to guarantee the fleet's safety.

At 6:30 that morning, the *No. 23 Nitto-maru*, a patrol vessel sailing off the east of Honshu, radioed that it had come across two American carriers 650 nautical miles to the east of Irozaki. However, it would normally have been considered impossible for carrier-borne planes to raid the Japanese mainland from this position, and Japan was still officially "keeping an eye on" the enemy when the totally unexpected happened. The *No. 23 Nitto-maru*, incidentally, was sunk by the American cruiser *Nashville*.

As Doolittle's bombing squadron took off 668 nautical miles from Tokyo, it split up into several groups which raided not only Tokyo but Kawasaki, Yokosuka, Nagoya, Yokkaichi, and Kobe as well. The

Enterprise was assigned to guard the task force itself, and none of the planes it carried went to Japan. As soon as the sixteen B-25s had taken off, the fleet began withdrawing to the east. The damage done by the Doolittle raid was not very great, and it was punningly remarked on the Japanese side that it was a "do-nothing" rather than a "do-little" affair; but the psychological effect was far from negligible. In a letter written on April 29—after the raid—to the same Niwa Michi as received the letter quoted above, Yamamoto wrote: "I was distressed to hear that Tokyo finally had a raid. Of course, it could hardly be called a real raid, but I feel it was just enough of a taste of the real thing to warn the people of Tokyo against their present outlook."

In fact, Yamamoto himself also seems to have received quite a shock. In a letter to Koga Mineichi dated May 2, he writes: "About the raid on the eighteenth of last month, one has the embarrassing feeling of having been caught napping just when one was feeling confident and in charge of things. Even though there wasn't much damage, it's a disgrace that the skies over the imperial capital should have been defiled without a single enemy plane being shot down. It provides a regrettably graphic illustration of the saying that a bungling attack is better than the most skillful defense."

Even after the Naval General Staff had agreed to the Midway operation, the date and time at which operations should start was still officially under consideration, but following the raid the date was brought forward—or, at least, the arguments in favor of putting it off were no longer heard.

5

On the morning of the day on which the Doolittle raid took place, the Japanese task force commanded by Nagumo Chuichi had completed its operations in the Indian Ocean and had reached a point on its way home where, passing through the Bashi Channel, the coast of Taiwan would soon be in sight. It would be just three months since the officers and men on board had set foot on home ground. Whatever one thinks of the abilities of the commander himself, the Nagumo fleet during the four and a half months since Pearl Harbor had waged war with indisputable and striking daring. It had sailed a total of fifty thousand nautical miles, going south to raid Rabaul and Port Darwin from the air, advancing into the central Pacific to pursue the enemy

300

task force that had raided the Marshall Islands, then penetrated far west into the Indian Ocean, where it raided Colombo and Trincomalee in Ceylon.

Wherever it went, its victories were almost completely one-sided. For example, the sinking of the British carrier *Hermes* outside Trincomalee harbor on April 9 was all over within fifteen minutes from the time that Lieutenant Egusa Takashige, commander of the attack force, gave the order to stand by; and not only the *Hermes* but a destroyer and large merchant vessel as well disappeared beneath the waves.

Even so, Fuchida Mitsuo has said that throughout all these operations he frequently wondered uneasily to himself whether they were really going about things in the right way. The ever-present doubt was whether they were not being kept incessantly on the move taking care of lesser foes when the strongest and most important foe of all then facing them—the American fleet—was left to its own devices.

He was also rather unhappy about the way the Combined Fleet command went about its business. If the need to coordinate operations on the basis of a broad view of the war situation required that it should maintain close liaison with the Naval General Staff, why did it not stay ashore, as did the commander and headquarters of the U.S. Pacific Fleet? If the idea was really that the C. in C. should lead his ships into battle, then Yamamoto and those under him should throw in their lot with the task force. To do neither properly, but to stay put on board the world's largest battleship, the *Yamato*, in the Hashirajima anchorage, was a waste of Japanese forces. Many of the flying men, in fact, rather contemptuously referred to the *Yamato* and other battleships with it as the "Hashirajima fleet."

Be that as it may, the fact is that though the aim of the Pearl Harbor operation had been to prevent the American fleet leaving Pearl Harbor for a period of six months, Japan's own main strength, including the *Yamato* and *Nagato*, had scarcely moved from the anchorage at Hashirajima for a full six months preceding the Midway operation. The only difference between the two sides was that one was damaged and the other not; both were alike in their immobility and uselessness.

"There they were, practicing with their big guns every day at Hashirajima," says Fuchida, "but what the hell did they think they were going to fire them at?"

The Nagumo fleet, on its way home through the Bashi Channel after the raids on Colombo and Trincomalee, heard reports of the appearance of a U.S. carrier off eastern Honshu and of the raid on Tokyo. Under orders, it proceeded under full steam to the attack, but was too far away to catch up. Halsey's group made a quick about-face and disappeared to the east, so the vessels under Nagumo relaxed their battle positions and returned to their home ports.

The fleet was tired, and urgently needed a change of crews and adequate rest and recuperation, but it arrived back in Japan for the first time in three months only to hear of the plan for the Midway operation and to be told that it must shortly sail into action again to the east. The heavy cruiser *Atago* and other vessels of the Second Fleet commanded by Vice Admiral Kondo Nobutake also came back from the South Pacific to hear of the Midway operation for the first time.

The timing of the operation had already been decided, and almost no chance remained for them either to call for a postponement or to study the plan of operations and query its advisability. Members of the task forces, who had already engaged in actual warfare, must surely have felt a great deal of dissatisfaction and apprehension. One advantage of the projected operation, however, was that it offered the strong possibility of a duel on the seas with their sworn foe, the American fleet. If anything, this assumed more importance than the occupation of Midway itself; it was the type of battle they most desired, and no one in the so far invincible Nagumo fleet seemed to doubt for one moment that they would beat the enemy hands down.

The apologists for the Combined Fleet command claim that by this time Vice Admiral Nagumo and other officers of his task force were suffering from a bad case of swollen heads; while those associated with Nagumo's group itself insist that the arbitrariness and arrogance of the Combined Fleet command was already getting out of hand. For four days beginning on May 1, a run-through was held on the *Yamato*. The whole ship was aglitter with brass; at mealtimes, everywhere was jammed with distinguished officers; the most junior among the vice admirals were turned out of the C. in C.'s wardroom and obliged to dine in the ordinary wardroom, while rear admirals went to the gun room, and mere captains and the like were reduced to eating standing on the deck.

The supervisor and chief judge of the maneuvers was the Combined

Fleet's chief of staff, Ugaki Matome. According to *Midway*, written jointly by Okumiya and Fuchida, when a group of hypothetical U.S. land-based aircraft delivered a bombing attack on a group of Japanese carriers, Lieutenant Commander Okumiya Masatake, one of the judges, threw a dice to decide how many hits they had scored and declared, in accordance with regulations for judging maneuvers, that nine direct hits had been scored. But Ugaki intervened: "Wait," he said, "we'll reduce the number of hits to three." As a result the *Akagi*, which was supposed to have sunk, got away with light damage. The *Kaga*, even so, was confirmed as having been sunk—but before very long it was miraculously "refloated" and enabled to go ahead with the next stage of operations. "This kind of supervision," says Fuchida, "was enough to disgust even the most hardened flying officers among us."

The same kind of sloppiness was also to be seen in the actual task force and landing forces. One seaplane squadron sent an extraordinarily careless routine cable requesting that mail addressed to the squadron should be forwarded to Midway from mid-June on—as though it had never even considered the possibility that the operation might be other than successful—while a report from C. in C. Nagumo summing up the situation shortly before going into action contained the following sentence: "Although the enemy's fighting spirit is poor, it seems probable that when our campaign to seize his positions gets under way he will come out to counterattack." One wonders what grounds he had for assuming that the enemy's fighting spirit was "poor." In fact, America was lying in wait only too anxious to do battle, and one can only conclude that Nagumo was too puffed up with success to see anything straight.

I have heard no one say, nor have I found any facts to suggest, that Yamamoto himself was overconfident. Nevertheless, the objective fact is that by this period he was coming to be regarded as a naval hero on a par with Togo, and an infallible strategist. The whole navy, including the operations division, seems to have succumbed to a feeling that if Yamamoto wanted to do something there was no help for it—and that it would probably be all right anyway.

There is a theory that in fact Yamamoto did not agree with the Midway operation. After his death, Arima Takayasu, torpedo staff officer of the Combined Fleet, apparently told Chihaya Masataka: "The C. in C. was actually opposed to Midway—I want you to remember that. It was the staff officers who insisted that the plan for the Midway operation, which they themselves had come up with after a lot of hard work, represented the C. in C.'s own wishes." This statement of Arima's is rather mysterious. If Yamamoto, who at the time of Pearl Harbor had brushed aside opposition from his staff officers and pushed his own ideas through so forcibly, had really not agreed with the Midway operation, why did he not say so clearly? Had he become so prone to sentimental consideration for his subordinates? Or was Arima trying to protect Yamamoto and shift responsibility for the Midway fiasco onto his own shoulders and those of the rest of the staff? Since Arima died not long after the end of the war, there is no way now of ascertaining the truth.

After the Battle of Midway was over, Yamamoto uttered not a word in defense of the way he went about the operation, but as a Kokuchokai reporter for the *Asahi Shimbun* has said: "If another man had been in his position . . . and had been responsible for the Midway debacle, Yamamoto would have given him a vicious tongue-lashing."

6

It was on May 5, 1942—the day of the Boys' Festival—that the following Imperial HQ order was issued to the navy:

> By command of His Imperial Majesty to Commander in Chief Yamamoto of the Combined Fleet:
>
> 1. The Commander in Chief of the Combined Fleet is to cooperate with the army in the occupation of Midway and strategic points in the west of the Aleutians.
>
> 2. Detailed directions will be given by the chief of the Naval General Staff.

The army at first said that it would not take part in the operation, but later proposed that it should do so, and one regiment—approximately three thousand troops forming the Ichiki detachment—was detailed to the occupation of Midway. The coasts and islands of the Inland Sea were just acquiring their new foliage, and an entry in Ugaki's *Sensoroku* reads:

> Tuesday, May 5; fine.
> The Boys' Festival spent preparing to go into battle. No chance

of even a glimpse of the carp banners. The new foliage is just at
its best on the islands dotting the sea:

> Day by day,
> The islands stand out
> Still greener on the waves.

At dusk that same day, however, a gun turret exploded on the battleship *Hyuga* during practice firing in Iyo Bay, killing fifty-one men and
seriously injuring eleven more—an accident that seemed to bode ill
for the Midway operation.

Two days later, on May 7, the carrier *Shoho*, escorting a transport
convoy on the way from Rabaul to occupy Port Moresby, was attacked
and sunk by carrier-borne planes of an American task force. The *Shoho*,
a light carrier of 11,000 tons made by remodeling the submarine
tender *Tsurugizaki*, thus became the first carrier of the war to be sunk
by the U.S. navy.

Of the six regular carriers in the Nagumo fleet, two—the *Zuikaku*
and *Shokaku*—had been detailed to the seas in this area and were serving
under the command of Vice Admiral Inoue Shigeyoshi, C. in C. of the
Fourth Fleet. The next day, May 8, these two vessels came across two
American aircraft carriers, the *Lexington* and *Yorktown*; they sank the
Lexington and badly damaged the *Yorktown*, but the *Shokaku* suffered
roughly the same degree of damage as the *Yorktown*, and was incapaci-
tated. However, the *Zuikaku* was unharmed. Yamamoto and his staff
officers, who were keeping an eye on proceedings at Hashirajima, were
eager that C. in C. Inoue should chase the remains of the enemy
group, but shortly after the crippling of the *Shokaku* Inoue gave up both
the attack on Port Moresby and the pursuit of the enemy. If the earlier
Battle of the Java Sea marked the end of premodern sea warfare, this
Battle of the Coral Sea can be called the beginning of the modern type
of sea warfare in which two task forces clash on the open seas. It seems
that many members of Combined Fleet command were highly incensed
by the way Inoue handled things, and accused him of lack of fight or
even of cowardice, but it also seems likely that there was considerable
personal prejudice against Inoue among the hawks who had previously
been opposed to his views on rearmament. In fact, there are very few
cases where Japan sought to follow through a victory on the seas. It did
not do so after Pearl Harbor, nor of course did it do so in the Battle

of the Java Sea. This may well be a question not so much of individual commanders as of an unwillingness in the Japanese as a nation to insist—to put it kindly—on anything too strongly, or—to put it unkindly—see anything through to its logical conclusion.

With the Imperial HQ order of May 5, the various units concerned got down in earnest to preparing for the trip to Midway and the Aleutians. This time, Yamamoto was himself due to sail on the *Yamato* as part of the supporting forces. Compared with the period preceding Pearl Harbor, however, security measures seem to have been extraordinarily loose. The naval harbor at Kure was like a battleground with ships entering and leaving, while launches from the carriers *Jun'yo* and *Ryujo*—which were due to sail northward—were plying between the quays and the carriers, carrying large quantities of winter clothing with almost no attempt at concealment. Even the barbers of Kure, it is said, would comment, as they cropped the officers' hair, "I hear you're up to something pretty big this time."

On the American side too, rumors that the Japanese fleet was coming to Midway were rife in Honolulu by the middle of May. Nevertheless, there is a very fine distinction between excessive pride and profound self-confidence, and it is only a partial truth to say that overconfidence on the part of the Japanese navy was responsible for the failure of the Midway operation. From the American point of view, their success at Midway was due once more to success in deciphering codes—to an overwhelming victory in collecting and synthesizing information.

At the headquarters of the U.S. Pacific Fleet in Hawaii, Admiral Chester·Nimitz and those under him had got wind of Japan's "MI-AL" operation some time before. According to David Kahn, America was readying a powerful "secret weapon" with which it hoped to recover control of the Pacific in one fell swoop, and which was kept in a long, narrow, windowless basement in the navy arsenal at Pearl Harbor. This "secret weapon" was the U.S. navy's code-cracking team, led by Lieutenant Commander Joseph Rochefort.

Japanese records show that the Naval General Staff changed the entire regulations for the use of the "*ro*" code, and all the random numbers charts, as of May 1. That a recently changed, unlimited random numbers code should immediately be deciphered would normally be considered impossible, unless a spy had been used to obtain a copy of the charts. However, there is one interesting factor in considering this question: the fact that in January that year contact had been lost with the submarine *I-124*, active in the Australian zone, with the duty of laying mines. The commands of both the Sixth (submarine) Fleet and Combined Fleet posted the submarine as missing after approximately one month, and ceased to worry any further about the matter, but in fact the *I-124* had been encircled and sunk off Port Darwin, at dusk on January 20, by an American destroyer and three corvettes of the Australian navy. At the site of the sinking the sea was only forty feet deep, with clear water free from strong tidal currents, and the U.S. navy immediately sent divers down from a submarine tender to cut open the *I-124*'s hull and bring up any important documents found inside. The documents thus recovered included a number of navy codebooks, among them the merchant vessel codebook.

Nothing is easier than to decipher codes once you have got hold of the original codebooks without the other side realizing it. From now on, it seems, a considerable portion of the navy's coded messages were unraveled by the Americans, and it also seems likely that the American find would have provided a valuable clue to the deciphering of codes following the revisions of May 1.

According to Kahn's book, however, the first stage of Japanese operations went ahead so rapidly that it was not possible to distribute the codebooks in time, and the revisions were postponed from May 1 to June 1. He also claims that the Allied decoding unit centering on the team commanded by Rochefort succeeded in deciphering ninety percent of the Japanese navy's principal coded messages using orthodox methods almost entirely.

It is not clear which of these two versions is true; either way, it seems certain that by the beginning of May the deciphering of coded messages had given the enemy the information that a major attack by Japan in the central Pacific was imminent. Nevertheless, even after they had got a general idea of the whole plan of operations, they were still rather uneasy as to whether the "AF" in the messages referred to Midway or not. Rochefort therefore suggested that they send an uncoded message saying that supplies of fresh water on Midway were running out due to a breakdown in the distilling plant. The signals unit in Japan chiefly responsible for intercepting enemy messages for the Japanese navy promptly snapped up the bait, and a coded message was sent to the units due to take part in the operation, informing them that there was apparently a shortage of fresh water on "AF." Japan even arranged to attach water supply ships to the attacking units—thus reassuring the Americans that "AF" was in fact Midway.

Ishikawa Shingo—who had stood in on the experiments to get "oil from water" during Yamamoto's period as vice-minister, and who was chief of the Second Section of the Naval Affairs Bureau by now—met Captain Kaku, commander of the *Hiryu*, during a visit by the latter to Tokyo in May. He asked Kaku his opinion of the proposed Midway operation. "If we succeed," he said, "it will do nothing but make headlines; if we fail, we'll be in the soup. Everybody in Tokyo is against it. What about you?"

Kaku seemed depressed about the whole business. "I think the operation is impossible and pointless," he replied. "But Yamamoto's set on it, so there's nothing more to say."

"Why don't you speak to him?" said Ishikawa. "Surely the commander of an aircraft carrier has the right to tell him clearly what he feels?"

"No, I couldn't," replied Kaku. "Even if I did, he wouldn't listen to me."

The next day, Ishikawa also met C. in C. Nagumo and asked him why he didn't try to dissuade Yamamoto from carrying out the Midway operation.

"I know what you mean," said Nagumo, "but remember—I didn't follow up the attack the last time at Pearl Harbor. Yamamoto went around criticizing me to his staff officers. 'Look at Nagumo,' he said; 'for all his bravado, he comes slinking home without following up his attack. He's no good.' If I opposed Midway this time, I'd almost certainly be labeled a coward, so I'd rather go and get killed at Midway, just to show him."

"Even admitting his long-standing grudge against Nagumo for the firing of Vice Admiral Hori," wrote Ishikawa after the end of the war, "I wonder why Yamamoto had to be so vindictive with C. in C. Nagumo." Ishikawa is equally hard on Yamamoto in other respects. He cites the view of some Americans that the Pearl Harbor attack was a slap on the cheek that only served to enrage the other side, and claims that although Yamamoto was an outstanding naval administrator, he was abysmal as a strategist, failing both in Hawaii and at Midway through excessive concern for the staff officers who had him under their thumb.

What Ishikawa has to say should perhaps be taken with a grain of salt, since he had been a member of the "fleet faction," one of those who, like Nagumo and under the leadership of Kato Kanji, had put up such spirited resistance to the disarmament treaty. Again, where the relationship between Yamamoto and Nagumo is concerned, some deny that Yamamoto was really so petty-minded and claim that, after the beginning of the war at least, he tended if anything to defend Nagumo. It is a fact, though, that after Yamamoto's death all the staff officers whom he had been fond of were shifted from central positions of responsibility where operations were concerned.

On the morning of May 13, two weeks before the operation was due to begin, the *Yamato* set sail from Hashirajima, entering Kure harbor that afternoon for repairs and refueling. During the six days they spent in Kure, all command staff officers and officers of the *Yamato* who so wished were allowed to bring their wives to Kure for a last few nights together. This was quite normal practice while the fleet was in port, but it had not been observed immediately before the Pearl Harbor attack. However, Yamamoto himself seems to have called Chiyoko in Tokyo several times that day, asking her to join him. Chiyoko had been suffering from pleurisy since mid-March that year. The attack had been severe, and once—around the time of the Doolittle raid—the doctors had given her case up as hopeless. She was still in need of complete rest, but finally decided to go whatever happened, and that evening had herself half carried onto the night train for Shimonoseki. She had a bad cough, and the doctor who accompanied her on the train gave her repeated injections. Arriving in Kure on the afternoon of the following day, she found Yamamoto waiting on the platform, in civilian clothes, with spectacles and a gauze mask disguising his face. He carried her on his back to the car he had waiting in front of the station.

They went to a Japanese-style inn in Kure, where they spent four nights together, though Chiyoko still had to have injections whenever breathing became difficult for her. This was to be their last meeting. Yamamoto seemed not to care what people thought of their relationship; he would take her up in his arms—illness had wasted her—to help her into the bath, and perform other such services for her. On May 27, after she had gone back to Tokyo and the *Yamato* had returned to Hashirajima, Yamamoto wrote her a letter in which he says:

> How did you feel on the way home after using up all your energy to come so far to see me in your present condition? . . . Just as you're struggling with the misfortunes you've taken on yourself for my sake, I myself will devote all *my* energy to fulfilling my duty to my country to the very end—and then I want us to abandon everything and escape from the world to be really alone together.
>
> On the morning of the twenty-ninth we leave for battle, and I'll be at sea in command of the whole force for about three weeks. Not that I'm expecting very much of it. Today is Navy Day. Now comes the crucial time. Bye-bye. Take good care of yourself. "Today too I ache for you, / Calling your name / Again and again / And pressing kisses / Upon your picture."

It is not clear what "now comes the crucial time" means. One might, perhaps, find it odd that the same Yamamoto who, a little earlier at the time of the Battle of the Coral Sea, had written a cheerful message to Furukawa Toshiko could use in this letter to Chiyoko on May 27 such oddly ominous-sounding phrases as "misfortunes you've taken on yourself" and "not that I'm expecting very much of it."

There were, in fact, a number of signs that might have dismayed the superstitious. Hori Teikichi, president of the Uraga Shipyards at the time, apparently told how the night before the fleet sailed into action for the attack on Midway he had an unpleasant dream in which a ship capsized as it was being launched. Again, at lunch on May 25, the day of the final map maneuvers on board the *Yamato*, a cook had served sea bream broiled in *miso* (fermented bean paste). In Japanese, "*miso o tsukeru*," or "to serve with miso," also means "to make a hash of things." Chief orderly Omi, who was in charge of menus, says that—though it might have been his imagination—he fancied that Yamamoto's expression changed when he saw it. Sailors in general are a superstitious lot, and Omi was told off by an aide for serving the dish at such a time. "The significance of it hadn't occurred to either the cook or myself," says Omi, "but if the C. in C. had been a more hot-tempered type, he could easily have flung the whole dish at my head!"

On the morning of May 27, the day on which Yamamoto wrote his letter to Chiyoko, the main body of the Nagumo fleet sailed into action from Hiroshima Bay. Twelve destroyers of the Tenth Destroyer Squadron led by the light cruiser *Nagara* took the lead in single file, followed by the heavy cruisers *Tone* and *Chikuma* of the Eighth Cruiser Division and the battleships *Haruna* and *Kirishima* of the Third Battleship Division. Bringing up the rear behind the *Kirishima* were the four large carriers—the *Akagi*, *Kaga*, *Hiryu*, and *Soryu*—of the First and Second Carrier Divisions.

Once out of the Bungo Channel, the fleet reformed into a circle with the four aircraft carriers in the center. The carriers *Ryujo* and *Jun'yo* of the Fourth Carrier Division, with the heavy cruisers *Takao* and *Maya* and three destroyers—the force due to go to the Aleutians—had left Ominato the previous day, May 26, under the command of Rear Admiral Kakuta Kakuji.

The twelve transports carrying the force due to capture Midway—two battalions of the navy's special land unit and the three thousand members of the army's Ichiki detachment—left Saipan on May 28, escorted by the light cruiser *Jintsu* and eleven destroyers of the Second Destroyer Squadron, whose commander was Rear Admiral Tanaka Raizo.

Two destroyers and the four cruisers *Suzuya*, *Kumano*, *Mogami*, and *Mikuma* of the Seventh Cruiser Division commanded by Vice Admiral Kurita Takeo, which sailed from Guam on the same day, were also due to provide direct cover for the force.

Vice Admiral Hosogaya Boshiro, commander in chief of the Fifth Fleet, who was in command of the northern operation as a whole, also sailed from Ominato on the heavy cruiser *Nachi* that same day. A further sixteen vessels—the Fourth and Fifth Cruiser Divisions consisting of the heavy cruisers *Atago*, *Chokai*, *Myoko*, and *Haguro*, the battleships *Hiei* and *Kongo*, the light cruiser *Yura*, and seven destroyers, together with the carrier *Zuiho* and one more destroyer, all under the command of Vice Admiral Kondo Nobutake, C. in C. of the Second Fleet—sailed from Hiroshima Bay on May 29, two days later than the Nagumo fleet. This force was to join up with the group due to occupy Midway in the assault on the atoll.

The three battleships *Nagato*, *Yamato*, and *Mutsu* under the direct command of Admiral Yamamoto, and the light cruiser *Sendai* and eight destroyers forming their direct escort, the carrier *Hosho* with one destroyer, the four battleships *Ise, Hyuga, Fuso,* and *Yamashiro,* commanded by Vice Admiral Takasu Shiro, C. in C. of the First Fleet, and the light cruisers *Kitakami* and *Oi* of the Ninth Division with twelve destroyers—all followed the Kondo force out of Hashirajima anchorage on the twenty-ninth. Of these, the force commanded by Takasu was due to part company with them on the way in order to support the Aleutian operation.

These forces together represented almost the entire strength of the Combined Fleet; they far exceeded the size of the fleet that had gone to Hawaii six months previously, and were vastly superior to the total strength of the U.S. Pacific Fleet. Almost certainly, it occurred to no one that such a massive fleet could possibly be beaten. Nevertheless— even granted that things such as Hori's launching dream and the episode of the sea bream were only remembered because of what happened afterward—it does seem that, compared with Pearl Harbor, when luck was all on the imperial navy's side, everything that could possibly go wrong went wrong this time.

Fuchida Mitsuo, flight commander on the *Akagi*, who had been having abdominal pains since before the fleet sailed, developed appendicitis; he was operated on aboard the ship as it sailed, and was unable in the end to take part in the fighting. Air staff officer Genda Minoru, a graduate of the same year at the Naval Academy, who came to see him in the sick bay and cheer him up with talk of raids on Sydney in a later operation, himself developed a high fever shortly after this. For some time he was suspected of having pneumonia, and though he was able to get up by the time the fleet reached the vicinity of Midway, he was still feverish. Even Yamamoto himself suffered acute pains at the height of the battle. It is not clear what made him write to Chiyoko that he was not "expecting very much of it," but one, possibly facile, interpretation might be that the gambler's instinct had told him that his luck was at last running out.

Type-2 navy flying boats from a base in the east of the Marshall Islands had been given the task of making a reconnaissance flight over Pearl Harbor late at night on May 31. The type-2 flying boat was the finest in the world at the time, but even this plane could not make the return flight without refueling, so they were due to meet up with a Japanese submarine at an uninhabited reef called French Frigate Shoals which lay between Hawaii and Midway, and to fly on to Pearl Harbor after refueling. However, when the submarine took a look at French Frigate Shoals through its periscope, it discovered two U.S. surface vessels and two flying boats already on the lookout there. It was obviously impossible for Japanese flying boats to touch down, and the flight was called off. The original reason for the flight had been that the Combined Fleet command believed the enemy to be quite unaware of the pending assaults on Midway and, assuming that any American counterattack would come from Pearl Harbor, wished to know what ships were at anchor there. In fact, the U.S. navy had already shifted everything it had available from Pearl Harbor to Midway and its environs, so as to be ready for any eventuality. Thus if the reconnaissance flight had been successful, it would have found Pearl Harbor empty—which would have made the Japanese suspicious, at the very least. Here again, the fleet's luck was not in.

Again—though these may seem relatively small matters—on June 1, when bad weather prevented the oiler *Naruto* from meeting up with the *Yamato*, it blundered by sending a signal giving its own position, and the *Akagi* also sent a weak signal on June 3 ordering the ships under its command to change course. Such things would never have happened at the time of Pearl Harbor.

There is no need to describe the Battle of Midway in detail. In the Japanese language, *Midway* by Fuchida and Okumiya provides a more or less complete record, and there are other works by Genda Minoru and Ito Masanori. In English, there is the voluminous *Incredible Victory* by Walter Lord. The assault on Midway was scheduled for June 7, and the attack force backing up the invasion was due to commence air raids on the atoll two days earlier. The first aim of the operation was to occupy Midway, and thus, secondly, to lure out the U.S. fleet—supposedly in Pearl Harbor—for a decisive battle on the open seas; if anything, this second objective was the more important of the two, but in terms of time the occupation of the atoll came first, and it was not entirely clear which objective should be given precedence if things did not go according to schedule. This fact would seem to have been one of the sources of the operation's failure.

Having reached a point 240 nautical miles to the northwest of Midway, the Nagumo fleet—at 1:30 A.M. on June 5 by Tokyo time, and as always thirty minutes before sunrise—set about launching the first attack force from its four carriers. It was a beautiful sight, those present say, as the red and green navigation lights flashed on the wings of the aircraft and mingled on the flight decks. Since Fuchida was ill, overall command was taken by Lieutenant Tomonaga Joichi, flight commander on the *Hiryu*. The force was made up of 108 planes, divided equally into horizontal bombers, dive-bombers, and escort fighters.

This first attack force, however, was tailed by an enemy seaplane from shortly after takeoff. As it came in over Midway, the seaplane dropped a flare to mark the position, and interceptor fighters came swirling up from the base. The covering force of "Zero" fighters led by Lieutenant Suganami Masaharu claimed the almost incredible feat of shooting down more than forty Grumman fighters for the loss of only two of its own planes and without letting them get at the bombers. But the airfield on the island was entirely innocent of its aircraft, which had been removed to safety previously, and the bombing achieved very little. Lieutenant Tomonaga accordingly sent Nagumo a message before turning back, saying, "Believe second attack necessary, 0400."

At this point, a dive-bomber unit led by Lieutenant Commander Egusa Takashige, another of torpedo bombers under Lieutenant Commander Murata Shigeharu, and a covering force of fighters under Lieutenant Commander Itaya Shigeru were standing by on board the four carriers as a second attack force awaiting the appearance of the American task force. However, on receipt of Tomonaga's message, it was hastily decided to replace with ordinary bombs the torpedoes already loaded on the bombers for the attack on the enemy carriers. Nagumo's report giving his estimate of the situation said: "We assume that no enemy aircraft carriers are active in the seas around Midway." This was, literally, only an assumption; to verify it, the fleet early that morning had sent out seven scout planes—one from the battleship *Haruna*, two each from the cruisers *Chikuma* and *Tone*, and one each from the *Akagi* and *Kaga*—in a fan shape with Midway atoll at its center. However, once again things went badly, and the reconnaissance seaplane from the *Tone* which took the course that was eventually to lead it to discover the American carriers was launched thirty minutes late because of a fault in the catapult. In fact, its pilot, a man called Amari Hiroshi, also made a mistake in calculating his course and flew in a slightly different direction from the one he was supposed to follow, so that it was fool's luck that led him to discover the U.S. fleet.

The other scout planes that flew on their correct courses either did not come near, or failed to sight, the enemy; it was the plane that was thirty minutes late on the wrong course that sent the message "Ten apparently enemy vessels sighted. Bearing 10°, 240 nautical miles from Midway, course 150°, speed twenty knots," by which time the second attack force on the decks of the *Akagi*, *Kaga*, *Soryu*, and *Hiryu* had already started loading ordinary bombs for another raid on the atoll.

The First Fleet command was momentarily taken aback, but seems to have been too wedded to its preconceptions to take the report very seriously. Nevertheless, an order was given for Amari's plane to keep the reported enemy in sight. Fifty-two minutes later, Amari sent a message saying, "One apparent carrier sighted to rear of enemy."

This report was the decisive factor: if a carrier was there, something was wrong. Pandemonium broke out on board the Japanese carriers. The attack planes lined up on the decks, loaded with ordinary bombs, were swiftly lowered to the hangars, where they were fitted once more with torpedoes. To carry out such an operation under such pressure was a major task. Up and down the elevators went carrying the aircraft, their warning bells setting up an incessant clamor, while the ground crew, drenched in sweat, uncomplainingly set about reloading the planes a second time. But they had no time to stow the unloaded bombs away in the hold, and left them lying about in corners of the hangars where, later, every one of them was to be touched off by other explosions.

Even as this went on, each carrier was faced with the task of taking back on board the planes of the first attack force, and of readying itself to do battle with any U.S. army planes that came from land bases. Fuchida Mitsuo, who had come up on deck despite feeling weak after his operation, asked Masuda Shogo, the *Akagi*'s flight officer, what time it was. "A quarter past seven," said Masuda with a sigh, looking at his wristwatch. "God, this is one hell of a long day!" Five minutes later, the order went out for the second attack force to take off as soon as it was ready.

The carriers turned into the wind, the propellers of the bombers— their loads finally switched to torpedoes—were already beginning to turn, and five minutes more would have seen all of them launched on their way to attack the American task force, when suddenly the black forms of three enemy dive-bombers came hurtling out of the sky toward the *Akagi*.

Three bombs scored direct hits, and before long the *Akagi* was shaken by fierce explosions as its own bombs burst in turn. By then, the *Kaga* and *Soryu*, which were visible from the *Akagi*, were both belching black smoke and rapidly succumbing to the same fate.

8

Around this time, the battleship *Yamato* carrying Yamamoto was sailing eastward at a point some eight hundred nautical miles northwest of Midway, followed by the *Mutsu* and other vessels of the main force. The distance separating them from the Nagumo fleet was about five hundred nautical miles, and command on the *Yamato* had no idea that the latter was wasting time frantically switching the armaments on its planes. Thus when the report of the sighting of the enemy fleet came from the *Tone*'s reconnaissance plane, they seem at first to have taken it as good news. If Nagumo's second attack force, standing by in readiness for the appearance of enemy carriers, set out now without wasting time, success—it was thought—was assured; and a gratifying current of optimism was detectable beneath the tension among Yamamoto's staff officers.

Yamamoto himself, however, spoke hardly a word as he stood on the combat bridge, his face pale after his recent stomach trouble.

It was shortly after this that the *Yamato* received the message: "Attacked by enemy land-based and carrier-based planes. *Kaga*, *Soryu*, and *Akagi* ablaze."

Yamamoto merely compressed his lips and gave a grunt, but the staff officers about him were appalled. The fact that the message came from the second-in-command of the Nagumo force on board the *Tone* suggested that the *Akagi* was incapable of sending messages and raised fears for the safety of Nagumo himself.

One staff officer of Combined Fleet command suggested excitedly that if only the Japanese planes took off at once with torpedoes they might, at least, ensure that both sides went down together. But the plates of the flight decks of the three carriers were already curling up with the heat, and flames were shooting up from below; to take off from them was obviously impossible.

The only thing the *Yamato* with the battleships under its command could do was increase speed to twenty knots and sail at once to the aid of the Nagumo force at Midway. The carriers *Ryujo* and *Jun'yo* of the Kakuta force to the north were ordered to sail south immediately and join the main force. Around this time, C. in C. Nagumo and Chief of Staff Kusaka had escaped through a window on the bridge of the *Akagi*, which was already enveloped in flames, and, leaving their vessel ablaze, were transferring their headquarters to the light cruiser *Nagara*. It was at this point that Fuchida Mitsuo, jumping from the bridge, broke his leg.

The only Japanese carrier still active in the sea around Midway was the *Hiryu*, flagship of Rear Admiral Yamaguchi, commander of the Second Carrier Division, with its captain, Kaku Tomeo, on the bridge.

The American aircraft that attacked the carrier were about a hundred and fifty in number, but the *Hiryu* was still afloat after being hit by twenty-six torpedoes and seventy bombs. Yamaguchi, a man of great insight and fighting spirit, had an extremely high reputation in the navy at the time; a number of naval men were to declare later that they wished he could have taken overall command of the task force. Although he was Yamamoto's junior—he had graduated from the Naval Academy eight years after Yamamoto—the two men were old friends, and it was Yamamoto who had arranged Yamaguchi's second marriage after the death of his first wife. The best type of old-fashioned naval officer, he often declared that in all his years in the navy he had never once regretted joining it; on leaving for Midway he told his wife quite simply, "We're going to a place where the enemy's expecting us—I may not get back this time."

Following the loss of the *Hiryu*'s three sister ships, Rear Admiral Yamaguchi took command of the air fighting. Confirming that the American task force consisted of the *Enterprise*, *Hornet*, and *Yorktown*, he put Tomonaga Joichi, who had come back from the first attack and was now awaiting further orders, in charge of ten torpedo bombers and six fighters, and ordered him to go to the attack.

The carrier-based attack plane that Tomonaga was flying was being repaired, the fuel tank on its left wing having been hit and ruptured in the morning attack, so it was not possible to take on adequate fuel. Nevertheless, he ordered them to fill the right tank full and, refusing his subordinates' offers of their own planes, took off from the *Hiryu* with enough fuel for one way only, never to return again.

The attacking planes inflicted heavy damage on the *Yorktown*, which was subsequently finished off by the Japanese submarine *I-168*. The *Yorktown*'s appearance at Midway had been a shock to the Japanese fleet. The Japanese carrier *Shokaku*, which had been damaged in the Battle of the Coral Sea in May, did not take part in this operation and was undergoing repairs at Kure which were expected to take three months. It had been believed that the *Yorktown*, having received roughly the same degree of damage in the same battle, would also be under repair for some three months. In fact, the U.S. navy had managed to patch it up in three days' intensive work at Pearl Harbor, then had dispatched it to Midway. By the time Tomonaga's squadron returned to its ship without its commander, the only planes left on the *Hiryu* were six fighters, five bombers, and four torpedo bombers. Since a strong attack by day was no longer possible, Yamaguchi decided to do battle at dusk and after dark, and set about making preparations accordingly. The long, weary day was drawing to a close and the crew were eating their battle rations when a shrill cry came from the ensign on lookout duty: "Enemy aircraft overhead! Beginning to dive!"

The *Hiryu*, by swerving violently, managed to dodge the first, second, and third waves of the attack, but the dive-bombers scored hits in all the next three waves. The flight deck was put out of action immediately, and before long the vessel's own bombs and torpedoes began to explode. Firefighting was still proceeding when dusk fell. Eventually, the electric power failed and the rudder became useless; still burning, the ship gradually began to list to port. The engine room was still coming through, although very faintly, over the intercom, and a cry of distress reached the bridge saying that the ceiling of the engine room was red-hot and that the men working there were dropping like flies. Kaku asked Yamaguchi for permission to order all hands out of the engine room, and Yamaguchi's feelings made him reluctantly agree.

Two vessels of the Tenth Destroyer Squadron, the *Makigumo* and *Kazagumo*, had drawn in close to the *Hiryu*. The commander of the squadron was Abe Toshio, who later became captain of the carrier *Shinano*. Using flashlights to signal to the destroyers, the *Hiryu* sent a message to C. in C. Nagumo saying that they must abandon ship. The survivors were assembled on the flight deck, and the second-in-command, Commander Kanoe, took a muster. The captain, Kaku, stood up on an empty can used for ship's biscuits and delivered a farewell message: "All of you fought well to the end; I can't thank you enough. It's a great pity that things have turned out this way—though one must expect it in battle—but the war has a long way to go yet. I hope you'll all survive and use this experience to build a still stronger navy."

Next, Rear Admiral Yamaguchi climbed onto the same biscuit can on the sloping deck. "The captain has already said everything for me," he said. "Let's face in the direction of Japan and give three cheers for the emperor." The company turned to face west, gave three *banzais*, and the only surviving signalman played the retreat while the ship's flag was lowered.

Yamaguchi and Kaku seemed to be having something of an altercation, each trying to persuade the other to leave, but in the end they both apparently decided to remain on board.

Second-in-command Kanoe and the ship's chief officers asked to be allowed to remain with them, but were refused. Parting toasts were exchanged, as is the custom, using water taken from the breakers below. The Midway operation had been timed to coincide with a good moon, and though the lights had failed, moonlight and the glare from the fires illuminated the flight deck.

Yamaguchi and Kaku went up to the bridge, which was still untouched by the flames. The ship's safe under the bridge contained some important papers and a considerable amount of money. It might still have been possible to retrieve them, so Chief Paymaster Asakawa asked the captain what he should do.

"You'd better leave them," said Kaku. "We'll need some money for the ferry across the Styx."

Senior staff officer Ito Seiroku called after Yamaguchi: "Sir—something to remember you by, please!" Yamaguchi halted and flung him his cap, which was marked with fluorescent paint to make it possible to distinguish the C. in C. in the dark. The cap is now in the possession of his widow.

The order was given to abandon ship, and they began to leave—first the wounded, then survivors from other ships, members of the fleet command's staff, and crew members in that order. By now a pale light was glimmering in the eastern sky. All night, enemy B-17s had circled the *Hiryu*, occasionally dropping bombs, but none of them scored a hit.

After the survivors had been transferred to the *Makigumo* and

Kazagumo, the commander of the destroyers sent a boat to try to take off the C. in C. and the *Hiryu*'s captain. But the two men signaled to the boat to go back and leave them; those on the deck of the *Kazagumo* could clearly see them waving.

Before leaving, the destroyer *Makigumo* fired two torpedoes at the *Hiryu* in accordance with a message from Yamaguchi. One passed right through the bottom of the ship and the other scored a direct hit, but the *Hiryu* still remained afloat.

9

On hearing that the *Hiryu* too had been put out of action, Yamamoto, on board the *Yamato* speeding toward Midway, finally decided to call off the operation and ordered his staff officers to write the order to withdraw. But they were too excited to agree at first.

"If we used the guns of the *Yamato* and our other ships to put the Midway airfield out of action, then sent the troops ashore, we could still occupy the island," said Watanabe. "Let's try!"

"You ought to know," said Yamamoto, "that of all naval tactics, firing one's guns at an island is considered the most stupid. You've been playing too much *shogi*!"

Senior staff officer Kuroshima was in tears. "The *Akagi*'s still afloat, sir," he said. "Supposing it was towed to America and put on show? We can't sink it with our own torpedoes!" Others asked how they could apologize to the emperor if they quit at this stage.

The *Kaga* sank at 4:25 P.M. that day and the *Soryu* at 4:30, but the *Akagi* and *Hiryu* still went on burning without sinking.

"I'll apologize to the emperor myself," said Yamamoto. Then, on his own responsibility, he had the destroyer *Nowake* sink the *Akagi*—the carrier with which he personally had been associated for so long. It was the first torpedo that the *Nowake* had ever fired at a real warship.

It was 11:55 that evening that the order to abandon the Midway operation and withdraw was given.

Thus the overwhelmingly superior fleet that had hoped to carry off such a spirited offensive limped away in defeat. Even allowing for the Americans' absolute superiority in the field of intelligence, their victory must have seemed, as in the title of Walter Lord's book, literally "incredible" to them. When the news of the outcome reached the American newspapers, they splashed it over their front pages, and the public went wild with joy. Sanematsu Yuzuru was in New York at the time, about to board the vessel that was due to take him back to Japan as part of an exchange of Japanese and U.S. diplomats. Noticing American seamen and sailors talking excitedly among themselves as they looked at something in the newspapers, he got hold of one himself—and found an article announcing the great Midway victory, together with a large photograph of the *Akagi* in flames.

Daybreak came at 1:40 Tokyo time. For a while after this, the *Yamato* continued to sail due east in the hope of taking on board survivors from the task force, but eventually it changed course to 310°. While they had been sailing full speed ahead, the wind had howled fiercely around the mast, but once they changed course to northwest and dropped their speed to fourteen knots, an unexpected silence fell over the flagship.

Yamamoto, his face greasy with sweat as he struggled with acute abdominal pains, retired to his private cabin, declaring that "it was all his responsibility, and they were not to criticize the Nagumo force." He did not appear again for several days. The chief medical officer eventually diagnosed the trouble as worms, and a dose of vermifuge cured the pains. Thus on June 10, when the *Nagara* came alongside and Nagumo, Kusaka, Genda, and others were taken on board the *Yamato*, Yamamoto was once again up and about. Even so, he had been out of action for rather longer than treatment for worms would normally have required.

Yamamoto's idea in the Midway operation seems to have been to score a victory that would give a second chance for an early peace settlement, and the shock of failure must have been correspondingly great.

Nagumo and Kusaka tried to commit suicide, but were dissuaded by their fellow officers and reached home alive. Kusaka, who had been injured, was transferred from the *Nagara* to the *Yamato* in a breeches buoy. The two men, worn and haggard, were a pitiful sight in the eyes of the orderlies who saw them.

The operation in the north had gone more or less according to plan, and the islands of Kiska and Attu were occupied on June 7. But the Midway force returned to Hashirajima on June 14 having lost four standard carriers and the cruiser *Mikuma*. On June 10, Imperial Headquarters announced its version of the outcome of the Midway operation: two U.S. carriers sunk, one Japanese carrier sunk, and one badly damaged. It was the beginning of the false reporting with accompanying fanfare that Yamamoto had dreaded.

To prevent news of the defeat from spreading, the surviving officers and men of the task force were dispersed to various bases in Kyushu where they were confined to base. The other ranks were transferred shortly afterward to the South Pacific, with no chance even to meet their families again.

TWELVE

1

For a while after this, there was little apparent change in the situation. Once again the *Yamato* and other battleships established themselves at Hashirajima. A brief rainy season gave way to high summer. It was exceptionally hot that year, and from the beginning of July almost no rain fell in the Inland Sea.

On the Pacific battlefront, far away in the southern hemisphere, the navy established itself on a line from the Bismarck Islands to New Guinea, then advanced still farther south, carrying the attack from Buka, Bougainville, and Shortland on to Tulagi and Guadalcanal, and was now engaged in constructing new forward bases for its air units at various points.

Thanks to all-out efforts by engineering units, one of these bases, the airfield in the Lunga district of Guadalcanal, was more or less completed barely two months after the Midway operation. But on August 7, just one week before fighters were due to start using it, an American marine division supported by a naval task force landed without warning on the island of Tulagi and on Guadalcanal, which lies to the south of Tulagi.

The next day, August 8, the Eighth Fleet in Rabaul—the flagship *Chokai* with four other heavy cruisers, two light cruisers, and one destroyer—hastily set out under the command of Vice Admiral Mikawa Gun'ichi in order to make a strike at the enemy anchorage. The attack with guns and torpedoes was made by night—a form of fighting in which the Japanese had had intensive training over many years. In a mere thirty-five minutes most of the five Allied cruisers and six destroyers were sunk, while Mikawa's force slipped out of Tulagi again almost unscathed. This attack is known as the First Battle of the Solomons. But the American landing was not so small in scale and

323

tentative as the Japanese authorities had overoptimistically thought; nor was it, at least in American eyes, so sudden as it seemed. It was, in fact, only the beginning of a real Allied counteroffensive.

Generally speaking, the Japanese army was at first thoroughly contemptuous of American infantry units. It seriously believed, for example, the legend that when subjected to sudden attack on the beaches they fled bawling at the tops of their voices. Particularly where the American marines were concerned, the army lacked almost any accurate knowledge whatsoever. Matsunaga Keisuke, who had served as aide and secretary to Yamamoto during his period as vice-minister, was at the front in the Rabaul area around this time. One day, he was asked about the American marines by an army staff officer who came specially for the purpose. "I see," the officer said when Matsunaga stopped, "—a kind of naval land unit, eh?" and went off satisfied. But the army units that—presumably reassured by this—went over to the attack disappeared, in Matsunaga's words, "without so much as a yelp."

Several days after the American riposte, Matsunaga was ordered by Kanazawa Masao, commander of the Eighth Base Unit, to fly over navy lookout posts and drop messages telling them to hold on a while longer, as help was coming. He took three land-based bombers and flew over Tulagi and Guadalcanal dropping the prepared messages. But the fighting did not go as Kanazawa had hoped. Realizing that the situation was serious, Combined Fleet command ordered the Second Fleet and most of the Third Fleet to proceed to Rabaul. The headquarters of the Eleventh Air Fleet in Tinian was also moved up to Rabaul, and command itself decided to shift its base to Truk.

In the early afternoon of August 17, the *Yamato*, accompanied by its destroyer escort and the liner *Kasuga-maru* (later remodeled to become the carrier *Taiyo*), weighed anchor at Hashirajima, went through the Kudako Channel, passed Cape Sata on the port side, then sailed via the fairway east of Okinoshima into the open sea and proceeded southward over pitch-black, moonless waters, keeping a strict lookout for submarines all the while. By dawn on August 18, the islands of Japan were no longer in sight. And Yamamoto was never to see them again.

On August 20, three days after the *Yamato* left Hashirajima, two vessels used in the exchange of Japanese and American diplomats— the *Asama-maru*, with Commander Sanematsu Yuzuru on board, and the *Conte Verdi*—came back to Yokohama. The spot designated for the exchange was Lourenço Marques, a harbor in Portuguese Mozambique. Shortly after the defeat at Midway, a Swedish vessel carrying 1,400 Japanese repatriates including envoys Nomura and Kurusu had set sail for Mozambique from New York via Rio de Janeiro. There it met up with the *Asama-maru* and *Conte Verdi*, which had come from Japan with Ambassador Grew and other foreigners returning to the States; passengers were exchanged, then the ships set sail for their respective countries. To Sanematsu, who as an aide and secretary during Yamamoto's period as vice-minister had been used to hearing the right wing talk of "punishing Yamamoto on Heaven's behalf," Japan and the Japanese navy must have seemed oddly changed.

He was posted to the Naval General Staff and before long was also appointed to lecture on American military affairs at Navy Staff College. Even so, the men at the Naval General Staff neither believed nor paid any attention to his accounts of American shipbuilding or his predictions that the activities of German submarines would begin to tail off in the near future. The students in the first year he taught at Staff College commented openly on what they called his "praise of America," and in private dismissed it as utter nonsense. From the next year, however, they began to listen to what Sanematsu had to say, while students in the third year, on their return to Japan after mortifying defeats, were to tell him, "Actually, sir, I think you underestimate America."

Lieutenant Commander Yoshii Michinori, arriving back in Japan from England, had had a similar experience. He too had been an aide and secretary to Yamamoto during the latter's period as vice-minister. From the beginning of 1939, he had been stationed in London. In November of the year the Pacific War began he left Liverpool for Japan, which he reached in December 28, after the outbreak of hostilities and one month later than Kondo Yasuichiro. Back home, he was astonished at the easy optimism engendered by the first battles of the war. Japanese journalists he had known during his stay in London had, in fact, complained of losing interest in their work because their papers in Tokyo were concerned only to play up stories of how London had gone on burning for three or four days as a result of German air raids, and completely ignored their own comments.

In the presence of Minister Shimada and Chief of the Naval General

Staff Nagano, he made an hour-long report on his work in London, in which he expressed the following view: "The press talks of England's being on its knees, but so far as I can see their standards of reference are all wrong. At one stage, some of the London underground was put out of action by the raids, but services were restored in a month. Sturdy two-tier bunks were installed on the platforms, and tickets put on sale in advance with the numbers of the beds on them, for the benefit of the general public. Trains are run throughout the night serving cakes and tea for the women and children. As you know, the London underground is extremely deep and offers an absolutely safe refuge; there is no panic, no defeatist talk, and almost no confusion. In the hotels, you can see military men and ordinary citizens dancing together in the basements as though nothing were up. I feel it's extremely dangerous to put too much emphasis on the decline in British strength."

Some of his listeners looked skeptical, as though to say, "Here's another fellow who's had his head turned by the West," while Nagano dozed comfortably in his seat. And in the months that followed, even Yoshii himself became so used to the atmosphere in Japan that it ceased to bother him.

2

It was August 26 when the *Yamato* steamed into the second Harushima anchorage at Truk. During its voyage, the Second Battle of the Solomons had taken place to the southeast, and the aircraft carrier *Ryujo* had been sunk, while the crack unit that the army had sent to make a counterlanding on Guadalcanal and recapture the airfield had been annihilated.

The unit in question was the Ichiki detachment that had left Saipan three months previously as a Midway occupation force. The Guadalcanal battle was increasingly assuming the aspect of a vital—and for Japan extremely awkward—battle of attrition. In his journal two weeks later Ugaki was to lament, "It's infuriating—we shoot them down and we shoot them down, but they only send in more."

Nevertheless, once the *Yamato* had established itself in the anchorage at Truk, Yamamoto's life on board was a surprisingly leisurely one. In the early morning and evening, when he was not directing operations, he began doing calligraphy for people who had requested it, and replying to mail he had received. Letters and even parcels arrived regularly from home, although they took some time.

In a letter to Niwa Michi dated "one day in September," he writes:

I'm reading your letter of September 11, which came by special mail, in the shade of a palm tree. Thank you for the cakes. It seems the weather has been fearfully hot this year in Tokyo, or rather the whole of Japan. We were there for most of it ourselves, but are now away from it for a while. . . . It's typical of you to say you're thinking of packing your bags and going off to the South Seas or somewhere. I'm sure things are most frustrating for you these days. Actually, though, what do you really think will happen in this war? It seems people back from the front are saying all kinds of irresponsibly optimistic things. . . . One man you can trust, though, if you want to know how things really are and what the future outlook is, is Vice Admiral Takahashi, who's going back home soon. Get Toyoda or somebody to bring him along, and listen to what he has to say. I'm sure he won't take it too seriously at first, but you must press him to talk things over properly with you. He'll probably say "Wait and see how things go for a while". . . . I hear there's been a lot of rain since autumn began, and I'm a little worried about the rice. I only hope there'll be such a crop that everyone will be expected to eat at least two pints a day. Take care of yourself, and don't talk about being forty-four—you're still a young woman. So take your time, take your time. . . .

Takahashi had been chief of staff at the time, in August 1939, when Yamamoto was posted to the Combined Fleet. Niwa Michi of the Shimbashi geisha house, whose business had been running into increasingly hard times, had conceived the happy-go-lucky idea that it might be better to pack her bags and set off to try her luck in the South Pacific—which might also give her a chance to see Yamamoto again. Eventually, she showed Yamamoto's letter to Enomoto Shigeharu and revealed her plans to him, but gave up all thought of the South Pacific when he said soberly, "Do you really think, then, that Japan's going to win this war?"

On September 24, Tsuji Masanobu, a staff officer from Imperial

Headquarters who had been posted to the Seventeenth Army and was directing operations on Guadalcanal, came to see Yamamoto on board the *Yamato*. The disparity between the two men's ranks was great—one was a major while the other was a full admiral—but Tsuji, who was not easily intimidated, intended to appeal to Yamamoto directly for more cooperation from the navy. Even so, his first encounter with the mighty *Yamato* seems to have startled him. In his book *Guadalcanal* he writes: "Going through the hatch into the interior of the ship was like entering a large hotel. The only difference was the innumerable pipes that ran here, there, and everywhere, presumably working together as an organic whole in keeping the seventy-thousand-ton bulk of this great monster alive. I had the feeling that if you cut one of them it would bleed, just like the innumerable blood vessels that keep the human body going. 'So this is why they call it the Yamato Hotel,' I thought. If you got lost in its interior it would be no easy matter to find your way out again."

After outlining his business to senior staff officer Kuroshima and Chief of Staff Ugaki, Tsuji was taken to the C. in C.'s cabin where he met Yamamoto. He appealed for the navy's cooperation in the army's attempt to recover Guadalcanal, by providing escorts for its supply convoys; by now, he told Yamamoto, the officers and men clinging to their positions there were "thinner than Gandhi himself."

"If army men have been starving through lack of supplies, then the navy should be ashamed of itself," said Yamamoto, as reported by Tsuji. "Very well—I'll give you cover even if I have to bring the *Yamato* alongside Guadalcanal myself." His eyes overflowed, and Tsuji too was moved to tears despite himself.

Whether this story is true or not is uncertain. Although Yamamoto was emotional by nature, he had shed no tears when, for example, the crippled *Akagi* had been sunk by torpedoes from the *Nowake*. The entry in Ugaki's *Sensoroku* for the same day notes merely: "Visits in the afternoon from a staff officer of the Seventeenth Army and two members of General Staff Headquarters on their way south."

In the end, the *Yamato* was never brought to Guadalcanal as Yamamoto had promised. It has been said that this was not because Yamamoto did not trust Tsuji (though this seems to have been a fact), but because the operation was forbidden, in the form of an imperial command, by the Naval General Staff. Another theory maintains that since the fleet's daily consumption of fuel had topped ten thousand tons, reducing reserves of heavy oil at Kure to sixty-five thousand tons, it was imperative that a vessel as large and comparatively useless as the *Yamato* should refrain as far as possible from doing anything. Yet it still seems rather odd that the commander in chief of the Combined Fleet should have had to stay put, cooped up in that great battleship, poised for action but doing nothing.

At the time of the Midway defeat, staff officers refused to allow any of the wounded to be accommodated on the *Yamato* on the grounds that the sight of blood might cloud the C. in C.'s dispassionate judgment. Similarly, Nagumo, Kusaka, and others who came from the *Nagara* to report were rapidly whisked away again. Even so, it would have been sufficient if the C. in C. had refrained from presenting himself anywhere where there was a chance of witnessing anything gory, and it seems that the traditional idea of a battleship as sacrosanct—the main strength and focal point of the navy—continually served as a restraint on Yamamoto's actions. Even the U.S. navy was not necessarily much more enlightened in this respect; the one difference, though, was that at Pearl Harbor it had lost a large number of battleships at one blow, with the result that the subsequent American switch of emphasis to strike forces was remarkably rapid.

Although the *Yamato* might be troubled by shortages of fuel, there was no shortage of foodstuffs. Tsuji Masanobu, eating dinner on board after his meeting with Yamamoto, was surprised to be given a meal that included raw sea bream, broiled sea bream, and chilled beer, served on black lacquered individual tables. He remarked with some sarcasm to A.D.C. Fukuzaki that the navy seemed to "like high living." Fukuzaki, apparently, smiled and replied in a low voice, "The C. in C. said that we were to lay on something decent for you." This was probably no more than a lie aimed at glossing over the awkwardness; it seems likely that the meal served to Tsuji was standard fare for the *Yamato* command. Whenever the food supply ships *Mamiya* and *Irako* called at Truk, the command orderlies were allowed to go and take first pick, and throughout Omi Hyojiro's period as chief orderly, Combined Fleet command's menus suffered no modification. Good food in the wardrooms seems to have been a kind of tradition in navies —a tradition which, though not without its virtues, was also part of an oddly aristocratic, snobbish tendency. On one occasion while the

Yamato was still at Hashirajima, the *Irako* came back with some eighty tons of sugar from Saipan. The fleet supply officer would have distributed the whole lot to the navy and navy installations, but Chief of Staff Ugaki is said to have ordered him to arrange for its distribution to children in the town instead. The story, doubtless circulated for its uplifting message, nevertheless bears witness to the taste for good living in the navy, that closed society in which the officers clung obstinately to their Scotch, English cigarettes, and spotless white collars. Later, when the flagship moved to Rabaul, Combined Fleet command was to take with it to the front, for a mere two weeks' stay, everything including Western-style plates, dishes, and knives and forks.

3

Yamamoto himself, though brought up in an impoverished, ex-samurai family, had a general antipathy toward anything that smacked of meanness or peasantlike "carefulness" over material things. He even objected, apparently, if a man he was with should start running to avoid a sudden shower. A similar story tells how in the late 1920s, when muskmelons were still worth their weight in gold in Japan, he insisted on plying a visitor with innumerable slices. The poor man complained that for some while afterward the very smell of melon was enough to make him feel sick.

The two orderlies, Kobori and Fujii by name, who attended to Yamamoto's personal needs on the *Yamato* in Truk are both dead, and apart from Omi the only surviving command orderly whose whereabouts can be traced is a Matsuyama Shigeo, whose rank was seaman at the time. Matsuyama, who was taken into the navy at Kure in 1942, was posted to command immediately on joining the crew of the *Yamato*. Here he soon got to know some of the personal peculiarities of his superiors. Among the staff officers, there were some who had their loincloths washed over and over again until they were yellow with age, but Yamamoto, although he never washed his own underwear, would not let the orderlies wash it either, and jettisoned his used loincloths through the porthole every day.

Matsuyama was then an attractive youth with a fair complexion. One day, he relates, as he was cleaning shoes in the cabin of an officer serving in command, he was suddenly embraced from behind and kissed. He struggled free, and the incident went no further, but he was sternly warned not to tell anyone about it. It is perhaps only natural that such irregularities should occur with so many men living close together in cramped, hot quarters. There is no sign that Yamamoto himself had any such inclinations—but, one is told, "he was very keen the other way." There was a branch of a Japanese establishment from Yokosuka in Truk. Labeled a "naval restaurant," it was, in blunter language, a brothel. If what the orderlies relate is to be believed, Yamamoto would sometimes go ashore to visit it, even though he was nearly sixty.

Once a week, popular movies of the day went the rounds of the fleet, beginning with the Combined Fleet flagship. In the Solomon Islands a desperate battle for supplies was in progress, but life on the *Yamato* went on comparatively normally. It was amidst such surroundings that, on October 7, Yamamoto had his first meeting in many months with Inoue Shigeyoshi, who had come aboard for an operational conference. That same day, Vice Admiral Kusaka Jin'ichi, cousin of Kusaka Ryunosuke and head of the Naval Academy, had arrived in Truk from Saipan on his way to Rabaul to take up his new post as commander in chief of the Southeast Area Fleet, and he too had come aboard the *Yamato*.

Following the operational conference, they and ranking officers of the various fleets had dinner with Yamamoto. During the meal, Yamamoto revealed that Inoue had been selected to follow Kusaka as head of the academy. Inoue seemed surprised and pleased, and it was decided that they should take the opportunity to discuss the changeover. After the meal, Kusaka and Inoue went to Yamamoto's cabin, where the three of them drank whisky and talked. In the course of the conversation, it seems, Kusaka asked Yamamoto what he was going to do when the war was over. "I imagine," said Yamamoto with every appearance of seriousness, "I'll be packed off either to the guillotine or to St. Helena."

Inoue's appointment became official on October 26, and he was transferred to Etajima, where he found the education to be far too narrow and earnest for his taste. The cadets, he complained, went around with a foxy look in their eyes that gave them the air of hardened criminals; the academy tried too hard to produce geniuses, and put too much emphasis on education as a means to future advancement. He forbade lecturers back from the front to tell their students stories about the war. He even refused to give up the teaching of English. As he once said to Takagi Sokichi, "English is a means of international communication like Morse code. To talk about giving up English is like asking one to discard a code that can be used for communicating with other nations. . . ."

Inoue's bold decisions were respected by the two principals who followed him. New students were regularly provided with a copy of a *Concise English Dictionary* and, odd though it may seem, the Naval Academy was one of the few Japanese schools that despite the war carried on teaching English to the end. It seems likely, too, that the Naval Academy under Inoue was about the only school where teachers were forbidden to talk to their students about the war.

During the seventy-year history of Etajima, the percentage of officers graduated from the academy who died in battle was five percent for the period from the Sino-Japanese and Russo-Japanese wars through World War I and up to the China Incident, but during World War II the rate is said to have gone up to ninety-five percent. In part this was due to the idea that a commanding officer or captain should share the fate of the vessel for which he was responsible—an idea derived, of course, from an old British tradition. Yet it was a pointless waste, in national terms, for able men to go out of their way to die at such a time. As Takagi Sokichi says, "even vessels such as the *Yamato* and *Musashi* can be built in four or five years, but it takes at least twenty years to produce a commanding officer with the rank of captain or rear admiral." Yamamoto, though moved by such deaths, did not necessarily approve of them; according to *Sensoroku* by Chief of Staff Ugaki, who was at the dinner for Kusaka and Inoue on October 7, Yamamoto hinted that he would prefer his captains to come back alive: "Unless people are pleased if a captain comes back alive when his ship has been sunk after a brave fight, it won't be possible to successfully pursue such a major and probably protracted war. The pilot of a plane is encouraged to save himself with his parachute—why should it be any different for the captain of a warship?"

It goes without saying, though, that views such as these never found their way into newspaper articles, radio broadcasts, or the communiqués of Imperial Headquarters; the army and the public at large both talked as though it were much better to die.

Between this time and the unofficial decision to withdraw from Guadalcanal in December 1942, there was a succession of fierce sea and air battles in the South Pacific, including the Battle of Savo Island, the Battle of the South Pacific, and the Third Battle of the Solomons. Some battles ended indecisively, others favorably for one side or the other. America lost the carrier *Hornet* which it had used in the Doolittle raid, and Japan lost the battleships *Hiei* and *Kirishima*. But a still more significant development was that the American forces' radar, whose threat Japan had begun to feel around the time of Midway, was reaching the point where a direct hit could be scored with the first shell fired on a dark night without any illumination.

In the entry for June 22, Ugaki's *Sensoroku* records, "The C. in C. was sunk in thought and seemed depressed." During his stay in Truk, Yamamoto's hair had become noticeably grayer. It is certain that he felt great distress that the Sixteenth Infantry Regiment—which included many natives of Nagaoka—was suffering gradual annihilation on Guadalcanal. In a letter to Sorimachi Eiichi, he writes: "Thank you for your letter of October 28. I am grateful for your congratulations, but find no pleasure in such things (please keep this to yourself), when I imagine the sufferings that young men from our district are going through."

In another letter, dated October 2 and addressed to Hori Teikichi, he says: "Things here are proving hard going. I felt from the start that America was not likely to relinquish lightly positions established at the cost of such sacrifices, and I pressed the view that a high degree of preparation and willingness to make sacrifices would be necessary on our side, but everybody here always persists in facile optimism until the very worst actually happens. I envy them. . . ."

On December 8, the first anniversary of the opening of hostilities, the estimated number of Japanese navy men who had been killed in action was 14,802.

On December 12, the emperor visited the Grand Shrines of Ise to pay his respects. There is no way of assessing what his true feelings were, but it seems likely that he went to report on his failure to prevent war and the sacrifices that that failure had entailed. In year-end letters written to various people, Yamamoto himself wrote: "One is struck with awe at the news that His Imperial Majesty personally visited the Grand Shrines of Ise, and overcome with shame that one's hair doesn't turn white overnight."

His letters to women, however, were somewhat different in tone.

One, written to Niwa Michi during the same month of December, has the following passage: "Everybody who comes here compliments me on looking so well. I wonder if I really am? Of course, though, since the prime minister, and the minister of finance, and the navy minister, and the minister of commerce and industry are all so 'well,' I suppose I must be too. . . . ."

The prime minister at the time was Tojo Hideki, the finance minister Kaya Okinori, the navy minister Shimada Shigetaro, and the minister of commerce and industry Kishi Nobusuke.

4

Yamamoto celebrated New Year, 1943, on board the *Yamato*, wiping away the sweat as he fished the moldy-tasting rice cakes from his *ozoni* (New Year's soup). That day, due either to a mistake by the cook or an oversight on the part of the orderlies, the *okashira-tsuki* (fish with heads and tails intact) that formed part of the New Year's meal came to the table with their heads pointing the wrong way—a remarkably "inauspicious" sign. Yamamoto contented himself with remarking, with mild sarcasm, that it looked as though the fish too had changed direction with the change of year. Chief orderly Omi Hyojiro still seems to feel rather guilty about the episode, just as he does over the "bean paste" incident at the time of Midway.

It was already three years and four months since Yamamoto had become commander in chief of the Combined Fleet. This was an unusually long record compared with the thirty-seven other commanders who had held the post since the time, before the Russo-Japanese War, when it had been referred to as "commander in chief of the standing squadron." But there was no suggestion yet that he should hand over to another man.

Although he never gave any hint to his staff, he was beginning to feel a little tired. His mind seems to have been divided between an easy acceptance of death on the one hand and, on the other, a hankering after the present world, and in particular Tokyo, where Chiyoko lived. Many of his letters bear this out. In one written on January 28, 1943, and addressed to Hori Teikichi, he says: "A full fifteen thousand men have been lost since the war began. I wrote a poem—

> Looking back over the year
> I feel myself grow tense

                    At the number of comrades
                    Who are no more

—and showed it to Takei. He praised it for once, but of course he was
being kind.''

Another letter was written on January 6 to Koga Mineichi, who was
now C. in C. of the Yokosuka station : "I am distressed to see the world
situation and our own operations steadily developing in the direction
I always feared. Things here look about as bad as they could ; to restore the situation will require even more bloody fighting and exceptional sacrifices. But it is no use complaining at this stage. How right
the man was who first said, 'One should choose one's friends'!''

The "choosing one's friends,'' of course, was a reference to the
Tripartite Pact with Germany and Italy. A letter written in February
to a retired rear admiral who had been in New York during Yamamoto's
period as naval attaché to the Japanese embassy in the U.S. has the
following passage : "At the moment I have acquaintances and beloved
subordinates both in this world and the next. Part of me feels that
it wants to go and meet them again, and another part feels that there
are things it still wants to do here ; I have two minds, but only one
body.''

I have already quoted part of a letter that Yamamoto wrote earlier,
on November 23, 1942, to Hori Teikichi. It also says : "I hear it's
quite cold in Tokyo. I envy you, but hope you'll take care of your
health. Everything is depressing here ; the trouble is not the enemy
but our own side. I have already served (!) from three to five generations of commanders and staff officers.''

In another letter to Hori written on November 30, 1942, he says :
"I leave things to you again, since I don't know when, if ever, I'll
be able to come home. . . . Here we are, one year since the commencement of hostilities, and I feel sad to see the handicap we were
given at the beginning being gradually whittled away.''

From a letter to Uematsu Shigeru, in September 1942 : "Received
your letter of August 18. Many thanks. I have resigned myself to
spending the whole of my remaining life in the next one hundred
days. . . .''

From a letter to Uchida Shinya, October 1942 : "Yours was the
first news I had had of Hasegawa's injury and Harada's illness. I too,
having laid low a considerable number of the enemy and killed off a

considerable number of my subordinates, expect soon to be called to account."

The recipient of this last letter, a former minister of railways, was governor of Miyagi Prefecture at the time. The "Hasegawa" and "Harada" are Hasegawa Kiyoshi and Harada Kumao. In a letter to Harada written at the end of December 1942, Yamamoto says: "In normal times, I would expect to have been replaced by now, but for some reason or other I have not heard a murmur about it, and find myself quite the oldest inhabitant of the fleet. To modify the old poem slightly:

> On the clamorous waters
> Of these rough seas
> Four years have passed;
> I am forgetting
> The manners of the capital.

"Ah me! . . ."

In the "ah me!"—a type of expression rare in his letters—one catches a glimpse both of self-mockery and of a hankering after the things he has left behind.

In a still earlier letter, to Matsumoto Kentaro, he says: "I wonder what Heaven must think of the people down here on this small black speck in the universe that is earth, or of all their talk about the last few years—which are no more than a flash compared with eternity— being 'a time of emergency.' It's really ridiculous."

To Niwa Michi, whose latest news was that she was learning to ride a bicycle, he wrote in early February 1943: "Please go on practicing as hard as you can, so long as you don't hurt your face (after all, what would happen to your limbs if you hurt your face, your toughest part?)."

Later in the same letter he goes on: "I've at last reached sixty, so I ought to be able to go anywhere by now without being treated as a naughty boy, but it seems they still feel the need to be careful where they put me, since my subordinates and the other commanders have all changed two or three—some of them as many as five—times, whereas I seem to have got left behind or forgotten. I feel that my face must have acquired a fed-up, bored look, but everybody who comes from Tokyo says tactless things like 'I was quite depressed when I left home, but I feel much better in my mind now I've seen you, sir.'

It makes you think, doesn't it?"

To Enomoto Shigeharu he laments that he has not played mahjongg for ages. He also seems to have been a little concerned about his health. He is still as good at *shogi* as ever, he says, so he'll probably last a while yet, but since August he has had some swelling in his legs and numbness in his hands. He also complains to Furukawa Toshiko that his fingers get a little numb and that his hand shakes when he holds his writing brush.

Whether it is true or not is uncertain, but Morimura Isamu, a Harvard classmate, claims that it was once suggested that Chiyoko should be taken by plane to Truk just to cheer Yamamoto up. Chiyoko, who had had a small cellar constructed in her house to serve as an air-raid shelter and also to hide Yamamoto in if it should ever be necessary, had still been working as the proprietress of Umenoshima, leaving someone else at home to take care of the house. She decided, however, to give up her business at the end of 1942. She canceled the bonds of all the geishas whom she had been employing, and at the beginning of the New Year settled down in Kamiya-cho with only a young girl to keep her company.

From the time he went to Truk, Yamamoto never once returned to Japan, but staff officers such as Miwa and Watanabe would go to Tokyo occasionally on business. At such times, Chiyoko entertained them at her home in Kamiya-cho, and occasionally gave geisha parties for them in Tsukiji and elsewhere at her own expense. It seems likely that in the course of these comings and goings, or through exchanges of letters, Yamamoto got wind of the talk of bringing Chiyoko to Truk. In a longish letter to Furukawa Toshiko at the end of January 1943, he writes:

Happy New Year. I was glad to get your letter written at 11:00 A.M. on New Year's Day, but at the same time got the feeling that you weren't too happy about things this New Year (I'm hoping of course that things are really going so well that you'll be put out with me for even thinking such a thing when you took all the trouble to write at such a busy time). . . .

As for myself, I ate my *ozoni* the first three days of the New Year, even though I sweated all the time and the rice cakes were more like dumplings; so now I'm a full-fledged sixty.

I've been ashore four times since August to visit the sick and wounded, to attend services for the dead, and so on, but apart from that I've been stuck on board. Somebody in the Navy Ministry said in a recent letter that a man from home who visited here said he cheered up when he saw my face. I wonder how they can carry on a war if they feel like that? If things are so bad at home, I've half a mind to take myself off to the South Pacific, get someone like Mr. Kawai to join me, and spend my days eating papaya from morning to night. That's all for now."

In practice—partly, probably, from fear of what people would say—the plan to send "Mr." Kawai to Truk never came to anything, and on February 11, 1943, just one year after moving to the *Yamato*, the headquarters of the Combined Fleet was transferred to the *Musashi* at anchor in Truk.

5

The withdrawal of troops from Guadalcanal had begun on February 1, shortly before the shift of command to the *Musashi*. With the third evacuation operation on the night of February 7, the removal of the thirteen thousand surviving officers and men of the army and navy was completed, and the island finally abandoned.

The public at the time was unaware of it, but the plight of Japanese forces on Guadalcanal during the six months following the American landings in August had been indescribably wretched. Guadalcanal was popularly referred to as "Starvation Island" (a play on *Ga-to*, the abbreviated Japanese name for the island, and *gato*, written with the ideographs meaning "starvation" and "island.") When finally rescued the troops were so undernourished that their beards, nails, and hair had all but stopped growing, and their joints looked pitifully large. Their buttocks were so emaciated that the anus was completely exposed, and on the destroyers that picked them up they suffered from constant and uncontrollable diarrhoea.

But their sufferings had been in vain; control of the sea and air south of the Solomon Islands passed completely into American hands. In more or less accurate fulfillment of Yamamoto's prophecy when he had said to Konoe "a year or a year and a half," Japan henceforth was to find itself clearly on the defensive.

One small achievement contributing to the success of the evacuation which deserves mention here is a false message put out by a navy signals and intelligence team. Taking advantage of the American custom of allowing uncoded messages in situations of emergency, the No. 1 Combined Signals Unit at the Vunakanau base at Rabaul seized a chance offered by poor communications between American Catalina patrol planes and their Guadalcanal base to pretend to be a Catalina and call the American base on Guadalcanal. When the Americans replied, a spurious message was sent: "Sighted two aircraft carriers, two battleships, ten destroyers, lat.—, long.—, course SEE."

The message was rapidly passed on to Nouméa and Honolulu, and about twenty minutes later was broadcast to the whole Pacific Fleet by a U.S. radio operator in Honolulu. All U.S. army bombers at the Guadalcanal bases were ordered to stand by, and by the time they realized they had been deceived the evacuation of Japanese forces was complete. When the officers commanding the Third Destroyer Squadron and the Tenth Division, which took part in the evacuation, returned to Truk, Yamamoto thanked them for what they had done and confessed that he had been resigned to losing about half their destroyers. There is no record, however, of his having sent any message praising the success of the false message. On the contrary, Ito Haruki, the communications staff officer who carried out the scheme, was reprimanded for acting in a way that gave away Japanese methods. It is not clear just how good an understanding Yamamoto had of problems concerning codes and signals intelligence—which were later to be the cause of his own death—but it seems likely, at least, that he did not attach any particularly great importance to them.

About two months after this, it was decided that Yamamoto should shift his headquarters from the *Musashi*, at anchor in Truk harbor, to Rabaul for a period of approximately one week.

Most of the crack units of the Naval Air Corps—which he had kept an eye on indirectly and directly, and whose growth he had encouraged ever since his days as second-in-command at Kasumigaura—including both land-based and carrief-based aircraft, had been obliged to proceed to land bases at Rabaul as a result of the increasingly serious situation in the Solomons area and the loss of carriers. The ostensible purpose of his forthcoming visit was to give on-the-spot encouragement to the naval air units in Rabaul. It does not seem, however, that Yamamoto had come up with the idea himself, but rather that he had to some extent allowed himself to be persuaded by the wishes of the commanding officers at the front.

On the evening of April 2, the day before his departure, Yamamoto said to liaison staff officer Fujii, who would be in charge on the *Musashi* during his own absence, "I shan't be seeing you for a while, so how about a game of *shogi*?" Yamamoto won, two games to one. After they had finished, Fujii said, "So at last you're going right up to the front, sir."

"Yes," replied Yamamoto. "It seems there's a lot of talk at home lately about commanders leading their own troops into battle, but to tell the truth I'm not very keen on going to Rabaul. I'd be much happier if they were sending me back to Hashirajima. After all, do you think it's desirable, in terms of the overall situation, that our headquarters should allow itself to be drawn gradually closer to the enemy's front line? Admittedly, it's an admirable thing from the point of view of encouraging morale. . . ."

On that same day, Yamamoto wrote Chiyoko what was to be his last letter to her:

Dear Chiyoko:
　　Your letters of March 27 and 28 finally reached me yesterday evening, April 1, having been delayed by the weather, which held up the plane. Thank you for the other things that came with it—the cotton kimono, the soap, etc. I was most pleased and grateful to hear that you entertained the chief of staff, Fujii, Watanabe, Kanooka, and Sanagi again; I'd been thinking they ought perhaps to refrain just for once. They seem to have enjoyed themselves thoroughly and took turns in coming to tell me about Kamiya-cho and what happened at Yamaguchi. I almost began to feel I'd been home and seen you myself.
　　Watanabe talked until past midnight, about three hours in all, telling me in detail about the house at Kamiya-cho, your health, and all the things you'd done for them. He told me how you insisted on giving him a new cotton kimono although the one for me was old, and how you washed his socks for him when they got soaked by rain and gave him a lot of new ones besides, as well

as feeding him any number of times. He said he felt bad about it, but I told him it was because you knew about him and were grateful, since I'd told you many times how hard he worked under me for three and a half years. 'You don't find many people so kind and thoughtful,' he said, and seemed to be genuinely moved.

Fujii, too, was praising you and saying how thoughtful you were; he told me how he came bursting in on you late at night and not only kept you up late but started talking official business with Kanooka, and how they found you'd had the good sense to go off downstairs. 'Actually,' I said, 'she's the only person I really bow my head to apart from His Majesty. I'm sure you can see why.' 'We're afraid we can!' they said, and they all laughed cheerfully. I was really happy. . . . I'm glad to hear that Umekoma has got permission, I'm sure it will be nice to know that the place can stay as it is. As for my health, as I told you the other day, my blood pressure is very good, the same as a man in his thirties. About the numbness in the hands, the only trouble was that I seemed to have a very slight numbness in the third finger and little finger of the right hand. But I deliberately exaggerated it when I told Tokyo, and it seems to have caused something of a stir (I wanted it to). However, I had forty injections of a mixture of vitamins B and C from the fleet medical officer, and it's quite cured by now (I let it be known for the benefit of others that it still wasn't quite right). So there's absolutely no need for you to worry, but please don't tell anybody the real truth—tell them, would you, that I just seem to be a bit run down through being in such a hot place and not even getting ashore. Tomorrow I'm going to the front for a short while. Senior staff officer Kuroshima and staff officer Watanabe will be going with me. I shan't be able to write to you for about two weeks, so don't worry, will you. I feel I can go cheerfully now I've heard all about you. April 4 is my birthday. I feel happy at the chance to do something. Well then, take care of yourself and good-bye for now.

Isoroku

Enclosed with the letter was a small lock of hair and a poem, written on a separate piece of paper. The Kanooka mentioned in the letter is

Lieutenant Commander Kanooka Empei, then serving as an information officer as well as secretary to the prime minister. The Sanagi was Lieutenant Commander Sanagi Takeshi, former air staff officer at Yamamoto's headquarters and now in the operations division of the Naval General Staff. Umekoma was a Shimbashi geisha and colleague of Chiyoko's who was to take over Umenojima.

Next morning, April 3, Yamamoto, accompanied by his staff officers, aides, the fleet medical officer, fleet paymaster, the fleet codes officer, and the fleet meteorological officer, went down the starboard ladder, boarded the C. in C.'s launch, and left the *Musashi*, seen off by the remaining members of command and the ship's crew. Arrived at the Natsushima seaplane base, the party split up and boarded two flying boats. After takeoff, the flying boats circled once over the *Musashi* to bid it farewell, then headed south and arrived in Rabaul at 1:40 P.M. that afternoon.

Yamamoto was welcomed by fleet commanders Kusaka Jin'ichi, Ozawa Jisaburo, and Mikawa Gun'ichi, and was installed in the official headquarters of the Southeast Area Fleet.

Before long Lieutenant General Imamura Hitoshi, commander of the Eighth Field Army, also came to welcome Yamamoto. He and Yamamoto had been bridge partners ever since the late 1920s and were on terms of friendly rivalry. It seems likely that Yamamoto was more at ease with him than any other professional army officer. On November 21 the previous year, when he had visited Yamamoto on the *Yamato* in Truk on his way to take up his post in Rabaul, he clearly remembers Yamamoto as saying, "There's no point in not being frank with each other at this stage. In the navy they used to say that one 'Zero' fighter could take on five to ten American aircraft, but that was at the beginning of the war. Since losing so many good pilots at Midway we've had difficulty in replacing them. Even now, they still say that one 'Zero' can take on two enemy planes, but the enemy's replacement rate is three times ours; the gap between our strengths is increasing every day, and to be honest things are looking black for us now."

Kusaka Jin'ichi, meeting Yamamoto for the first time in six months, noticed how muddy the whites of his eyes were, and had the immediate impression that he was exhausted. Not far from Kusaka's headquarters, there was a hill about a thousand feet high, commonly known as "Residency Hill'' because the German governor had lived there in the days when the island was under German control. Yamamoto was installed in a cottage on this hill, where the nights would be cool.

THIRTEEN

1

The day following Yamamoto's arrival, the air units in Rabaul were due to carry out Operation "I," an all-out attack on Guadalcanal. However, April 4—Yamamoto's birthday—brought violent squalls, and takeoff had to be postponed for three days. Finally, on April 7 a large-scale assault by a combined force of fighters and bombers was launched against the island of Guadalcanal and Allied vessels in the vicinity. Attacks were carried out at intervals on four separate days—the seventh, eleventh, twelfth, and fourteenth—and a total of 486 fighters, 114 carrier-based bombers, and 80 land-based attack planes took part, including some that flew from forward bases in the Bougainville area.

Each time aircraft took off, Yamamoto appeared in white dress uniform and waved his cap in farewell, then went back to Kusaka's room in the Southeast Area Fleet HQ, where he seated himself on the sofa and passed the time discussing operations with, perhaps, Kusaka, Ozawa, and Ugaki, or simply chatting, or playing *shogi*. At other times he would go to visit the sick and injured in the hospital; he seemed to dislike inactivity—his liveliness, in fact, suggested that his muddy eyes had been only a temporary symptom. He ate as heartily as ever. It was considerably later that Rabaul started trying to supply its own food; at this stage there was plenty of fruit, as well as all kinds of stuff brought from Japan. They also tried making *sukiyaki* using the flesh of sea turtles.

Kusaka, who suffered almost continuously from severe tropical diarrhoea, ate practically nothing. "You should try to get *something* down, at least," Yamamoto told him. One morning, when Kusaka came on horseback to call at the cottage on "Residency Hill," Yamamoto himself picked a cucumber growing nearby and tried to get Kusaka to have some. The two men were on terms of complete familiarity and openness. According to Kusaka, the navy, though not without its class distinctions, traditionally avoided many of the excessive formalities of language and address that afflicted the army. "Later on," Kusaka says, "they began to imitate the army and use 'your excellency' and the like, but I don't see what was wrong with just 'you'!"

One day Kusaka, with Ozawa, decided to hold a small reunion for five graduates of the thirty-seventh year at the Naval Academy who happened to be in Rabaul. When Yamamoto heard of it he said, "I don't suppose they'll mind my joining in," and turned up at the meeting with a bottle of Johnny Walker Black Label. The excuse was that in 1909, when the class graduated from the Naval Academy and set off on a training cruise of distant waters, Yamamoto, then a lieutenant, had been divisional officer on board the training ship *Soya*, the ship on which the class went on the ocean cruise that followed graduation. When the party was at its height, someone suggested they mark the occasion by making a *yosegaki* (collection of their signatures), and Yamamoto proposed that they send one each to admirals Suzuki and Koga. At the time of that training cruise thirty-four years earlier, Suzuki had been captain of the *Soya*, and Koga had been an ensign on board. Yamamoto himself started the collection for Suzuki by writing, with a brush, his own name and his posts at that time and at the present: "Yamamoto Isoroku, divisional officer on the *Soya*, now Commander in Chief Combined Fleet." The others followed suit. Yamamoto could not have known that the two collections of signatures were to be delivered immediately after his own death.

As he played *shogi* with Watanabe Yasuji in the staff officers' lounge, Yamamoto kept his ears open for American broadcasts over the shortwave radio. From these he realized that notification of the commencement of hostilities must have taken place following the Pearl Harbor attack after all, and that the American government and people were both deeply outraged. "So we were too early, all the same," he said to Watanabe. "That's bad. I don't know which of us will get killed first, but if I die before you, I'd like you to tell the emperor that the Combined Fleet certainly did not plan things that way originally. We thought we were doing things according to schedule."

The days passed. Operation "I" ended more or less successfully, and Yamamoto's scheduled stay in Rabaul was drawing to an end when he suddenly announced that to wind up his stay he wanted to make a one-day tour of bases in the Shortland area—closest to the front line on Guadalcanal—in order to raise the morale of the men stationed there.

The planned tour was officially decided on by C. in C. Yamamoto personally on April 13, and late that afternoon a message was sent to base units, air flotillas, and garrisons in the area saying in part: "Commander in Chief Combined Fleet will personally inspect Ballale, Shortland, and Buin on April 18. Schedule as follows: 0600 leave Rabaul in medium attack plane (escorted by six fighters); 0800 arrive Ballale and proceed immediately by subchaser to Shortland, arriving 0840. . . . 1400 leave Buin by medium attack plane; 1540 arrive Rabaul. . . . To be postponed one day in case of bad weather."

Approximately one hundred and eighty miles southeast from Rabaul on New Britain Island lay the island of Bougainville, with the Buin base at its southern extremity. A mere five or six minutes to the south of Buin by plane was Shortland Island, and directly to the east of this the tiny island of Ballale, which consisted of little more than an airfield. Southeast from Bougainville again lay Choiseul Island, Santa Isabel Island, and Guadalcanal; these formed the Solomon archipelago.

Quite a few of Yamamoto's associates were opposed to the projected tour. The first to object was Ozawa Jisaburo, C. in C. of the Third Fleet. When Yamamoto refused to be dissuaded, he appealed to senior staff officer Kuroshima: "If he insists on going," he said, "six fighters are nothing like enough. Tell the chief of staff that he can have as many of my planes as he likes." But Chief of Staff Ugaki was in bed with dengue fever, and Ozawa's proposal never reached him.

Two months earlier, on February 10, Lieutenant General Imamura had, in the same way as Yamamoto was preparing to do, got a navy plane to fly him to Buin on a visit to officers and men under his command who had been fighting for a long time without food supplies. Ten minutes before they were due to land at Buin, a squadron of thirty American fighters had appeared out of the blue. The petty officer who was piloting the plane told Imamura, in a rear seat, that he was going to take evasive action. He flew straight into the clouds, and after twisting and turning inside them announced this time that he was going out to take a look. And with admirable coolness he flew out above the clouds. The enemy fighters had been given the slip, and they landed at Buin none the worse for this hair's-breadth escape from death.

Imamura told Yamamoto of this experience, hoping indirectly to warn him of the dangers involved, but Yamamoto merely expressed satisfaction at Imamura's escape and the skill shown by the petty officer, and showed no sign of being deterred himself.

When Rear Admiral Joshima, commander in chief of the Eleventh Air Flotilla on Shortland, saw the radio message of April 13, he said to his staff officers: "What a damn fool thing to do, to send such a long and detailed message about the activities of the C. in C. so near the front! This kind of thing must stop." On the seventeenth, the day before Yamamoto's departure, he went over to Rabaul and warned Yamamoto personally that he should give up the plan, since it was too dangerous, but Yamamoto would not listen.

"I have to go," he said. "I've let them know, and they'll have got things ready for me. I'll leave tomorrow morning and be back by dusk. Why don't we have dinner together?"

2

Every day so far in Truk and in Rabaul Yamamoto had worn white dress uniform, but the following morning, April 18, he emerged from his lodgings wearing a new, dark green, simplified uniform. Kuroshima and Watanabe were to stay behind in Rabaul; Chief of Staff Ugaki and the other seven staff officers who were to accompany Yamamoto followed Yamamoto by car to the Rabaul east airfield, together with Vice Admiral Ozawa and others who were going to see him off.

Two type-1 land-based attack planes belonging to the 705th Squadron were waiting there. Four passengers—Yamamoto, fleet medical officer Takada, air "A" staff officer Toibana, who had taken over from Miwa, and an aide, Fukuzaki—boarded the first plane; the second plane was to carry Chief of Staff Ugaki, fleet paymaster Kitamura, fleet meteorological officer Tomono, communications staff officer Imanaka, and air "B" staff officer Muroi.

The captain and chief pilot of the first plane was Chief Petty Officer Kotani. The captain of the second plane was Petty Officer

First Class Tanimoto, and the chief pilot Petty Officer Second Class Hayashi. They were all highly experienced, reliable men who had already taken part in many battles.

The two attack planes took off at six, precisely on schedule, from the east airfield. Following them, six "Zero" fighters belonging to the 204th Squadron took off in a cloud of dust and immediately split into two groups of three in order to fly as escorts on either side of the plane carrying Yamamoto and the others.

An hour and a half later, the planes were flying along the west coast of Bougainville Island at a height of about 6,500 feet, with dense jungle visible below. Buin and Ballale were already close at hand, and the captain had just passed back a slip of paper saying "Expect to arrive at Ballale 0745," when one of the escort fighters suddenly accelerated and went ahead of their plane. It dipped its wings, and the pilot could be seen pointing to something.

Looking down to the right, they saw a dozen or more American P-38 fighters flying in a southerly direction at an altitude approximately 1,600 feet lower than their own. They were at more or less the same spot at which Imamura had encountered enemy aircraft two months earlier.

Spotting the Japanese planes, the P-38 squadron immediately discarded its extra fuel tanks and with obvious intent to do battle divided into two formations, one of which climbed steeply while the other moved around to the front so as to obstruct the path of the two type-1 attack planes. The first of the Japanese planes seems to have tried to evade them by hurtling down to fly immediately above the jungle and turning sharply to the left in the direction of Buin base, which lay immediately ahead.

Making no attempt to avoid the counterattacking "Zeros," the P-38s seized this opportunity to swoop down on it from above and directly behind.

All kinds of reports have been circulated as to what happened from this point on. Only two persons on the Japanese side are still alive to give direct evidence—Yanagiya Kenji, who was one of the survivors of the escorting "Zero" squadron, and Hayashi Hiroshi, chief pilot of the second plane. As the only person who can describe what took place on board the plane carrying members of Combined Fleet command,

Hayashi's testimony is particularly valuable. The remaining twenty-odd men at headquarters and the plane crews are all dead by now.

Hayashi, who is still hale and hearty, keeps a fish shop on Yakushima Island in Kagoshima Prefecture, where he serves as head of the local fire brigade. He is well known and popular on the island. He still has the flight record of the time in his possession, but it seems possible that, in the course of twenty-six long years, certain errors have crept into his memories of the day.

The account given by Ugaki in his *Sensoroku* is very detailed, but he was seriously injured in the crash and did not set his impressions down until April 18, 1944, a full year later. Here too, therefore, it may be too much to expect complete accuracy in every respect. There are, in fact, discrepancies between *Sensoroku* and Hayashi's account, so it is best here to go over the ground again, setting the two accounts side by side where they differ.

Hayashi's first knowledge of his own flight plan for the eighteenth came from orders posted on the evening of April 17. At first he thought it was the regular flight to Buin, but his unit commander came in and told him that the next day he must dress up properly in the regulation flying uniform. Hayashi, who was used to flying comfortably with just a jacket over his heat-protective clothing, asked why, and was then told for the first time that he would be flying Commander in Chief Yamamoto and other high-ranking officers from Combined Fleet headquarters.

The type-1 bombers of the 705th Squadron were at Vunakanau base on top of the hills, so Nos. 323 and 326, which had been selected to carry the party, took off from Vunakanau at dawn on the day and were flown down to the east airfield by the sea. The pilots switched off their engines to wait, and before long Yamamoto and his group arrived. Takada and Kitamura alone were in white dress uniform, the C. in C. and the rest in dark green. It had been decided the day before, at the chief of staff's suggestion, that they should all wear the latter, since it would be inappropriate for members of headquarters to appear before officers and men in the front line in anything else; but the decision seems not to have reached Takada and Kitamura. Yamamoto seems to have been rather put out, but it was too late to do anything, so the party divided in two and immediately boarded the aircraft. First the plane carrying

Yamamoto, then the second plane, then the escorting fighter squadron took off on schedule. The weather was fine and visibility good—a pleasant day for flying. Before long, Chief of Staff Ugaki, who was sitting in the captain's seat immediately behind chief pilot Hayashi, nodded off. When Petty Officer Tanimoto, captain and observer of the plane, who was in the copilot's seat, went to report that they would arrive in Ballale in fifteen minutes' time, Ugaki was still half asleep. It seems that the radio mast of their plane had lost a screw or something, for it had started to wobble. Turning around, Hayashi reported the fact and said that it would delay them slightly, but Ugaki merely grunted sleepily.

Almost immediately after this, one of the escorting "Zeros" was seen to approach the first plane, which promptly turned its nose down. The instruments showed that it must have increased speed to about 240 knots. Hayashi remembers thinking to himself that it was dangerous to drop altitude at such a rate.

Sensoroku notes: "Plane No. 2 was flying in excellent formation to the left and slightly to the rear of plane No. 1—so excellent that at times the wingtips seemed almost in danger of touching, and I could clearly see the profile of the C. in C., sitting in the captain's seat, and the forms of people moving about inside the plane. It was a comfortable flight as I sat listening to explanations, with reference to flight maps, of objects visible on the ground below."

But subsequently, while Ugaki was dozing, plane No. 2, which had tended to lag because of the problems with its radio mast, got still further separated on the same account.

It must have been an awareness of something untoward that made Ugaki wake up. Later, in *Sensoroku*, he wrote: "Everyone sensed that something was wrong. I asked the captain, who was in the gangway, 'What's up?' and he replied, 'It must be some mistake.' This reply was itself a gross mistake, and intolerably slack."

Suddenly Hayashi, who was at the controls in the chief pilot's seat, saw a red tracer bullet pass over his head. Simultaneously the captain, Petty Officer Tanimoto, struck him on the shoulder with a cry of "Enemy aircraft!" Startled, he glanced up and caught sight of a P-38 through the roof of the cockpit. From then on he scarcely had time to realize what was happening, much less worry about the flutter on the radio mast. A sudden dive, a high-speed turn of more than ninety degrees, and he was flying his craft over the jungle treetops in a desperate effort to avoid attack.

By now plane No. 1 was flying about two and a half miles to the right of plane No. 2, at a low altitude and decreasing speed, and was already spurting black smoke and flames.

Ugaki ordered air staff officer Muroi, who was standing in the gangway, to keep an eye on the C. in C.'s plane, then turning to the pilot shouted, "Follow plane No. 1! Follow plane No. 1!"

To Hayashi, who was performing desperate escape maneuvers, sometimes using only his feet and sometimes only his hands as he banked the plane and put it into sharp turns, the order came as a momentary shock, and he admits to having been at a loss. Since the enemy aircraft were not paying much attention to their own plane, there was a good chance that they could save themselves at least. But the order had come from the chief of staff of the Combined Fleet; he decided, as he had been told, to get as close as possible to plane No. 1. However, after a number of quick turns they lost sight of the other aircraft.

By the time they switched to level flight again, the C. in C.'s plane was nowhere in the sky, and a tall column of black smoke was rising out of the dense green of the jungle.

The P-38s, having made sure of the first plane, immediately turned to attack the other. Petty Officer Hayashi headed the plane out over the sea, fearing that they would quickly be disposed of over the jungle. The engines were at full throttle. He took the plane about a hundred and sixty feet out from the coast and brought it down until the propellers were in danger of hitting the water. Almost immediately, though, it must have been shot through the controls or flaps, for he suddenly lost control and the plane plunged straight down into the sea. It must have tilted quite sharply as it hit the water, for he saw one of the engines fly off at an angle.

Hayashi lost consciousness momentarily, and when he came to found himself in the water by the base of the left wing of the plane, which was on fire, lying half on its side with the tail and right wing sticking up high out of the sea.

Their position was a little to the north of Moila Point at the southwestern extremity of Bougainville Island. Hayashi started swimming for the shore. Ugaki also started swimming, a little later, it seems, than Hayashi. He had felt a number of the P-38s' shells score direct hits on the plane, and had given himself up for lost. As the plane dived into the sea, he was thrown out into the gangway and everything went black. When things became light again, he looked around him in surprise and found that he had risen to the surface of the water.

Both Ugaki and Hayashi seem to have been thrown out of the plane, through the canopy over the cockpit, by the shock of impact. The plane was burning fiercely, and there was no sign of the other staff officers and crew members. A large number of wooden boxes came floating by. Ugaki clung to a particularly large, gray-colored toolbox and started swimming, using only his legs. Catching sight of a crew member in a flying helmet swimming strongly some way ahead of him, he shouted to him.

From the shore came the busy sound of guns being fired; the army lookouts there were trying to kill them, under the impression that they were the enemy. "Signal to them! Signal to them!" Ugaki called frantically to Hayashi. The latter heard and looked around, but bullets were flying all about him, so he continued swimming toward the shore, shouting and keeping under water as much as possible. There was a fast current, and Ugaki found himself being carried along parallel to the shore without getting much closer to it, but soon a soldier— informed by Hayashi who by now had been dragged out of the water— stripped and came plunging into the sea in his direction. As he got closer to Ugaki, after swimming about ten yards, the soldier suddenly gave an excited shout: "It's a staff officer!" Thus Ugaki was brought safely to shore. Hayashi's memory of the episode and Ugaki's account do not agree as to whether the site was Moila Point as such, where a detachment of the navy's land units was stationed, or another place farther to the north, but both are agreed that they were given first aid by an army orderly.

Ugaki was seriously injured, but Petty Officer Hayashi had little more than light bruises and a slightly cut mouth. Despite this, the army orderly kept staring at him oddly. Scrutinizing the orderly in his turn, Hayashi had the feeling that he had met him somewhere before. In fact, by an extraordinary coincidence, the man had worked with Hayashi before the latter joined the navy, when both of them had been streetcar conductors in Yahata in Kyushu.

As Hayashi remembers it, he and Ugaki were treated by Hayashi's former colleague, then the two of them were sent by truck to Moila Point.

Rear Admiral Kitamura, who had been discovered and rescued by a navy seaplane as he was swimming alone and injured in the water, was brought directly to Moila Point. He had a hole in his throat, and could only reply with meaningless noises to Ugaki's exclamations of encouragement.

These three men were, in fact, the only survivors among those who had been on plane No. 2. After about an hour, the chief medical officer of the First Base Unit in Buin, Lieutenant Commander Tabuchi, arrived in a subchaser and gave them emergency treatment, then they were conveyed to the base unit's sickbay. It was decided that Hayashi, who was a petty officer and not seriously injured, should be sent back to Rabaul that same day. On his arrival at the east airfield in Rabaul around dusk, he was promptly isolated in the Eighth Naval Hospital. The purpose, of course, was not to treat him but to prevent any leakage of information. Even so, he says, once he had been submitted to routine questioning in hospital he was not subjected to further restrictions.

The flight record in his possession records the two-hour, one-way flight made by plane No. 326 on Sunday, April 18, 1943, from RRF (Rabaul) to RWP (Buin), but after that remains blank until he began flying again on June 15. During the interval Hayashi was paid the sum of twenty yen by way of solatium, in the name of Vice Admiral Kusaka, commander in chief of the Southeast Area Fleet.

3

It was around noon that day that Kuroshima and Watanabe, the two staff officers who had stayed behind in Rabaul, together with Kusaka and Ozawa, heard about the crash of Yamamoto's plane via a message from Buin and the reports made by the escort fighters on their return. It was not known whether the C. in C. had survived or not.

At 2:30 P.M. the following cable was sent to the navy minister and chief of the Naval General Staff:

Cable No. 181430, official secret
From: Commander in Chief Southeast Area Fleet
"A" Report No. 1

The land-based attack planes carrying members of the Combined Fleet command, together with six escorting fighters, encountered and engaged in combat more than a dozen enemy fighters in the vicinity of QBB around 0740.

The No. 1 land-based attack plane (carrying: the C. in C. [A], the fleet medical officer [C], staff officer Toibana [E], and an aide [F]) was seen to dive at a shallow angle into the jungle eleven nautical miles to the west of QBV emitting flames, and No. 2 plane (carrying: the chief of staff [B], the fleet paymaster [D], the fleet meteorological officer [G], the communications staff officer [H], and staff officer Muroi [I]) made an emergency landing in the sea, to the south of Moiga [sic]. So far as can be ascertained at the moment, only B and D (both injured) have been rescued. A search and rescue operation is at present being arranged. (This cable will henceforth be referred to as report "A.")

This cable was sent at 2:30 P.M.; its number shows the date and time. It was received by the Tokyo Signals Unit, housed in the Navy Ministry, at 5:08, and deciphering was completed by 7:20. It was treated as a "military secret." The "Moiga" in the text is probably a cipher clerk's mistake for "Moila."

According to an account written by Sagara Tatsuo, a member of the Aeronautics Department who also worked as an aide in the Naval General Staff, Commander Asada, a member of the Naval Affairs Bureau, came into the minister's secretariat—which was more or less deserted by that time of the evening—with an extraordinarily tense expression and handed a copy of the message to Captain Yanagisawa, the senior aide, who was working late. As he read, Yanagisawa's face grew steadily more solemn. Soon the ministry began to bustle with activity, and late that night a stream of navy leaders began secretly to arrive, among them Navy Minister Shimada, Navy Vice-Minister Sawamoto, Chief of the Naval General Staff Nagano, Vice-Chief Ito, and Fukudome, head of the First Division.

In Rabaul, administrative staff officer Watanabe, having arranged to have this first report sent to Tokyo, intended at first to fly immediately to the spot, but a plane could not be readied in time, and a fierce squall blew up as well, so his departure was delayed until the following day. Arriving in Buin by land-based attack plane at something after eight on the morning of the nineteenth, accompanied by Captain Okubo, chief medical officer of the Southeast Area Fleet, Watanabe hastened straight to the officers' sickbay, which stood in a palm grove.

Ugaki's injuries were fairly severe, involving a severed radial artery and compound fracture of the right arm, but he was a tough man who, even as they pumped the umpteenth injection into him to prevent infection, could joke that this would probably "cure his 'R.'" "R" stood for gonorrhea (*rimbyo* in Japanese) and was the slang term for a disease of which many naval officers had had experience at some time or other. Even so, when he saw Watanabe his eyes filled with tears, and looking up, swathed in bandages, from his truckle bed, he could only say repeatedly; "The C. in C.'s 4.5 miles northeast of Point Camau. Get there quickly, quickly!"

"Point Camau" is the name of a place at the southern extremity of the Indochina peninsula; there is nowhere of that name on Bougainville. If Watanabe's memory is not mistaken, it must have been a slip of the tongue for "Point Moila" due to Ugaki's feverish state.

Watanabe commandeered a type-94 reconnaissance seaplane and set out to search for the missing plane from the air. The place where plane No. 1 had dived into the jungle was easily identified by the scorched trees round about. Watanabe had brought with him a number of rubber balls; he slit them open, inserted into each a piece of paper with a scribbled note reading, "This is Watanabe. Please wave your handkerchiefs," put each ball into a long net bag, and dropped fifteen or sixteen of them at the site of the crash.

There was no reply from the ground. Even so, he had the seaplane repeatedly circle low over the jungle, just in case some signal from below had been hidden by the dense foliage. Eventually he gave up and had the seaplane fly out to sea, where it alighted beside a waiting minesweeper. As had been previously arranged, some sixty men of both watches were ready to form a search party. He himself took command, and they went ashore by boat at the estuary of a small river. The afternoon was already fairly far advanced.

The river's meandering course led deep into the Bougainville jungle. It was the party's intention to proceed upstream by boat with supplies of food, clothing, and medicine, but the stream was shallow and blocked in places by fallen trees, so they abandoned the boat halfway and split into two parties which started to make their way up the left and right banks respectively. This too proved impossible, so they joined forces again and waded together up the center of the stream. No one remembers the name of the river in question. A large number of streams rise high on the mountain known as Tabago, which looms behind the Buin base, then flow down into the sea to the northwest of Moila Point. According to a large map stuck on the wall of the local Australian government office on Buin today, it seems likely that the river that Watanabe and his party followed was the Wamai. The distance from the coast up the Wamai to the spot where Yamamoto's aircraft crashed is not far as the crow flies, but the jungle is extremely dense—it invites clichés such as "dark even at midday" and "untouched by ax since the beginning of history"—and the river itself is full of loops and curves. Watanabe had already estimated, by observation from the air, that the crash site was so many miles to the east of the river and so many bends upstream, but he must have got his direction wrong, for they trudged on until late at night, plagued by mosquitoes all the while, without reaching the site. Sometime past midnight, they were all so exhausted that they sprawled out on the ground and went to sleep where they were.

4

Another search party had set out overland directly from Buin. The Sasebo Sixth Special Land Unit, stationed in Buin, organized a party consisting chiefly of a medical team and set out around 11:00 A.M. on the eighteenth under the command of a special duties lieutenant called Furukawa. They searched all that day and the next, but were equally unsuccessful in finding the C. in C.'s plane. In the end, it was an army search party that found it. The Seventeenth Army command was located on Bougainville, and various units belonging to the army were stationed here and there around the island. The leader of the party that discovered Yamamoto's plane was Second Lieutenant Hamasuna. Hamasuna, who had been drafted shortly after the outbreak of the China Incident, had already seen six years of active service in various places, during which time he had risen from the ranks to become an officer. At the time in question, he and his men were camped close to the native village of Aku, about eighteen miles west of Buin, engaged in the construction of an army road.

The eighteenth being a Sunday, they were not working but resting and going over their weapons and equipment. Sometime before eight in the morning, a dogfight suddenly started at an extremely low altitude above them. The jungle echoed with explosions and the rattle of machine guns, and several American P-38s and Japanese navy "Zero" fighters were seen chasing each other to and fro just above the treetops. Hamasuna and his men were soon on their feet, bawling encouragement to the Japanese fighters. When they saw a large column of black smoke rising above the jungle in the distance, they danced with delight, believing that a "Zero" had shot down one of the American planes. Several hours later, an order was delivered from regimental headquarters about one-third of a mile away, and was passed on verbally to Second Lieutenant Hamasuna: "A plane carrying top navy brass has crashed. You're to organize a search party and go to look for it. You were watching, so you'll know roughly where it crashed."

Wondering who the "top navy brass" might be, Hamasuna selected a sergeant and nine other NCOs and men from his own platoon, and the eleven-member party plunged into the jungle with only a single compass to go by.

The jungle was a dense mass of banyans, palms, rattan vines, and other, unidentifiable plants and trees; it was gloomy beneath the trees, and no hills, banks, or other landmarks such as might help them find their bearings were visible. They could never have found their way back again unaided, so as they went they shaved pieces of bark off the trees, or hung things from the branches, in order to give them some sign.

They scoured the jungle all day in the area where they had seen the black smoke, but failed to find the plane, and returned to their unit at Aku just before sunset. On going to regimental headquarters to report, Hamasuna was told that the naval search party had also been unsuccessful so far, and he was ordered to try again the next day.

The following day, the nineteenth, was the day on which Watanabe and the rest reached Buin. Around eleven o'clock, a friendly plane arrived in the sky over Hamasuna's party, so they found a clearing and waved the Rising Sun flags they had brought with them, whereupon the plane dropped them a message tube. They hoped it might explain the whereabouts of the crashed plane, but when they opened it all they found was a paper with the message, "Have you found the wreck? If there are survivors, let us know by waving a white cloth or flag in circles." The friendly plane in question may have been the type-94 reconnaissance seaplane carrying Watanabe.

Hamasuna's party trudged on through the jungle. Dusk approached, and they were thinking of giving up for the day again when one of the men said he thought he could smell gasoline. They sniffed the air eagerly. He seemed to be right. It had been a weary trek through the jungle (malaria was rampant on Bougainville at the time, and none of the men in the party had escaped), but now they plunged ahead again in the direction from which the smell seemed to come.

Before long they caught sight of what seemed to be a bank rising ahead. A bank, though, was improbable in such a place, and as they drew closer they found that it was the large tail fin of the wrecked type-1 land-based attack plane. The wings and propellers had survived, but the massive fuselage had broken just in front of the Rising Sun mark, and the section extending from there to the cockpit was a burned-out hulk. Dead bodies were lying about the wreckage. Among them was a high-ranking officer. He sat as though abstracted, still strapped into his seat, amidst the trees. He had medal ribbons on his chest, and wore white gloves. His left hand grasped his sword, and his right hand rested lightly on it. His head lolled forward as though he was sunk in thought, but he was dead. This officer was the only one who had been thrown out of the plane in his seat.

The glove of the left hand gripping the sword had the index and middle fingers tied up with thread. The gilt epaulettes each bore three cherry blossoms. A full admiral with only three fingers on one hand. . . . Hamasuna remembered reading somewhere that Admiral Yamamoto Isoroku, commander in chief of the Combined Fleet, had lost two fingers during the Russo-Japanese War, and was the first holder of the Japanese equivalent of the Purple Heart. For the first time he realized that the "top navy brass" must include Yamamoto.

Putting a hand into the breast pocket of the corpse's jacket, he drew out an expensive-looking diary in which he finally found the signature "Yamamoto Isoroku," together with a large number of copies of poems by Emperor Meiji and the dowager empress Shoken. Oddly enough, he says, even when the body was identified as that of Admiral Yamamoto, nobody showed any great surprise. What seems to have impressed itself most strongly on Hamasuna and his men was the thick wad of pure white toilet paper and the clean white handkerchief that emerged from Yamamoto's pockets. The rank and file at the time suffered from an extreme shortage of, among other things, toilet paper. As one of the search party said, "You get to use good paper when you get to be C. in C.!"

Yamamoto still wore his black flying boots, but his cap had disappeared. With his lightly closed eyes and the half-white stubble on his cropped head, he reminded Hamasuna, the latter says, of a picture of a regent of the Kamakura shogunate that he had seen in a primary-school reader as a child. Yamamoto's body was on the left of the fuselage, and close by him the body of an elderly medical officer in white uniform lay spread-eagled, face up, on the ground. This was Rear Admiral Takada, the fleet medical officer. Beside him again lay another body, and on the other, right-hand side of the fuselage toward the front the body of a staff officer lay face up with all the buttons of its uniform undone. This was probably Toibana. Besides these, there were a number of burned bodies piled on top of one another, among them that of the chief pilot, Chief Petty Kotani.

None of the bodies was maggoty yet, but their faces were all swollen and puffy except Yamamoto's, which was relatively presentable. Odd though this may seem, it is apparently the truth; it was to give rise to all kinds of speculative legends in later days—that Yamamoto had looked as though he was still alive; that he had in fact been alive, but had committed suicide after leaving the plane; that his eyes were wide open and staring; that he was in such-and-such a posture. . . . These spread still further and took still more elaborate forms after the war. Some American writers have suggested that, on the contrary, a man in a plane that had been shot down could hardly have looked so presentable, and that the Japanese had fabricated the story in order to make a god of Yamamoto.

Unfortunately, the only people who saw plane No. 1 as it was just after it crashed were Hamasuna and the other ten members of his party, since they promptly cut down trees round about and set up a temporary shelter in the clearing that the aircraft itself had made, transferring into it Yamamoto and the other ten bodies. The corpses were covered with banyan leaves, and offerings of water—drawn in navy cups from a jungle spring nearby—were placed beside them.

(The interior of the rear section of the fuselage, which survived the flames, was empty save for navy enamelware scattered about the floor.)

Almost all the members of the Hamasuna party seem to have been killed by the end of the war or cannot be traced, but Hamasuna himself was ordered to a home unit four months after this. He arrived safely back in Japan, and thus survived the end of the war. Possibly his transfer back home was made in recognition of his service in discovering Yamamoto's plane. Today he runs a small shop in Saito City, Miyazaki Prefecture. The account that he gives today is substantially the same as that contained in the report that he submitted at the time, via regimental headquarters, to Combined Fleet command, and one must conclude that it represents the closest thing to the truth that we have.

Yamamoto's corpse showed no sign of his having committed suicide. If anyone from plane No. 1 survived after the crash and conflagration, it was probably Rear Admiral Takada, fleet medical officer. He was discovered lying right next to Yamamoto, and his body was almost totally free of visible injuries. A sense of the responsibilities of his post may have made him wish to leave the C. in C.'s remains in as decent a state as possible, and he may have taken appropriate steps in his last moments of semiconsciousness before expiring. This would satisfactorily explain why Yamamoto was so presentable in death; but it can never be more than a hypothesis.

5

The sword that Yamamoto was gripping at the time was made by a swordsmith called Amada Sadayoshi, of Shibata in Niigata Prefecture; it had been given to Yamamoto by his elder brother Kihachi. Yamamoto had seven or eight other swords besides this one, including some with far more distinguished pedigrees. The reason why he chose this new sword to wear when he went to the front was that it was a gift from his deceased brother, while the swordsmith's given name was the same as that of his deceased father, so that he felt, somehow, that the other two were always with him.

Some of the staff officers were carrying small, stylish pistols that Hamasuna and the others eyed rather covetously, but Yamamoto had nothing on him apart from his sword, diary, and his handkerchief and paper. He had intended to be back by nightfall.

By the time Hamasuna's party had more or less finished clearing away the bodies, it was time to get back if they did not want to be benighted in the jungle. Leaving the wrecked aircraft, the remains of Yamamoto and the others, and most of the dead men's belongings, they turned back onto the main track that led to Aku, where they came across an utterly exhausted naval party taking a rest. This, it would seem, was the search party sent by the Sasebo Sixth Special Land Unit at Buin. Delighted at the news of the discovery of Yamamoto's plane, the navy men announced that they wanted to camp where they were that night and proceed to the crash site at dawn the following morning, and asked Hamasuna's party to take them there.

Thus on the morning of April 20 Hamasuna and his men joined forces with the navy unit and plunged into the jungle for the third time. Around the same time, Watanabe and his men, waking on the banks of the river, set off once more in search of Yamamoto's plane, but again failed to reach it. They were still struggling on, their hands and faces swollen from the mosquito bites covering them, when a plane came flying over, banking its wings steeply in the prearranged signal that meant "aircraft discovered, bodies recovered."

Watanabe's party decided to go back to the assembly point at the mouth of the river. There they found the navy search party from Buin waiting with stretchers. The Hamasuna party had taken them to the site, helped them get the bodies out, then taken its leave and gone back to its base at Aku. At a request from the unit commander, Hamasuna drew up a detailed report giving places and times for their three-day search, and submitted it together with diagrams. This was forwarded to Combined Fleet command, and somewhat later Hamasuna received a letter of thanks from Watanabe, written with brush and ink, in which the latter thanked him and his party for their cooperation "in such difficult terrain and under the blazing sun." Nevertheless, the letter ended by enjoining him to strict secrecy about the crash until such time as there should be an announcement from Imperial Headquarters. No mention at all was made of the name "Yamamoto."

The place-name Aku, incidentally, was known among Japanese

forces in the area at the time as "Ako." There is a popular theory that Hamasuna's party was led to the site of the crash by local natives, but according to Hamasuna himself it is mistaken. They caught absolutely no sight of any natives during their search, and the place—a marshy area entirely devoid of paths, where water oozed up through a thick layer of dead tropical vegetation—was one that even the natives did not normally frequent. Although all the bodies were recovered, the plane was left where it was. Today, almost thirty years later, type-1 land-based attack plane 323 still lies in the jungle of Bougainville Island. Its number is no longer visible, its propellers are covered with moss, the red of the Rising Sun mark on its fuselage has almost faded away, and it is covered with tropical vegetation. If you take the regular flight to Buin via Port Moresby and Rabaul, and ask the young men of Aku or the neighboring village, they will take you to the spot—which they know well—cheerfully singing Japanese songs on the way. There are less mosquitoes than there once were, and there are no poisonous snakes or fierce animals, but there are many historical relics that can be viewed in greater comfort.

It was around 4:00 P.M. on the twentieth that the navy search party from Buin handed over the remains of Yamamoto and the rest to Watanabe at the mouth of the Wamai River. A tent was set up on the forward deck of the minesweeper that had come to fetch them, and the bodies were laid out in its shade. During the trip to the pier at Buin via Moila Point, Watanabe and chief medical officer Okubo went into the tent and carried out a preliminary examination.

Seeing the marks of the bullet that had pierced Yamamoto's lower jaw and emerged at the temple, Okubo said, "This alone would have killed him outright." Yamamoto's watch had stopped at 7:45. Quite obviously he had been killed on the plane before it crashed into the jungle.

At this point, it seems, one of Yamamoto's admiral's insignia on the collar of his uniform was missing. Watanabe apparently suspected that the local natives had stolen it (when, arriving fresh from the splendors of Combined Fleet headquarters, he first set eyes on the Melanesians, he had felt that "you almost expected to find they had tails"), but, as we have seen already, no native had so much as set eyes on Yamamoto's body. If both insignia were in fact there when he was first discovered, it probably means that someone in Hamasuna's

362

party or the naval search party had surreptitiously made off with one as a souvenir.

The eleven bodies were put in coffins and placed in a tent set up for the wake in front of the offices of the First Base Unit in Buin. The next day, they were cremated at the Sasebo Sixth Special Land Unit's farm, about fifteen minutes away by car. The man who performed the autopsy on Yamamoto's body at Buin and drew up the official autopsy report was Lieutenant Commander Tabuchi, chief medical officer of the First Base Unit.

On the morning of the eighteenth, hearing that the C. in C. was coming to Buin that day and that on arrival he was scheduled to go directly to the hospital to visit sick and wounded men there, Tabuchi went to the hospital personally to see that everything was clean and in order. He was still there when a message came from senior staff officer Tomita Sutezo of the base unit asking him to come immediately to headquarters with the necessary medication for treating wounded and feverish patients. When he got back to the base office, he found Tomita, who told him in great dismay that the C. in C.'s plane had been shot down and that the second plane carrying the chief of staff and other officers had crashed into the sea near Moila Point. Ugaki had apparently been rescued. Tabuchi was to go there immediately. Tabuchi set off for Moila Point in a subchaser, taking with him a young medical officer and several men from the Sasebo Sixth Special Land Unit.

In the meantime, Lieutenant Shinkawa, chief paymaster of the Sasebo Sixth Special Land Unit, had suggested that natives should be employed to take the search party to the site, but his suggestion had been turned down. He also held the job of chief public relations officer, and as such knew the local headmen well. As he saw it, the quickest way to find a plane that had crashed in the jungle was to seek the aid of the local natives, but the idea was rejected because it was a top-secret matter.

Arriving at Moila Point, Tabuchi gave Ugaki and Kitamura first-aid treatment, then sent them back to Buin. He himself, however, stayed on with the idea that there might be survivors from plane No. 1 as well, and that he would have to give them treatment if they were brought to the coast. He waited up all night, gazing disconsolately at the fireflies dancing about outside, but learning of the search party's failure to reach the site and the apparent absence of any survivors, he returned to Buin the next day, the nineteenth. Of the eleven bodies that reached the First Base Unit around dusk on the twentieth, Tabuchi examined only five—those of Yamamoto, fleet medical officer Takada, air "A" staff officer Toibana, A.D.C. Fukuzaki, and chief pilot Kotani; it is not known who examined the bodies of the six enlisted men. Four other officers were present—Rear Admiral Itagaki, commander of the First Base Unit and younger brother of Itagaki Seishiro; Captain Okubo, chief medical officer of the Southeast Area Fleet; Captain Uchino, chief medical officer of the Eighth Fleet; and Commander Watanabe of the Combined Fleet.

As Lieutenant Commander Tabuchi examined the bodies, he spoke aloud his findings, which were recorded by medical officer Fukuhara, attached to the First Base Unit. A fair copy was then made by a chief petty officer called Ikeda, and on this basis five copies each of the autopsy report and autopsy record were drawn up. According to these, Yamamoto's body had wounds about the size of the tip of one's little finger where a machine-gun bullet had entered at the angle of the left lower jaw and emerged at the right, and an entry wound the size of the tip of one's index finger in the center of the left shoulder blade. The latter hole went upward and to the right, but there was no exit wound. Watanabe himself put a finger up into the wound, but could not contact the bullet. The left half of the undershirt was stained with blood. The uniform jacket was slightly burned, and had L-shaped tears in two or three places. One of the flying boots was slightly damaged, but the foot was uninjured. Several maggots were already crawling about the face, but it was still remarkably well preserved and recognizably that of Admiral Yamamoto as Tabuchi had seen it in newspaper photographs.

Dr. Tabuchi, who at present runs a surgical clinic at Saidaiji in Okayama Prefecture, has carefully preserved copies of both the autopsy report and the autopsy record. These two, being official documents, contain the information just given in considerably stiffer and more technical terminology, which might give the impression that they are extremely detailed and faithful accounts of the facts. However, if one reads them carefully, one finds places where they differ from the facts as I have related them here. Oddly enough, moreover, it is the official record that is wrong, as Dr. Tabuchi himself bears witness.

The record contains the phrase "examination carried out on board minesweeper No. 15," but chief medical officer Tabuchi was not on board minesweeper No. 15 at that time; he was waiting for the arrival of the bodies at Buin. The record, again, contains the words "sixty hours were estimated to have elapsed since death." The original figure was "seventy hours," but this had been amended to "sixty hours," with an official stamp beside the amendment saying "one character corrected." In fact, it was approximately seventy-two hours after Yamamoto's death that the autopsy record was made, so the uncorrected version is, in fact, the correct one. The account, in short, was tampered with, on orders from above, in order to make things look better. It is a notable example of what Takagi Sokichi means when he writes "it is extremely dangerous to swallow whole official records concerning the history of the war."

There is no need to discuss in detail the autopsy reports where the others are concerned. Toibana had suffered a fracture of the base of the skull, and the body was already badly decomposed. A.D.C. Fukuzaki and chief pilot Kotani had suffered "fourth-degree burns all over their bodies," and carbonization had made them scarcely recognizable as human beings, identification being possible only by such things as the names on their flying boots.

The oddest case was that of fleet medical officer Takada, whose autopsy record states: "burns on the upper half of the body and signs of a violent blow to the head were noted, from which it is concluded that a broken neck led to occlusion of the vital organs and instant death." This account is still more fictitious than that relating to Yamamoto. "He was also completely free from apparent injury," says Dr. Tabuchi, "—so much so that one wonders how he could have died."

Lieutenant Fukuhara, who took down the record as Tabuchi spoke, had gone to Rabaul with Petty Officer Ikeda four or five days previously, partly to take care of the wounded from Operation "I" and seriously sick patients from the First Base Unit hospital, and also, on orders from the chief medical officer, to take a short rest. His work at Rabaul finished, he took things easy for two or three days, and was due to fly back on the morning of the eighteenth to resume his post. Word came, however, that a large contingent of brass was due to take the flight on the eighteenth, and that he and Ikeda were to extend their stay for a day. Arriving back in Buin on the morning of the nineteenth, he heard for the first time what had happened to the C. in C.'s plane, and realized his own narrow escape.

Fukuhara had frequently visited the Naval Academy at Etajima in his middle-school days and later, and the bloodstained uniforms of heroes of the Russo-Japanese War that he saw in the museum there had made a strong impression on him. He felt somehow that Yamamoto's uniform and undershirt should not simply be burned with the body but should, if possible, be preserved as historical relics. He also wanted to check once more for himself the blind bullet hole in Yamamoto's back. Before cremation took place at the land unit's farm, therefore, he bent over the corpse with the idea of removing its clothing. Just then, someone bawled at him suddenly, "That's enough!" Looking up, he saw Watanabe towering over him threateningly. Permission was, in fact, given in the end for one of Yamamoto's collar insignia to be preserved as a memento, but all trace has since been lost of it.

A separate pit was dug to cremate Yamamoto's body, on the other side of the road from those dug for the rest. Each pit was packed with brushwood, then the coffin was placed on top and covered with more brushwood. The whole was doused with gasoline and set on fire; then, after making sure that the flames has taken a good hold, those present at the cremation site retired to the base at Buin, leaving only one man to keep guard.

The ashes were collected at 3:00 P.M. Watanabe jumped into the still-warm pit and, using papaya twigs as chopsticks, began to gather Yamamoto's ashes. The first remnant he found, he says, was the Adam's apple. They had no urns of the kind normally used in Japan, but stout wooden boxes had been readied. Yamamoto's was lined with papaya leaves, on which his ashes were placed.

One of the other ten men, Toibana, was a former classmate of Watanabe's, so the latter carefully gathered his ashes with the idea of taking them back personally to Toibana's children.

Once the ashes had been collected, the pits were filled in and earth mounds erected over them. Beside Yamamoto's mound they planted two papaya trees, since he had been particularly fond of the fruit. Until the end of the war, these graves were tended carefully by naval units, but since papaya trees live twenty years at the most the site is impossible to locate by now.

Commander Watanabe had been worked off his feet for days past; his uniform was salty from sweat, and he felt as though the nails in his boots would sizzle audibly if he were to dip them in the nearby stream. That evening, he recalls, the base commander laid on beer for him. It tasted unbelievably good, but directly afterward he began to have pains in his joints. Soon it hurt even to sit in his chair, but he managed to get through supper somehow, only to be seized with acute chills. He had been bitten by mosquitoes in the jungle and had contracted dengue fever.

Chief of Staff Ugaki did not attend the cremation, being still in bed, encased in plaster, but he kept repeating that it was all his fault and that he should have been more careful. It occurred to Watanabe then, he says, that Ugaki might commit suicide sometime in the future. The story is well known of how, two years and four months later—on August 15, 1945, the day of Japan's surrender—Ugaki, who was then commander in chief of the Fifth Air Fleet, led eleven of the "Suisei" carrier-based bombers under his command in a final suicide raid, from which he did not return, on Okinawa. At his side he wore a short sword that had been given to him by Yamamoto.

The following day, although he had a high fever, Watanabe took the remains of the eleven men back to Rabaul by plane, in a party that also included Ugaki, fleet paymaster Kitamura, and Captain Okubo.

Captain Honda—who as a lieutenant had been a divisional officer during Yamamoto's days as second-in-command of the Kasumigaura Aviation Corps, and had been encouraged by him to study ways of lengthening the lives of their planes—happened to be in Rabaul as fleet engineer of the Southeast Area Fleet and Eleventh Air Fleet. He clearly remembers the arrival of the ashes in Rabaul on the afternoon of the twenty-second.

The remains of the eleven men were contained in wooden boxes wrapped in white cloths and distinguished only by the code letters written on them. Yamamoto's death was kept strictly secret even from the units in Rabaul, and the wake was carried out in a dugout opposite headquarters, in the presence of a few members of headquarters staff. Under a dim electric light, two candles were lit in front of the boxes, and two beautiful tropical flowers were stood by them in lemonade bottles.

The next day, Yamamoto's ashes were seen off by Kusaka, Ozawa, Honda, and many others, as they left on the next leg of their journey, back to the flagship *Musashi* where it waited in the anchorage at Truk.

The box containing the ashes was deposited in the C. in C.'s cabin. Shortly afterward, Watanabe collapsed and was prostrate for the next fifteen days.

FOURTEEN

1

Once they had recovered from the shock of Yamamoto's death, the first thing that occurred to those responsible, both in the Southeast Area Fleet at Rabaul and in Combined Fleet command, was a suspicion that the navy's top-secret codes had been cracked. Even prior to Yamamoto's accident, Kusaka Jin'ichi, commander in chief of the Southeast Area Fleet, had on two or three occasions, including the experience with the land-based attack plane carrying Imamura Hitoshi, had the uneasy feeling that information was leaking to the enemy through the deciphering of Japanese codes, and had sent a message to the Fourth Division of the Naval General Staff, which was responsible for naval codes, urging it to take special care. But the reply—whether due to pride on the part of those responsible or to bureaucratic sectionalism—was that such a thing was quite impossible. Chief of Staff Ugaki himself is said to have declared, prior to his departure for Buin with Yamamoto, "How could they possibly break the Japanese codes?"

Once again, therefore, and despite the obvious doubts that remained, the affair was accounted for as sheer coincidence; it was not until after the war that it was revealed by the Americans that the shooting down of Yamamoto's plane was a deliberate ambush made possible through the breaking of Japanese codes.

The outfit responsible for the ambush was a mixed U.S. army, navy, and marine air group from Henderson Field on Guadalcanal, commanded by Rear Admiral Marc Mitscher. The commander of the P-38 squadron was a major called John Mitchell, while of the sixteen P-38s, the one that scored direct hits on Yamamoto's plane and brought it down is supposed to have been that flown by Captain Thomas Lanphier, Jr.

Marc Mitscher was commander of the carrier *Hornet* at the time of the Doolittle raid on Tokyo, and became famous, after his promotion to rear admiral, for the prominent part he played in the air battle over the Solomons.

On the afternoon of April 17, Rear Admiral Mitscher at the base on Guadalcanal saw a top-secret message that had come from Nimitz via Halsey. It stated that the Japanese admiral Yamamoto was due to go from Rabaul to Ballale on the morning of the following day, the eighteenth, then proceed by subchaser to Kahili (Kahili is the name of the coastal area that includes Buin; the Japanese used the name "Buin" for the area as a whole); that he was expected to arrive in Ballale at 9:45 (7:45 Japan time); and also that, since Yamamoto liked punctuality, he was likely to move according to schedule. The message also provided detailed information as to the type of plane due to carry Yamamoto, and even the number of escorting fighters. It directed that every possible means should be employed to shoot the plane down, and was signed with the name of Frank Knox, secretary of the navy.

One theory has it that Admiral Nimitz, in Hawaii, was not taken with the idea of killing the enemy admiral by means that depended on the breaking of a code, and at first passed responsibility for the decision to Washington. Nimitz was temperamentally a different type of man from Halsey; if William Halsey was America's Onishi Takijiro, then Chester Nimitz was its Yonai. This character difference is the probable origin of the legend; yet in fact even the most moderate, intellectually minded of military men could hardly have afforded to be so gentlemanly in the midst of a fight to the death. What Nimitz feared in reality was that the operation would reveal to the Japanese the truth about American code-breaking activities. Thus he vacillated at first, caught between the pros and cons of action, but once he felt assured that there was a suitable means of allaying Japanese suspicions, and that even if Japan changed its codes America could still deal with them, he gave the go-ahead.

Nor, in fact, did he know enough about Yamamoto to feel any real reluctance to kill him. It was only after the end of the war that Nimitz learned that Yamamoto had risked his life in opposition to the Tripartite Pact and had been an obdurate opponent of war with America and Britain, and that he recognized the true worth of the man.

On receipt of his orders, Rear Admiral Mitscher promptly drew up a plan of operations and set about preparations. The question remains, however, as to which particular coded message containing the schedule for Yamamoto's tour of inspection was deciphered, and how. As in the case of Pearl Harbor and Midway, this question remained for a long time shrouded in mystery. Even Potter and Nimitz's *The Great Sea War* says merely that information was received thanks to the cracking of Japanese codes, and that Yamamoto's plane was shot down precisely according to plan. Beginning the day after Yamamoto was shot down, the P-38s at Henderson Field—in the same way as on the morning of the eighteenth—made many sorties in formation in the vicinity of Bougainville, although they had nothing particular to do there, so as to give the impression that the encounter on the eighteenth was quite coincidental and utterly unrelated to codes and the like. The Southeast Area Fleet command at Rabaul, for its part, sent false coded messages saying that fleet commander Kusaka Jin'ichi was going to tour the front, but the Americans ignored these completely.

The conclusions reached by the former navy men who tackled the question after the end of the war were as follows. There were, in all, six different messages giving details of C. in C. Yamamoto's visit to Buin and Shortland. One of them, from the army lookout unit stationed at Ballale, where Yamamoto's plane was due to land, reported that fact back to the Seventeenth Army command on Bougainville.

Those responsible in the navy would naturally have liked to assume that if any code was broken it was the army's rather than their own. After the war, however, when someone pressed an American navy officer concerned with intelligence to reveal, at least, whether it was an army code or a navy code that was broken, the officer, without speaking, drew the single letter "N" on his desk. This, if true, cleared the army lookout unit's message of any suspicion.

Next, there was a message sent at 6:05 A.M. on the day of the flight by the base commander at Rabaul east airfield, informing the base commander at Ballale of the departure of two land-based attack planes and six "Zero" fighters.

Another message was sent after takeoff by the chief pilot of the plane carrying Yamamoto, informing Ballale base that they were "due to arrive 0745." These two messages, which were sent in simple flight codes, could probably have been deciphered by anyone with a mind to do so, but they would not have allowed the necessary time to prepare an attack.

The fourth message was the long and most detailed cable of April 13, which, as we have already seen, so angered Rear Admiral Joshima when he saw it. This used the *"ha"* code, employing five-digit random numbers in the same way as the *"ro"* code. As already stated, it would normally be considered impossible, short of stealing the actual codebook, to crack in the short space of ten days or two weeks a random numbers code which had just been altered, and the Naval General Staff's Fourth Division was not entirely unjustified in insisting that such a thing was quite unthinkable.

The fifth message was the cable outlining the fighting in Operation "I" that was sent on April 16 in the name of C. in C. Combined Fleet to, among others, the chief of the Naval General Staff in Tokyo. At the very end of this cable occurs the sentence, "Following inspection of the Shortland area on April 18, will transfer flag back to the *Musashi* on April 19." It is not clear precisely which code was used for this cable, but it was customary, in reports of fighting sent in the name of C. in C. Combined Fleet, to use the most advanced codes available.

The idea that codes were cracked is apt to suggest that every single one of the imperial navy's coded messages immediately became an open book to the Americans—nor can it be asserted definitely that this was not the case—but there are a number of indications that they were not always quite so successful. One of the most convincing proofs of this involves the bloodless withdrawal from Kiska that took place three and a half months later. On July 29, 1943, the naval units on the island of Kiska successfully withdrew all their personnel under cover of mist, so that half a month later, when American forces threw in one hundred vessels including battleships and landed on the island after a fierce bombardment from the sea in which a large number of their own men were killed or wounded by mistake, they found nothing living save a few dogs. This could never have happened if the Americans had been able to decipher all the imperial navy's codes.

If one assumes that the *"ha"* code with its newly changed random numbers and other similar advanced codes were not in fact cracked, then the likeliest candidate is the one remaining message. Some two hundred miles farther to the southeast from Shortland Island, there was a seaplane base called Rekata, on Santa Isabel Island. Immediately to the south of the latter lay Guadalcanal, so that the area at the time was in the very front of the front line. The forces at Rekata were a detachment of those on Shortland, but communications between the two were already restricted—urgent documents being dropped by plane and foodstuffs brought by submarine—so that Yamamoto obviously could not be expected to include Rekata in his tour.

On receipt of the coded message of April 13 from Southeast Area Fleet command in Rabaul, giving the schedule for Yamamoto's tour, somebody at the Shortland base suggested that they should let the people at Rekata know too; they were having a hard time, and it would improve their morale to know that the C. in C. was coming so close. Someone else queried whether it would be safe to send them a radio message—the only rapid means of communication available—since the only codebooks they had were those used by aircraft. But the message seems, in the end, to have been sent. If it was in fact sent, it would have been in an easy code which the Americans might very well have cracked almost immediately.

Moreover, on the Solomon Islands, then occupied by Japanese forces, the Americans had infiltrated over two hundred and fifty bands of agents known as "coast watchers," who enlisted the help of the natives in gathering information. The Japanese navy was itself aware that suspicious, weak radio signals were constantly emanating from various parts of the islands. At Kieta on the east coast of Bougainville, there was a detachment of the Sasebo Sixth Special Land Unit. The commander, a chief petty officer, made use of two overseas Chinese servants to get him information and maintain contact with the native village chiefs. Ironically, it seems that he himself first heard of the imminent arrival of the "number one" of the Japanese navy from the local chief.

Until comparatively recently, the only theory as to what really happened that seemed possible in Japan was that the factors ultimately responsible for Yamamoto's death were the intelligence activities of the coast watchers—making use of the natives, overseas Chinese, and missionaries—and the sixth Japanese message, sent from Shortland to Rekata. The year before last, however, the publication of David Kahn's *The Codebreakers* radically upset this theory. According to Kahn's book, the radio intelligence unit of the U.S. Pacific Fleet command did not rely on coast watchers, nor did it pay any attention to messages sent by local units, but went straight to source and succeeded in cracking the NTF (Southeast Area Fleet) top-secret message No. 131755 (sent at 1755 on the thirteenth)—the long message beginning "Commander in Chief Combined Fleet will personally inspect Ballale, Shortland, and Buin on April 18. Schedule as follows. . . ."

Kahn states simply that the fleet radio unit succeeded in cracking the larger part of the random numbers code newly changed on April 1 by using random number tables punched on IBM cards, and details of the process are not clear. However, the book includes a clear, full-page photograph of a Japanese navy five-digit number codebook (probably copied from the basic codebook used for sending the "*ha*" code), so that almost no doubt remains that the Americans did in fact read this message.

In the event, thus, it seems probable that Joshima Takaji, the man who was so angered by the "NTF top-secret message No. 131755" when he saw it on Shortland, was the only one who showed a correct apprehension of the dangers involved.

Another point which the book makes clear is that the "suitable means of allaying Japanese suspicions," which, as stated above, was devised by Nimitz, involved, in fact, deliberately spreading rumors of Yamamoto's impending visit in areas occupied by Japanese forces, so that the Japanese got the idea that it was coast watchers who had first got wind of it. The local chief who told the individual commanding the detachment at Kieta that the "number one" of the Japanese navy was coming was probably put up to it by others in the background.

2

Nevertheless, there still remain many other areas of the conflict between Japan and America that are still unclear. Although only thirty years or so have passed—or, depending on how one looks at things, precisely *because* these years have passed—a number of these riddles seem likely to remain forever unsolved. The survivors among those who took part in the events concerned are dying off rapidly and, as we have already seen, it is dangerous to put implicit trust in available records just because they happen to be "official."

One of the most intriguing of these riddles is the question of who was responsible for actually shooting down land-based attack plane

323 carrying C. in C. Yamamoto. For many years, this was believed to be Captain Thomas Lanphier, Jr., of the U.S. Army Air Corps, and no one, either in Japan or America, cast doubt on this assumption. Moreover, Lanphier took part in and won a *Reader's Digest* competition for essays containing personal accounts of the war; the essay in question, which provides a more or less clear account of that day's fight as seen from the American side, was published in the January 1967 issue of the Japanese edition of the magazine under the title "I Shot Down Yamamoto Isoroku."

According to this account, the number of P-38s that attacked Yamamoto's plane—previously cited variously as twenty-four, eighteen, and sixteen—was in fact sixteen. Eighteen planes set out on the mission, but two of them returned to base shortly afterward with engine trouble.

However, according to Lanphier's story, immediately they launched the attack the American planes shot down one "Zero" fighter, and shot several more of them down during the subsequent air battle. This is a mistake. Of the six escort fighters of the 204th Squadron, not one, in fact, was brought down. The story is different if one includes the battle with the "Zero" fighters that set out, too late, from Buin base for a rescue attack, but nothing in Lanphier's account suggests that he is referring to these. The names of the men in the escort fighters and their ranks are all known. Five of the six were killed before the end of the war, but one of them—Yanagiya Kenji, who piloted plane No. 3—survived thanks to losing his right hand in some later action, as a result of which he was brought back to Kure on a hospital ship. Takagi Hajime, sponsor of the magazine *Maru*, found Yanagiya living in Tokyo and in 1968 published a book called *Six Escort Fighters*, which bears out the fact that the Japanese escort squadron suffered no losses.

The combat record of the escort "Zeros" also survives; it runs:

0540: Takeoff from Rabaul
0715: Engage 24 P-38s
0745: One plane lands at Ballale, 5 at Buin
1200: Assemble over Buin
1350: Land at Rabaul
Six enemy aircraft downed: Tsujinoue 2, Sugita 2, Hidaka and Yanagiya 1 each

Unfortunately this record, with the exception of the "no losses" item, is a mass of misinformation. The times given for departure from Rabaul and engaging the enemy both seem to be too early, the number of P-38s is wrong, and the figure for enemy losses is particularly wide of the mark.

The Americans themselves are clear about the losses they suffered. Of the sixteen P-38s, only one was shot down—the plane piloted by Second Lieutenant Raymond Hine. The official U.S. army record runs: "13th Fighter Command Detachment—Subject: fighter interception—Date: April 18, 1943—Time: takeoff 0725, return 1140." The makeup of the P-38 fighter squadron on the day in question was as follows: attacking section—Captain Thomas G. Lanphier, Jr., Second Lieutenant Rex T. Barber, Second Lieutenant Besby F. Holmes, Second Lieutenant Raymond K. Hine; cover—Major John W. Mitchell (commander), Second Lieutenant Douglas S. Canning, and ten other planes.

Despite the apparent weight of such official documents, it seems in practice to be particularly difficult to give an accurate account of what happened in combat, and of gains and losses. It seems to me that, rather than the various records preserved in Japan and America, one should place credence in what the natives in and around Buin say today—that the only planes in the jungle are one large Japanese plane and one small American plane.

It is, perhaps, unavoidable that, in the heat of battle, the Japanese should have convinced themselves that they had downed six planes when in fact they had downed one, and that the Americans should have believed they had downed several "Zeros" when in fact they had downed none. Recently, however, an American has cast doubt not just on the number of fighters bagged by each side but on the very identity of the man who downed the type-1 land-based attack plane carrying Yamamoto. Shortly after Lanphier's account of his exploit won the *Reader's Digest* competition, an American magazine called *Popular Aviation* published in its spring 1967 number a short piece by U.S. air force Lieutenant Colonel Besby Holmes entitled, "Who *Really* Shot Down Yamamoto?"

Holmes who, as shown already, was a second lieutenant at the time, was in one of the P-38 Lightnings that took part in the direct attack on Yamamoto's plane over Bougainville Island. He confirms that he himself sent one "Betty" (as the Americans called the type-1 land-based attack plane) down into the sea, then turned back to base, but his plane was hit and ran out of fuel, and he was obliged to make an emergency landing on Russell Island. Thus his return to Henderson Field on Guadalcanal was several days later than that of his colleagues, and on arrival he found that Thomas Lanphier, Jr., and Rex Barber had already been cited for their prowess in downing two "Bettys."

Holmes says that he personally witnessed the "Betty" that he had shot down go into the sea, but this would mean that there were three "Bettys." Since there were in fact only two, one must conclude that one of the three pilots—either Lanphier or Barber or Holmes—either lied or was under some misapprehension.

Holmes, it seems, was extremely annoyed, and at one point engaged in a fierce argument with his colleagues. After the end of the war, he realized from Japanese records that it was not he who had brought down Yamamoto's plane, since the plane that went into the sea was the one carrying Chief of Staff Ugaki. This posed the question, then, of who really had shot down Yamamoto. For more than twenty years following the end of the war he kept quiet, on the principle of letting sleeping dogs lie, but the renewal of interest in the circumstances of Yamamoto's death, together with the serious errors he found even in accounts by historians, finally persuaded him, Holmes says, to speak up.

The truth of the matter, in short, is not clear. It is not even clear to me at the moment whether the third man, Rex Barber, is alive or not, or whether he has written anything. One personal experience of my own, however, may be added here as a kind of appendix. In March 1967, on my way back to Japan from Europe via the United States, I felt I would like to meet Thomas Lanphier, Jr., and hear his story personally. I got someone to introduce me, and wrote him a letter requesting a meeting. It was just around this time, I believe, that the issue of *Popular Aviation* carrying Besby Holmes's article appeared in American bookstores, but I knew nothing about it.

Lanphier today is a businessman living in the town of La Jolla near San Diego in California, but his work keeps him traveling to and fro between there and the East Coast. When I arrived in Los Angeles, I found a reply from him waiting for me at the JAL counter at the airport. The letter, which was very friendly, said that he would be glad to meet me, and that since on Tuesday he was going to New York again via Los Angeles, it would be convenient if I could call him at his home on Monday evening to arrange a meeting. That day happened to be the Monday in question, so I called La Jolla from my hotel, and we arranged that he should contact me at 6:00 P.M. at my hotel the following day. Since he was taking the night plane from Los Angeles to New York, he would have some free time in the evening in which we could meet.

A call came from him at six in the evening of the following day, but it was from his home in La Jolla, apologizing and saying that urgent business had prevented him from leaving, so that he could not meet me. I returned to Japan frustrated at having heard his voice and nothing more. It was shortly after this that I saw Besby Holmes's article in *Popular Aviation* and wondered whether, perhaps, Lanphier had been reluctant to meet me for some reason or other. Some time later, I mentioned what had happened to Mizota Shuichi, who had been Yamamoto's friend and interpreter, and he told me that he, too, had had a similar experience.

On a visit to America four or five years previously, he had conceived a desire to meet the man who had killed Yamamoto. It was arranged, thus, that he and an American friend, a former classmate of his at Stanford, should drive to La Jolla for a game of golf with Thomas Lanphier, Jr. Lanphier, a member of a La Jolla golf club, promised faithfully to be there, but they waited for him in vain.

The impression, in short, is that Lanphier was avoiding both Mizota and myself—though even if this were so, it would not, of course, prove that his account of the crash of Yamamoto's plane was wrong. Mizota subsequently received a letter in which Lanphier apologized deeply for not having met him, saying that he had gone to the wrong golf course by mistake. He also mentioned my name and said that he hoped to meet us both in Japan before long.

If we could only meet and talk to him, there might be some clue as to whether he did in fact avoid us—and if so why—and also as to the truth about the shooting down of Yamamoto's plane. As things are, however, I can do no more than record the coincidence—if coincidence it be—of these two episodes.

On the afternoon of April 25, 1943, Admiral Koga Mineichi arrived on board the *Musashi* at Truk to take over Yamamoto's post as commander in chief. Strict secrecy regarding Yamamoto's death was observed even in the navy. It was put about that Koga's departure to take his place was a tour of inspection of the South Seas area by the C. in C. of the Yokosuka station; even at the party held to see him off, his place-card read "C. in C. Yokosuka station."

When Koga called on Suzuki Kantaro to pay his respects before going to join the Combined Fleet, he found the *yosegaki* written in Rabaul displayed on the family Shinto altar. A similar *yosegaki* had recently arrived at Koga's home. *Gohoroku* records the text of this one too:

> We are holding a class reunion on the southeast front, and swapping stories of our days as cadets.
>
> Far away though we are, we are praying for your health and happiness.
>
> Graduates of the thirty-seventh class:
>
> (Honorary member) Yamamoto Isoroku
> Kusaka Jin'ichi
> Ozawa Jisaburo
> Samejima Tomoshige
> Takeda Tetsuro
> Yanagawa Norishige

The six men signed their names, and the date was April 13—the evening of the day on which details of Yamamoto's planned tour of the front were radioed from Rabaul. Somewhat earlier, on April 4— Yamamoto's birthday—Furukawa Toshiko had gone to Yokosuka at the invitation of Koga. The camellias and cherry blossom were in full bloom in the garden of the naval station, and Toshiko had the idea of pressing some of the cherry blossoms and sending them to Yamamoto. "You'd do better to send them pickled in salt rather than pressed," said Koga, "then Yamamoto can eat them."

Toshiko spoke of letters from Yamamoto in which he complained of trembling hands and swollen legs. Koga had already heard about it. "I told the minister," he said, "that it might be a justification for bringing Yamamoto back to Japan. But the minister's so slow to act that nothing ever gets done."

A week later, the *yosegaki* from Yamamoto and the former cadets had been delivered; Koga never imagined that death would come so soon.

The message confirming Yamamoto's death in action reached the Navy Ministry on April 20, but no one was informed outside a very small circle including Koga and Hori. Even members of his family did not hear of it until some time later.

That day, Enomoto Shigeharu was working in his office in the ministry when Hori came in and grasping two fingers of his left hand in his right muttered, "You know who."

"Has something happened to Yamamoto?" asked Enomoto, startled. Hori closed his eyes and threw back his head, then went out of the room without another word.

On May 18, about a month later, the bag in the safe in the vice-minister's office which Hori was supposed to be given "if necessary" was handed to him by Vice-Minister Sawamoto. It contained 1,600 yen in clean new hundred-yen bills, a statement of Yamamoto's beliefs written as vice-minister, a copy of the memorandum concerning the Hawaiian operation and the replacement of the C. in C. Combined Fleet dated January 1941, and another statement of beliefs written on December 8 of the same year, the day the war broke out.

In a drawer in the C. in C.'s cabin on board the *Musashi* at Truk was found what can be seen as an official "last letter." It is written in the alternating five- and seven-syllable lines of Japanese poetry, and the sense is as follows:

> Since the war began, tens of thousands of officers and men of matchless loyalty and courage have done battle at the risk of their lives, and have died to become guardian gods of our land.
>
> Ah, how can I ever enter the imperial presence again? With what words can I possibly report to the parents and brothers of my dead comrades?
>
> The body is frail, yet with a mind firm with unshakable resolve I will drive deep into the enemy's positions and let him see the blood of a Japanese man.
>
> Wait but a while, young men!—one last battle, fought gallantly to the death, and I will be joining you!
>
> Yamamoto Isoroku
>
> Late September, 1942

It is understandable that his staff officers should have been moved when they read this, and one can guess the mood in which Yamamoto wrote it, but the piece smacks rather of the popular patriotic ballads that he used to hum to himself while playing mahjongg or *shogi*. One feels, after all, that Yamamoto was very far from being a natural poet; in that respect, Ugaki Matome, whose *Sensoroku* contains so many haiku, was far and away his superior.

In the C. in C.'s cabin they also found a letter to Yamamoto from Hori Teikichi:

> I was setting out for Uraga this morning when I heard that Watanabe was suddenly due to leave to rejoin you, so I'm writing this in pencil on the train on my way there and back.
>
> The cherry is late this year—perhaps because the cold went on so long and there was little rain—and the buds are still tightly closed. Even so, the cherry blossom season, the second since I last saw you, can only be about ten days away now.
>
> There's something forlorn about such things under wartime conditions, isn't there? I hope your trouble, which you say is due to beriberi, will be better soon. . . .
>
> Everything is all right with your family. The addition to the house is more or less completed, and I'm having the worst places in the old part repaired. Yoshimasa has moved to the Shikamas' and is studying hard. He goes at it very hard, and was saying that one month nowadays seems the equivalent of one year in the past. My own son Tadashi seems very much impressed by the way Yoshimasa has changed. . . .
>
> Koga is very fed up, and whenever I see him lets off steam by saying things he couldn't say to anyone else.
>
> I can't say anything much about the situation at home as a whole, but the Diet session has come to an end without anything untoward happening, and the political world seems to have settled down for the moment. I know no details, of course, nor do I want to know.
>
> It's a year now since the first raid on Tokyo. Everybody is training like mad, but most people, I feel, don't fully realize just how serious the situation is getting. I try picturing various possible futures to myself, but none is particularly appealing. . . .

Somehow, the towns seem rather forlorn without the *chindonya* [see below], but if it means that people are really beginning to think seriously about things, I'm all for it. It would be dreadful if optimism were to give way progressively to uneasiness, pessimism, and finally apathy.

It's just a year since your call at Tokyo Bay was canceled. I imagine you're getting steadily busier these days. Take good care of yourself.

The train has passed Shinagawa and will soon be at Shimbashi, so I'll stop now.

Tei

March 27

The Koga mentioned here is, of course, Koga Mineichi. The "*chindonya*" (normally, a band of two or three strolling musicians employed to advertise the opening of a new shop, etc.) may be a reference to the Information Section of Imperial Headquarters. The "call at Tokyo Bay" refers to the fact that in June the previous year, if the Midway operation had gone well, the fleet had been due to call at Yokosuka, and Hori and Yamamoto had been looking forward to meeting again there. The reference to the cherry blossom, though almost certainly written with nothing particular in mind, might almost have been inspired by a premonition of Yamamoto's death.

Both the date on the letter and the reference to Watanabe's impending departure suggest that this letter is the one that Watanabe brought back to the *Musashi* at Truk on April 1, together with Chiyoko's. But—though it seems impossible that Yamamoto should have been so preoccupied with a letter from the woman that he forgot his friend's—the envelope was still sealed. It was later returned, still untouched, to Hori, along with other personal items of Yamamoto's.

At 10:00 A.M. on May 7, the *Musashi* set sail from the Harushima anchorage at Truk carrying the ashes of Yamamoto and the others, together with their belongings. On May 21, it entered Tokyo Bay and dropped anchor off Kisarazu.

Chief orderly Omi says that in all his long navy career no voyage affected him so deeply as those four days in which he kept watch over Yamamoto's remains. Ensign Tayui Tamotsu, only son of Tayui Yuzuru, who was also aboard the *Musashi* as officer of the deck (and was later to die on the heavy cruiser *Chikuma* in the Battle of Leyte Gulf), told members of his family of seeing a *shogi* board that someone had placed next to Yamamoto's ashes.

Most of the crew were kept in the dark concerning Yamamoto's death even after the ship had left Truk. Even so, as Yoshimura Akira's *Battleship "Musashi"* records, suspicions as to the real truth were growing on board the vessel. Some of the crew found it odd that passages in the area around the C. in C.'s cabin should be closed off; many men had seen Chief of Staff Ugaki in his bandages, as well as the white boxes containing the ashes; others reported that there was a smell of incense coming from somewhere near the C. in C.'s cabin. Finally, Arima Kaoru, commander of the vessel, obtained Koga's permission for his second-in-command, Captain Kato Kenkichi, to announce the news of the C. in C.'s death to the assembled crew in the course of the voyage.

It was on May 18 that news of Yamamoto's death was conveyed to his immediate family by the Navy Ministry. The previous day, Hori Teikichi, as representative of the deceased's family, had been summoned by Navy Minister Shimada Shigetaro, who told him that a messenger was going to call on the family the following day and requested him to see that everyone behaved in seemly fashion.

"I suppose I can inform Kamiya-cho too, can I?" asked Hori.

"I suppose so," replied the minister.

On May 19, Hori arrived at Nakamura-ya. From his request to see Umeryu at once and his agitated appearance, Toshiko immediately sensed that something was seriously wrong. "Has something happened, Mr. Hori?" she pressed. "To Admiral Yamamoto, perhaps? . . . What's happened, is he sick—or dead?"

"He's dead," said Hori. "But under no circumstances are you to tell Umeryu until I can do so myself."

Chiyoko was not in her home at Kamiya-cho, having gone to Ryogo-ku to watch the eighth day of the summer sumo tournament. When she got back, her maid gave her a phone message from Hori saying that he would call on her at nine the following morning. When he arrived, he was very pale and said immediately, with a tense expression, "I want you to prepare yourself for what I have to say." Then he added, simply, "Yamamoto has been killed in action." Chiyoko almost fainted, but managed somehow to pull herself together.

The Imperial Headquarters announcement for the benefit of the nation as a whole was made on the afternoon of the following day, May 21, the day on which the *Musashi* entered Tokyo Bay. The following is the complete text of the announcement: "In April this year, Admiral Yamamoto Isoroku, commander in chief of the Combined Fleet, met a gallant death on board his plane in an encounter with the enemy in the course of directing overall operations at the front line.

"Admiral Koga Mineichi has been appointed by the emperor to succeed him, and has already assumed command of the Combined Fleet."

On the same day, an announcement from the Bureau of Information stated that Yamamoto had been posthumously awarded the Grand Order of the Chrysanthemum, First Class, and the posthumous rank of fleet admiral, and would be accorded a state funeral. The navy had requested in addition that he be given the posthumous title of baron, but this request was turned down.

At the crack of dawn on May 23, the *Musashi*, as it lay off Kisarazu, was cleaned in preparation for the shipboard farewell service. At 11:30, Yamamoto's ashes were transferred to the destroyer *Yugumo*, which had come to fetch them. Then the *Yugumo*, accompanied by its sister ship the *Akigumo*, set sail for Yokosuka, the entire crew of the Combined Fleet flagship *Musashi* lining the decks to watch it go.

The box containing the ashes was carried by Watanabe Yasuji. On the pier at Yokosuka, Yamamoto's son and heir Yoshimasa was waiting together with Hori Teikichi and others; bearing the ashes, he boarded a special train at Yokosuka Station. On the train, Captain Isobe Taro, a staff officer who represented the ship's aides, handed Hori a paper package. Opening it, he found a lock of Yamamoto's hair, together with a piece of paper bearing a poem that Yamamoto had written on April 3.

Many people, having heard about the special train, were lining the tracks to watch it pass. So long as he could be seen by them, Watanabe was obliged to sit by the window holding the box containing the ashes, but when the train entered a tunnel Hori said impatiently, "Here, let us have it a while." Thus both Hori and Yoshimasa held the box in their arms for a time.

At 2:43 P.M., the train drew into Tokyo Station, where some two hundred people, including imperial representative Jo Eiichiro (military aide to the emperor), representatives of the various imperial princes, Yamamoto's widow Reiko and other members of his family, and representatives of the government and military were waiting. Tojo, Shimada, and Nagano were there on the platform, and so was Konoe Fumimaro. As the box containing her father's ashes was brought off the train, Yamamoto's second daughter Masako, standing in line with other family members, buried her face in her handkerchief.

The ashes were taken first to a special room where those present paid their respects, then carried in a procession of cars headed by that of Captain Yanagisawa, senior aide at the Navy Ministry, past the Sakuradamon Gate of the Imperial Palace and the Navy Ministry to the Navy Club in Shiba. A Buddhist altar had been readied in a Japanese room in the annex, which Yamamoto had known so well.

4

From February through April of that year, Tsurushima Masako, proprietress of the teahouse Togo in Sasebo, had been confined to bed, seriously ill. However, finding herself rather better in May, she wrote Yamamoto a letter on the twenty-first, the first she had written in a long while. Not long after she had been to post it, someone who had heard the Imperial Headquarters announcement over the radio came to tell her of his death in action. She resolved at once to go to Tokyo. On the evening of the twenty-third, when she arrived in the capital, she visited the home of Katayama Noboru, a retired admiral and former classmate of Yamamoto's whom Yamamoto had always taken a great delight in teasing. In his house hung a large photo of Yamamoto standing on the deck of his flagship with binoculars slung around his neck. Turning to this photograph, Katayama said to it: "Look—she's come all the way from Sasebo!" He placed before it the box of Japanese cakes which Masako had brought with her—such delicacies were almost unobtainable at the time except for someone in her sort of profession—then said to her kindly, "There, you see—he's smiling!"

Although Masako had known Yamamoto longer than Chiyoko and longer even than his wife Reiko, he had kept her out of the public eye more than the others, and she was obliged to pay her respects to his remains, both at the Navy Club and at Yamamoto's home in Aoyama, without revealing her identity.

Among the other offerings before the altar at the Navy Club was an expensive-looking box of cigars. It was from Imperial Household

Minister Matsudaira Tsuneo, with whom Yamamoto had worked in London when Matsudaira was ambassador there. They were the cigars that Matsudaira had wanted to give to Yamamoto at the time of the outbreak of the China Incident. Yamamoto had asked him to keep them for him, since he had stopped smoking until the incident was settled. Some years later, Matsudaira had reminded him that they must be getting musty, but Yamamoto had asked him to keep them a while longer. So, in the end, they remained with their seal unbroken; Yamamoto was never to get the chance to "smoke till the smoke came out of his ass."

Oharu, daughter of the proprietor of Takaraya in Sasebo, was living not far from Yamamoto's Aoyama home at the time, and since Reiko had been staying at the Navy Club ever since the day the ashes arrived, she and her elder sister, Tomi, had gone to the Yamamoto house to help with the work. One day, when Hori Teikichi happened to be visiting the Aoyama house to discuss some business, a messenger came from the chief of General Staff Headquarters bringing an offering for the deceased. Oharu was about to place it in front of the altar when Hori forbade her absolutely to do so. "Yamamoto would not be pleased," he said.

Masako, who was "elder sister" to Tomi and Oharu in the world of geishas, used her connection with them in order to go to Aoyama to pay her respects to the dead. While she was in the house, however, she was approached by a man, apparently from Yamamoto's home district of Nagaoka, who asked in a loud, accusing voice what her relationship was with the deceased. "No relationship, actually," she said. "My sister happens to be looking after the house for them here, so I just . . . ." And she fled the house. She was asked by Hori to make a parcel of the letters from Yamamoto in her possession and send them to Tokyo, but she equivocated, and on her return to Sasebo locked them away in a suitcase so that the navy should not get them. American B-29s, however, were to burn every one of them two years later.

The state funeral was scheduled to take place fifteen days after the announcement of Yamamoto's death. Prior to this, Yamamoto's ashes were divided into two portions at the Navy Club. When the box containing them was opened, the papaya leaves lining the bottom were still green. One portion was to be placed in the Tama Cemetery, the other to be taken home to Nagaoka. Chiyoko would have liked a share of them, but that was too much to hope for. However, a lock of his hair came back to the house at Kamiya-cho, along with quilts, a pillow, a wallet, and a needlecase she had made for him from some cloth left over from an everyday kimono of her own. As soon as the general public was admitted to the Navy Club to pay homage, on May 24, she went herself. A steady stream of people, none of whom looked as though they had had any personal connection with Yamamoto, were weeping as they offered up incense before the photograph placed on the altar.

That evening, Commander Watanabe came to her house in Kamiya-cho to offer his condolences. "I don't know how to apologize for coming back alone," he told her. "I could scarcely bring myself to cross the threshold of this house." So heartbroken did he seem that it was Chiyoko, rather, who ended up feeling sorry for him. In the Kamiya-cho house, there was a clock belonging to Yamamoto, a gift from the emperor. Hori took it away, saying that it was one thing he could not possibly leave with her. He also came on June 1, announcing that he was acting on instructions from the Navy Ministry, and took away all her letters from Yamamoto, including the final letter written on the *Musashi* at Truk on April 2. The letters seem to have been kept for a while in a safe at the Navy Ministry, but were later returned to Chiyoko, in whose possession they remain. Before the state funeral, Furukawa Toshiko, Sano Naokichi, Shirai Kuni (proprietress of Yamaguchi), and others, most of them women from Shimbashi who had known Yamamoto well, gathered at the house in Kamiya-cho for a private funeral ceremony of their own: "This is where his spirit really is," they told each other.

Hori took the crisp hundred-yen notes that had been found among Yamamoto's possessions—he had always liked banknotes to be so crisp that you could almost cut your hand on them—wrapped each of them in a piece of paper on which he wrote "Hori: for Yamamoto," and presented them to women whom Yamamoto had known. "Hardly a keepsake," he told them, "so think of it as payment from Yamamoto, to keep you quiet about his faults. . . ."

According to Chiyoko, a certain army major visited her several times after that, urging her on Tojo's behalf to commit suicide. Every night for some time after these visits, she would gaze timidly at places on the lintel from which one might suspend a rope, and even asked Oi

Seiichi, the doctor who accompanied her when she went to Kure, for some pills. Oi himself, it should be added, agrees that she asked for the pills, which he refused to give her, but says that he never heard of any outsider urging her to kill herself.

During the two weeks or so before the state funeral, Reiko, the children, and other relatives took turns at staying at the Navy Club. Never had the Yamamoto children spent so much time close to their father as in these days following the return of his remains to Japan. The eldest son, Yoshimasa, was in second grade at the Seikei High School at the time. Sumiko, the eldest daughter, was attending the Yamawaki Girls' High School and Masako, the second daughter, Girls' Science College. The youngest child, Tadao, was in fifth grade at the Seinan National Elementary School. "We hardly know anything about Father," said Yoshimasa over and over again to his father's subordinates and their wives. "I hope you'll tell us all kinds of things about him. . . ."

Both for navy men and the general public, Yamamoto's death was a source not only of deep grief but of anxiety about the future course of the war. At the moment when Yonai Mitsumasa received the report from the Navy Ministry confirming Yamamoto's death in action, he was in conversation with politician Ayabe Kentaro, who was later to be parliamentary undersecretary for the navy in the Koiso-Yonai government. "Yamamoto himself may have felt satisfied to die when and where he did," Yonai told Ayabe. "But he was a man whom both Japan and the navy could very ill spare." He closed his eyes, making no attempt to wipe away the tears that spilled from them.

The men who were aides when Yamamoto was vice-minister, along with many others associated with the navy, agree that for them Yamamoto's death marked the beginning of the end for Japan. Takagi Sokichi, who was chief of staff of the Maizuru naval station at the time, heard the news of Yamamoto's death in a car in Kyoto, where he had gone to meet scholars of Kyoto Imperial University. He was deeply shocked. His first thought was, "This will be the end of the war for Japan." His next was more specific: "The only men who could have succeeded Yamamoto as C. in C. of the Combined Fleet were Yamaguchi Tamon and Ozawa Jisaburo, but Yamaguchi was killed at Midway, and the navy's too bound by the seniority system to allow itself to appoint Ozawa."

Tayui Yuzuru was in Shanghai as chief of staff of the China Area Fleet. He remembers Yoshida Zengo—who, his illness cured, had succeeded Koga Mineichi as commander in chief of the China Area Fleet—telling him one day that he was sure Yamamoto wanted to die, since he had said things in a recent letter that could only be interpreted that way. It was shortly after this that they heard the report of Yamamoto's death in action.

According to Matsunaga Keisuke, who was well aware how quick Yamamoto had been to sense the way things were going, his first thought was that, though Yamamoto's death might not have been suicide, Yamamoto had deliberately set a term to his own life.

"I feel that he set out, if not with the intention of dying, at least quite willing to do so," says Kondo Yasuichiro. "After all, he deliberately threw himself into what, in the army, would be considered the thick of the enemy's fire."

Fujita Motoshige was commanding an air unit at Tateyama in Chiba Prefecture. He was deeply depressed, both by a personal sense of losing someone he had greatly admired and also by the idea that a commander in chief of the Combined Fleet could have been killed in action. From then on, he says, he too somehow felt that it was all up for Japan.

From the American point of view, the most important outcome of the shooting down of Yamamoto's plane was, perhaps, the psychological shock to the Japanese people, and to the higher echelons of the imperial navy in particular.

In business circles, a number of men seem to have been privately hoping that Yamamoto would be of use in bringing the war to an end; but they, too, were disappointed. Some time after the state funeral, Matsumoto Sankichi called on Ishibashi Tanzan (later to become prime minister) at the offices of the *Toyo Keizai Shimpo*, an economic journal. "A terrible pity about Yamamoto," said Ishibashi with quiet intensity. "I never met him personally, but to tell the truth we'd had a vague idea that he might take things in hand after the war. You see, if a man with such an illustrious war record took over, the public could be persuaded to put up with their dissatisfactions just by the idea that it was 'Admiral Yamamoto' who was responsible. The very fact that he'd been labeled pro-British and pro-American before the war would have worked in his favor, as we saw it, in trying to integrate public opinion in the postwar period."

Yamamoto's state funeral was held in Hibiya Park, in the center of Tokyo, on June 5, 1943—the same day of the same month as the funeral of Admiral Togo Heihachiro nine years previously. The president of the funeral committee was Yonai Mitsumasa. The chief officiant was Shiozawa Koichi; both he and Yoshimasa, the chief mourner, wore Shinto-style robes and hats, and Yamamoto's widow Reiko wore formal dress of the kind worn by court ladies.

At 8:50 that morning, members of the *Musashi*'s crew carried Yamamoto's coffin, draped with a white cloth, from the room in which it had been lying in state in the Navy Club and placed it on a black gun carriage standing before the front entrance.

Led by a naval band playing Chopin's Funeral March, the procession descended the slope from the Navy Club, turned right, passing directly in front of Chiyoko's house in Kamiya-cho, then went slowly on via the Toranomon crossing and the Uchisaiwai district. The people in the stand erected by the roadside for special acquaintances of the deceased were annoyed, they say, by press cameramen who, guessing that Chiyoko must be among them, tried to get a picture of her.

Turning the corner by the navy minister's official residence, the procession arrived at the site of the funeral ceremony in Hibiya Park at 9:50. The sword that went with Yamamoto's posthumous rank of fleet admiral was carried by Watanabe Yasuji; the Grand Order of the Chrysanthemum was carried by Miwa Yoshitake. Miwa, who had been in hospital in Tokyo with dengue fever contracted in Rabaul, was painfully emaciated, but he had insisted on taking part in the state funeral. No sooner had he placed the box containing the decoration on the altar than he withdrew to one side and collapsed. The altar and other structures customary at Japanese funerals were constructed simply of unvarnished wood with black-and-white striped curtains, a touch of color being provided by a bunch of roses sent by Mussolini. The military personnel present were commanded by General Doihara Kenji, and the approximately one thousand five hundred mourners included Prime Minister Tojo and many others whom Yamamoto himself would hardly have been delighted to see.

The representatives of the emperor, the empress, and the dowager empress paid their respects, followed by other members of the imperial family or their representatives. Then the twenty-two-year-old, bespectacled chief mourner stepped forward in his straw sandals and offered up a sprig of the sacred tree of Shinto; as he did so, a military band briskly played the first eight bars of the navy's ceremonial march "Casting My Life Aside," and guns fired a salute of three salvos.

That afternoon, tens of thousands of ordinary citizens came to pay their last respects. When this was over, half Yamamoto's ashes were taken by car to the Tama Cemetery, just outside Tokyo, and placed in a grave next to that of Admiral Togo.

The other half of his ashes arrived home in Nagaoka on June 7. His elder sister, Takahashi Kazuko, was seventy-eight by now and her back was rather bent. Four days before the state funeral, on June 1, she had gone up to Tokyo, supported by close relatives and carrying two cloth-wrapped bundles containing the cakes and other local delicacies that her brother—who had been so fond of his food, and especially sweet things—had particularly liked. A week later, when the official ceremonies were over and she arrived home together with Reiko and her nephews and nieces, she seemed relieved and said, still clasping to her the urn containing her brother's ashes, "Don't worry, Iso, from now on I'll look after you!"

Yamamoto's grave in Nagaoka stands in the grounds of a Zen temple, the Chokoji. The stone is carved with Yamamoto's posthumous Buddhist name, which was chosen by his old friend Hashimoto Zengan, and the words "killed in action in the South Pacific, April 1943." It stands in a pebble-covered plot some twelve feet square that also contains the graves of his adoptive father, Yamamoto Tatewaki, and other Yamamoto family ancestors. Tatewaki's gravestone—erected after the Boshin War of the Meiji era at a time when the Nagaoka clan was considered an enemy of the emperor—was a very simple affair, so Isoroku's gravestone was kept equally simple and, at the suggestion of Yonai and other friends, one inch shorter and half an inch narrower. Costing only seventy yen in the money of the day, it is said to be the cheapest monument ever erected to a Japanese admiral or general killed in battle.

On June 3, in Tokyo's Marunouchi district, a group of men including former justice minister Obara Sunao, Doi Akihira, governor of Niigata Prefecture, Matsuda Kohei, mayor of Nagaoka, and Sorimachi Eiichi had met at the Japan Club to discuss the possibility of some undertaking to honor Yamamoto's memory. One of the proposals was

the establishment of a "Yamamoto Shrine" in Nagaoka City, and after
the state funeral they began negotiations with the various authorities
concerned. Society at the time would have found nothing particularly
odd in the creation of a Yamamoto Shrine; there were, indeed, prece-
dents in the Nogi and Togo shrines in Tokyo, but Yonai Mitsumasa
and Hori Teikichi strongly opposed the plan. Better than anyone else,
they knew that Yamamoto had believed—to borrow Inoue Shigeyoshi's
words—that "however glorious his achievements, to make a god of a
military man is absurd." On this question, Yonai was adamant. "Yamamoto hated that kind of thing," he said. "If you deified him, he'd be
more embarrassed than anybody else."

So the matter was quietly dropped, and the site of Yamamoto's
birthplace in Nagaoka, where the shrine was to have stood, is today
a small memorial park for the use of the children and adults of the
area.

INDEX

Abe Isoo, 136
air raid on Tokyo, 298–300
Akagi, 16, 76, 87–89, 175, 218, 241,
    255, 278, 316, 317, 320, 321
Arita Hachiro, 155–57
Arizona, 252
Atago, 16

Berengaria, 24–25
Black Chamber, 27
Bokyo Gokokudan, 136
Boshin War, 17–18, 68, 391
Bougainville, 346
Bungei Shunju, 19, 21, 68
Byrd, Richard E., 86–87

California, 252
Chatfield, Lord, 26, 41, 48
Chiang Kai-shek, 124
Chihaya Masataka, 219
Chikuma, 255, 311, 314, 383
China Incident, 4, 14, 106, 123, 124,
    131, 138
Chiyoko. *See* Kawai Chiyoko
Chokai, 16
codes, 27, 244–45, 274–78, 306–7, 369–
    74
Combined Fleet, 11, 14, 16, 19, 172;
    exercises, 173, 175–76, 199–201
Craigie, Sir Robert, 35, 39

Davis, Norman, 35, 38–39
Diet building, 102

emperor. *See* Hirohito, Emperor
Enomoto Shigeharu, 22, 23, 24, 36, 41–
    42, 215, 380
Enterprise, 252, 280, 299, 317

Exeter, 289

February 26 Incident, 95–97, 102, 118
Friedman, William, 276
Fuchida Mitsuno, 173, 175–76, 227, 236,
    253–54, 255–57, 262–63, 270, 282,
    301, 312
Fujii Shigeru, 259, 289, 340, 341
Fujita Motoshige, 7, 8, 10, 16, 389
Fukazawa Motohiko, 66
Fukuda Keiji, 93
Fukudome Shigeru, 11, 209, 211, 213,
    297
Furukawa Toshiko, 62, 64, 65, 96, 147,
    163, 379
Furutaka, 174, 200
Fushimi, Prince, 43, 51, 92, 129, 208,
    210, 213
Fuso, 16

gambling. *See* Yamamoto Isoroku
geishas. *See* Yamamoto Isoroku; *also*
    Furukawa Toshiko, Kawai Chiyoko,
    Niwa Michi, Tsurushima Masako
Genda Minoru, 221, 312
Germany, relations with, 143–44, 186
Gohoroku, 196, 379
Great Kanto Earthquake, 75–76, 112
Grew, Joseph, 219
Guadalcanal, 323, 328, 333, 338, 344

Haguro, 288
Hakozaki-maru, 22
Halsey, William F., 282, 299, 370
Harvard University, 73, 177
Hasegawa Kiyoshi, 84, 117, 119, 335,
    336
Hashimoto Kingoro, 134–35

393